The Politics of Memory

The Politics of Memory

THE JOURNEY OF A HOLOCAUST HISTORIAN

Raul Hilberg

Chicago • Ivan R. Dee • *1996*

Library of Congress Cataloging in-Publication Data:
Hilberg, Raul, 1926–
The politics of memory : the journey of a Holocaust historian /
Raul Hilberg.
p. cm.
Includes index.
ISBN 1-56663-116-5
1. Hilberg, Raul, 1926– . 2. Holocaust, Jewish
(1939–1945)—Historiography. 3. Jewish historians—
United States—Biography.
I. Title.
D804.348.H55 1996   96-11953
940.53'18—dc20

Preface

M UCH OF MY LIFE has been devoted to the study of a
subject that in fundamental ways is different from
any other: the destruction of the European Jews. Often
enough, acquaintances as well as strangers have wanted to
know why I undertook such an exploration and what sort of
reactions I encountered in the course of my work. In this
account of my experiences I have consolidated and elaborated my answers to these questions. The result is a personal story but one which touches upon a range of
phenomena that are part and parcel of the politics of memory in America, Israel, and Europe from the late 1940s to
the early 1990s.

I have shared drafts of these pages with my old friend
Eric Marder, my longtime literary agent Theron Raines, my
newly found kindred spirit Walter Reich, my wife Gwen-
dolyn, my son David, and my daughter Deborah. Each approached the manuscript with special perspectives, and
from all I received valuable insights and suggestions. I thank
them for everything they have given me.

Contents

History without tragedy does not exist,

and knowledge is better and more wholesome

than ignorance.

—H. G. Adler

The Politics of Memory

I
The Review

ON TUESDAY, SEPTEMBER 15, 1992, I received a call from my literary agent Theron Raines, a man of learning who was born in Arkansas and who earned degrees at Columbia College and Oxford University. Raines is always to the point, always clear. My new book, he said, was going to be reviewed on the following Sunday in the *New York Times*. I thanked him for the call, but in a relaxed manner as if to suggest that I was now at an age when such news was not about to make me euphoric. Still, I was pleased. I no longer had any professional enemies who might want to tear me down in print. Consequently there was everything to look forward to and nothing to fear. But then, Theron Raines added, "You are not going to like the last sentence of the review."

That evening my wife brought home facsimile copies of two reviews sent to her office by my editor at Harper-Collins, Aaron Asher. The review in the *New York Times* was one of them. I read both quickly and decided to put them aside, because my daughter was visiting me and I did not wish to spoil our time together. On Sunday I would leave for a book tour, starting in Boston, and she would return to Jerusalem. Aaron Asher, however, was worried. He called me on Thursday and asked whether the two reviews, particularly the one in the *Times*, should be answered. My immediate reply was no, because these were sophisticated discussions, and I did not wish to refute them. He countered that in the *Times* I had been accused of lack of scholarship. True, I said, in a manner of speaking my research had been found wanting, but still I did not wish to write a letter.

I knew the reviewer in the *Times* personally. He had invited me to lecture at his university and had written glowingly about the second edition of my large book, *The Destruction of the European Jews*, in the London *Times Literary Supplement*. Now he not only dismissed my new study but revised his thoughts about the second edition of the earlier work. In his reevaluation he was reviewing my whole life, starting with the first edition of *Destruction* published more than thirty years before. He praised *that* edition and asked pointedly, "What does one do when such a work is completed?" He explained that I had taught political science at the University of Vermont until my retirement; I had inspired a new generation, serving as mentor and guide. When the second edition of *Destruction* was published in 1985, reviewers had paid homage to my "original achievement," but some were "disappointed" with the new version. Finally, in my new book, *Perpetrators Victims Bystanders*, I had remained "aloof" from younger scholars who had created new work with new documentation and new questions. I had become, he said in his last sentence, "less a pathfinder than a conscience."

Always in my life I had wanted the truth about myself. Here was an assessment by a man who was in no sense ignorant and who bore me no ill will. What if he were right? When I first embarked upon my self-imposed task at the age of twenty-two, I was working alone, trying to grapple with my enormous topic which stood for the epitome of human destruction in our time. I had immersed myself in this history, delving deeper and deeper into the documents of the German bureaucracy of the Nazi era in an attempt to touch bottom. I was thirty-five when my first word on the subject appeared in print. What had I done in the last thirty-one years? What had happened to me?

I shared the review with my old friend Eric Marder. It was not so bad, he said, considering the flattering sentences in those paragraphs devoted to my early accomplishments. I asked him to read the whole review over again, assuring him that I myself had studied it five times before its full impact was clear to me. He called me back after he too had read the review five times. It was not so good, he confirmed, but to him the real question was, Why should I accept the premises of this reviewer? Why should I agree with these conclusions? I countered with the argument that, above all, I had to remain clear-sighted. Never had I tried to delude myself, and now especially the truth was most important to me. Perhaps my creative potential had been exhausted three decades ago. Conceivably I had lingered on this earth since then.

Yet I was not completely sure. When I had completed the new work, with its focus on people rather than events, I had shipped it without mental reservations to Theron Raines. At HarperCollins, Aaron Asher had read the manuscript and accepted it without hesitation. It was still early;

the book was just on its way to the stores. Why not wait? Although the footnotes had been banished to the back of the book, they were not lost, and someone might call attention to the variety of my sources. If, as Eric suggested and my son believed, the book was too subtle, another reviewer might nonetheless discover its intricacy. As for sales, major stores might have piled up copies for strollers wandering through the aisles.

On the Sunday morning of September 20, I boarded a plane to Boston. It was still morning when I arrived. I bought a copy of the *Boston Globe*, in which I had once reviewed a book, but it was silent. I visited the large Barnes & Noble store—the only bookshop open before noon—but the book was not there. In American politics there are election nights when a candidate, fighting for survival, awaits the result of a vote in a single crucial precinct, because a negative outcome there signifies the loss of the entire contest. For me, Boston was such a test.

I returned to the hotel for my lunch in a dining room just above the street-level restaurant The Last Hurrah. The food was unexpectedly good, and even more excellent was the guitarist whose sounds filled the room. I listened to his masterful playing of Francisco Tarrega's *Recuerdos de la Alhambra*. Suddenly I felt an indescribable sadness. So this is the end, the real end, regardless of what may still happen. That moment I was alone with myself, saying goodbye to my life.

II
Background

Origins

M Y FATHER ONCE TOLD ME that even before I was
born I was sufficiently unruly to cause a serious
problem for my mother, and that in the hospital he was
asked by the obstetrician whether, in the event of a dilemma
necessitating a choice between the survival of my mother
and the life of the child, he would prefer the one or the
other. At that moment—so he confided to me—he made a
decision that was wholly inappropriate in the light of all the
teachings of the sages, but that was nevertheless compelling
in his eyes. In such an eventuality, he told the physician, it
was my life he wanted saved. This secret he shared with me
while I was still a schoolboy, in one of the conversations we
had about his own childhood and his adolescence, employment, and military service. I was impressed with all his accounts, and I have always thought of my father as a wise and
considerate man. To me he was a guide from whom I have
tried, not always successfully, to draw my ideas, attitudes,
and style.

There was a vast difference between my father, who had
experienced and suffered much, and my mother, who did
survive my arrival. It is difficult to talk about them in the

same paragraph or on the same page, and so I will begin by describing them separately.

My father was born on September 15, 1889, in what he remembered as an unpaved village in the northeastern part of the Austro-Hungarian Empire: Dzuryn (or transliterated from the Russian: Dzhurin). Much later I looked up the place, which is now located in the western portion of Ukraine, and found it clearly visible on a good map. It had evidently become a town, considerably larger than I had expected. The Hilbergs, my father said, had come to Dzuryn from Bavaria in 1648, but I did not verify this information. One Hilberg, perhaps a cousin of my paternal grandfather, was a rector of the University of Czernowitz (subsequently Cernauti and thereafter Chernovtsy) sometime before the First World War. Considering the utterly humble circumstances of my father's extended family, I always thought the story of the successful Hilberg to be apocryphal, but searching at one time in a library catalog of Southern Methodist University for cards with titles of my own literary output, I discovered that the Hilberg of Czernowitz was real, and that he had written several books on such subjects as the formation of syllables in ancient Greek. From then on I resolved never to disbelieve anything my father had told me.

My father left Dzuryn shortly after he had completed his schooling at about the age of fourteen. Europe was still at peace, optimism reigned, and choices could be made with an expectation of improving one's life. He told me that he had visited Zurich and Berlin before settling in Vienna. Because I was still very young, it did not occur to me to ask him whether his travel was financed by his parents. They must have been very poor, because my father never gave me any details about the occupation of my grandfather. In fact, he did not say very much about him altogether. All I heard was the story of my grandfather's flight from the advancing Russian army in the First World War and his death during that war as a refugee.

My father, one of ten children, had a living sister and three living brothers, the usual residue from deaths in infancy. The oldest brother and the only sister lived in New York, where they too were poor. A younger brother, Josef, followed my father to Vienna. My father was heavily preoccupied with Josef, and after Josef's death with his memory. Josef was a man who left no mark at all. He was dependent on my father immediately on his arrival in Vienna. During the First World War he pretended to have a bad leg, and limped throughout the four years of the conflict. So successful was Josef in this act of draft evasion that he had trouble resuming a normal gait after Austria's defeat. He was childless, and his tiny apartment, in which he lived with his wife, was not even suited for the briefest visitor. I always hated to go there, for I stood in the middle of the small living room, which was also the bedroom, where I had to listen to his sighs about the terrible state of the economy and his unending hardships. After Vienna became a part of the German Reich, Josef crossed the Belgian border illegally and fled again in 1940, to be interned in a camp where stateless and stranded people just like Josef and his wife were held by the collaborationist French Vichy regime. My father, by then in New York, received Josef's frantic appeals for help, but there was no money for tickets which might have enabled Josef to escape to America. When the deportations from the Vichy-French zone began in 1942, Josef disappeared. "The blood of my brother is upon me," my father would say at that time, and years later he repeated these words to signify that this failure to pay for the berths on a ship was his greatest sin, never to be expiated. In 1978 I looked for Josef on a list of deportees from France. There was no record of a Josef Hilberg. How invisible could a man be? Then it occurred to me that my grandparents had been married only in a religious ceremony, and if Josef had not taken formal steps to change his name he would have had to carry the maiden name of my grandmother, Gaber, on his personal documents. Although the postwar French transcribers of the deportation lists had trouble deciphering some of the original entries, I found Gaber, Joseph, born October 23, 1893, in "Dzwyen." He was deported on August 14, 1942, and arrived in Auschwitz two days later. Since he was already forty-eight years old, he must have been gassed immediately.

Unlike Josef, my paternal uncle Jakob was a soldier in the First World War. As an artilleryman he fired heavy Austrian shells in support of German forces on the Western front. Although never wounded, Jakob returned from the war half deaf. He never left Poland again, and I never met him, his wife, or their children. The German occupants of Poland in the Second World War, I must surmise, thanked him for his help by killing him and his family.

All my knowledge about my paternal grandmother comes from my father, and all he really told me about her concerned her extreme pacifism. When he was discharged from a military hospital and visited her in Dzuryn after the war, she burned all his uniforms and papers, and threw away all his medals. She overlooked only a creased photograph which shows him as a sergeant in the Austro-Hungarian army. By 1942, in her eighties and blind, she lay in bed most of the time. Apparently that is where the German raiders found her and where they shot her on the spot.

I could understand how a woman with two sons at the front could have become peace-loving. What I could not grasp so easily was my father's description of himself as a pacifist. War, he said, is not what the chauvinists and romantics write about it. He had spent twenty-six months in the trenches, twenty-two months on the Russian front, and, after being wounded in the neck, four more months on the Italian front, where a shell smashed his shinbone and left him in the hospital with gangrene. But, I interjected, he had also been decorated. His silver medal, as I learned later, was at least the equivalent of an Iron Cross First Class in the German army or a Silver Star in the American army. True, he would answer, but what had he received these decorations for? Once he rescued a major, whose guts had been ripped out. Another time he had to repair a torn wire of the Austrian telephone lines at night. Losing his way, he hooked it up by mistake with a Russian wire. Since he understood Russian, he overheard a conversation signaling an attack on a regimental front to begin at dawn. He was going back, he thought, as he came, but lost his way again and arrived at a neighboring German regiment from which he called his colonel, Herrn Oberst von Wipplinger. "Do you know what you are saying?" the colonel asked him. "If you are right I must withdraw the entire regiment to the reserve trench, the B-Line, and if you are wrong . . ." The Austrians withdrew and for several hours the Russians bombarded an empty trench. When Russian infantry began their assault, the Austrians filtered back into their old positions. The first Russian wave collapsed in no-man's-land, and the second barely reached the Austrian line. The third turned back in flight. That is what he had gotten one of his medals for: three thousand Russian dead as a result of his inability to orient himself on the ground.

No, he was a pacifist, and he served for only one reason: honor. Jewish honor. For this attitude he could give a concrete example. Once he led a patrol into no-man's-land where he was suddenly confronted by an enemy patrol. The Russians, however, were just as surprised. He addressed the Russian patrol leader quickly and discovered that in both patrols there were several Jews. They decided not to fight but to talk. Sitting in a shell hole, they traded alcohol and food—the Austrians had the rum and the Russians the bread. At the end of this meeting my father said to his Russian counterpart, who was also Jewish, "Alcohol is prohibited in your army; come, surrender to us and you will drink." The Russian replied, "No, you are starving in your army; come, surrender to us and you will eat." Inasmuch, however, as both sergeants were men of honor, they bid each other goodbye, and each returned to his own lines to continue the war.

When my father returned to Vienna he had to build his life anew. His first task was to walk. Lying in the hospital, he overheard a military doctor remark to a colleague that he was not likely to live. Then an Austrian surgeon inserted a silver shinbone in my father's leg. The Austrians gave him crutches, assuring him that he would need them for the rest of his days. After some months my father discarded the crutches and walked with a cane. Then he put aside the cane and simply walked. While he was still crippled, the postwar Austrian government asked him whether he wanted to avail himself of a tiny pension or an income tax deduction for his disability. When he chose the deduction, the bureaucrats laughed. He persisted, even though an older partner in the minuscule business they had founded before the war had become bankrupt while my father was at the front, and even after the economic depression of the 1930s dealt him a further blow. He had my mother and he had me, and his life seemed fulfilled.

Not so fulfilled, it seems, was my mother's life. Recapitulating her experience is a problem. Although I spent much more time in my childhood with her than with my father, I do not recall any real conversations we may have had. I could learn something about her only by asking repeated questions about her childhood and family, and even then her disclosures were sometimes incomplete or misleading. She claimed that her original home was in Buczacz, a city in Galicia, also in the northeastern corner of the Austro-Hungarian Empire. Buczacz, I heard, was important enough to have a *Gymnasium*, the sort of school that was a stepping-stone to higher education in a college or university. Much later, however, I learned that she was actually born and raised in the insignificant village of Podzameczek, which is adjacent to Buczacz but clearly separated from it by the river Strypa. In describing her extended family, she was most prepared to talk about one individual, Naphtali Herz Imber, who was related to my maternal grandmother, and who is immortalized in the *Encyclopedia Judaica* as the poet responsible for the words of Israel's national anthem, the Ha-Tikvah, or "The Hope." For many years I had assumed that he had composed the music as well—"He wrote the Ha-Tikvah," my mother had said—but the *Encyclopedia* corrected my misapprehension. The famous Imber had written only the words. Moreover, they were derived in part from the Polish anthem "Poland Is Not Yet Lost."

My mother was one of eighteen siblings, half of whom survived their infancy. Her oldest brother, a promising classicist, died of an infection following a tooth extraction before the First World War. Most of the other brothers and sisters, who were older than my mother, had migrated to the United States. In Europe I knew my aunt, Augusta Szigeti, who lived in Sighet, Romania, with her son Alexander. Augusta, who manufactured violins, had much more money than we. She owned a house and garden and was driven by a chauffeur in a Mercedes-Benz. In March 1939, as the war clouds gathered, Alexander, who was known as Sanyi, traveled to the Middle East, including Palestine. He was in his early twenties then, already mustered out of the Romanian army, in which he had performed his obligatory duty, and I thought that his trip was an exploration to determine whether the Holy Land was as hospitable and livable as his own Romania. Sanyi returned, possibly dissatisfied with his discoveries. He was already an expert in fine living, and I was particularly impressed with his taste in women.

Although I was only eleven when I saw him in Prague, I was awestruck by a young lady he escorted there. I am sure she was Jewish, but she looked almost Japanese to me, and very beautiful. I had an infatuation then with all manner of things Japanese—no doubt influenced by my father, who told me that during the Russo-Japanese War the Jews of Austria-Hungary, thinking of their oppressed brethren in Russia, had prayed fervently for a Japanese victory. Sanyi at any rate did not marry this woman but, as I heard after the war, another who, I hope, was no less beautiful. The couple had a little son before Augusta, Sanyi, and his family were swept up by the deportations to Auschwitz in the spring of 1944. There they disappeared into the night.

My mother had one younger brother, Heinrich, who was born at the turn of the century and who was an officer candidate in the Austro-Hungarian army before it collapsed in 1918. His uniformed service was not completed, however. He served as a lieutenant in the Polish army, fighting the Bolsheviks, and after that war he was a Polish captain of artillery in the reserve. This military career is remarkable because Heinrich had become a physician without relinquishing his status as an artillery officer. He lived in Gdynia on the Baltic coast, and I saw him only once, when he visited us in Vienna. To my great regret I never met his family. I still have a small photograph of his two daughters, which they sent me, addressed to *den lieben Raul*, and I studied it for a long time, concentrating on the older Sziutka, a handsome teenager. I do not know precisely what happened to Heinrich. From my mother I heard that sometime between September 1939 and June 1941 he was supposed to have been in Soviet-occupied Lvov. That is where the trail ended. No further word was received about him, his wife, or Sziutka and her little sister.

Only one aunt had remained in the Buczacz area, but for decades I barely knew that she existed. Her name was Frieda. My mother was reluctant to divulge anything about her. After persistent questioning I found that Frieda had been divorced. That is why nothing more could be said about her life. She too vanished in the 1940s during the German occupation of Poland.

My mother was far less reticent to talk about her father. She was already in her seventies when she visited me once in Vermont and revealed how much she had suffered in his house. Her troubles began when she was a sensitive girl, about thirteen years old. At that time her mother had died and her father, without waiting a year, had remarried. "Really?" I asked as I brewed tea for both of us. "Yes," she said, "that is what he did to me. So now you know." My grandfather, I must add for the record, also died in Adolf Hitler's Europe.

So unhappy was my mother in the northeastern part of the Austro-Hungarian Empire that she left it—I do not know exactly when—to live in Vienna, where, at last content, she became a bookkeeper, and where, at the age of twenty-six, she met my father. "Why did you marry him?" I would ask her. "I do not know," she would answer in an irritated voice. "I was influenced by friends who told me that I should." True, true, I said to myself, that would have been the advice to a woman who was not attracted to a man. Tens of thousands of Jewish soldiers had been killed in the Austro-Hungarian army, and many a young Jewish woman was consigned to spinsterhood. It must have been my father who was the pursuer. My supposition was confirmed after her death, when I inherited her collection of family photographs. Among dozens of portraits of my uncle, the classicist who died after a visit to his dentist before the First World War, I retrieved a photograph of my mother that she had given to my father. Here she was in the glow of her youth, yet stately, at the edge of that maturity which characterizes a woman who already knows how to dress, move, and pose. "Your mother was an attractive woman," my reliable father had told me. She was not as beautiful as Augusta, whose face was almost blinding, but . . . He wanted my mother, really wanted her, I concluded after I read a brief notation on the back of her photograph. She had written only two words, "*Bitte wenden*" (Please turn), and he had added, evidently after she had agreed to become his wife, "*veni, vidi, vici,*" the only brash words he had ever permitted himself.

One should think that three people in a very modest apartment would constitute a closely knit family, but in retrospect I realize that I spent time with my father and with my mother, but not so much with them both simultaneously. Although my father habitually returned home midday for his major meal, I do not recall any conversations between them. Subjects they deemed inappropriate for my ears were in any case discussed in Polish, a language both of them had mastered in childhood. Yet on a few occasions, while speaking in German, a disagreement between them welled into an argument, always initiated by my mother, who would shout, *"Du bist ein Niemand!"* (You are a nobody!). It was the one expression my father did not accept with equanimity. His principal pride in life was his self-sufficiency. This accomplishment was not minor, and if he did not demand verbal recognition, still he could not ignore her outburst, which he answered with the assertion that he was certainly not a nobody. In her reply to this rejoinder, she called him Count Potocki—an allusion to the seventeenth-century Polish lord who had granted privileges to the Jews of Buczacz.

Their exchanges made a lasting impression on me. I was convinced of my father's sense of worth, and I adopted his values, but I could not miss the undertone of my mother's message that he had fallen short, that she had been shortchanged by her marriage, and that she deserved better. Thus, even while agreeing with him, I resolved to be better armed. Meanwhile my father did not help me when I tried to take his side, because then he would say that my mother had always done her duty. She was a superb cook, kept the house immaculately clean—albeit with the help of a housekeeper—and, above all, took very good care of me.

Only once did I overhear my mother defend my father. It was in November 1938, just after my father had been arrested in a major roundup of Jews, when a man with a pistol aimed straight at my mother demanded that we vacate the apartment at once. The Jews, he screamed, had always exploited the German people, cheating them of their earnings and wealth. At this moment my mother replied calmly that my father had always worked honestly and that he had never broken the law.

My father was not kept under arrest very long. He had presence of mind, and when he noticed a "D" next to his name on a list, he quickly surmised that he was destined for the concentration camp Dachau. "Gentlemen, you cannot do that," he said politely to the two Gestapo men sitting behind a table. "Oh, we can't?" they answered. "No," he insisted, "I fought in the World War." "One moment, you Jew, where did you fight?" My father recited regimental locations. "We cannot send him to Dachau," said the older of the two Gestapo men. "He is not lying. I was there myself."

My father was released, but he was a broken man. He had not been tortured, and he was reunited with us in an apartment of friends who had taken us in. From this moment, however, he lost his independence. His business had been that of a middleman. It consisted of buying household goods for people who needed credit and who paid him in installments. In 1938 and 1939 the Aryan or Aryanized stores demanded all the money owed to them by Jews, but many of my father's customers could not or would not pay off their debts to him. Finally, it was my mother's family in the United States that enabled us to emigrate, and when my father and mother arrived in New York in 1940, both of them became factory workers. That was when my father concluded that he no longer had any say or claim in family matters. He had been robbed of his principal attainment, and henceforth he deferred to my mother for all those decisions still to be made. The issues, to be sure, had been narrowed considerably. Money had to be saved, dollar by dollar, and my father took as little as possible from the till. He was keenly interested in Israel, but he never went there, even after his retirement. Although he would have been more generous than my mother in allowing me to work fewer hours in a factory while I was still in college, or to forgive my monetary debt, which I accrued in later years by living in my parents' New York apartment, and which I calculated to be a third of the household cost for the time that I spent there after my sixteenth birthday, he never insisted that I be given any concessions. He had promised my mother in the early 1920s that she would never have to work, and in their middle age he could no longer keep his word.

My mother took good care of him when he became old. When they were both retired with social security benefits, she also had a small pension and he received a monthly check of approximately ten dollars paid to him by the Austrian government in recognition of his physical impairment resulting from his service in the First World War. My mother had time to watch his diet of pot cheese and assorted foods recommended for people with a heart condition, and he read books, which he selected not so much from the works of his beloved Heinrich Heine or even the biblical commentaries as from a club offering adventure novels in digest form. His life became narrower and narrower, and one day I was summoned from Vermont to see him for the last time. "He did not make it," the surgeon announced after my father had succumbed to a heavy dose of anesthesia. At that moment my mother burst into tears.

Formative Years

OUR APARTMENT IN VIENNA consisted of four rooms. I was told that at first it was shared with a previous tenant, an elderly gentleman, who died in due time. The rooms had higher ceilings than those to which Americans are accustomed, and they were relatively spacious. One of them, however, the foyer, was half filled by a large white linen closet in which my father stored goods for sale. By contrast, the living room furniture was all black, including the glassed bookcase which housed the works of Goethe, Heine, and Dostoevsky, as well as those of the Jewish historian Heinrich Graetz. This is the room I remember the most, and to this day I am partial to black, including black book covers and book jackets. Our furniture, like the house, was made to last for generations. In 1938, when we sold it, some of these pieces were purchased by the people who had ejected us.

Lest there be a mistaken impression about our comforts, I should emphasize that there was no running water in the apartment. A single spigot in the hallway served the entire floor. The toilets, one for each family, had separate doors in the hallway as well. The entrance to the house was a narrow corridor, and the spiral staircase was made of stone. We had an icebox, a telephone, and a radio, but I paid little attention to these conveniences, at least until 1938, when listening to the news took up much of my time.

The XX. District, in which we lived, formed with the II. District an island between the Danube River and the Danube Canal. We were close to the canal, and I spent many hours on stretches along its XX. District shore. Inasmuch as I had no brother or sister, I would often walk by myself, flanked by bushes and staring at the sky. At one time I looked up and said to myself: tomorrow I will be eight. I still like to take a walk every evening before a birthday for stock-taking.

It was during my early years that I encountered a problem that surfaces for almost everyone: We do not live forever. This cognition is not so simple for a schoolboy who has just started his life. I remember standing in the stone hallway, looking out a window into the courtyard where beggars sang for a groschen and where my mother beat the dust from our carpets. Momentarily I had the thought of jumping out. It was the only time I have had such a temptation. As a mature man I became convinced that in a manner of speaking we are trapped in our bodies, which will self-destruct eventually if not before. At that point I settled for continuity in lieu of eternity, allowing only a purpose *in* life, as distinct from a purpose *of* life, to serve as my last bastion.

Martin Luther said that if he did not have his God he would rather be a pig wallowing in dirt. The fact is that I have had no God. My father is at least partially responsible for this state of affairs. His idol was Baruch Spinoza, who taught that God in His extensions was everywhere, in every

rock and every human being. Much later I came to the conclusion that such a proposition could easily be reduced to a
tautology: one may as well say that one is one, two is two, or
three is three. My father did not tell me that the Dutch Jews
of the seventeenth century had clearly seen the implication
of a philosophy in which God was so completely at one with
the universe, and that they had promptly excommunicated
Spinoza. I suspected, however, that in my father's case, beliefs or nonbeliefs had little to do with religion.

He dragged me to the synagogue in order that I might
acquire an identity. He wanted me to know the biblical
words in Hebrew. Inevitably it was there I became a rebel.
Already I was contrary-minded, turning away from religion,
which at first became irrelevant to me and then an allergy.
Yet I was captivated by the arts of religion, particularly religious music, and not only Jewish music. To this day I listen
enraptured to the liturgy of the Russian Orthodox church.
There is something penetrating in the voice of a Russian
basso profundo, something soaring in the Russian choir. I
am ensnared by the great Italians, notably the fascist tenor
Beniamino Gigli in the Verdi *Requiem*. A stranger in a
record store once told me that he could not live without Vi-
valdi's setting of Psalm 109, the *Dixit*, and I nodded with
full understanding. In Paris I had the supremely good fortune of hearing a live performance of Rossini's *Stabat Mater*,
and when I first listened to a recording of the young
Mozart's "Italianate" *Laudamus Dominum*, the melody was
piercing. In a conversation with a highly intellectual mon-
signor, I asked why Beethoven's *Missa Solemnis* was not
heard more often in churches. He replied that the music

was so powerful that the listener would be paying homage not to God but to Ludwig van Beethoven. And so it is with my homage when I enter the mosque of the Dome of the Rock, or when I gaze at Jusepe Ribera's painting *The Holy Agnes*, or when I read Genesis.

In the Austria of the 1930s it was impossible even for a Jewish child to be completely insulated from the pervasive Catholicism of the country. One of my teachers in public school, a Jew who had become a Catholic, led the class in the Lord's Prayer. Carefully he stated that the Jews need not participate, but since the prayer was so "beautiful," he invited them to recite it anyway. Nothing this man could have done would have created a greater aversion in me for all the words in the New Testament. More than a half-century passed before my interest in this document was aroused. To understand the actions of a priest, Bernhard Lichtenberg, who prayed for the Jews openly in the Berlin of 1941, and who was tried and convicted by a German court for his act, I reached for the Gospels and read them in one evening. That is when I appreciated their power.

A child is influenced not only by elders. One of my friends, Heinz Aschkenasi, who was a year older than I, imparted to me a great deal about his interests and hobbies, especially geography. I must have accommodated myself to him for several years, until he expanded into astronomy, but I still heard from him after his emigration to Tarija, in southern Bolivia, from where he sent me detailed letters about local flora and fauna. Whatever he said, the word *Geographie*, which he pronounced with gravity, remained in my consciousness.

In my childhood, both my mother and father constantly reminded me of my good fortunes. I was shielded from privation. Never did hunger or want cloud my days. I should have been unqualifiedly happy. Indeed I was, with my daily coffee, or on those momentous occasions when my mother and I boarded a train in the summer to leave for some destination, the farther the better. The linear experience of being on a train was my awakening to space. I needed a window not only to see what was outside but to estimate speed. I had to listen to the rhythmic sounds which one can no longer hear, now that the tracks are seamless. The train opened the world to me. In my pre-atheistic period I imagined that after the completion of a reasonably long life, I would continue to ride in these trains, invisibly, as a ghost or a soul, without having to purchase or reserve a seat. This magnetism of the railroad never deserted me. In my adulthood I kept it a secret, of course, thinking that it would be regarded as an element of infantilism, even though I already realized that this contrivance of the industrial revolution had had an immense psychological impact, notably in Germany and Austria. The traveler in a modern German train, which is mostly bereft of the all-important compartments, still receives a schedule marking the kilometers between halts, and the time of arrival at each of these stops, so that the speed may be calculated en route. In the United States, where passenger trains are relatively slow and are no longer an optimal mode of travel between many cities, I have had to transfer my loyalty to airports and aircraft.

My cognizance of trains has affected my work, and for a long time I was preoccupied with them in a research project. Specifically I was interested in the transport of Jews to their deaths. Germany relied on railways not only for moving supplies and troops, but also for the so-called Final Solution, which entailed the transfer of Jews from all parts of Europe to death camps or shooting sites. The railway apparatus was not only very large; its administrative procedures were almost incomprehensible. I went from archive to archive, pondering the special trains, the assembly of their rolling stock, their special schedules, and their financing. After I had just completed my study, Claude Lanzmann visited me in Vermont to discuss his idea of making a major film about the Jewish catastrophe. He showed me a railway document he had found and I seized it like an addict to explain the hieroglyphic contents to him. "This I must film," he said, and I repeated my analysis before his camera. Lanzmann also borrowed a train from the Polish government. A retired locomotive driver, who had hauled Jews to the death camp of Treblinka, took the controls one more time. The train encircles the film, emerging, as if from a tunnel, again and again, to mark the end of the Jewish people in Europe.

At the age of ten I was presented with a precious book. Although it was bought not for my pleasure but as a required text for the *Gymnasium* I was to attend, it mesmerized me immediately. The book was an atlas. A masterpiece of cartography, it was made for the eye, with maps so finely shaded that they highlighted the distinctions between major and minor rivers, deeper and more shallow waters, higher and lower mountains. Railroad tracks were always sketched in red, and cities were shown with circles and lettering denoting their size. Soon I leaped across the topographical features to the international frontiers. Here was something new: the political world, the world of power. Needless to say, Germany's and Austria's territorial losses in the First World War were indicated on several maps, and understandably Palestine was absorbed in an Arab desert. The omission of Palestine, however, was made up later when my school, the Chajes Realgymnasium, which was a Jewish institution, supplied us with a map on which we could locate every settlement in the Jewish homeland.

I never became a geographer. When I was about eleven I did try to make use of Latin, which we were forced to learn, to write a short text of geography in that language. I must have believed mistakenly that my work would be admired. A few years later I had forgotten all my Latin, along with my Hebrew, but the maps were imprinted in my mind for decades to come. In 1938 and 1939 my geographic expertise was actually appreciated by prospective Jewish emigrants who would ask me, "Raul, where is Barbados? Where is Trinidad?" Geography, however, became for me something more than an array of place names. I was beginning to think in spatial terms. When I studied international law I understood without need for explanations what "territory" meant in the context of that law, and when I delved into the German Reich, its occupied areas and satellite states, I saw it in a specific space, widening and extending its measures against the Jews.

That I did not explore geography as such more deeply is primarily a result of my shortcomings, particularly in mathematics; but to a certain extent I also attribute my stoppage of progress in the cartographic arts to my discovery of history. We had been introduced to the subject of chronology in our history classes, of course, but the recital of Holy Roman emperors had instead produced a nebulous impression of perpetuation. The Viennese instruction in history had for all practical purposes smothered any sense of change or even of progression. Then came a man who imparted to everyone a powerful demonstration of historical presence: Adolf Hitler. The impact of his appearance was unmistakable. In the hallway a Christian neighbor was crying because her thousand-year-old Austria had ceased to exist. The next day giant swastika flags were draped from the upper stories of apartment houses; photographs of Hitler were hung from windows; and marching youths with drums were moving through the streets. Jews, huddling in their apartments, breathed the ominous air and wondered what would happen to them if they did not emigrate in time. "Hitler will put us to the wall," my father said.

My childhood had ended in one stroke. I listened to all the conversations of the adults, and I was not excluded from their anxieties. I was riveted to the specter of unfolding events. Nothing escaped me now: the endless truck convoys filled with troops moving to the Czechoslovak border; Hitler's ultimatum that, come what may, he would march into the Sudetenland on October 1, 1938; the occupation of Prague; Japanese offensives in China; the Phalangist victory in the Spanish Civil War. As I gazed from the window, observing the scene, a thought fleeted through my mind: Some day I will write about what I see here.

On April 2, 1939, we were on a train moving slowly across the Rhine bridge linking Kehl, Germany, to Strasbourg, France. A German woman approached my mother in the corridor of the railway car and, full of curiosity, asked my mother for her reactions to the Nazi regime. She was a fashion expert on her way to Paris for a look at *haute couture*, the only field in which Germany still conceded superiority to the French. My mother replied that she would not speak until we had reached Strasbourg. A few minutes later we were free and—to be precise about our new status—refugees. In my mind this change, despite the advent of rootlessness and poverty, was completely positive. My parents still provided for me, and so far as I was concerned it was *they* who depended on my mother's family or occasionally on Jewish refugee relief agencies along the way. I was carefree. Not only had I escaped from Nazi Germany but I was expanding my acquaintance with the world exponentially. For a week we remained in Paris, waiting for a ship to Cuba that we would board in La Rochelle. Paris was a revelation to me. I noted that the poet Heinrich Heine had lived there. The Rhine in Düsseldorf, from where he came, is wider than the Seine, and he sometimes pined for the Altstadt—Düsseldorf's old core, where he was born and where he grew up—but he must have been drawn irresistibly to Paris, as I was. Paris, perhaps more than any city I know, had everything for everyone. One could not be lost there; one could only find oneself. I had occasion to test my reaction at intervals during later decades, and it never mattered what I did there. On my sixty-second birthday in 1988, I was still able to take an intoxicating walk through the throngs on the Champs Élysées.

My excitement in April 1939 was not dimmed when we

went on by train to La Rochelle. As we moved south I noticed the many soldiers, some of them Africans, at the stations, and permitted myself a conclusion that turned out to be my first error of judgment in world affairs. If Germany tried to attack France again, I thought, it would bleed to death there.

The ship, the *Reina del Pacifico*, was English, and so was its food. For most of the eleven-day voyage I was seasick, but for a few days, as the vessel moved into the tropics, I tried to walk on the deck reserved for third-class passengers. There was a single small social room with a single phonograph and a single record that played the "Donkey Serenade" over and over. Perhaps this music was an unsubtle message of what the British management thought of the passengers assembled there: Jewish refugees embarked for Havana, Cuba; middle-class Chinese on their way to South America from Canton, a city occupied a few months earlier by the Japanese; and Cuban communists who had fought as volunteers on the losing side in the Spanish Civil War, just ended, and who were going home.

My Cuban interlude lasted a little more than four months. I would not have minded a longer sojourn in Havana, for I felt alive there. We lived in a "hotel," in the old part of the city, on the corner of Calle Habana and Calle Muralla. It was filled with Jewish refugees and its rooms were partitions, without a ceiling, capped only by a roof. When someone turned on a light it illuminated the other cubicles as well. The showers and washroom were at the end of the hall, and each family had a table with chairs in the corridor. The summer was hot and insects were everywhere, from flying cucarachas to ordinary sugar ants. I remember a poor refugee who found ants inside her loaf of bread and exposed the cut bread to the sun in the hope the ants would leave.

My father and I walked a great deal in Havana, and I listened to the cacophony of musical sounds blaring from the open windows of street-level apartments. Some of the sidewalks were so narrow that a passing trolley would force pedestrians to press against the wall of a building. Everywhere there was loud conversation and shouting. The ubiquitous oranges, sold from carts, were cut in half and eaten by their buyers on the street. Coffee and milk were poured with both hands into the cup of a patron who would regulate the proper mix with continuous instructions. A chain of fifty Chinese restaurants, the Fonda, dotted the city and offered meals for a few cents. In an amphitheater police and army bands entertained the public free of charge. The concerts were always offered in two parts: the first half was classical, featuring such works as Wagner's *Tannhäuser* overture, which were applauded politely; but for the second half the instruments for the Cuban rumba and conga were added, and the audience became more animated until it went wild with the rhythmic playing of the dances.

In Cuba I also had my freedom. I do not mean the feeling of an adult who has just left a totalitarian country, but the elimination of the constrictions imposed by school. Most all our books were in storage, but I had three, including the atlas, which I always carried with me. The other two books were a novel, written by a German who had crossed the United States as a tramp on freight trains, and a volume of plays by Shakespeare, in German, of course. I read both the novel and the plays for my amusement. Two tutorials were nevertheless imposed on me. My father himself took charge of my Hebrew, which he feared was slipping from my mind. He tried valiantly to have me memorize in the original as much of Genesis as possible. The brevity of Hebrew, he assured me, was one of the marvels of the world; the power of its sentences could not be duplicated in any other language he knew. The more of these sentences I could retain, the better a man I would be. I fully understood Genesis, and its literary impact on me was unmistakable. "You write short sentences," an editor once complained to me. I still do, though sometimes I hide this quirk with suitable connectives and, on rare occasions, semicolons. My Hebrew, however, was not to be salvaged. It went the way of Latin. The fact is that I started with the wrong languages. Many years later I read an article by a colleague about the fate of the Norwegian Jews. One of his footnotes puzzled me, and so I called the author for an explanation. He struggled with an answer, comparing his source with his note, and finally blurted out: "Raul, why don't you know an important language like Norwegian?" He was right, of course, and he might have added Latvian, or Lithuanian. . . .

I also had to learn a new language in Cuba, not Spanish—for soon I would have to leave this island—but English, which was to be my next vehicle of discourse. In Vienna I had already heard English in broadcasts of the BBC. I knew that in order to speak it I had to adjust my mouth, and I practiced these contortions in the mirror, also lisping as one was supposed to. In the *Gymnasium* the instructor in English was practical. He did not burden us with grammar (I soon learned that there was none, at least by German, Latin, or Hebrew standards) but taught us "Pat a cake, pat a cake, baker's man." In Havana my tutor, thinking that Kipling's jungle stories were appropriate for my age, introduced me to that author. But when I came to the United States I could not tell someone the time.

The United States used annual quotas to regulate immigration. They were assigned on the basis of birth in a foreign country. My parents, born in a part of Austria-Hungary that was Polish between the two world wars, were admissible only under the relatively small Polish quota. Austria, where I was born, was considered for quota purposes to be a part of Germany, and therefore I was eligible to enter the United States under the much larger German quota. My father had registered himself, my mother, and me at the American consulate in Vienna on the same day, but for them the waiting period was ten months longer than for me.

After traveling by ship with a Cuban couple to Miami, where I arrived on September 1, 1939, I saw the tabloid headline WAR STARTS. Having heard that the American press would print anything to sell papers, I ignored them. For two days on my way to New York I did not think about Europe. On the bus, which had tiny windows, I caught a glimpse of America. The one sight that remains in my memory as we traversed the South was that of benches marked "For Colored." I reflected on the fact that I, who was not allowed to sit on a Viennese park bench stenciled *Nur für Arier* (For Aryans Only), had instantly been catapulted into a position above that of many Americans who had been born here.

On September 3 in New York I met several family members on my mother's side: the matriarchal aunt Adela and most of her children. The first cousins were considerably older than I. One of them, with whom I lived for the first two weeks, had a small daughter, the first of yet another generation. I was then shifted to Adela's apartment, where I joined her husband and her two adult unmarried children. Adela's daughter Gertrude, who played the violin, was the sort of person who could teach little children how to hold a bow and move it across the strings. I liked Gertrude immensely.

On my first day in New York I was naturally in the center of my family's attention, but the questions I was asked were interrupted as everyone gathered around the radio to listen to the British and French declarations of war on Germany. War had indeed begun, at least for the Poles, who were being overrun by German armies. For me this development was a signal to start a diary. Each day was allotted a line, and the only entries pertained to the progress of the war. In other words, I read the war communiqués and carefully noted invasions and the capture of cities.

In New York I was no longer spared from school. Only days after my arrival I was registered in the Abraham Lincoln High School, where I would spend the next three years. While one of my cousins and I were waiting in a small room for an interview and forms, I noticed an older man and his son who were there for the same purpose. The man

walked up to me and asked me in German whether my name was Hilberg. He had never seen me before but had known my father in Vienna. His son Erich (later Eric) Marder became my lifelong friend. Both Eric and I lived three or four miles from school, and to save the cost of the trolley ride (five cents) we walked home together, discussing Jewish politics and the larger questions of life. In the fifty years or so since, we have largely dropped Jewish political issues, but we are still engaged in exploring selected existential questions.

Even in retrospect my overall impression of Abraham Lincoln High School is such that I must pause in the middle of the sentence to regain my composure. The atmosphere struck me as totalitarian. Student patrols were posted in the corridors. When I first received my program, I was supposed to report daily to a room with a three-digit number and an "L." Day after day I looked frantically for a number with an "L," but there was none. Finally I learned that the room was "prefect class," which met only for the purpose of checking attendance, and that the "L" stood for "late session." For several decades I relived this horror in my dreams. Gymnastics was an abomination, destroying every vestige of dignity and privacy a human being of any age should be entitled to in civilian life. "I don't like your rotten attitude," the gymnastics teacher told me. I did not have much to look forward to in my other classes, either. Science and mathematics were taught to elevate geniuses and brand the untalented. These subjects, as I should have known right away, would not be the bedrock of my career. The course in European history, on the other hand, taught by a

woman who could not hide her communist sympathies, was laughable.

As I look for saving graces in this system, I can think of only three. One was a speech class for foreigners, in which accents were worked on. I now wish I had received more of this instruction. Another was the "creative writing" class, which was noteworthy not for what was taught there, namely next to nothing, but because it was an island of freedom. Finally I must mention a teacher in American history, Alfred Nussbaum, who pronounced the "u" in his name as in "us." Mr. Nussbaum was a follower of the now half-forgotten Charles Beard, who had emphasized the economic basis of history and politics. For me such an approach was much too confining, and I would probably have forgotten Mr. Nussbaum were it not for his manner and one particular incident, both of which were unusual.

Mr. Nussbaum was utterly convinced of the importance of what he was teaching, which is a fundamental prerequisite for any effective classroom presentation. "Can't you see," he would say with reference to some point that, if missed, would assuredly result in a permanent perceptual disability. One day I did not bring my homework, which he would inspect by walking through the rows at the beginning of the class hour. It was Monday, and the date was December 8, 1941. On the Sunday before, I had dropped all my usual activities, acutely aware that Japan's attack on the United States and Great Britain had opened a new chapter in history. When Mr. Nussbaum asked why I had not done my homework, I made no attempt to conceal my reaction to his question. "Because I am not a historian," I said sarcasti-

cally. "But you *are* a historian," he answered calmly. Some forty-five years later he came to a lecture I gave at the Graduate Center of the City University of New York, which hosted a small Holocaust conference. During an intermission I told the story of my December 8, 1941, exchange with Nussbaum to a colleague, Lucjan Dobroszycki. "Funny," said Dobroszycki, "Nussbaum just told me the same story."

Not very long ago the principal of the high school called me in Vermont to ask whether I would speak to the school. No, I said immediately, my schedule was already more than full, and I could not muster the time for a trip. In truth, I had never set foot there since my graduation, and I had always been convinced that virtually all the graduates of this institution kept their incarceration in the place a secret. But then a colleague who was in the biochemistry department of our medical school, and who, it turned out, was also an alumnus of the high school, shared with me a two-page newsletter that the principal had mailed to several of the alumni. Evidently some of them had accomplished something. One was the novelist Joseph Heller, who probably had the same creative writing teacher. In addition there were three Nobel laureates in the sciences.

I was a thirteen-year-old high school student in 1939 and a sixteen-year-old college student in 1942. The first two years in Brooklyn College were even more depressing than the preceding three in high school. I worked part-time in Manhattan factories, and at the insistence of my father, who strongly believed in the practical value of chemistry, I concentrated my major study in that discipline. My misery grew. When I had a seat in the subway I read irresponsibly, be it Hemingway or Tolstoy, Spengler or Nietzsche. Finally I became eighteen. The war was still on and the United States Army liberated me from chemistry.

Crossroads

WHEN I WAS STILL in basic training, an unusually perceptive sergeant told me that I could be a corporal or a colonel, but that I could not be a military man between these ranks. I was a poor soldier at the start, because I could not accept shibboleths like the senseless "general orders," which I refused to memorize. When the company commander decreed that I would not have the privilege of a pass to the city of Spartanburg, South Carolina, he found me quite content to stay in the camp on Sundays. I then obtained the pass as a punishment. When he asked me *why* I was the only man in the company who had not learned the general orders, I replied that evidently I could not master them. He became angry and actually considered sending me to officers' training school. I did not become an officer, but I was intensely interested in the war and was given the task of explaining it to the other trainees in the company.

Grand strategy was not my only interest. I began to wonder why the American infantry was equipped with the clip-fed Browning automatic rifle—with which an expert could fire single deliberate shots but which had 103 parts that could jam easily—while the German army had a light

53

machine gun, which was a terror weapon with a high cyclic rate of fire and a barrel that could be changed in seconds when it became overheated. The American hand grenade seemed to me a tribute to the game of baseball, and I seriously considered the possibility that, beyond all the calculations involving the need to fight overseas and the attendant problems of supply, infantry arms could also be an expression of national character. The American, I believed, had a faster reaction time than his German opponent, and he sought ways of acting quickly in crisis situations, but for this reason he also dreaded and felt trapped in an artillery barrage, not armored by the psychological stamina and fatalism of his European adversary. Such were some of my thoughts during my first months in uniform.

From the moment I boarded a troopship to Europe, I became hyperalert. Everything within view and hearing I imprinted in my memory. I did not, however, have the searing experience that was the lot of millions of people in wars. I cannot compare my record with the long agony my father endured. I was not wounded and received no medals. Unlike so many American soldiers, I was not shelled at Anzio, did not cross the Rapido River, and did not wade ashore under withering fire on Omaha Beach. For years and decades I was told that I could not imagine what it was like. I heard this phrase over and over, not only from Americans but from a one-legged German veteran who had been trapped in the Demyansk pocket in 1941, and from survivors of Auschwitz. My brush with the war was very brief. Although I carried a rifle, I felt less than I observed.

I do remember a moment at two o'clock in the morning

when our troopship was rocked by explosions. Having always made distinctions between kinds of death, the watery one was especially threatening. Lying in my bunk, I imagined the waves rushing in and the ship going down with its thousands of soldiers trapped inside, a pandemonium and a drowning. The explosions, it turned out, were caused by our own depth charges to discourage what might have been an enemy submarine penetrating the cordon of warships in our convoy. On land I somehow felt more secure, even when I was awakened by explosions shaking the ground under me in a replacement depot. Was I the European in an American uniform?

One time I came away with an image rather than an experience. It was April 1945 in Bavaria. I looked at a field bathed in the sun. During the night the Germans had attempted to assault our lines. Our machine gunners had mowed them down. All over the field the bodies of the Germans lay motionless, rifles stuck in the ground to mark their location. One corpse was on its back, its eye sockets filled with blood. What, I asked myself, could have compelled these men at this late stage of the war to run into almost certain death? Was it the forlorn hope of being spared? I already knew that the state, and its political order, rests on the possibility of an ultimate resort to force by a government acting against its own citizenry. The men who, with barking officers behind their backs, made their suicide run were proof of the viability of this system. But why had they followed such an order? Why did they not mutiny?

I gathered impressions at a furious rate, but as a soldier I was, of course, a novice, and the war was over before I could be anything else. Our division stopped in Munich, and there we were quartered for several weeks in the former Nazi party headquarters. I had reached the center of the Nazi movement just after its demise, fingering the books of the Nazi party library, including a party edition of Martin Luther's treatise *About the Jews and Their Lies*. I mistrusted that publication until some years later when I read the original sixteenth-century book in the New York Public Library. In the party building I also spotted about sixty wooden cases. Still in possession of my skills as a shipping clerk, I opened a few and discovered that they contained Hitler's private library.

When I returned to the United States I was sent to intelligence school. Now I learned all manner of things that I should have known before I interrogated any German prisoners. My major course was "Order of Battle," the organization of foreign armies, a subject I recognized later as a proper subcategory of political science. For the first time I plunged into my studies with eagerness. It was during this assignment that I was promoted to technician fifth grade, the equivalent of a corporal. One of my classmates, a sergeant, Francis Winner, was one of the brightest men in the army. At the school we fought the war over, and in our competitive exercises I beat him only once, when I drew a situation map of the Battle of the Bulge. He had crowded his map too much, a familiar failing of American cartographers.

One weekend, Winner and I drove to his home, a pig farm in Iowa. It was an all-night drive, and so we had to have an agenda. He proposed his favorite topic: land mines, one of which he had sent home by parcel post from Germany for closer study. I countered with comparative machine guns. When our weapons discussion was exhausted, he came to the real point. He wanted to stay in the army. He wanted to be a cadet at West Point. He wanted to become a general. My immediate thought was, You can be a sergeant or a general, but what about all the intermediate ranks? Out loud I reminded him that he was over twenty and that he had been wounded on the Remagen Bridge. Furthermore he had another problem: Would there be another war? He wanted to be a major player and he understood, even in his sergeant's uniform, that a military man could not find fulfillment without a real test, a real contest. I lost track of him, but some forty years later I learned that he had become a major general in the reserve, dealing with legal matters. Had he reached his goal? And I, what was to become of me?

Returning to Brooklyn College, I jettisoned my chemistry. My remaining subjects of concentration were history and political science. In political science I found my intellectual home. I hungered for a structure, and soon I found two of them in the context of political science courses: government and law. Yet it was a historian at college who, more than any of his colleagues in the political science department, was to have a deep and lasting influence on me. His name was Hans Rosenberg. An expert in Prussian bureaucracy, he labeled his course "The Rise of the National State." He spoke in complete sentences and paragraphs, and each lecture was a chapter. In his presentations the bureaucracy became an organism. Its cells underwent amalgamation and interfusion as it took root in the territorial domain of the state, evolving and developing with a tenured meritocracy into an indispensable and indestructible system. As I listened to his lectures I began to identify "government" more and more with public administration, and I became aware of the concept of jurisdiction, that bedrock of the legal order, which appeared to be both the basis and the basic tool of the bureaucrats. These potentates were an unstoppable force. As administrators they would always follow precedent, but if need be they would break new ground, without calling attention to themselves or claiming a patent, trademark, or copyright. The bureaucracy was a hidden world, an overlooked world, and once I was conscious of it I would not be deterred from prying open its shuttered windows and bolted doors.

Like me, Rosenberg was a refugee from Germany, but from what I heard he had no connection with the Jewish community. His course covered the years from 1660 to 1930, a stopping point that at the time was customarily observed by historians who shied away from the present. Once, he overstepped his self-imposed limit and spoke of the German resistance movement during the Second World War. Another time he remarked, in parentheses, that the Napoleonic atrocities in Spain had not been equaled since. At this point I raised my hand and asked, "What do you call six million dead Jews?" Ah, said Rosenberg, that was an interesting problem, but one which was very complicated, and he was constrained by time and the outline of the course to forgo a discussion of my question. The whole incident took but a minute, and I believed that I was very calm. Many years later, however, a woman who had been in the class and who remembered the exchange exactly, said that I had been so tense that my fellow students were concerned about me.

Although I perceived in Rosenberg's remark about Napoleon a plain denial of Adolf Hitler's Germany, I used everything he taught. I did not even discard the word "complicated," with which he had answered me. To the contrary, the idea that the destruction of the Jews was complex became a fundamental hypothesis that guided my work. This complexity was to be uncovered, demonstrated, and explained. The killing, I became convinced, was no atrocity in the conventional sense. It was infinitely more, and that "more" was the work of a far-flung, sophisticated bureaucracy.

As yet, however, the inchoate thoughts swirling in my head had not reached tangible form. I had to entertain, however briefly, a choice dictated by the division of more advanced studies into law schools and graduate schools. You must go to law school, said one of my professors. You should earn law *and* graduate degrees, I was advised by a professor in graduate school, who held both. I could afford only one program, even with the help of veterans' benefits, so I became a student in the Department of Public Law and Government, as political science was called in the graduate faculties at Columbia University. I would concentrate on public international law, a field that soothed me and gave me peace. I mastered the logic of this law and spent long days reveling in such topics as state succession and reservations to multipartite treaties. Briefly I weighed the possibility of writing a dissertation about an aspect of war crimes, and then I woke up. It was the evidence that I wanted. My subject would be the destruction of the European Jews.

As I thought about my plan concretely, I was able to enroll in classes of two highly knowledgeable men. One was Salo Baron, who had set himself the task of writing about the entire sweep of Jewish history, in twenty or more volumes if need be. His vision was more complete than that of any of his predecessors. It was to encompass all the domains of the Jewish experience: political, economic, social, and religious. Later I heard it said that he was in a trance, writing incessantly as he became older until he was enfeebled and died—his work still unfinished.

Baron would come to his class directly from his apartment nearby, take off his coat, sit down at his desk, and lecture without notes like a pianist embarking on a sonata. Moreover, Baron was not only the player but also the composer. He delivered his chords faultlessly, and I wrote down what he said as completely as I could. The yellowed pages are still in my possession—the only such folder I have saved from my student days—and when I decided to reread them after many years, I was amazed by the extent to which I had incorporated his thinking. It was a course in modern Jewish history, which Baron had divided into eras before and after emancipation, but in which he constantly stressed the independent life and separate fate of the Jews in all the lands of their residence. He spoke of the Spanish certificates of purity—*limpieza*—issued by the Inquisitorial courts of the fifteenth and sixteenth centuries and showing the Jewish descent of professing Christians, sometimes to one-sixteenth of their ancestry. He would point out that a book published by a Jew in Salonika would be read by his brethren in Amsterdam and Krakow, even while the Krakow Jews were ignorant of a Polish book published in their own city. Yet there was safety in this isolation, he said. When the emancipation was promulgated in several countries of Europe, it was not only uplifting but threatening. It was not an act of goodwill toward the Jews but a necessity of the national state. Jewish society responded nervously, he indicated, by making efforts to shift Jews into more "productive" pursuits, such as agriculture and manufacture.

I came away from Baron's course with an impression of Jewish apartness, of a long-lived self-contained community that had to cope with the new expectations of governments and that had become newly vulnerable as it emerged from the ghetto. Already I was thinking of Jewish defenselessness under the Nazi regime. When I asked Baron for bibliographical references to explore my subject, he asked me whether I wanted to write my doctoral dissertation under his direction. No, I said, I was a student of public law and government, and I was going to ask a professor in that department to be my guide. His name was Franz Neumann.

I had already decided to write about the German perpetrators. The destruction of the Jews was a German deed. It was implemented in German offices, in a German culture. I was convinced from the very beginning of my work that without an insight into the actions of the perpetrators, one could not grasp this history in its full dimensions. The perpetrator had the overview. He alone was the key. It was through his eyes that I had to view the happening, from its genesis to its culmination. That the perpetrator's perspective was the primary path to be followed became a doctrine for me, which I never abandoned.

Franz Neumann was to bring me closer to my goal. As a new visiting professor in 1948, he taught a course in German government which was packed by more than one hundred graduate students. He was forty-eight years old. Because he was hard of hearing, he would respond to questions with a bellowed "What? What?" His lectures were delivered in a staccato manner. His observations came like hammer blows, and conclusions sounded like announcements: "Germany became a democracy twice—both times by decisions of military authorities." Neumann began with the Middle Ages, holding his class in suspense until he reached the Nazi regime. That subject was his specialty, and he had explored it in an audacious book which he called *Behemoth*.

I read Neumann's work, which was one of our texts, from cover to cover several times. Its style, like that of the lectures, was dry, declarative, unadorned. The opening sentence of his concluding chapter begins with the words, "We have finished our discussion." But what a discussion and what a conclusion! With one decisive, sweeping motion he determined that Nazi Germany had no political theory, that it had no Marx, that it was not missionary in character, that unlike communist or democratic systems it sought no converts. In a single, startling generalization he pointed out that under National Socialism the whole of German society was organized into four solid, centralized groups, each operating under a leadership principle, and each with legislative, administrative, and judicial powers of its own. These four hierarchies were the civil service, the army, industry, and the party. Operating independently of one another, without a legislature specifying their prerogatives, they coordinated their efforts with agreements that, in class, he caustically referred to as "social contracts." Here then I found a Nazi Germany that in its roots was anarchic, an organized chaos, but with a freedom to march into completely uncharted areas of action.

When Neumann wrote his *Behemoth*, the war was still in progress. He did not have the benefit of using captured records. All his sources were library materials, such as legal gazettes or industry journals. My own intention, on the other hand, was to exploit the internal correspondence of the perpetrators, which was secret from the Allied powers and the general public during the war but which was being sifted in Nuremberg for introduction as evidence in the trials of war criminals. From a few printed samples of this collection I formed my first assumption: The destruction of the Jews was not centralized. All four of Neumann's hierarchies were involved in this operation. I called this bureaucratic aggregate the machinery of destruction. As I read on, I discovered my second hypothesis in an affidavit by Rudolf Kastner, a Jewish leader in Budapest who had observed the fate of the European Jewish communities before the Hungarian Jews were inundated in the catastrophe. In one sentence of his description of events he noted that "The plan of operation was almost identical in all countries: at first the Jews were marked, then separated, divested of all property, deported and gassed." It appeared, therefore, that the Jews were destroyed in a progression of steps and that everywhere the sequence was the same. Considering, however, that the machinery was not unified and that it did not follow a basic blueprint from the beginning, such patterned action was remarkable. The Germans did not know in 1933 what they were going to do in 1935 or 1938. The ultimate goal of annihilation, which in German correspondence was called the "Final Solution," was not even formulated until 1941. There was, however, a direction that was characterized by ever more intensive, more drastic anti-Jewish activities. Along this path, the logic of the development emerged, for the simple reason that earlier, more harmless measures were always the administrative prerequisites for later, more harmful ones. In short, the destruction of the Jews had an intrinsic, or latent, structure. I called this phenomenon the destruction process.

Kastner had given me an indication of this process, but I needed a more exact specification of the steps. I had to construct an outline, rigid and comprehensive enough to hold any document that I would find, so that even if there were thousands of notes, I would be able to file all of them precisely in the order in which I would use them in my narrative. At this point I was stymied, and I felt there was only one man who could help me: Eric Marder. A conceptualizer and problem solver unlike anyone I knew, he listened to me one evening at the Port Authority Terminal in New York, where he was about to take a bus home. With a sheet of paper he untangled the maze right then and there. Three of the steps were organic: the definition of the Jews, their concentration, and their annihilation. The Germans had to define the concept of "Jew" before they could move further against their target, and they had to isolate the Jews physically from their neighbors before they could proceed with the Final Solution. The economic measures against the Jewish community, which I could not easily place in the scheme without Eric's help, had another, secondary logic of their own. They too followed the basic steps in a precise order: dismissals from jobs and transfers or liquidations of Jewish enterprises after the definition; special taxes and wages up to forced labor after marking or ghettoization; confiscations of the Jewish "estate" after the killing.

One of my professors in international law, who was born in Moscow at the beginning of the century, asked me why the Jews could not have been simply killed with bricks and bats. The answer, of course, lies in the limited effects of a pogrom. As I discovered later, Adolf Hitler already understood this basic limitation in 1919 when he discounted temporary and relatively ineffectual outbursts in the streets and advocated rational measures that would lead to a final result.

I had become sure of myself, secure in my decision, certain that I would fill in the pieces of my jigsaw puzzle. It would take all my limited knowledge, all my limited talents, but precisely for this reason it was the right project for me. "Man," said Goethe, "may turn wherever he will, he may undertake whatever it may be, always he will return to that path which nature had marked out for him." As yet, however, I was not prepared to approach Franz Neumann with the full scope of my plan and to disclose my nature to him.

I was only a first-year graduate student. Neumann, who had many protégés and who granted only fifteen-minute interviews, did not know me at all. I broached the subject of a term paper. It would be titled "The Role of the German Civil Service in the Destruction of the Jews." He nodded and asked me whether I knew who Franz Schlegelberger was. At the time I did not know that ranking official of the German Justice Ministry. He sent me to the poorly lit four-teenth floor of the Butler Library, where mimeographed copies of the Nuremberg trial documents were kept. Later I said to him that the topic was too big for a term paper. Would he agree to sponsor it as a master's essay? He nodded again. After he had read my trial run of two hundred pages, he objected only to one passage in the conclusion. It was my statement that administratively the Germans had relied on the Jews to follow directives, that the Jews had cooperated in their own destruction. Neumann did not say that this finding was contradicted by any facts; he did not say that it was underresearched. He said, "This is too much to take—cut it out." I deleted the passage, silently determined to re-store it to my larger work. Then I said to him that the civil service was only part of the story. I would have to add the military, industry, and the party. Neumann nodded for a third time. Would he, I asked, sponsor me for a doctoral dissertation entitled "The Destruction of the European Jews"? I was prepared to hand him a tightly constructed twenty-page outline. Neumann said yes, but he knew that at this moment I was separating myself from the mainstream of academic research to tread in territory that had been avoided by the academic world and the public alike. What he said to me in three words was, "It's your funeral."

III
The Gamble

Documents

FOR MANY YEARS after my decision to write the dissertation, I was alone. I do not mean that I was cut off from all contacts with colleagues and friends. In the course of my employment in various jobs I met with other people, and I was always in touch with Eric Marder. To all outward appearances I led at least a seminormal life.

Yet I was living in a closed world, one in which I was isolated with my documents and the story that evolved from them. Now and then I would share a discovery with a young fellow specialist in Nazi matters, Frederic S. Burin II, or with Eric, but on the whole I was engaged in a lone endeavor. In the prevailing atmosphere, which drew the attention of American Jews to Israel and the Arabs, and which directed the thinking of Americans as a whole to the cold war with the Soviet Union, my subject was relegated to the past. This was the time when those—like survivors—who were plagued by memories, were told to forget what had happened, and when the Nuremberg trials were conducted not so much to understand Germany's history as to conclude unfinished business in order that Germany might be reconstituted with a clean slate in the North Atlantic community of nations confronted with the threat of communism. Under these circumstances I was reluctant to mention my preoccupation in conversations with strangers.

In fact, I believed I was the only person who was trying to unearth and describe the German upheaval against the Jews. Fred Burin, who was fluent in French and who kept up with new books in the French language, called my attention to a book by Leon Poliakov. Titled *The Breviary of Hate* (later translated as *The Harvest of Hate*), it was a succinct summation of the Holocaust, albeit concentrated on the drastic phase of the process. I quickly looked at the footnotes—they were references mainly to the Nuremberg trial records. Whereas I was in the midst of looking at virtually all the nearly forty thousand prosecution documents, and a number of defense items as well, he had used relatively few. His thesis, expressed in the title, that the root of the process was hatred, seemed in my eyes to be an antiquated supposition. The bureaucrats, I already knew, were not "haters."

A few years after Poliakov's book appeared, another colleague mentioned that he had seen a British monograph on my topic. He did not remember the author, and he thought the title was something like "The End of the Question." Before I even found the book, whose author was Gerald Reitlinger and whose title was *The Final Solution*, I called Eric Marder. Here was the possibility of a personal crisis. If the work was based on the same sources, if my project had already been done, I would have to cease my efforts. After I read the book I was more at ease. Reitlinger had dug into documents more extensively than Poliakov, but he belittled—was this a British trait?—what had happened. He stressed that the destruction of the Jews was an "attempt" which had not entirely succeeded. After all, entire communities of Jews, especially in the West but also in the Balkans, had been left alive. He reduced some of the perpetrators to mere bunglers. One of them, a young man in a key position who expedited the deportation of Jews from France, he described as "puerile" and "ridiculous," a "pettyfogging lawyer of the least possible consequence." I could not endorse such an approach and saw no compelling reason to abandon my work. My coverage would be greater, and I would describe the deed, and those who had implemented it, in full.

By the spring of 1951, however, I had exhausted my savings. Neumann offered me a temporary job to escort a delegation of Germans in Washington. I said no. They were social democrats, he explained. Again I said no. Shortly thereafter he offered me another position, one which would unite me with my documents as a member of the newly formed War Documentation Project.

The project was housed in a building near the waterfront in Alexandria, Virginia, which had been converted from a torpedo tube factory into a federal records center. What I found inside was absolutely extraordinary. The United States government had gathered up captured German records of the Nazi era, shipped them across the ocean, and reassembled them in that building, where they filled 28,000 linear feet of shelf. Each piece of paper was in its original German folder and each folder, usually with other folders, was in a box, several inches wide, standing upright next to other boxes. It took but one glance at all these documents to realize that their contents could not be read by one individual in a lifetime.

The collection was sparse in industrial records or those of old established ministries; some of them had already been returned to the newly created Federal Republic of Germany. There was, however, much military material, including documents dealing with such topics as procurement, forced labor, and the military regime in occupied territories. I was a member of a team that consisted, on average, of eight people. We had been brought in to examine folders and to fill out cards about them for government clients, principally the air force, which wanted to know what the Germans had discovered about the Soviet Union during the Second World War. As I understood our mission, we were engaged in target research, not merely or even primarily physical targets but all the strengths and weaknesses of the USSR, including the morale of the Red Army and the civilian population. No objective, however, was clearly spelled out for us, and our aims remained murky.

The director of the project, Fritz T. Epstein, who had been chosen for his library experience and his knowledge of German and Russian, turned out to have limited analytical abilities. He was a prewar refugee who loved all Germans, and he took great care, because of his name, to explain that he was a practicing Lutheran. "He looks like a Jewish cattle dealer from Hesse," one of my older coworkers, who was a Jewish refugee, declared in a conversation with me, hissing as he spoke. Epstein's son Klaus became a well-known historian, who later gained notoriety for a derogatory review of William L. Shirer's *The Rise and Fall of the Third Reich*.

The Federal Republic of Germany mailed the review to many historians and political scientists in the United States, without explaining, of course, that the Epsteins might not be practicing Jews.

Our Epstein wished to establish contact with members of other projects in the building. One of the individuals he found in his explorations was Gustav Hilger, an official of the German Foreign Office during the Nazi regime, who had processed the reports of killings by Security Police for Foreign Minister Ribbentrop, and who had also been the conduit for plans to deport the Jews from northern Italy. Hilger was to address us, Epstein announced triumphantly. In that case, I would walk out, I replied. Epstein retreated and said nothing more about his German diplomat.

Hilger was not the only German recruit in our vicinity. There was also a German colonel who taught some American military officers in a room next to ours. One of my young colleagues, who was excited about intelligence work and national security, was tempted to look into the German personnel folder of the colonel, which was kept in our building. He showed me the record and asked me to explain the colonel's assignments on the eastern front. I could see immediately that our German neighbor had been the transport officer of the Eleventh Army at a time in 1941 when that unit lent the Security Police enough trucks to transport ten thousand Jews from the Crimean city of Simferopol to a shooting site. The Jews could then be killed quickly enough to allow the German army to enjoy Christmas without their presence. The colonel and I, however, had something in common. We would both stand in front of the locked gate before the records center was opened at eight o'clock in the morning. He said "Good morning" on one of these occasions, and I stared at him, not answering.

My eagerness at the gate had a profound reason. I had just begun to understand what a document really is. Here I could see that it is first of all an artifact, immediately recognizable as a relic. It is the original paper that once upon a time was handled by a bureaucrat and signed or initialed by him. More than that, the words on that paper constituted an *action*: the performance of a function. If the paper was an order, it signified the *entire* action of its originator.

Documents also store information. They are texts which contain a great deal of what we call history. A vast number of the documents in the federal records center had never been examined. Since the government did not know precisely what was in the folders, all of them were labeled confidential or secret. For me the pristine nature of this collection provoked suspense. What would I find there? Virtually all the work I performed for the government was automatically of benefit to me as well. The sheer disentanglement of German jurisdictions, such technical questions as to whether a military Ortskommandantur in some small city was a unit or a local office—all these problems would have to be addressed whether I was doing the government's work or my own. Moreover, the Jewish fate, as I learned quickly, was not isolated from the events that exploded all over the East. I had to know a great deal about the German occupation and its ramifications in order to grasp the setting and conditions in which the destruction process took place. Finally, however, I was interested in my subject specifically—the mention of Jews and the separate actions taken against them. I was looking especially for these passages, and I knew that the more I looked, the more of them I would find. When I was rewarded with a discovery, I experienced a sensation that is best known to my fellow page-turners. It is an excitement that still comes to me when I run a microfilm through a machine. I recall traveling with teams of specialists for the United States Holocaust Memorial Council to the Soviet Union and the German Democratic Republic just before their demise. As we sat in the cramped archives of these countries, Robert Wolfe, a veteran keeper of records, who once headed the Modern Military Branch of the United States Archives, remarked that looking at all these files, which had been locked behind the Iron Curtain for so long, was like being at the creation again.

I cannot help thinking of the isolated archivists in communist Eastern Europe who had held the other half of the story. The USSR had its sophisticated missiles and hydrogen bombs, but it kept its German records wherever they had been captured, in dozens of regional and local archives. Finding aids were often handwritten for the few researchers who were permitted to set foot there, and in one of these archives a Natasha with sixteen years of experience still did not know what was in her collection. The archives in Potsdam or Leipzig were different. Communist controlled but efficient, the German personnel knew everything. One of the clerks in Potsdam talked about a list of special trains as a "famous" register. It was, of course, famous to the other six clerks.

Often I have been asked whether in all the years of my research any of the material in the documents has ever made me ill. In the main I have been immune from such a reaction, but I do recall an exception. Early in my work I came across a wartime record of a court action brought by a Jew who had been denied his ration of pure coffee on the ground that he had received the coupon by mistake. *That* story made me slightly nauseous.

In the gathering of my sources I have always remained a brute-force man. My watchwords have been comprehensiveness and quantity. The more agencies whose materials I could examine, the better, and the more paper in the files, all the better. Because the destruction of the Jews was so decentralized, it required the participation of all those agencies that had the means to perform their share of the action at the moment when the need for their contribution arose. The spectrum of offices that were ultimately involved in the process is synonymous with the concept of German government or the whole of Germany's organized society. That is the reason I could not dispense with any agency collection, why nothing seemed too remote. I would sit in an archive in Lvov reading the correspondence of local German officials dealing with gardens and ornamental horticulture to discover that the greens were used as camouflage in the camps. I would learn that church records of births and marriages dating to the middle of the nineteenth century were essential in proving who was of Aryan descent and hence not a Jew. I found that a Berlin company that manufactured flags also produced bales of yellow Jewish stars. But I did not always recognize the importance of every single document, nor was I consistently successful in interpreting key pieces of paper. Such failures were galling to me.

Once, at the beginning of my research, I discarded a record because it seemed superfluous. Heinrich Himmler, as Reichsführer-SS und Chef der deutschen Polizei, had placed an announcement in a newspaper depriving the Jews of their drivers' licenses. I was still in Vienna when this edict was issued, and I distinctly recall that in the adult circle of our friends the measure occasioned some hilarity. No one in this group had a car. It was a young German researcher, Uwe Adam, who in the 1970s pursued this subject further and was led to a significant realization about the fundamental nature of the Nazi regime. Apparently there was a Jew with a driver's license who claimed that a mere announcement in a newspaper, as opposed to a promulgation in a legal gazette, was without effect. One might ask what importance a legal gazette had in a country so absolutist as Nazi Germany. The answer, of course, was that an order directed at a segment of the public had to be issued by the office that had jurisdiction in the regulation at hand. Himmler may have thought of himself as solely in charge of Jewish matters even before the war, but he had not been named to such a command post, and drivers' licenses, which were a traffic matter, were within the sphere of the Transport Ministry. A legal gazette was a means to assure that the proper authority was taking the action. If a particular measure touched the competence of two or more agencies, a prior agreement between them was necessary. That is why the *Reich Legal Gazette*, which was the most important of its

77

kind, would sometimes publish a decree signed by several ministers, the top name being that of the man in charge, but the others signifying with their signatures a participation in the origination and enforcement of the measure. That is the step that Himmler had omitted, and that is why the courts had a serious problem. Finally the highest court ruled that if the Reichsführer-SS had placed an announcement in the newspapers without arousing the protest of the Highest Reich Authorities, as the ministries were called, then his measure was law. Here I had overlooked an important development in the Third Reich. I did not clearly see the creation of an engine for the taking of initiatives. Not only Himmler but any number of potentates began to rely on the silent assent of their fellow functionaries to take ever more drastic and unprecedented measures.

Inattention to the value of a document was bad enough. Misconstruing the content of a communication, especially one that I regarded as pivotal, was worse. The item in question was an order signed by Göring, the Number Two Nazi, to Reinhardt Heydrich, chief of the Security Police, on July 31, 1941. It is but three sentences long and charges Heydrich with organizing the Final Solution of the Jewish Question in Europe. I took this order to mean that Hitler himself had decided that day to annihilate the Jews, and that Göring was acting as his deputy. There was evidence of restlessness in the bureaucracy now that forced mass-emigration plans had collapsed. In Poland the Jews had already been concentrated in ghettos, and in areas wrested from the Soviet Union the Security Police and SS brigades had begun sporadic killing. The time for widening these measures had come, and Göring's authorization appeared to be evidence that the thought was now being translated into action. My reasoning was not altogether wrong—the time *had* come, and Hitler had not only signaled his intentions in preceding months, he had underscored them later. But *this* piece of paper was not one of his orders. My misunderstanding was already in print for some years when Uwe Adam published his obscure book to demolish the Göring letter thesis. If a written order had been issued, he reasoned, it would have been handed by Hitler to Himmler, not by Hitler's subordinate Göring to Himmler's subordinate Heydrich. As soon as I read this argument it convinced me. Now, however, a new question arose: How was one to account for Göring's letter?

The answer came to me one day when a politically conservative publisher in New York asked me to look at a memoir to determine whether it was authentic. The author displayed the consummate knowledge of an insider. Unquestionably I was reading a slightly edited version of Adolf Eichmann's recollections, which he had dictated in Argentina. In his account Eichmann disclosed that he himself had drafted the three sentences for Heydrich, who submitted the text to Göring for his signature. Heydrich was seeking an open-ended authorization, and because of his excellent relations with Göring he obtained it. Heydrich did not know what Hitler would decide—he wanted to be the official with power in his hands once a decision was made. Eichmann went on to say that one day he was called in by Heydrich who told him the grave news that Hitler had decided upon the physical annihilation of the European Jews.

The order had been given orally to Himmler who had passed it orally to Heydrich.

I read the three sentences again. They had been drafted in bureaucratic language. This was not Göring's prose. Uwe Adam had unlocked yet another important characteristic of the process. I had thought only of the decisive steps in the destruction; I had paid no attention to the fact that the decisions themselves were taken in steps. Nor had I appreciated that there was an evolution in the procedure of decision-making, that gradually laws gave way to decrees, and decrees to announcements, written orders, oral orders, and finally no orders. The functionary who sensed the purpose of the operation had come into his own.

Uwe Adam was a young man who died young. He was a researcher with deep insights, and he asked questions that others had failed to raise. At a meeting of a United States–German committee which dealt with intellectual and academic reactions to the Jewish catastrophe, I asked the German side to provide academic positions for just three young historians who were known to me as pioneers in the field: Hans-Heinrich Wilhelm, who dealt meticulously with mobile killings in the occupied Soviet Union; Götz Aly, who first pointed to the role of statisticians and economists in the process; and Uwe Adam. Nothing happened, of course, in response to my plea, and shortly thereafter Uwe Adam was gone.

An Art

M Y POSITION IN THE federal records center did not
last long. At the beginning of 1952 Fritz Epstein
began to talk to me in a fatherly fashion about my need to
write my doctoral dissertation. His admonition was
prompted by a number of his own concerns. He wanted to
replace the existing crew in order to hire men who would be
totally beholden to him. I was most certainly not one of his
favorite researchers, inasmuch as I had expressed some
doubt about his ability to maximize the exploitation of our
documentary collections, and I had even shared my opinion
with Professor Neumann and another Columbia University
professor. Epstein must have been aware of my evaluation
of him, and his conversation with me was an understandable
act of self-preservation.

Leaving was not so simple for me. I could not be indifferent to money, and I did not wish to be jobless again.
When I explored other opportunities in Washington, I
quickly discovered a stumbling block. I could put on a uniform or I could join the newly created Central Intelligence
Agency, which was an equal-opportunity employer, but
other offices in my range of interest rejected me because I

was foreign born. Like Gustav Hilger and the German colonel, I could be used for a special purpose, but I was not trusted in principle. Years later I would explain to my class in American Foreign Policy that under the law Henry Kissinger could not have been appointed to the ranks of the Foreign Service. He could only be a high official, a secretary of state.

At the same time I knew I had a deeper problem. During the first few months of my stay in Washington, I had utilized my evenings and weekends to full advantage in the Library of Congress. I still remember leaving the library when it closed and walking along magnificent avenues deserted in the night. After a while, however, the War Documentation Project occupied all my thoughts. Instead of simply filling out cards, I was concerned about its direction and accomplishments. I could not write any chapters with leftover thoughts in leftover time.

Reluctantly I returned to New York to take up residence in the small apartment of my parents, assuring them that I would be responsible for a third of the household costs, which I would pay as soon as I had the means. In the living room I set up a bridge table every morning. There I sat for the next three years. My mother would occasionally ask me with an insistent tone when I would be finished, and then my father, sighing, would ask me the same question.

My plan had no room for compromises. With my handwritten notes on three-hole paper in sixty folders piled in front of me, I would write chapter after chapter in pencil, again on three-hole paper. All the documents were arranged in the order in which I would consult them. I was restricted only in my use of material in the federal records center. My knowledge of the confidential folders sometimes insured me against making a mistake, or more often it enabled me to see a connection, which might otherwise have remained invisible, between facts gathered from other sources, but I was not allowed to cite these files directly. In 1955 I returned briefly to the records center to make notes about newly declassified items; I had to wait many more years for the remainder.

Meanwhile I worked daily. When I had completed a major passage I read it aloud to Eric Marder for his reactions. I would not show anything to Neumann before the entire manuscript was complete. It was for him that I was preparing the dissertation.

To portray the Holocaust, Claude Lanzmann once said to me, one has to create a work of art. To recreate this event, be it on film or in a book, one must be a consummate artist, for such recreation is an act of creation in and of itself. I already knew this fact on the day I embarked on my task.

The artist usurps the actuality, substituting a text for a reality that is fast fading. The words that are thus written take the place of the past; these words, rather than the events themselves, will be remembered. Were this transformation not a necessity, one could call it presumptuous, but it is unavoidable. What I say here is not limited to my subject. It is applicable to all historiography, to all descriptions of a happening. My subject, however, was mighty, as the novelist Bernard Malamud would have said, or a Tremendum, as the theologian Arthur Cohen would label it, and to

slip or fall in this effort would have been tantamount to failing tremendously.

No literature could serve me as an example. The destruction of the Jews was an unprecedented occurrence, a
primordial act that had not been imagined before it burst
forth. The Germans had no model for their deed, and I did
not have one for my narrative. Yet later I became aware that
I was appropriating, transcribing, arranging something. It
was not a work of literature but a body of music. While I sat
at my bridge table during rest periods in the evening, I
would listen to the radio, which in New York afforded an
abundant choice of recorded symphonies, concertos, quar-
tets, and sonatas. My childhood musical training was such
that I remembered almost nothing anymore. I could only
listen and gradually assimilate what I was hearing.

There are Mozarts and Beethovens in this world.
"Mozart wrote masterpieces when he was fifteen," said a
college psychologist who specialized in the problems of ado-
lescents, Peter Blos, after I had shown him a feeble effort of
mine at writing during the academic year 1942–1943, when
I was sixteen. It was the most devastating comment ever
made to me about my abilities, and I have not been able to
put it out of my mind, even after I learned more about Blos,
a not quite Aryan refugee who was a Protestant admirer of
Luther and the Reformation. Mozart would forever be out
of reach. He could not be emulated; he could not even be
copied. I am stunned, listening to his music, be it an early
composition like the *Divertimento in D* or a later, overpow-
ering organ fantasia. Everything he did seemed effortless. It
is as if his mind produced a series of explosions, in the

course of which his hand was driven to write the notes or to glide across the keys of his piano. This was a god whom the ancient Greeks, were they alive in his century, would have celebrated and worshiped with abandon.

Not so Beethoven. *He* had to work, to build his music like an edifice, draft after draft, slowly, painfully. Four opening notes in his Fifth Symphony—I listened only to his odd-numbered ones—followed by four more, and thus he laid down his building blocks. I imagined him with four measures like these creating a phrase, and with this phrase a theme, and upon the theme the variations. But what architecture this structure became! The chords—those tones played simultaneously—were varied in turn. Not for naught is Beethoven called a master. All was controlled, taut to the ultimate degree.

I had to control my work, to dominate it as Beethoven had fashioned his music. Writing, like music, is linear, but there are no chords or harmonies in literature. For this reason I concentrated more and more on chamber music, which is sparse, and in which I could hear every instrument and every note distinctly. The Schubert Quintet in C—a Germanic work—gave me the insight that power is not dependent on simple mass or even loudness, but on escalations and contrasts. Beethoven's *Appassionata*, that supreme achievement of piano music, which proves that one keyboard can be the equivalent of an orchestra, showed me that I could not shout on a thousand pages, that I had to suppress sonority and reverberations, and that I could loosen my grip only selectively, very selectively.

I grasped for an overall symmetry. Beethoven, I learned

in a book by the musicologist Lewis Lockwood published in 1992, had sketched the finale of his *Eroica* symphony by pairing what he placed first with what he put down last, and then what followed the first with what preceded the last, and so on in candelabra fashion toward the middle. I had done something very similar with my twelve-chapter work. The first chapter was thematically reflected in the last. The second was matched with the next to the last, and the third with the tenth. The longest of my chapters was the one on deportations. It was the *andante* of my composition, with a theme and multiple variations that mirrored the special conditions under which deportations were carried out in each country.

The specific content of my text was given to me, of course, primarily by the records that the Germans had left behind, but there was a problem of rendition. Because these documents were in German, I could not embed them in my story without reproducing their substance in English. Languages are not the same. There are agglutinative words in German, as well as a great deal of heaviness, redundancy, and exclamation. One would think I did not have this difficulty when my books were later translated *into* German. But the German of the Nazi era is different from the German that emerged after the war. Extreme positions, and the absolute certainty with which they were stated in Nazi times, have been attenuated. Pristine German words have given way to a mélange of foreign and imported expressions. I was not fully aware of the extent of these changes until I received the drafts of the German translators. No, I would say, you cannot do that, a *Beamter* is not a *Manager*, a

Niederschrift is not a *Protokoll*, *misshandelt* does not mean *malträtiert*. You are losing the original style and feeling. You are ignoring the fact that every German sentence that one finds in a document of the early 1940s incorporated the whole culture and atmosphere of that time. You are actually translating one kind of German into another German. In my quandary I thought I might produce document books, but even if I were to do so in the original German, this exercise would be a compromise. Documents never stand alone. As fragments they should be interpreted and explained. If they are to become ingredients of a coherent account, they must first be selected, excerpted, and ordered. All of these manipulations are a way of imposing a meaning on the pure texts for the sake of intelligibility. In short, whatever the genre, I would still have the task of synthesizing my work in a manner that would retain, to the maximum extent possible, the thoughts of all those who created this history.

My training in the social sciences took place in the 1940s. The methodological literature that I read emphasized objectivity and neutral or value-free words. I was an observer, and it was most important to me that I write accordingly. At one time I said to Eric Marder that when, if ever, my manuscript appeared as a book, nothing should be said on the dust jacket about the personal experiences of the author. Needless to say, no publisher allowed me such anonymity, but the printed pages at least would be devoted to the subject, not the person who wrote them. To this end I banished accusatory terms like "murder," as well as such exculpatory words as "executions," which made the victims into delinquents, or "extermination," which likened them to vermin. I added charts and numbers, which added an air of cool detachment to my writing. I did yield to some temptations. Herman Wouk said to me that the work contained a suppressed irony, in other words, an irony recognizably suppressed. I also wanted capsule lines at the end of passages and chapters. I really weighed this decision, listening to Beethoven's extended finales but also to a violin concerto by Prokofiev that seemed to end in midair. In my resolution of this particular predicament I leaned toward Beethoven.

Above all, I was committed to compression. I had to avoid elaborations, detours, and repetitions, not only because they would diminish an effect but for the simple reason that I had to watch the size of my work. My estimates of length had been wrong. I needed more space and more time than I had thought. The task demanded comprehensiveness and it required balance: if this, then that. Brevity did not mean omissions, and the pages were piling up. I never regretted my tenacity in this regard. Claude Lanzmann did not miniaturize the event in his nine-hour film, and Herman Wouk did not do so in his two-volume novel. When I participated in the planning of the United States Holocaust Memorial Museum, I expressed the hope that it would not be small, and when the building was opened its sheer size was large enough to make a statement. Eric Marder approved of what I was doing. He suggested, half-jokingly, that I should hand my completed manuscript to Professor Neumann with the words: Here is my funeral.

By the fall of 1954 I could allow myself an encompassing glance at my work. Most of the pages were down on paper.

Even though I was teaching, I was still advancing toward my goal. I was in Puerto Rico then, and delayed news reached me that Franz Neumann had died in an automobile crash in Switzerland. Momentarily I broke down. Neumann had been important to me to a far greater extent than I had acknowledged. He was not only the political scientist who in his *Behemoth* had given me an indispensable tool of analysis, and he was not merely a professor on whom I was going to rely for the furtherance of my career. He was a presence that sustained me.

For the first time I reflected on *his* life. I had learned so little about him. Some of the details of his youth and family had surfaced in time, and so had the bare facts of his career, but I could not muster much more. I knew that he was a Jew who was born in Silesia and educated in Frankfurt, where he obtained a law degree; that he practiced labor law in Germany before moving to England; and that he studied under Harold Laski in London, where he earned a doctorate in political science before moving on to the United States. In 1942 he joined the Office of Strategic Services and later the Department of State, two agencies which employed refugees to decipher Nazi Germany. During his last seven years, in the Department of Public Law and Government at Columbia University, he was a phenomenal success. I heard that at the time of his death he was the sponsor of some twenty-six doctoral students. He had also published articles, which were quoted reverently, about such subjects as power and anxiety. To me they did not matter. What, after all, can a man do after he has written *Behemoth*? But this is a question that preoccupies me now and that I would not have asked aloud while he was alive or for as long as he might have lived. All I would have said then is that *Behemoth* would remain as the milestone that it was, and that I would henceforth be an academic orphan.

IV
On Struggling

Securing a
Teaching Position

FOR THIRTY-SEVEN YEARS I was engaged in teaching. A professor in my field will stand in front of a class and essentially tell a story two or three times a week over a span of approximately four months. The telling is supposed to flow, and that is why the lectures are called a "course." I taught one particular course, in basic international relations, at least sixty times.

My portfolio of offerings, especially during my first decade as a faculty member, was quite large. It included my first love, international law, and my primary offering, American foreign policy, but also world politics, geographic backgrounds to politics, American government, public administration, defense policy, and even methodological considerations in political science. All these courses were a part of the usual curriculum, and a new entrant in the profession had to be flexible. Fortunately I was an eclectic practitioner in my discipline. I actually felt a psychological need to investigate political institutions that were centered on everyday life. These laws, agencies, and policies were a wall of stability on which I could lean. Only later, much later, did I teach a course labeled "The Holocaust."

Obtaining a teaching position was far from easy. I battled three obstacles. The first, which affected all applicants, was the teaching market: Whereas many war veterans had been encouraged by available government benefits to pursue graduate studies, thus swelling the supply of men who were academically qualified to teach in colleges, the enrollment in classes was beginning to thin out, because the pool of potential students had to be drawn from the shrunken generation born during the economic depression of the 1930s. A second problem was discrimination against Jews, particularly in private colleges. The third was, of course, the peculiar subject of my doctoral dissertation.

I remember my first appointment, which consisted of teaching a night course in a business school training secretaries and sales people for service in Latin America. In February 1954 I obtained a lectureship at Hunter College in New York to teach four sections of American Government for four-fifths of $320 a month. Hunter College was one of the four colleges operated by the city of New York. In an effort by the city to promote a cultural "melting pot," it was the custom to install a Jewish president in Queens College, which had a predominantly Protestant student body, and a Protestant president in Brooklyn College, which was overwhelmingly Jewish. Hunter College, which was already a melting pot of students, albeit with few Protestants, had a Catholic president, George N. Shuster. I promptly looked up his qualifications and discovered that he had been a professor of German as well as a publicist who had written books about Nazi Germany before the war. In two of these publications he had also mentioned Jews, with references to the "fishmongers" of Krakow and the aesthetic appeal of the "daughters of Sarah." The Department of Political Science at Hunter College had three full professors, one Protestant, one Catholic, and one Jewish, all them women who looked somewhat elderly to me. Their sex and age may be explained by the fact that Hunter College had been a school only for female students before the war. I was handed a detailed syllabus, prepared by the Catholic professor, with which I was expected to teach. It emphasized the Constitution of the United States.

I loved the Constitution and could recite many of its provisions from memory. Had I been a member of the Supreme Court I would surely have slept with a copy of this document under my pillow, lest I awake in the middle of the night worrying about the wording of a particular clause without having the text immediately at hand. As a lecturer, however, I also wanted to teach something about the actuality of American government, and I wanted to be very broad in my presentation of its institutions. In this respect I was only following the greatest political scientist in America, Lord James Bryce, whose two-volume textbook, *The American Commonwealth*, first published in 1888, did not fail to include all kinds of bodies, among them universities. Having thrown the syllabus away, I obtained colored chalk and drew organization charts, discussing such ingredients of our commonwealth as the Defense Department, the independent regulatory commissions, and the educational establishment. The Jewish full professor, walking into one of my classes unannounced to observe my teaching, could immediately spot my heresies on the blackboard. Later in the semester I wanted to say something about prejudice and discrimination, giving as a prize example the writings of the college president, George N. Shuster. When I discussed my plan with Eric Marder, he counseled against a public showing of this particular illustration in my class, basing himself on the supposition that I wanted to keep my job. I followed his advice, but now I wish that this one time I had not consulted him.

In the summer of 1954 an acquaintance working in the office of the president of the City Council called me. We had been employed for six weeks in a local Republican election campaign in 1949, and now, a Democrat, he offered me a modest position with a salary ordinarily payable to a typist. I thanked him, explaining that I already had employment at Hunter College. In that connection I told him about a letter that the chair (the Protestant woman) had sent me, thanking me for the work I had done and wishing me a pleasant summer as well as a successful next year. In other words, he said, I had been fired. For a moment I was dumbfounded. Could I have been so naive? He picked up the telephone right then and there and made me ask for a clarification at the college. He was right. I was unemployed.

I was dispirited by the prospect of working full time in a municipal office, so far removed from the national and international scenes, even though I was impressed with the fact that New York City had the second-largest public budget in the United States. Going to the placement bureau of Columbia University I asked if there was another teaching position. Did I have any geographic restrictions? I was asked. No, I replied, I would go any place where the American flag flew. In that case, I was told, I could take advantage of an immediate opening in Mayaguez, Puerto Rico, a city on the west coast of an island wrested from Spanish control fifty-six years earlier.

The position was in every sense an impossible assignment. The recruiter was William Hunter Beckwith, director of general studies at the Mayaguez campus of the University of Puerto Rico. We talked only on the telephone, because his time in New York was exhausted and he had to return to Mayaguez right away. He was interested in me, even though—or precisely because—I was unable to lecture in the Spanish language. Puerto Rico was United States territory, and it was important, he said, that college students there learn their subjects in English. After I arrived, I found that I was the only one *not* teaching in Spanish. Many of my students would nod in my classes, but not many understood what I was saying. Moreover, the course I was teaching was an introduction to the social sciences, with a syllabus synthesized by social science faculty members. It was clear to me that even if I spent all my time mastering the rudimentary elements of the subjects in which I was untrained, I could not do justice to the course outline. To be sure, the vast majority of my students were underprepared as well. The university stuffed itself with young people for whom there were no employment opportunities on the island, and in 1954 it accepted without much question Puerto Rican veterans of the Korean War, for whom the United States government paid tuition and monthly support.

The Puerto Ricans, unlike the Cubans, had never re-
volted against anyone. They were a most peaceful people,
with a touch of sadness. Even their national anthem, the
Borinquen, struck me as sad. In 1954 Puerto Rico looked like
an American colony. A minority political party, the Inde-
pendendistas, were striving to establish a republic. Another
small group, the Estadistas, wanted to be like Massachusetts
or Texas, with senators and representatives in the Congress.
Most Puerto Ricans, however, saw viability only in the status quo, as a relatively tax-free, low-wage island which could
attract American manufacturing enterprises to Puerto Rican
cities and export its own surplus population by the plane-
load to New York.

Yet Puerto Rico affected me in ways I had not foreseen.
My Puerto Rican colleagues accepted me unreservedly as I
was, without saying "if only" I would do this or that, without wanting to remold me in any way. I would listen to the
popular music, especially the *merengue*, but also to the
stately *danza*, which was old music of Spain, preserved on
the island by the Figueroa string quartet. In December
1954 I was invited to a Christmas party. The centerpiece
was a puny, possibly plastic Christmas tree, and everyone
sang the *Arbuelito*. It was almost as if I were in a trance.

I could not remain there. After Franz Neumann's death
all my expectations had become precarious. My only certainty was my resolve not to write another doctoral dissertation. I offered the first 22 percent of my manuscript as a
fragment for my degree, and approached Professor William
T. R. Fox to be my sponsor. Once, he had asked me whether
I wanted to write about the German satellite states—his

wife, Annette Baker Fox, also a political scientist, was interested in small countries—and I had declined. Although he had every right to turn me down in turn, he agreed in a magnificent gesture of magnanimity to my plan. By January 1955 I had my degree. By March of that year I learned that I had no job.

William Hunter Beckwith had sent a letter to six members of his faculty, asking for their resignations. He had not written six letters but one to all of the recipients. My notice was a carbon copy. I knew little about Beckwith. A middle-aged bachelor who had been a dean at Hofstra College on Long Island, and who reputedly had a substantial financial interest in a Brooklyn shipyard, he was a man of multiple talents. He knew Spanish and other languages, had been a missionary in the Philippines, and played Mozart on the piano as well, perhaps, as Albert Schweitzer played Bach on the organ. Some of my colleagues who had been imported from the mainland assured me that Beckwith was an outspoken bigot. One day they came to the restaurant, Johnny's Bar, where I had my supper every day, and asked me to lead a revolt to oust him. To an instructor in English, the folklorist Billie Wallingford Boothe from West Virginia, Beckwith had said trustingly that the Puerto Ricans were worse than the New York Jews. I agreed to be the leader. With the quiet support of the Catholic church and a key member of the Independendista party, we prepared our case. On April 26, 1955, we read our sixty-one-page statement aloud before a packed audience. We won and I returned, unemployed, to New York.

At the age of twenty-nine, my calculated debt to my father and mother was almost as much as I could hope to earn after taxes in a year. My only income in the fall was provided by an institute which sent me for a few weeks to Washington to survey the newly declassified documents in the federal records center. I salvaged these materials also for my own use, copying them frantically by hand. Then the winter came.

In January I received a call from William T. R. Fox. The University of Vermont had a temporary opening which had been created by the absence of two faculty members on consecutive leaves, and which was good for a year and a half. I told him that discrimination against Jews was widespread and that I probably would not even survive an interview. He tried to reassure me, saying that a state university was not allowed to discriminate. When I arrived in Burlington, Vermont, I learned that I was safe. The discrimination was directed at Catholics. Counting me, the nine-man Department of Political Science consisted of six Protestants and three Jews. An east-west street in this city of fewer than forty thousand people divided the Protestant and Catholic communities. Twenty years earlier, Catholics had not even been able to obtain employment as bank tellers.

During my interview I was not fully aware of these divisions, nor did I soon become acquainted with all the compartmentalizations within the university. Half the students came not from Vermont but from other states, and there was a considerable difference in the economic circumstances and career orientations between the two groups. Many of the out-of-staters, whose parents could pay the high tuition, were self-segregated in fraternities and sororities. Jewish students, most of whom also came from other states, had their own two fraternities and a sorority. In the women's dormitories, students were assigned to rooms by religion, wealth, and physical height. The social life of the students was closely monitored by the administration, lest there be inappropriate associations across religious or social boundaries, and the handful of young unmarried faculty were adrift.

The university had only about three thousand students, and when I was shown the library, a turn-of-the-century building with much interior wood, I asked where the principal collections of books were kept, only to be told that I was looking at them. From the dean I gained the impression that my research was my own private business and that I would be paid for my teaching. The pay, incidentally, was a thousand dollars less than my salary in the War Documentation Project four years earlier. All these drawbacks and limitations notwithstanding, I accepted the position unhesitatingly. Bolstering my morale, Eric Marder pointed to several positive elements in my new situation: I was going to be an assistant professor before I had reached my thirtieth birthday, and the university was instantly recognizable because it was named after a state.

After I returned to Vermont with my two suitcases a few days after the interview, I was told that my tight three-day teaching schedule had been changed to six mornings and five afternoons of classes. Instead of international relations I would be offering American government, and in addition to teaching my four sections of three different subjects, I would be participating in a seminar called "Popular Government." From the first day I decided that, no matter how heavy my load, I would never neglect my lectures. I plunged into the classroom with all my mental resources, relegating the completion of the remaining chapters of my book to my abbreviated weekends and typing finished pages before breakfast. At the same time I suppressed the thought that, given my rate of progress, the manuscript would not be finished for years.

One night I looked at myself as I was, and had insomnia. It was the evening of June 1, 1956. The next day I would be thirty. I stared at the ceiling from the ultrasoft mattress in the furnished apartment I had rented. A curtain separated the "bedroom" from the kitchen, where I had never cooked anything. I had rented this place in the middle of the Catholic French-speaking section of town as a gesture of protest, after a faculty wife had warned me that I was looking for accommodations in the "wrong" area of town. I walked from here to the office every morning, stopping for coffee on the way. Now I reflected on the fact that I had met only my departmental colleagues and that I had no private life whatever. What had happened to me?

In the summer I resolved to move out of the French section to rent a more spacious one-bedroom apartment near the university. Were it not for my furnishings, one might have concluded that I had already joined the middle class. They consisted of a plain bed with a five-dollar night table, an inexpensive sofa and chair, bricks and boards for my very small collection of books, and a dining table with a single leftover matching chair, which I acquired at a greatly reduced price, and which I used for my work. No curtains, no rugs, no television set, and no telephone. Also, no car. When I first set foot in the United States I had admired cars, often stopping to gaze at them in the streets of Brooklyn. Now I still could not afford one, and with the passage of time my hunger for a vehicle passed as well.

My employment was stabilized during the spring of 1957 with a change in my position in the university. Owing to the increasing popularity of political science among the students, the departmental teaching staff was to be increased by one person. Since I was already on board, I could remain. The alternative would have been yet another temporary position in a college situated in central Ohio.

An additional change in my fortunes was a grant, financed by a Jewish organization that received German reparations funds for the support of needy victims who were pursuing research projects in the realm of Jewish cultural reconstruction. Since I was considered a victim by virtue of my status as a refugee, and inasmuch as I was needy enough on the basis of my salary, I met two of the verifiable criteria for eligibility. As to my contribution to the enhancement of Jewish culture, I am not sure about the thoughts of the grantors. The title of my project, at any rate, clearly indicated that I was dealing with something that had happened to the Jews. I received $1,500—almost enough to repay all the remaining debt to my parents.

Although I had finally gained a steady position with financial freedom, I did not augment my living standard to any appreciable extent. One of the reasons for this forbearance was my continuing rootlessness. "Vermont is a disaster," my father said at one time. He did not see me walk in the icy wind to eat my supper in a cafeteria, but he sensed what my life was like. Although I had feigned happiness, talking about my friendships with younger departmental colleagues, especially the erudite L. Jay Gould, who grew up in Puerto Rico and who would call me *hijo* (son) while he listened patiently to all my troubles, my father knew that years after my arrival in that state I could have left it instantly with my two suitcases and a couple of boxes containing my books. I should note, however, that my social isolation was not the only cause of my restraint as a consumer. The additional consideration was a very specific worry. I had to ask myself how much money I might need to finance the publication of my book.

The Road to
Publication

IN NOVEMBER 1955, before my appointment in Vermont, I was notified by the dean of the graduate faculties of Columbia University that I was the recipient of a Clark F. Ansley Award. This honor was conferred by the university once a year on two persons, one who had submitted a doctoral dissertation in a department of the social sciences, the other in a department of the humanities. That year more than seventy degrees had been granted in the social sciences alone. My dissertation was selected in a two-step competition. First I had been nominated by the Department of Public Law and Government, and then I won a contest with the nominees of the other social science departments. The prize consisted of a contract offered by Columbia University Press for publication of the chosen dissertation.

A door had been opened for me: I could look forward to seeing my work in print. I felt not only uplifted by this development but also grateful, particularly to William Fox, who had already rescued me after Neumann's death, sheltering me under his protective umbrella. When I told him later that I could not repay him, he said only that I should help others who might need me, and this I have tried to do, to the extent possible, from my base in Vermont.

Soon, however, a potential problem surfaced in a letter written to me by the publication manager of Columbia University Press, Henry H. Wiggins. The dissertation, for which the prize had been awarded, was not the complete manuscript. Would I, he asked in his letter of December 30, 1955, absolutely refuse publication of this fragment, if the faculty and the Press were to agree that "that and that only" should be published as the Ansley Award winner, and that publication of "more" of the work would have to be the subject of "separate and later" negotiations between the Press and me? I was disturbed by this guarded attitude, by the negative implication in his question, by the hint that a line could be drawn. I could imagine him drafting a memorandum to the faculty urging that in the future Ansley awards not be given to candidates whose dissertations exceeded a certain length.

My correspondence with Mr. Wiggins went on for three and a half years. In 1956 he revealed to me, in stages, the position of the Press. First of all, the financial responsibility of the Press was definitely limited to the dissertation portion. A subsidy would have to be obtained from a foundation for the remainder of the manuscript. Then he mentioned a reader. "Technically" the complete work would not be accepted by the Press for publication until a favorable verdict had been received from a designated referee.

I filed these letters while I was trying to complete my labor. What I had drafted before coming to Vermont I could edit and type with deliberate speed. All but the last two chapters were finished in 1956, but these concluding passages, which dealt mainly with consequences and implications in the postwar era, became an albatross with which I struggled until the spring of 1958. During that time I added not only pages to my manuscript but also dollars to my savings account. The sums were much too small to guarantee the publication of my work, but I stockpiled the money for the contingency that all else would fail and that I would have to provide a subsidy myself.

In October 1956 a complete stranger became interested in my manuscript. His name was Frank C. Petschek. He lived in New York and was a refugee from Czechoslovakia, where his family had owned coal mines. In an early chapter that was part of my dissertation, I had described the Aryanization of the Petschek properties, that is to say their forcible passing into German hands. "We have never had anything to do with banks," Mr. Petschek said at one time. When I looked at him questioningly, he explained that the Petscheks had never *owned* any banks.

Mr. Petschek's curiosity was aroused by a conversation reported to him by his daughter, who was a graduate student in political science at Harvard University. She had talked to one of her professors, Carl Friedrich, who had been one of the judges for an award presented by the American Political Science Association to the writer of the best political science dissertation of the year. I had been edged out for this award by Judith Sklar, a political theorist who had obtained her doctorate at Harvard for a study of "Utopia," but Friedrich was impressed with what I had written. He could not remember my name or the title of my dissertation, but he was certain that I had done my work at Columbia University and that I must have interviewed the Petschek family. Frank Petschek remembered no such interview and wondered how I had covered the story. Looking under "coal mines," "industry," and "German economy," in the Columbia University library, he could not find my dissertation. Finally he was handed my manuscript titled "Prologue to Annihilation." In the footnote references to the Petschek enterprises he could see citations of Nuremberg trial documents drawn from the files of German industrialists, bankers, and the Finance Ministry.

The library did not permit removal of a manuscript from the premises, and Mr. Petschek wished to read my account at home. He wrote to me for a copy, but those were the days when duplicate pages were made with carbon paper. The clear ribbon copy that I had typed myself was in the hands of the Press, and I asked Mr. Wiggins to lend it to Mr. Petschek.

By April 1957 Frank Petschek had read all of the sixteen hundred typewritten pages I had finished by that time. He asked casually whether the publication of the work was financially covered, and I replied that funds for the expected deficit had not been secured. Later that summer he told Wiggins that he was not the man who could provide the needed subsidy. Wiggins took that statement to be final. Why then had Mr. Petschek read all those chapters that dealt with the Final Solution? He was a Jew. His wife's family had been killed. In addition, he had a sense of responsibility, undoubtedly derived from the fact that he had once been a major businessman. He wanted to see this manuscript become a book; he did not want to drop it or me. At the same time he was acutely aware of how much his resources had shrunk. His small foundation supplied colleges with slides of his favorite Dutch landscape paintings. He had shown me a copy of a world almanac in which he had put check marks next to some of these needy colleges. Clearly Mr. Wiggins wanted more than slides.

Another interested person was Philip Friedman. When I defended my dissertation in January 1955, he was on the examining committee, where he had replaced Salo Baron. Friedman was not a philanthropist but a survivor, marginally employed as a lecturer in history by the university. He was interested in the Jewish scene in Poland and hoped to write a book about ghettos. It did not come to that because he died early, before undertaking the project. He did read my dissertation with care, and he had various connections with institutes. Since he lived in the Jewish world, he recommended joint publication of the complete work by Columbia University Press and an organization formed in Jerusalem a few years earlier: Yad Vashem, Israel's official "Remembrance Authority of the Disaster and Heroism." The book was to be printed in Israel, where costs of production were less than those in the United States. The Israelis wanted $10,000. If Columbia University Press allocated $5,000 from its Ansley reserves, said Dr. Friedman, the acquisition of the remainder might not be so difficult. The Press was receptive to this idea. The imprint of Yad Vashem might attract the missing funds. Mr. Wiggins left me with little doubt that he meant Jewish funds.

When I consulted the copyright law I discovered that the importation of books by Americans printed abroad was limited, but I was in no position to set conditions. In April 1958 the entire manuscript arrived in Jerusalem. Yad Vashem's answer was written on August 24, 1958. The complete text of the letter is as follows:

Dear Professor Hilberg,

Your manuscript on the extermination of the Jews has been read in the course of the last two months by several of our staff, each of whom is an expert in one of the aspects involved.

At a meeting of the editorial board which took place on the 15.8.1958, a joint readers' report was considered. In this report it was stated that while the manuscript possessed numerous merits, it also had certain deficiencies:

1. Your book rests almost entirely on the authority of German sources and does not utilize primary sources in the languages of the occupied states, or in Yiddish and Hebrew.

2. The Jewish historians here make reservations concerning the historical conclusions which you draw, both in respect of the comparison with former periods, and in respect of your appraisal of the Jewish resistance (active and passive) during the Nazi occupation.

On the basis of what has been said, our foundation cannot appear as one of the publishers without running the risk that expert critics who know the history of the Nazi catastrophe thoroughly and possess a command of the languages of the occupied states in question, might express hostile criticism of the book.

On the other hand we are prepared to act as mediators between the University of Columbia and the printer here, in order to make possible the book's appearance under the auspices of the Columbia University.

Yours faithfully,
[handwritten signature]
Dr. J. Melkman
General Manager

Here was the first negative reaction to my manuscript, and these bullets were fired at me from Jerusalem. For ten years I had imagined that the Jews, and particularly the Jews, would be the readers of my work. It was for them I labored. And now this. I knew very little about Yad Vashem, and at the time I knew nothing about Dr. Melkman, though I wondered who he was. As I learned later, he had arrived in Israel in 1957. Before the war he had been a teacher of Greek and Latin in a secondary school in the Netherlands, and during the German occupation his Zionist connections enabled him and his wife to hold on to a precarious privileged position, first in Amsterdam, then in the transit camp of Westerbork, and finally in Bergen-Belsen. In writing his letter to me he clearly relied on his staff. To discover the source of his argument about "resistance," I merely had to glance at Yad Vashem's letterhead, which proclaimed the parity of the disaster and heroism. Next to that ideological statement, I could see only an attempt at parochial self-preservation. Did his experts really believe that their Yiddish or Hebrew sources had altered the basic history revealed by the German documents? Could they really stand on the "primary sources" in the languages of the occupied countries when in fact these materials were largely inaccessible to the public and therefore unexplored by Yad Vashem itself? Where were the publications of these experts? Where was the evidence of their expertise? Dr. Melkman did not question the qualifications of his associates, but in referring to my work he permitted himself the use of the phrase "certain deficiencies," knowing that I would have to share his letter with Columbia University Press.

At this point I knocked down the negotiating table, answering Dr. Melkman in a manner that diplomats call "frank." Wiggins was startled by the tone of my remarks. Unlike me, he still harbored a spark of hope that Jerusalem would change its mind. I did not believe in and no longer cared about such a possibility. Nor was my appraisal mistaken. Thirty-seven years later Dr. Melkman wrote to the Hebrew newspaper *Haaretz* that Yad Vashem's decision had been the right one.

In New York the Press's next step was the submission to an outside reader of "portions" of the manuscript segment that followed the pages already judged worthy of the Ansley Award. On December 29, 1958, Wiggins sent me word of the reader's judgment. The crucial sentence in that letter was the following: "The reader felt that the sections 'contained a good deal of important and well documented material,' but thought that many of your comments were more like those of a 'polemical prosecutor' than of an historian and felt that it was impossible for such comments to appear in a scholarly work to be published under the Press imprint."

Was I now accused of indicting the Germans? The anonymous reader had indicated that the manuscript would require "extensive revision" before it would be suitable for publication. Under the circumstances, Mr. Wiggins wrote, the Press could only offer me a contract for the fragment on a take-it-or-leave-it basis. I knew I was going to leave it. How could I find a publisher for the publication of the segment that constituted more than three-quarters of the work? I scarcely even asked myself how, if I succeeded against all expectations, I would deal with two editing styles, two indexes, and two books that belonged together but would be sold separately. The whole idea seemed impossible, and the winter day was bleak. In my savings account I had $1,600. How many years would pass before I had accumulated enough money to satisfy a publisher?

I sent the dismal news to Petschek. He replied immediately, "I cannot help the thought that the size of your thesis is the prime and true deterrent for their readiness to publish the whole work." Then he added, "I would like to help you overcome that obstacle, if this is within my means." He wanted to see me soon. When I visited him in New York he promised $10,000, saying that it was a large sum but that he would continue to eat the same breakfast every day.

A friend of Eric Marder, the philosopher Hilary Putnam, suggested that I send the manuscript to Princeton University Press. I did so without mentioning Petschek's backing. If at all possible, I wanted to walk without financial crutches. Princeton's reply, dated March 25, 1959, and signed by Gordon Hubel, was rapid. It was with "great disappointment," Mr. Hubel said, that he had to report that my study would not be published there. My manuscript did not "constitute a sufficiently important contribution as a case study in public administration to stand alone on that ground," and "readily available" books, such as those of Reitlinger, Poliakov, and Adler, existed "in sufficient detail for all but a very few specialists."

The Adler mentioned by Hubel was H. G. Adler, who had written a major work in the German language about the Theresienstadt ghetto. The book was published in Germany in 1955, but it has not appeared in English translation to this day.

After I received the letter I called Hubel to ask him whether the decision would have been different if he had known that I had backing in the amount of $10,000. There was a moment of silence at the other end of the wire before he answered that Princeton University Press did not act on the basis of financial considerations.

While the manuscript was still at Princeton, an anthropologist at the University of Vermont, John Teal, who specialized in Eskimos and Indians of the Arctic region but who was housed in our department, talked with me about the University of Oklahoma Press. One of the attractions of that publisher, he said, was the physical quality and beauty of its printing and bindings. Since I did not know where to turn, I wrote to Oklahoma, mentioning at the outset the availability of $10,000 for the purchase of books. The University of Oklahoma Press held my manuscript for sixteen months. The editor, Savoie Lottinville, was warm and friendly, but it was almost six months before he received the most excellent reports about my manuscript from his readers. It was a very large one, after all. He then wanted $10,000 as an outright grant. The edition, in a printing of 1,650 copies, would generate costs of $24,000, and at a list price of twenty dollars yielding a net of twelve dollars to the Press, that kind of subvention was needed to recover Oklahoma's investment. Later Lottinville revised the cost estimate to $28,000 for a printing of 2,500 copies, of which 2,000 could be sold, and demanded $17,000 with an offer to rebate a part of the contribution to the extent there might be a surplus.

I was increasingly perturbed. Frank Petschek had had a stroke, and I was corresponding with his son-in-law, Maurice de Picciotto, who undertook to conduct all the foundation's negotiations in selfless labor. Like all university presses, the University of Oklahoma Press did not accept author's funds, but it was prepared to collect money from my university, and the University of Vermont was willing to transmit in its own name any amounts that I could contribute. My savings had reached $3,100. Since my credit with my mother and father was sound, I could borrow the remainder from them. I explained that situation to Mr. Petschek. Sitting in his chair, barely able to speak, he wrote the entire amount, $17,000, on a sheet of paper and handed it to me.

That was still not the end. Savoie Lottinville requested a list of all the organizations to which the Petschek Foundation might recycle the hypothetical rebates. During a one-hour meeting in New York, Lottinville questioned me closely about my background and said that my passages about Martin Luther might offend religious groups. Since the University of Oklahoma Press was not merely a university press but the press of a *state* university, he said, these passages might have to be changed. In the interest of impartiality, he also hinted at modifications of unsuitable comments I might have written about cardinals and rabbis. I said that if he had any specific editorial suggestions, I would listen to them. At the same time I called his attention to the headlines proclaiming Adolf Eichmann's capture by Israeli agents in Argentina. There would be a trial, I said, and we would be missing an opportunity if we did not take advantage of this development with timely publication. Lottinville did not seem to listen. A few months later he demanded the power to make any and all editorial changes, whether or not I approved of them.

During the early stages of my dealings with the University of Oklahoma Press, I talked casually with a representative of Random House, Charles Lieber. He visited the University of Vermont not only to sell textbooks for adoption in courses but to solicit manuscripts. I told him that I had not written anything for classrooms, that my subject was the destruction of the European Jews, and that I was negotiating with the University of Oklahoma Press. While we stood outside my building in the gentle October sun, I also mentioned the sum of $10,000, which Mr. Petschek had already pledged to finance the book. "For $10,000 I will hand-print it for you," he said. "Done," I replied, half playfully, half seriously. As we walked up the stairs, Lieber had second thoughts. Wait, he said, Random House was not really the kind of company that would publish my work. I showed him the carbon copy of my manuscript. "It looks Germanic," he announced, glancing at my footnotes. They were actually brief, but there were thousands of them. The right publisher, he decided, was Alexander Morin, a good friend of his who had been managing editor of the University of Chicago Press and who was now the president of a new, small, independent publishing company in Chicago, Quadrangle Books. He was willing to talk to Morin right from my office if I paid for the telephone call.

Eleven months later I sent Morin the manuscript. He was enthusiastic, full of admiration for my work, and—dispensing with outside readers—he accepted $15,000 of Mr. Petschek's money in payment for copies that were to be shipped as donations to libraries. Before long he sold printed sheets for another $2,900 to a British publisher and obtained an advance order, amounting to a few hundred dollars, for books I would present to my family and friends.

Later I learned that his production costs were only about $18,500. In short, he had recovered the entire investment before publication, and he still had several thousand copies, priced at $14.95 each, which he could sell to the general public. Later his successor, Melvin Brisk, told me that the Petschek Foundation's subvention was not really needed. Most of the books sold to the foundation for free distribution to libraries would have been purchased by these libraries in any case.

To contain his expenses, Morin made some compromises. I did not expect lavishness, and I did obtain all the essentials: the tables, the maps, and the placement of the notes at the bottom of the pages. Nevertheless, I could not help noticing the cheapness of the paper and the binding, which seemed to be an announcement that the book was not made to last. I was pained by the appearance of Table 87, which became Table 87A and Table 87B. The original table was a flow chart, which I had drawn to show the disposition of the last possessions of the Jews who had been transported to the death camps. This chart was not merely an illustration accompanying a case study of public administration, but a portrayal of involvement. It was important to me to encompass in a single drawing all the German offices that had processed these Jewish belongings, and all the categories of people who had been designated as the recipients. I remember working an entire month on the chart, drawing crisscrossing diagonal lines in black and red to replicate this complex of operations and to reflect the mentality of the participants. In my naiveté I assumed that my table would be preserved intact, that it would be a foldout chart in the book. By the time Alexander Morin had completed his surgery, the overview was gone, the clarity obliterated. He had created two half-tables, printed back to back, and my diagonal arrows had given way to horizontal and vertical lines, some of which were formed into rectangles—confusing, incomprehensible, useless.

Morin also chose a double-column format, which irritated me. Many more words were hyphenated; spaces between sections were reduced; and there was an appearance of crowding on the page. After asking me whether I would like black for the cover, he chose brown.

The book jacket was a special problem. I could not help

comparing it with the mantle of the phenomenally successful ten-dollar volume on the rise and fall of Nazi Germany
by William L. Shirer. Like that best-seller, my book was
decked out in white, black, and yellow, albeit in different
proportions. Both books were fitted out with swastikas. It
seemed that my publisher was trying to ride the Shirer
bandwagon. I was slightly, ever so slightly, depressed by this
thought.

V
Aftereffects

The Thirty-Year War

I n 1985 DAVID WYMAN, the author of *The Abandonment of
the Jews*, reviewed the second edition of my book in the
New York Times. In that discussion he remarked that the first
edition had received little notice from the wider public.
Again, in 1989, Judith Sklar came to a similar conclusion. As
president of the American Political Science Association and
a professor at Harvard, she had been invited to lecture at
the University of Vermont. On that occasion she said to me
that books must appear at the right time, and that *The Destruction of the European Jews* had been published too early.

Topics may be suppressed or catapulted to public attention, but always for reasons that reflect the problems and
needs of a society. In the United States the phenomenon
now known as the Holocaust did not take root until after
the agonies of the Vietnam War, when a new generation of
Americans was searching for moral certainties, and when
the Holocaust became a marker of an absolute evil against
which all other transgressions in the conduct of nations
could be measured and assessed. For Germany the time did
not come until the 1980s, when the perpetrators were either
dead or in old-age homes, and when for the first time their

sons and daughters, grandsons and granddaughters, could openly ask questions about the activities of their elders during the Nazi era. In France, a complicated country where former resisters lived next door to former collaborators, time had to pass as well. In both Germany and France decades passed before my work was translated, but then the reception exceeded my expectations.

In the days when the first edition appeared, in 1961, I could sense a general unpreparedness for my subject. I was already aware of realities in the literary world. I was prepared for the difficulty of a small publisher trying to sell a large book. That much was clear to me. What I had not anticipated was the *nature* of the reactions I received, what it was that reviewers accepted as a matter of course, and what aroused controversy.

I had thought my fundamental thesis would become a critical issue. After all, I had asserted that the process of destruction was bureaucratic, that for its successful completion it fed upon the talents and contributions of all manner of specialists, that a bureaucrat became a perpetrator by virtue of his position and skills at the precise time when the process had reached a stage that required his involvement, that he was a thinking individual, and that, above all, he was available, neither evading his duty nor obstructing the administrative operation. This all-encompassing readiness, which had to be deep-rooted, carried certain implications for the question of what Germany was all about. Given the prevailing notion that the Nazis had imposed their will on an unwilling German population, and that the whole regime was an aberration of history, I was braced for a protest: the resurrection of the old emphasis on the role of seducers, deceivers, henchmen, and sadists in Nazi Germany, and the reaffirmation of the essential goodness of ordinary people the world over. Yet there was hardly any objection to my description of the machinery of destruction. Most commentators simply bypassed my analysis or considered it a matter of course. One of them thought about it more deeply and, treating it as a discovery, said that after reading my book he could never see the Final Solution in its old light. That reviewer was Hugh Trevor-Roper.

Trevor-Roper, a wide-ranging historian who refused to barricade himself behind a "Maginot Line" of highly concentrated subject matter, became Oxford University's Regius Professor of Modern History after writing a heavy work about Archbishop Laud and a popular, accessible book about the last days of Adolf Hitler. He also crafted several dozen masterful essays, many of them reviews of books or based on books. Here too, most of his topics were people, like Machiavelli, Sir Thomas More, Gustavus Adolphus, or Karl Marx, but also congeries of individuals, like the Jesuits of Japan, the Quakers, and the Jews. About Jews he had published three essays, one of them in the magazine of the American Jewish Committee, *Commentary*. It must have been Trevor-Roper's books about Hitler and his essays on Jewish subjects that made him *Commentary*'s choice as a reviewer of my book. His essay about my work was eight thousand words long, and for anyone who could not muster the energy to read my eight hundred double-column pages, he provided a summary, guide, and evaluation of my findings. His grasp was total, and he wrote more about my volume in another, different review in the *New Statesman*, where he made the crucial observation that the destruction of the Jews was a "national act," and that "disguise it as they may, the Germans were involved in it as a nation."

National character analysis is not pursued in the United States as in Europe, where several writers like Ernest Barker and Salvador de Madariaga have explored this domain. In the United States one treads lightly in matters of national traits, so much so that the principal works about *American* national character have been written by Europeans, like Alexis de Tocqueville, Gunnar Myrdal, or Denis Brogan. In the main, therefore, American reviewers who saw clearly and accepted unequivocally what I wrote about the participation in the destructive labor of German diplomats and soldiers, lawyers and accountants, policemen and clerks, stopped short of attempting to draw ultimate conclusions. For practical purposes I had ignited no controversy about Germany.

The quiet, however, was shattered when Trevor-Roper, whose interest encompassed also the Jews, noticed my description of the actions of the victims during the catastrophe. I had included the behavior of the Jewish community in my description because I saw Jewish institutions as an extension of the German bureaucratic machine. I was driven by force of logic to take account of the considerable reliance placed by the Germans on Jewish cooperation. I had to examine the Jewish tradition of trusting God, princes, laws, and contracts. Ultimately I had to ponder the Jewish calculation that the persecutor would not destroy what he could economically exploit. It was precisely this Jewish strategy that dictated accommodation and precluded resistance. Trevor-Roper now called special attention to my discussion of that topic. He saw immediately that from 1933 to the end, the Jewish leadership was not a new oligarchy installed by the perpetrators, that Rabbi Leo Baeck had been the Jewish leader in Germany before 1933, that the administrative tasks performed by the Jewish councils in German-dominated Europe relieved the German apparatus of a burden, that Jewish resistance was negligible and German casualties almost nil. The active role of the Jews in their own destruction he called the "most surprising revelation" and, prophetically, "the least welcome" to my readers.

And so it was. In *Commentary* itself, Professor Oscar Handlin of Harvard, whose specialty was immigration, including Jewish immigration to the United States, wrote an entire article as a rebuttal to my argument. The title of his essay was "Jewish Resistance to the Nazis," and its tone was set in one of the opening paragraphs in which he referred to my interpretation as an "impiety" that was "defaming the dead." The Jews did resist, he went on, but since he did not wish to "exaggerate," he would point to the fact that collaboration was a general European phenomenon. As to "that awesome moment at the edge of a grave," he found that there, in the final extremity, the victims could comfort themselves with the thought of God's magnificent creation.

After the appearance of Handlin's comments, and a small flood of letters supporting his views, I still thought such reasoning would collapse of its own weight. My assessment, however, was mistaken. The fragile nature of the objections hurled against me did not impair their durability. I had underestimated the importance of myths and had placed too much reliance on soberness. I had not reminded myself enough of Franz Neumann's words: "This is too much to take." The opposition did *not* die. Even in 1993 an article appeared in the German mass-circulation magazine *Der Spiegel* replete with many of the disapprobations I had read in the intervening decades. Added to the repetition of these charges was the accusation that in my subsequent writings I had reiterated and elaborated what I had first said in 1961 about compliant Jewish reactions to destruction. I had waged a thirty-year war against the Jewish resistance.

The author of this article was Arno Lustiger. He was not a professor but an Auschwitz survivor who had become a businessman in postwar Germany. I first met him in 1984 when he introduced himself to me on the occasion of my first public lecture on German soil. He asked me whether the name Lustiger was familiar to me. Yes, I replied, the archbishop of Paris was a Cardinal Lustiger. It was his cousin, said Arno, and he wanted me to know that unlike his cousin he had not converted from Judaism to Christianity. I refrained from complimenting him, but I could not help asking myself, What is he doing in Germany? Is his residence in that country after his Auschwitz experience not as radical a step as the conversion of his cousin in France? Did not both of them achieve success, the cousin as a prince of the Catholic church and he as a potentate in a sector of German business?

There were but fifty thousand Jews in Germany in 1993, and few of them were professors. The criticisms advanced by Lustiger would not be offered by a non-Jew in the German Federal Republic. They were an internal Jewish matter but of considerable interest to the German magazine, which printed them as a one-time opportunity and which hoped to arouse a "controversy," just like the one that had lasted so long in the United States.

It has taken me some time to absorb what I should always have known, that in my whole approach to the study of the destruction of the Jews I was pitting myself against the main current of Jewish thought, that I did not give in, that in my research and writing I was pursuing not merely another direction but one which was the exact opposite of a signal that pulsated endlessly through the Jewish community. This message has three elements, and I had countered all three.

To begin with, there is an insistence that the major effort of Jewish learning and remembrance must be focused on the Jews, *their* circumstances and *their* experiences. Placing the victim rather than the perpetrator at the center of attention is the cornerstone of virtually all the edifices—be they encyclopedias, institutes, or museums—which have been created in the United States or Israel. The largest, most imposing effort is the United States Holocaust Memorial Museum in Washington. I have been associated in minor ways with the creation of this museum. The building is the work of a genius, the architect James Ingo Freed. It has towers and an atrium that recall the watchtowers and parade ground of a concentration camp. During its construction a member of the German federal legislature, the Bundestag, privately expressed the fear to me that *this* building would represent Germany in the heart of the American capital. In the end, however, his concern was too great.

Nestled between other buildings by virtue of its placement in an available space, and limited in height and the choice of materials by government restrictions, it can be seen clearly for what it is only from an aircraft or a helicopter. Once inside the newly opened museum, the visitor was invited to draw a card showing a photograph of a victim. During the walk through the museum halls the person on the card was a constant companion. Indeed, this silent attendant became more familiar along the way as the card was inserted into machines which printed out more information about the victim's fate. Among the exhibits, the visitor could see mounted photographs of an extinct Jewish community, a Gypsy cart and violin, a Danish rescue boat, and many other reminders of the victims' lives. What then about the perpetrators? What may be seen of them?

I had planted the idea that the museum should house a German railroad car in which Jews had been transported to their deaths, and the Polish government actually donated a freight car that had been left on Polish soil. Here then we had obtained a large product of German manufacture, but the exhibitors provided a structural addition for a second perspective. A bridge was built through the open door of the car, so that the visitor may peer into the dark interior and imagine the Jews locked in. I had also proposed that we ask the Polish government for a can of Zyklon gas, with which the Jews were killed in Auschwitz and Maydanek. I would have liked to see a *single* can mounted on a pedestal in a small room, with no other objects between the walls, as the epitome of Adolf Hitler's Germany, just as a vase of Euphronios was shown at one time all by itself in the Metropolitan Museum of Art as one of the supreme artifacts of Greek antiquity. Instead a whole pile of gas cans donated by generous Polish authorities was heaped in the middle of the floor to be stumbled on and noticed with a downward glance. Finally I had suggested that one wall be covered with the photographic portraits of sixteen or twenty perpetrators, known and unknown, to represent the civil service, the military, industry, and the party. The "Hilberg" wall, as the planners called it jokingly, became a display of the Allied war crimes trials. Some of the perpetrators are still there, but in the role of defendant.

The fadeout of the perpetrator is no accident. One editor who compiled accounts of victims chose a characteristic title for his book. He called it *Out of the Whirlwind.* This practice is the ultimate effect of an admonition in Deuteronomy, where one may find the words, "You shall blot out the remembrance of Amalek from under heaven." It is that tradition which is observed also during the Jewish holiday of Purim, when the Scroll of Esther is read and when children with rattles drown out the name of Haman, who sought to kill the Jews of Persia. Once, at a meeting of the United States Holocaust Memorial Council, I heard a presentation of the director, an Orthodox rabbi, Seymour Siegel, who mentioned Adolf Eichmann and, between commas, added the ritualistic words, "May his name be erased." Then and there I reflected on the countless hours I had spent in archives and libraries, searching for the first names of bureaucrats who habitually signed their memoranda only "Klemm," or "Krause," or "Kühne."

Modern Jews know, like their ancient forebears, the hazard of giving the perpetrators a face, of endowing them with identity and thought, of allowing them a modicum of doubt or regret, of making them human. Remember only what they did. And what have *I* done? I insist on delving into forbidden territory and presenting Amalek with all his features as an aggregate of German functionaries.

The prevailing emphasis on the victims has its corollary in the embrace of Jewish sources. The victims do not have much individuality in German documents. There they coalesce indistinguishably into categories: foreign Jews, Jewish laborers, Jewish children; or into numbers: 20,105 Jews, 363,211 Jews, 1,274,000 Jews. Because I used so many of these materials, Arno Lustiger wrote that I banished all the victims "into the anonymous grave of concealment of forgetting," and that I covered the dead "with the records of the murderers," pouring on the graves the "thousands of footnotes" of my books.

I shall not dwell on the fact that the proponents of Jewish sources have paid relatively little attention to the contemporaneous correspondence of the Jewish councils. These collections, however fragmentary some of them may be, are invaluable indicators of the desperate adjustment strategies pursued by the communities in the wake of strangling German measures. My critics are primarily interested not in those records but in the testimony of survivors. In oral history projects a major effort has been made to interview as many of these survivors as possible. There is, however, a sharp built-in limitation in this undertaking. As an early compiler of such accounts, David Pablo Boder, pointed out, he "did not interview the dead." The survivors are not a random sample of the extinct communities, particularly if one looks for typical Jewish reactions and adjustments to the process of destruction.

In their accounts, survivors generally leave out the setting of their experiences, such as specific localities or the names and positions of persons they encountered. Even when they talk about themselves, they do not necessarily reveal mundane information about their financial circumstances or their health. Ghetto life and the early labor camps are not given prominence. The principal subjects are deportations, concentration camps, death camps, escapes, hiding, and partisan fighting. Understandably the survivors seldom speak of those experiences that were most humiliating or embarrassing, and whereas they may mention their hunger, thirst, pain, and fear, it is precisely in these passages that one confronts the implicit or open dictum: "No one who was not there can imagine what it was like." Only one fact is always revealed clearly and completely. It is the self-portrait of the survivors, their psychological makeup, and what it took to survive.

I have read countless accounts of survivors. I looked for missing links in my jigsaw puzzle. I tried to glimpse the Jewish community. I searched for the dead. Most often, however, I had to remind myself that what I most wanted from them they could not give me, no matter how much they said.

The focus on Jewry and Jewish sources is tied to a third imperative. The Jewish victims must be seen as heroic. The Jews in this pictorialization engaged in resistance, many of them, and in many ways. Arno Lustiger, for example, extends the roster of the resisters by including Jewish soldiers in Allied armies and even those Jews who joined the international brigades in the Spanish Civil War, which ended before the Second World War began. More often the concept of resistance is redefined to accommodate such activities as feeding or hospitalizing people in the ghettos, even if the German overlords permitted these functions as part of the maintenance of the ghetto system before the onset of deportations. And more: In 1968, at a conference at Yad Vashem, Meir Dvorjetski of Bar Ilan University presented a paper on "Resistance in the Daily Life of Ghettos and Camps," and enumerated under this rubric the "Individual Renunciation of Chance to Escape" out of loyalty to relatives and fellow workers, and the "Desire Not to Be an Exception," "The Sense of Family and Going Together to Death." Martin Gilbert concludes his book *The Holocaust*, published in 1985, with a paragraph in which he says, "Even passivity was a form of resistance. . . . To die with dignity was a form of resistance. . . . Simply to survive was a victory of the human spirit."

Active, armed acts of self-defense within the destructive arena have nevertheless remained the centerpiece of a historiography and celebration. That these acts have been magnified and popularized should not be surprising. The image of a resister with gun in hand is comforting. Something that is uplifting can be salvaged from the catastrophe. To resist is not to cooperate with the perpetrator, not to follow his orders, not to be meek in the face of death. In Israel such an elevation of the ghetto Jews has been especially important. Before the founding of the state, the Jews who inhabited Palestine, who called themselves the Yishuv, distanced themselves from European Jewry not only geographically. Tom Segev writes of a "common stereotype that depicted the Exile as weak, feminine, and passive, and the Yishuv as strong, masculine, and active." The native-born Palestinian Jew, called the Sabra, represented an ideal, and the Holocaust survivor its reverse. In Yishuv slang, he states, the survivors were called "soap." Given such sentiments, one may understand why an attempt was made to create a sloganized, equally stereotypical response featuring widespread ghetto heroism.

Needless to say I had a problem with this campaign of exaltation. When relatively isolated or episodic acts of resistance are represented as typical, a basic characteristic of the German measures is obscured. The destruction of the Jews can no longer be visualized as a process. Instead the drastic actuality of a relentless killing of men, women, and children is mentally transformed into a more familiar picture of a struggle—however unequal—between combatants. To the perpetrators themselves, the idea of a Jew as such an adversary was psychologically important. A German mobile killing unit would even invent a Jewish "spirit of opposition" to justify a small massacre, and after the largest engagement between Germans and Jews, in the Warsaw ghetto, the SS commandant, Jürgen Stroop, listed every one of his sixteen dead and eighty-five wounded by name, as if to emphasize the magnitude of his losses. When I was testifying in a Toronto case against a purveyor of literature asserting that a holocaust had not occurred in the first place, I heard echoes of Stroop's report in questions posed by the defendant's attorney. The Germans, he intimated, had acted as the responsible authority in an occupied city when they put down the Warsaw ghetto rebellion.

The inflation of resistance has another consequence which has been of concern to those Jews who have regarded themselves as the actual resisters. If heroism is an attribute that should be assigned to every member of the European Jewish community, it will diminish the accomplishment of the few who took action. When Jewry was threatened with destruction, the independently minded breakaway Jews made a sharp distinction between themselves and all those others who had not joined them. "Do not walk like sheep to slaughter," they said, and they meant every word. After the war, some of them still retained the view they had formed in the days when they faced battle. Yisrael Gutman, who was in the Warsaw ghetto, Maydanek, Auschwitz, and Mauthausen, wrote a five-hundred-page book, *The Jews of Warsaw 1939–1943*, more than half of it devoted to the Jewish underground movement and to the conduct of the fighting. Noteworthy is his estimate of the active Jewish combatants, because it is even lower than my own initial figure, which I based partially on Stroop's report. He refrained altogether from estimating how many casualties this small aggregate of poorly armed fighters had inflicted on the Germans and their collaborators. Rachel Auerbach, who stood at the side of the underground Jewish historian Emmanuel Ringelblum, was at pains to tell me that the public did not understand that, if even a hundred Germans were killed or wounded in the ghetto revolt, the result was a major achievement.

Finally, and perhaps most important, the preemption or

magnification of resistance has obscured the reality of Jewish life in the ghettos and camps. One of the most sophisticated and astute observers of the catastrophe is Bronia Klibanski, who was a courier for the Jewish resistance in the Bialystok area of Poland. In a conversation with me in 1968 she expressed her reservations about the equalization—she used the German word *Gleichschaltung*—between the underground fighters and those who did not fight at all. To her the blending of the two groups was not merely a form of dilution, which blurred the multitudinous problems of organizing a defense in a cautious, reluctant Jewish community; it was also a way of shutting off a great many questions about that community, its reasoning and survival strategy. Jewish history could not be written, she said, before these questions were asked.

For thirty years, between the articles of Oscar Handlin and Arno Lustiger, I was almost buried under an avalanche of condemnations. But just before this campaign began, a noteworthy article appeared in a Yiddish newspaper, which—like the other Yiddish dailies—was read mainly by the elderly, and which was therefore already in decline. Although the Yiddish press had barely mentioned my work, the journalist Aaron Zeitlin, whose father, a Yiddish writer in Warsaw, had been killed in 1942, devoted six paragraphs of his column of February 2, 1962, in *Der Tog—Morgen Journal* to reflections about my conclusions. He spoke of Jewish trust and optimism in history, and said yes, this optimism of ours had always been a cane with two ends—more than once it had supported us, but then it had also brought the worst blows on our heads.

Questionable Practices

W HEN THEODOR ADORNO condemned those who would write poetry after Auschwitz as barbaric, I had a problem. I am, of course, no poet, but I have been a footnote writer. Are footnotes less barbaric? In his column "From Friday to Friday" of February 2, 1962, Aaron Zeitlin, who wrote verse himself, noted with a tone of resignation that the Jewish catastrophe would be fashioned into a catastrophology, an academic field of research, and that nothing could be done about such a development. All that had happened would eventually be documented and written down. Even that which was most horrible would in time become history.

And so I try to nod wisely when poets or novelists step forward with their art, which in its very nature is much less disguised than mine. Nor am I disturbed when popularizers of history excavate the monographs of the footnote writers and, distilling the contents, highlight story and drama for a large reading public. The Jewish historian Heinrich Graetz recognized the distinction between researchers, the *Geschichtsforscher*, and writers, the *Geschichtsschreiber*. Not wanting to abdicate in either capacity, he was both.

There are, however, limits. Those I draw are not necessarily enshrined in law, yet in my eyes they mark out areas of inappropriateness or illegitimacy.

Among the practices that give me discomfort is the creation of a story in which historical facts are altered deliberately for the sake of plot and adventure. I remember a time many years ago when my only diversion in Burlington was going to the cinema. Once I watched a film in which ancient Macedonians fought a naval battle with Romans. I was completely absorbed with the scene when I suddenly heard an agonized critique of a few rows behind me. It came from the chairman of our Department of Classics. My own composure was shaken in a bookstore when I spotted a novel with a glittering cover adorned with a large golden swastika on a crimson background. I opened the book at random and discovered more than a whole page containing my translation of a German document that the author of this international best-seller had lifted from a document book I had compiled. Together with this real record he presented fictional texts of bureaucratic correspondence that he had made up to complete his amalgam of history and fantasy. The reader, however, was not informed that my document was fact and that the other, apparently verbatim passages were the author's inventions.

I realize that the example of the golden swastika is far from rare. The creators of a serious film, *The Wannsee Conference*, which was a reconstruction of a high-level bureaucratic discussion about the Final Solution held in wartime Berlin, also took liberties with the facts. The *New York Times* asked me to write an article about the dialogue depicted in this film, precisely because the ordinary viewer could expect a faithful rendition on the screen of everything that could be gathered about the meeting from documents and testimony. I do not know whether my comments destroyed any chance of a meaningful distribution of *The Wannsee Conference*, but I certainly fired on the makers of the film, giving them no quarter. My colleague Samuel Bogorad of our Department of English thought that my attitude toward artistic works was much too rigid. What, he asked, would I say about Shakespeare?

If counterfactual stories are frequent enough, kitsch is truly rampant. In my small collection of art books is a volume of essays, compiled by Gillo Dorfles, about the world of bad taste. The compendium is richly illustrated, and when I look at these reproductions during a late evening hour, I dissolve in laughter. In my subject, to be sure, I do not regard such examples of the aesthetic spirit as comical. The philistines in my field are everywhere. I am surrounded by the commonplace, platitudes, and clichés. In sculpture, Jewish resistance fighters are memorialized in the center of Warsaw by a large heroic statue in Stalinist style. In poetry I regularly encounter graves in the sky. In speeches I must listen to man's inhumanity to man. In some of my own works, the publishers have added their flourishes on jackets, covers, and title pages. The stylized barbed wire appeared on one of my paperbacks. The publisher of the first German translation of *The Destruction of the European Jews* added a subtitle, *Die Gesamtgeschichte des Holocaust*—The Whole History of the Holocaust, to the oversized double-column volume. When I handed an expanded text of this book to an American publisher it was plainly marked "Second Edition," but when the finished three-volume set was sent to me I discovered that he had changed these words to "Revised and Definitive Edition." The editor of an American magazine solicited a paper I had presented at an academic meeting on "The Role of the German Railroads in the Destruction of the Jews" and unilaterally substituted for this title "German Railroads/Jewish Souls." The first German publisher of a small volume, containing my introduction and documents about the railroads, inserted a poem for which, he said, he had paid good money, describing human beings in freight cars, including children whose eyes glowed like coal. Something else happened to the American edition of Claude Lanzmann's book *Shoah*, which comprises the testimony of his multilingual film, including also my statements. Lanzmann had designed this book so that each subtitle on the screen forms a separate line on the printed page. With this format, which preserves the intonations of the speakers and crystallizes the meaning of their utterances, he achieved a special power. The American publisher, however, believed that his reading public was not receptive to poetry. The lines were run together and the book was reduced to a rhythmless, lackluster prose.

The manipulation of history is a kind of spoilage, and kitsch is debasement. What may be said of both is that they are almost routine. Many historians can give personal examples of such experiences, so that my own are certainly not exceptional. I have, however, had disturbing encounters which are distinctly less common. I have in mind the handiwork of three authors who were sufficiently inspired by the muses to think of themselves as special, one as a narrator of events, one in the role of historian, and one as a philosopher interpreting history. Each of them regarded her specific contribution as a capstone to be placed on the work of others. Each considered her work to be a summation in which everything of importance that had been missed was finally resolved, and each complicated my life in her own special way. Their names were Nora Levin, Lucy Dawidowicz, and Hannah Arendt.

Nora Levin wrote a book called *The Holocaust*, with the subtitle *The Destruction of European Jewry 1933–1945*. The volume of 768 pages was published in 1968 by Thomas Y. Crowell, a firm established in 1834. On the opening page Levin makes a grateful acknowledgment to Robert L. Crowell, "who, in a spirit of bold and generous faith in an amateur writer," originally suggested that she undertake the task of writing the book. In a disarming way she points to her "very limited credentials" and her "very limited resources." She was born in 1916 in Philadelphia, where she lived all her life. With a bachelor's degree in education and another degree in library science she had been a teacher in public schools and had taught English and history in high school before she embarked on her career as an author. After her book appeared, I read a review of it by Gerald Reitlinger in the *New York Times*. "I found myself wading," he wrote, "through oceans of stated facts before encountering a single footnote. Then it became apparent," he continued, "that footnotes were scarce because each had been preceded by long recapitulations from single authors." Finally he said, "I began to notice sentences of my own, then whole paragraphs, slightly altered. No quotation marks, no acknowledgments."

If this is what she had done to Reitlinger, I thought, what has she taken from me? The answer was: even more. Her copying was so pervasive that I soon tired of looking for all the passages that paralleled mine. Crowell never withdrew the book, and neither did Schocken, which distributed *The Holocaust* as a paperback. Schocken did not desist even after I reminded representatives of the house, which contacted me in one matter or another, that there was a problem.

Levin, however, paid a continuing price for her literary activity. She was helpless against a rumor network in which facts were sometimes alloyed with imaginary happenings. On January 29, 1982, she sent me a letter, telling me about a "poisonous tale" to the effect that she had made an out-of-court settlement with me. She asked me whether I had heard the rumor and pleaded with me to deny it in writing, so that she might make copies of my answer for ten or fifteen scholars around the world. Since I had never heard this particular tale, I began to compose a letter, certifying that I had not initiated a suit for copyright infringement against her and that she had not made any payment to me for any damage I had suffered, but then I tired of working on my draft.

Lucy Dawidowicz, born in 1915, held a bachelor of arts degree awarded in 1936 and a master of arts degree earned in 1961. She worked almost all her life for Jewish institutions, and she received quite a few grants from Jewish foundations. Her books were devoted to Jewish subjects. She was a New Yorker, moored to the city in which she was born, and when she served on the President's Commission on the Holocaust in 1978–1979 she was the only member of the group who refused to sign its final report on the ground that a museum commemorating the Jewish catastrophe properly belonged in New York City, not in Washington. Just before the war she had visited Vilna, then a part of Poland, where a Jewish Institute, the YIVO, which devoted itself to Eastern European Jewish history and the preservation of Yiddish, was located. When the institute was reconstituted in New York, she could avail herself not only of its facilities but also the knowledge of its staff. In 1975 she published a 460-page book, *The War Against the Jews*, consisting of two disconnected parts, one about the Germans, the other about the Jews. Upon its appearance, the volume received words of praise, such as "distinguished," "trenchant," and "authoritative."

I approached this book as I would any other in my field. Were there any new facts I should know? Was there any insight I had overlooked? In the first chapter I found an extensive discussion of Hitler's *Mein Kampf*. On the first page the author posed a question, which was just short of an answer, suggesting that Hitler had already formed the idea of a Final Solution, that is, the physical annihilation of the Jews, in the 1920s. Really? The next few chapters, based largely on secondary sources and conveying nothing whatever that could be called new, jumped from topic to topic as though the author were anxious to come to the conclusion of Part I. She arrived there, on page 150, asking another question: Did Adolf Hitler decide on the destruction of the

Jews as early as November 1918? "It is a hazardous task," she said, "to construct a chronology of the evolution of this idea in Hitler's mind." The sparse evidence, she added, would no doubt be inadmissible in a court. Lucy Dawidowicz, I am sure, was careful not to enter courtrooms. She was content to leave testimony in war crimes cases, including answers in cross-examinations, to people like me.

The second part of *The War Against the Jews* consisted of a chapter about Germany's Jews and a number of chapters about the Jews of Eastern Europe, in the main, Poland. The Jewish councils in the ghettos, which she called the "official community," were treated briefly as powerless entities. She allotted more space to institutions not directly controlled by the councils, including welfare organizations, house committees, and the rabbinate, all of which she labeled the "alternative community," and to the resistance movement, which she named the "countercommunity." She wrote no chapters about the rest of the European Jews. An appendix, with short, almanaclike entries, took care of them.

I tried not to be mystified by the success of this book. Now and then I glimpsed a semihidden reward for nostalgic Jewish readers. Nothing could really be done, Lucy Dawidowicz seemed to say, not by the Jewish leaders and not by anyone else. Indeed, she reserved her approval mainly for the soup ladlers and all those others in the ghettos who staved off starvation and despair as long as possible. In the end, she observed, everyone was carried away by the tide, including those young men and women who were fired by "the medieval virtues of Christian chivalry" to offer physical resistance. Perhaps such a book was bound to be produced and, given its vaguely consoling words, could easily be clutched by all those who did not wish to look deeper.

In a free market there is a place for every idea and for every product. Yet Lucy Dawidowicz was not wholly satisfied with her rewards. She wanted preeminence. Now that she had spoken, there was no need for other efforts. Hers was the ultimate word. She became a critic, weighing the contributions of researchers and dispensing judgments, some of which she sprinkled into her footnotes. In 1982 Harvard University Press published an entire book of her views, *The Holocaust and the Historians*. I read a discussion of this work in the *American Historical Review* by Henry Friedlander, a survivor of the Lodz ghetto and Auschwitz, whose knowledge of Holocaust historiography was probably unmatched. Friedlander noted some authors of monographs whom she had omitted or dismissed. The list included Poliakov, Reitlinger, and me, as well as H. G. Adler, Uwe Adam, Christopher Browning, Gavin Langmuir, Telford Taylor, Henry Feingold, Saul Friedlander, Meir Michaelis, Randolph Braham, Bernard Wasserstein, David Wyman, Leni Yahil, Elie A. Cohen, Josef Wulf, Helmut Eschwege, Hans Buchheim, Heinz Höhne, Adalbert Rückerl, Jozef Marszalek, Alan Bullock, A. J. P. Taylor, Hugh Trevor-Roper, and Franz Neumann.

There are other problems in her book about the historians. In criticizing an interpretation of a document by an English writer, she states that on November 30, 1941, a transport with Jewish deportees went from Berlin to Prague. This kind of mistake is not an ordinary one. It is not the result solely of carelessness, conjecture, or the failure to see a complication. Rather, it is an error of unfamiliarity that *no* historian specializing in the Jewish catastrophe would be capable of making. It is almost the equivalent of declaring that on December 7, 1941, the Japanese attacked not Pearl Harbor but the Panama Canal.

To be sure, Dawidowicz has not been taken all that seriously by historians. I do not recall a single professional conference in which I saw her as a participant. Nevertheless she had standing enough, not only to publish books but to write about them. Evidently in America there were as yet no standards that could enable even an experienced editor to distinguish between her work and the contributions of so many of the people she looked down upon. And that was a troubling thought.

Hannah Arendt, says my agent Theron Raines, is an icon. Books have been written about her, and in the Federal Republic of Germany her name was given to an express train and her face appeared on a postage stamp. She was born there in 1906. Her field of study was philosophy, and her mentors were Martin Heidegger and Karl Jaspers. Twice she had to flee, in 1933 from Berlin and in 1941 from France. In the United States she began to identify herself as a political theorist. Two of her specialties were totalitarianism and revolution. Both were popular concepts at the time. Totalitarianism in particular was a watchword in the United States, as Americans tried to find common denominators between the Nazi Germany they had just helped to defeat and the Soviet Union, their new foe. Naturally I looked at Hannah Arendt's treatise on the origins of totalitarianism, but when I saw that it consisted only of unoriginal essays on anti-Semitism, imperialism, and general topics associated with totalitarianism, such as the "masses," propaganda, and "total domination," I put the book aside. I never met or corresponded with her, and I heard her in public only twice. All I recall from these two lectures is the emphatic, insistent manner in which she spoke.

In 1961 Hannah Arendt covered the Eichmann trial for the *New Yorker* magazine. Judging from her subsequently published correspondence with Jaspers, she left Jerusalem after a stay of ten weeks, just three days *before* Adolf Eichmann's own extensive testimony began.

When I read the second installment of her account in the February 16, 1963, issue of the magazine, I noted a flattering comment about me. Referring to the difficulties the prosecution faced in untangling the labyrinth of German institutions, she wrote: "If the trial were to take place today, this task would be much easier, for the political scientist Raul Hilberg, in his book 'The Destruction of the European Jews,' published in Chicago in 1961, has succeeded in presenting the first clear description of this incredibly complicated machinery of destruction." I could not help fantasizing what she might have added had she suspected that the experts at Yad Vashem, who supported the prosecution with evidentiary material, had already been introduced to my description of this machinery in 1958, and that, such awareness in Israel notwithstanding, I had not even been asked for assistance in the preparation of the trial.

Hannah Arendt's five articles in the *New Yorker* were densely packed with facts. When the Viking Press published her report in book form later that year, as *Eichmann in*

Jerusalem, I looked for footnotes. There were none. On two pages in the back of the book she stated that her chief sources were the transcript pages and other items that had been handed to the press while she was at the trial. Apparently copies of original German documents introduced in evidence were not part of these packages. A revised and enlarged edition of the book, again under the Viking imprint, appeared in 1964. This version contained a postscript in which Arendt noted that a complete record of the trial had not been published and was not easily accessible. Then she wrote: "As can be seen from the text, I have used Gerald Reitlinger's *The Final Solution* and I have relied even more on Raul Hilberg's *The Destruction of the European Jews.*"

Her reliance on my book had already been noticed by several reviewers before the publication of her second edition. Given the extent of her dependence on me, such a discovery was not difficult. Several commentators, however, went beyond the factual terrain and also attributed her opinions to mine. In constructing this linkage, which has persisted for decades, they unfortunately failed to observe two significant differences between us.

The subtitle of Hannah Arendt's *Eichmann in Jerusalem* is *A Report on the Banality of Evil.* That subsidiary title has the rare distinction of being recalled more clearly than the main one. It is certainly a description of her thesis about Adolf Eichmann and, by implication, many other Eichmanns, but is it correct? In Adolf Eichmann, a lieutenant colonel in the SS who headed the Gestapo's section on Jews, she saw a man who was "déclassé," who had led a "humdrum" life before he rose in the SS hierarchy, and who had "flaws" of character. She referred to his "self-impor-tance," expounded on his "bragging," and spoke of his "grotesque silliness" in the hour when he was hanged, when—having drunk a half-bottle of wine—he said his last words. She did not recognize the magnitude of what this man had done with a small staff, overseeing and manipulat-ing Jewish councils in various parts of Europe, attaching some of the remaining Jewish property in Germany, Aus-tria, and Bohemia-Moravia, preparing anti-Jewish laws in satellite states, and arranging for the transportation of Jews to shooting sites and death camps. She did not discern the pathways that Eichmann had found in the thicket of the German administrative machine for his unprecedented ac-tions. She did not grasp the dimensions of his deed. There was no "banality" in this "evil."

The second divergence between her conceptions and mine concerned the role of the Jewish leaders in what she plainly labeled the destruction of their own people. It had been known before, she said, but now it had been exposed "in all of its pathetic and sordid detail" in what she called my "standard work." The whole truth, she said in a sentence that was quoted over and over, was that if the Jewish people had been unorganized and leaderless there would have been chaos and misery, but not between four and a half million and six million dead.

In writing about the Jewish councils I had emphasized the extent to which the German apparatus counted on their cooperation. The accommodation policy of the councils had ended in disaster. For me, however, the problem was deeper. The councils were not only a German tool but also an instrument of the Jewish community. Their strategy was a continuation of the adjustments and adaptations practiced by Jews for centuries. I could not separate the Jewish leaders from the Jewish populace because I believed that these men represented the essence of a time-honored Jewish reaction to danger.

In Israel itself there had never been a splitting of the Jewish councils from the ghetto Jews in general. During the early years of the Jewish state, the victims were still considered to have been trusting and weak individuals. As late as 1957, only a year before Dr. Melkman's letter rejecting my manuscript for the way I treated this history, *Yad Vashem Studies* featured an article by Benzion Dinur, Yad Vashem's chairman, who stated in unvarnished language that the councils could not be considered in isolation because they constituted an "expression basically of what had remained of the confidence Jews had in Germany even under the Nazi regime." The Jews, he said, "carried out regulations" even if they could have evaded them at some risk to themselves. In the Netherlands they had "hurried with their luggage" to the trains that would carry them to the east, and "even in Warsaw and Vilna, in Bialystok and Lvov, reports of death journeys were discredited for a long time."

Dinur's train of thought had not completely disappeared in Israel when the Eichmann trial began; the view was maintained by Israel's youth in particular. When Jewish survivors testified about their experience publicly in the court proceedings, the issue was therefore joined. It was the witnesses who were on trial. If they could not explain their behavior to the new generation, the old image would be confirmed and they would be judged to have been automatons. To the dismay of Hannah Arendt, the prosecution asked several of the survivors *why* they had followed orders. Thus the attorney general: "Dr. Buzminski, you knew it was a death train, didn't you? Why did you enter these cars?" The witness, as it happens, had jumped out of the train, but the questions remained, and now the repair work was pursued methodically from Jerusalem to New York. The Jews, it was said in metronome fashion, *had* been heroic, *had* resisted, and this assessment covered leaders and followers alike. Not surprisingly, when Hannah Arendt's *New Yorker* articles appeared, the wrath of the Jewish establishment, as she called it, descended upon her and simultaneously upon me.

In March 1963 the Council of Jews from Germany, an international organization of Jewish emigrants from that country, published a statement in the press. Referring to "recent opinions" about the Nazi period, the council declared that a historical picture influenced by such opinions would be a falsified one. "This is especially true," it said, "of the book by Raoul Hilberg which appeared in 1961, '*The Destruction of the European Jews*,' and of the articles published by Hannah Arendt in '*The New Yorker*.'"

Hannah Arendt and I were coupled so often that I could even act as her stand-in. On October 18, 1963, the New York literary critic and political commentator Irving Howe chaired a symposium about "Eichmann and the Jewish Tragedy." He wrote about this event twice, in the *Partisan Review* that same year and again, at length, in his autobiography eighteen years later. In the *Partisan Review* he stated that he and his fellow organizers had invited Hannah Arendt "herself" to speak. "She declined," and so did Bruno Bettelheim, who was invited next as a man whose views were thought to be similar to those of Arendt. "We then asked Raul Hilberg, author of a scholarly volume on which Hannah Arendt leaned." The meeting, he said, was "excited and passionate," but "at no point—I repeat, at no point—was anyone shouted down." In his autobiography Howe described the meeting as "hectic" and "sometimes outrageous," but also "urgent and afire."

My own impressions were slightly different. When I was invited to this symposium I was told in writing that I would have thirty minutes to speak. I knew I would have difficulty with such a time frame, but I did not wish to reduce the scope of my topic. I was still thinking of dealing with Eichmann *and* the Jews, a combination that was almost unmanageable.

The hall in the hotel was filled with hundreds of people. One of them was the poet Robert Lowell. I asked him why he was present at such a gathering and he replied, "I've got to be where the action is." So this was going to be spectacle. On the dais Irving Howe informed me that I would have just twenty minutes. I was not adamant enough to demand the half-hour I had been promised, and I was not experienced enough to throw away my prepared thoughts immediately, to assess the audience before me, and to address it directly. I had come with transcript pages of the Eichmann trial, and I read from the testimony of a woman who had lived in the primitive village of Volhynia, and who was herded with her family to the edge of a mass grave where her young daughter asked her why they did not flee. The impatient guard had asked whom he should shoot first, and he shot the child. The mother, wounded, dug herself out of the grave. *This* is a scene, I wanted to say, that illustrates what happens when orders are followed. *This* was the outcome of Jewry's age-old policy. I was not friendly. I did not yield, and I was oblivious to the fact that I was tearing open unhealed wounds. I was not allowed to finish. A panelist pounded on the table with his fist. His banging, magnified by the microphone, was followed by a cascade of boos. Irving Howe invited the audience to ask questions and make comments. Now one after another individual rose, one to accuse me of sadism, another to read from a prepared written statement challenging my figures on the German dead in the Warsaw ghetto battle, and so on, on and on.

In later years I have given hundreds of public lectures. A few times I was honored with standing ovations, but I will not forget that particular evening in the seedy New York hotel.

When Hannah Arendt wrote her postscript to the second edition of her Eichmann book, she had grown bitter. It was not she who had claimed "that the Jews had murdered themselves." The "well-known" construct "ghetto mentality," which she attributed to the Israelis and which, she pointed out, had been espoused by Bruno Bettelheim, was not hers. Then she said that "someone who evidently found the whole discussion too dull had the brilliant idea of evoking Freudian theories and attributing to the whole Jewish people a 'death wish'—unconscious, of course." But who was *that* individual? When I first read these lines, I could not solve this riddle. I simply did not know anyone who wrote or spoke about death wishes in connection with the Jewish fate. More than twenty years passed before I read Arendt's correspondence with Karl Jaspers. On March 24, 1964, he asked her whether I had defended her. She wrote back on April 24:

> I have heard nothing about Hilberg taking my side. He is pretty stupid and crazy. He babbles now about a "death wish" of the Jews. His book is really excellent, but only because it is a simple report. A more general, introductory chapter is beneath a singed pig. (Pardon—for a moment I forgot to whom I am writing. Now I am going to let it stand anyway.)

The correspondence was published by Piper Verlag in Munich in 1985. The American translation, which appeared in 1992, did not contain the sentence with the words "stupid" and "crazy." Curious, I inquired about this omission and was told that the statement was struck on legal advice.

In the 1960s Piper Verlag was much more concerned with libel than in 1985. When that publisher considered her *Eichmann in Jerusalem* for the German market, the possibility of lawsuits became a stumbling block. In the absence of footnotes, her multitude of statements about a great many living individuals, most of them in Germany, were unsubstantiated. Struggling in a four-page letter, dated January 22, 1963, with answers to Klaus Piper's detailed questions, she said at one point:

> Here as elsewhere I have used material presented in the book by Raul Hilberg that appeared in 1961. That is a standard book, which makes all the earlier investigations, such as those of Reitlinger, Poliakov, etc., appear to be antiquated. The author has worked for fifteen years only with sources, and if he had not, in addition, written a very foolish first chapter, in which he shows that he does not understand much about German history, the book would have been perfect so to speak. No one at any rate will be able to write about these things without using it.

I found this letter among her papers in the Manuscripts Division of the Library of Congress. Coincidentally, in that same collection I also unearthed a letter addressed to her on April 8, 1959, barely four years earlier, by Gordon Hubel of Princeton University Press. In that letter I discovered that the press had turned to *her* for an evaluation of my manuscript. Thanking her, Hubel enclosed a check. Here then was the source of Hubel's argument—which he invoked in rejecting my work—that for all practical purposes Reitlinger, Poliakov, and Adler had exhausted the subject. This assessment was Hannah Arendt's thinking a year before Eichmann's capture in Argentina.

I still wonder what triggered her reactions to my first chapter. Was she really aroused by my search for historical precedents, such as the roots of anti-Jewish actions from 1933 to 1941 in the canons of the Catholic church, or the origin of the Nazi conception of the Jew in the writings of Martin Luther? To be sure, she had a personal need to insulate the Nazi phenomenon. She went back to Germany at every opportunity after the war, resuming contacts and relationships. With Heidegger, who had been her lover in her student days and who was a Nazi in Hitler's time, she became friendly again, rehabilitating him. But in dismissing my ideas she also made a bid for self-respect. Who was I, after all? She, the thinker, and I, the laborer who wrote only a simple report, albeit one which was indispensable once she had exploited it: that was the natural order of her universe.

V I
What Does
One Do?

The Second Edition

IN 1948 I HAD CHARTED A COURSE that I pursued heedless of my prospects. In 1961 I had no course. Rudderless, adrift, I waited. By 1963 I was tempted by an opportunity to extend my research. My publisher in Chicago, Quadrangle Books, employed a literary agent who tried to sell *The Destruction of the European Jews* to European publishers. In Munich the Droemersche Verlagsanstalt Th. Knaur Nachfolger bought the German rights and made arrangements for a translation. The library of the University of Vermont had obtained an English transcript of the Eichmann trial, and I could not resist reading its six thousand mimeographed pages. I purchased microfilm copies of those trial documents that I had not yet seen in my research. This small augmentation had a few other items I weaved into the book for the German edition. It was work for one and a half summers, plus the free hours between them. I sent the insertions to Munich in July 1964.

I traveled to Europe after mailing the package. Germany was not a country I wished to visit, but I stopped in Munich for one day on August 24, 1964, to meet with anyone at the publishing house who could see me, and if possible to talk with the translator about any problems.

When I arrived at the hotel I was met by a Droemer/Knaur representative who was not my editor and who professed to know nothing about the progress of the translation or any other publishing plans. He did not invite me to the offices of the company but to a coffee house. I remember nothing of that casual conversation other than his remark, which I took to be deliberate, that he was partly Jewish. Then I left immediately.

It was not until June 1965 that word came from my editor at Droemer/Knaur, Fritz Bolle. "If you have not heard from us in so long," he wrote, "it is because we have been preoccupied again and again with the difficulties of publishing a German translation of your work." It was not my documentation that was the issue but my thesis of Jewish—and here he used quotation marks—"collaboration." After long reflections and thorough discussions, the company had decided that a German edition could have "very dangerous consequences," because malevolent people could pose the question, "But why have the Jews collaborated? Why did they not resist?" and could draw anti-Semitic conclusions from such questions. "That there are malevolent people, you know," he said. "That they can be dangerous, we know." A newspaper like the neo-Nazi *Die Deutsche Nationalzeitung*, he said, could create much damage and poison the atmosphere.

I could not take Fritz Bolle's arguments very seriously. From newspaper reports I knew that hundreds of trials for National Socialist crimes were being prepared in Germany and that there was opposition to these proceedings. One prosecutor had written to me in 1962 and again in 1964 to inquire whether a German translation was in the offing. He said that he had been asked about this matter again and again by his colleagues. I could imagine that my book might be a tool in the hands of a prosecutor and that a publishing house responsible for its distribution in the German language could arouse the ire of all those who sympathized with the defendants. At the time I could think of no other pertinent reason why Droemer/Knaur, which had already paid an advance to Quadrangle Books, would take the serious step of breaking a contract.

To be sure, there were Germans who might have read my book nostalgically, admiring their incomparable Final Solution. They might conceivably have looked in the index for their names, nodding. Such readers could also have considered the Jews who surrendered themselves and their families to be despicable. What they would never have done, however, is to share their feelings with anyone publicly. The *Deutsche Nationalzeitung* did have a respectable circulation in Germany—it was sold openly in kiosks—but that paper was not likely to say that the Jews failed to resist the honorable German army, SS, or police; it would brand me, as it did on March 3, 1967, as the "standard Zionist author," and it would describe the destruction of the Jews as the "Lie of the Six Million."

The "malevolent people" did not suddenly appear in 1964 or 1965; there were at least as many of them in 1963, when Droemer/Knaur made the contract, as two years later. Yet something to which I paid little attention did happen in the interim: the appearance of the German version of Hannah Arendt's *Eichmann in Jerusalem*. On August 7, 1964, just before my visit to Munich and the publication of Arendt's book, Paul Arnsberg wrote a long article in the *Rheinischer Merkur* about the reactions to her work in the United States, calling the debate the "Affair Hannah Arendt." In her correspondence with Jaspers, she wrote on September 24, 1964, that her German publisher Piper—like Droemer/Knaur in Munich—had just told her that some booksellers were actually boycotting her *Eichmann in Jerusalem*. The store owners had informed Piper that they did not *want* to sell the book.

Here then, after all these years, I had found a kernel of truth in Bolle's letter. Jewish accommodation and cooperation, which Bolle called "collaboration," *had* become a problem, because taking Ms. Arendt's side or mine in the "controversy" was to risk offending a significant segment of the Jewish community worldwide.

My short-lived relationship with Droemer/Knaur did not upset me. Without a full understanding of the tortured thinking in the offices of German publishers, I saw only a concern for former perpetrators. Many a practitioner of the Nazi era was still at his desk in the Federal Republic of Germany, and every forty-year-old had lived through that time.

But the failure in Munich did underline my isolation. No institution of higher learning in the United States was really interested in research about the destruction of the Jews. I already knew by 1963 that I would be staying in Vermont for the rest of my career, and I solidified that situation when, newly married, I bought a house, the one in which I still live. My house became my refuge. From my rear windows I look out at nothing but trees, which are green in the summer and completely covered with the pristine white of snow in the winter. Here, gradually, almost imperceptibly, the decades rolled away.

In 1965 I closed my eyes to my subject, but then, a few years later, I resumed my search for documents. Again, I took advantage of an opportunity. This time no friendly stranger had deposited a collection in the university library. I had to look for new materials elsewhere. The possibility was created by the University of Vermont, which had abolished sabbatical leaves during the Great Depression of the 1930s but reinstituted the practice in the more prosperous 1960s. A waiting list of old-timers in the faculty preceded me, but my turn came in the spring of 1968. With paid leave for six months, I could travel to archives abroad to examine records that had never been brought to the United States. I began to think about the gaps in my book, particularly the role of the German railways and the relatively unknown death camps of Belzec, Sobibor, and Treblinka. The place to explore these topics was Germany, but I could not imagine living there with my small family even for a few months. I chose, instead, Jerusalem, in which the Yad Vashem archives were located. This was a mistake.

For an entire month I was not allowed entry into the archives. Clearly I was persona non grata. Literally knocking on one door after another in the administrative building, I was given all sorts of explanations and advice. The chairman of Yad Vashem was out of the country, said one of the staff members, and nothing could be done in his absence. I should have written for permission before coming, said another. Since I was already in Israel, said a third, I should go to the oral history archives in Tel Aviv, where access was unrestricted. In Tel Aviv I spent several weeks examining statements of survivors. Then I went back to Yad Vashem where I met the remarkable Bronia Klibanski.

During the war she had been at the side of Mordechaj Tenenbaum-Tamaroff, a young man who had tried to organize resistance in several ghettos and who was killed in the short battle of the Bialystok ghetto. She must have studied languages, for—as she told me—she could read all the materials in her archives except those in Hungarian. She had never written much, despite her insights into the dilemmas of the Jewish population under German rule in Poland, and she had a subordinate position at Yad Vashem, categorizing records and, I believe, using her linguistic skills and her noble, graceful gestures to conduct important visitors to various exhibits in the place.

When we first met, I introduced myself: "My name is Hilberg." "You—you are Hilberg!" She began to laugh. On her own, violating the rules that had been recited to me, she allowed me to sit in the archives, from which her superior, Josef Kermisz, did not eject me. Very few staff members exchanged any words with me, and it was some weeks before I discovered that after six years my book had been reviewed in the latest volume of *Yad Vashem Studies*. The review was thirty-six printed pages, and its title was "Historical Research or Slander?"

In later years I visited Yad Vashem again. I was even invited to be on one of its editorial boards and to deliver a paper on Jewish councils. In 1968, however, I was wrestling with problem after problem: my inability to find an apartment in crowded Jerusalem, the hours spent on buses commuting from Tel Aviv, and the limited hours when the archives were open. As I contemplated ruefully the meager yields of my research, I decided to give myself a short time in efficient German archives, which were not barricaded for my arrival and which held significant collections. The time in Germany was too short, and I was returning to Vermont with a diversity of materials which did not constitute a coherent whole.

I was in my forties, and for men in America this particular passage through life was known by the title of a popular novel as the "hurricane years." It was the age at which a man might face unexpected misfortunes or reverses. He might experience a sign of mortality, like a heart attack, or a failure in his career, like a lost appointment or promotion, or the collapse, as in my case, of a marriage. At such a time of disequilibrium and disorientation, the organism seeks reflexively a new stability on a secure plateau, salvaging its remaining resources and possibilities.

During my absence from Burlington in the spring of 1968, my colleague Jay Gould had unwittingly provided me with a psychological base. He had seen to it that I was elected to a small university committee that passed on all reappointments and promotions of faculty members. A year later I was also elected to the chairmanship of a faculty committee that was charged by the university's board of trustees with seeking a new president, it being understood by several key members of the board that the winning candidate should be a white native-born man of a Protestant denomination. Finally I was appointed to the chairmanship of my department. The university absorbed me almost completely. I studied it in all its characteristics: its administration, faculty, and students, the sources of its revenue, and the allocation of its funds. In this microcosm I was simultaneously a participant and observer, fascinated, buoyed. And then I stopped.

In the spring of 1976 I had another sabbatical leave. This time I went straight to archives in Germany and Austria. It was clear to me that I was returning to my documents, but I was not sure what I would do with them. In 1969 and 1970 I had spent late evening hours in my study, translating some of them for a small compilation which Quadrangle Books published. In the later 1970s I imagined an enormous expansion of this initial exercise, a multivolume undertaking. In my reveries I thought of myself as commander-in-chief of a project that would employ researchers and translators, all of them working on items under my supervision, producing a storehouse in the English language of materials gathered from archives all over Europe. The selection, organization, and explanation of these documents would be my contribution. The dream spurred me to look wide and far. When I testified in courts for the governments of the United States, Canada, and Australia, I was strongly motivated by the prospect of obtaining any new evidence these governments could obtain through official approaches to the Soviet Union, where archives were still closed to the public. When I joined the President's Commission on the Holocaust and its successor, the United

States Holocaust Memorial Council, I lobbied for the creation of an archive that would be filled with microfilms of pertinent records from European archives. Considering the heavy emphasis of the council and its museum on the oral statements of survivors, it is a veritable miracle that an archive was established for documents and that such collections were filmed in the Soviet Union, East Germany, and Romania. A document project of the kind I had in mind for the benefit of future researchers in the United States was, however, the sort of investment that—even if vanishingly small in comparison with the cost of a museum—would have been considered an unjustifiable luxury.

There was only one remaining possibility. The documents I was collecting enriched my knowledge. With them I could fashion a description that would be more accurate, complete, and incisive. In short, I was moving toward a second edition of *The Destruction of the European Jews*. From a practical point of view the proposition was nightmarish enough. Revisions of monographs are not welcome ventures for publishers. If the first version was a failure, why try a second? And if, as in my situation, the original edition could be sold in modest, predictable quantities continually, why spend the money for a new one? I had to work steadily while remaining poised for any opening, domestic or foreign. Eventually these opportunities did arise, and I produced, if translations are counted, second, third, and fourth editions. Each time I inserted new material painstakingly into a preexisting text. No other approach was feasible, inasmuch as I had to respond to developments when I encountered them.

Because I was not the master of my fate, I was tense, often on edge. Of necessity, my eyes were simultaneously fixed on my documents and publishers. The publishing world, in turn, seemed to be in turmoil, and starting with Quadrangle Books it presented me with surprises. By 1971 Quadrangle had become a house that stood for high quality. By dint of effort, the second president, Melvin Brisk, and his capable young editor, Ivan Dee, had built a list of some three hundred respected titles. That year the New York Times Company bought Quadrangle. A few years later Quadrangle (now Times Books) sold some eighty of its titles, which were deemed "textbooks," including my first book and the new document volume, to a publisher of children's literature, Franklin Watts. To me this transaction was so bewildering that I visited an editor of Times Books in New York and asked him why I had been sold without so much as a letter explaining the action. When I talked with this man I became aware that he had been associated with Irving Howe and I suspected that he had been one of the organizers of the symposium in the Diplomat Hotel. The editor did not really answer my questions, but I remember him saying that Times Books would publish "other good books."

For the first time I realized what the grant of a right to print really means. It could be passed on and the author's work might be nothing but a commodity in the hands of total strangers. Franklin Watts sold the two books for several years until they disappeared from *Books in Print*. I called Theron Raines, who had become my literary agent, and he advised me to engage a lawyer for the purpose of regaining the rights to my book. Soon I was free again, and

Raines sold the rights for a five-year period to Harpers, so that I could work purposefully on a second edition. My only remaining problem was the total lack of interest in such a project on the part of publishers everywhere. Theron Raines began to talk about the need for a sizable subvention, and I had a sense of déjà vu. After all these years, the subject was still in limbo.

I did not even think about a translation into German. In 1967 a friend of a friend had suggested my work to Rowohlt, a major publisher near Hamburg. The answer, by F. J. Raddatz, was that Rowohlt was already "burdened" with nonfiction and that my book would mean the abandonment of several literary works. In 1979 a much smaller company, the Verlag Darmstädter Blätter, inquired about the book but then decided it could not manage publication financially. A literary agent in Switzerland wrote to Raines on March 5, 1980, that C. H. Beck, an old established German publisher specializing in legal commentaries, had turned down the book as well. "You will not unload more than 600-800 copies," the agent wrote. "I doubt whether more than 20 people would read the edition. It is far too long."

In Germany, however, members of a new generation were coming to the fore. They were born during or after the war. One of them, from a family of railroad men, was a publisher of railroad books. His typical readership consisted of people who were interested in timetables of the Transsiberian railway during tsarist times. He found out about my study of railroads in the Nazi era and in a daring move offered to publish a documents book with my commentary about the trains that transported Jews to their deaths. That small book, which appeared in 1981, was the first German publication with my name on the cover.

Before the close of 1980 I received a letter from a small West Berlin publisher, Olle & Wolter. This firm wished to publish my large book. Ulf Wolter, who corresponded with me, was in a hurry, and in 1982 I went to Germany frantically researching material for last-minute inclusion in his edition. While there I became curious about this man. Why did he want to bring out this work, which apparently no one else in Germany would touch? Seeking an answer to this question, I boarded a plane to Berlin to meet him.

He was a young man whose family had managed to cross into West Berlin from East Germany just before the wall cut off escapes. Like several of his friends, he was a bachelor. His office was in an inconspicuous building reached through a courtyard. The space was cavernous but inexpensive. He prided himself on spending very little money for rent. That is why, he explained, his costs were considerably lower than those of his larger competitors. To prove his point he quartered me for the night in a pension where one had to switch on the hall light, which went out automatically before the guest had found the room. I had almost always chosen modest accommodations on my research trips, but this time I felt uncomfortable. Perhaps because the pension occupied an upper floor of an apartment house, perhaps because of the stairs of stone, the sounds, the cell-like nature of the room with its 1930s furniture, I imagined the brown-shirted SA downstairs and men in boots ascending the steps and banging on doors.

The next day I asked Wolter why he was publishing my book. His list had given me no clue. He had been interested in a translation of a work by one of my University of Vermont colleagues, the Sovietologist Robert V. Daniels, who wrote about the Trotsky deviation from communist orthodoxy, and I had spotted titles by radical or socialist German authors as well as books by feminists. By why mine? Wolter, who had mastered English, said he had read my book while still in college and had decided then to publish it in German translation as soon as he had established himself as a publisher. His books, he said, were centered on one theme: injustice. He could not have omitted mine.

I was impressed by Wolter, even though he had rushed me much too much, and I was impressed by the masterful translator to whom he had introduced me, Christian Seeger, another young bachelor. I asked Seeger why so many young men I encountered in publishing and journalism had not married, and he answered that he himself had several siblings and that there were enough Germans in the world.

At this point I was also on the threshold of another edition in the United States. Discouraged, I had not been looking for a publisher, but a very small house that I had never heard of asked me to evaluate a manuscript, and after I had done so, the owner, who turned out to be a survivor, asked me what I was doing. I am reasonably sure he did not expect the answer I gave him, but he was not fazed. I in turn was attracted by his choice of titles and the mode of his publication. He had never had a best-seller, he said almost with pride, but he chose good acid-free paper as well as fine designs for covers, and in keeping with such devotion he had never remaindered a book. What he did not tell me is that he would charge an unheard-of price for my three-volume set and that he regularly denied a standard trade discount to distributors. Thus he would be mailing these sets direct to libraries and private purchasers, deriving a relatively large profit from very small sales. He died, but the book languished, comatose, in his publishing house.

This new American edition, which I labeled the second but which was really the third and which he had restyled "revised and definitive," appeared in 1985. By then I had invested a great deal of work in it, splicing the additions seamlessly into the text so that a new reader might see no vestige of the old limits. In this endeavor I had succeeded only too well, for now most of the reviewers did not notice most of the augmentations either. For Lucy Dawidowicz the three volumes were sheer bulk in any case: a sign of my inadequacy as a writer. I was consoled, however, when, on the other end of the scale, Christopher Browning, the highly sophisticated researcher who had explored a wide range of subjects pertaining to the Jewish catastrophe, found every significant insertion and highlighted it in his review.

Not until 1988 and not fully until 1992 did I realize that I had become a European author. In 1988 a major French publishing house, Fayard, brought out the book. The contents were further expanded—my fourth edition. No doubt Fayard had become interested in the project after the showing of Claude Lanzmann's film *Shoah*. Unquestionably the success of the book was assured by the efforts of my young editor, Eric Vigne, who combined intelligence and sensitivity with driving energy. In addition, the subject was new in

France, and books still mattered there. "Do not forget," my American publisher said in self-defense when I compared his dismal sales performance with the success in France, "that there your book is a first edition, and do not assume," he added, "that the two markets are at all alike." Finally, however, I knew that in France the time had come, for Lanzmann's film, for Vigne's talents, and for my work.

In Germany, Ulf Wolter became ill, and his publishing company disappeared. Yet even this marginal entrepreneur had sold more copies than anyone would have thought possible when he asked for my book. In 1990 S. Fischer Verlag, a major publisher in Germany, produced a three-volume set—a second edition in Germany—in paperback. "We will lose money," my editor, Walter Pehle, predicted. But he found a donor, Dieter Dirk Hartmann, who enabled him to cover some of the costs and to lower the price of the published work. In the end the book became a commercial success.

Again and again I went to Germany to lecture and be interviewed. The Germans probed deeply, not only into the contents of the work but also its genesis. How had I begun? Why? In particular, they wanted an answer to a mystery that troubled them especially. They seldom phrased the problem succinctly or posed the question outright, but once, in Berlin, a young person asked simply, "Why did we do it?"

The Diary of
Adam Czerniakow

D O YOU KNOW WHAT WE HAVE?" The rhetorical question was put to me by Josef Kermisz, the archivist of Yad Vashem, at the end of my stay in Jerusalem in the spring of 1968. He was a short, slightly built man, and his tone suggested that despite his small physical stature and his subordinate status in the organization, he was in a position to grant or deny access to documents in his custody, thus holding the direction and success of outsiders' research projects in his hands. "What do you have?" I asked, playing his game. "The diary of Adam Czerniakow," he answered.

His words had the desired effect. I remembered immediately that in the 1950s Alfred Sloane edited the diary of Emmanuel Ringelblum, the Warsaw ghetto historian who had been seized and killed after going into hiding. Sloane had to use a sanitized version that had been published in Warsaw, because he was not given permission to view the original Ringelblum diary in Warsaw or its copy in Jerusalem. The Sloane edition was consequently published without crucial passages in which Ringelblum had mentioned the Sobibor death camp and had asked why the Jews went like sheep to the slaughter. Josef Kermisz was the jailer of the Jerusalem copy. Yet Kermisz did have a problem. He was in the position of all those who have a secret but who cannot impress anyone with their power unless they divulge it and thereby relinquish their monopoly and indispensability. In the case of the Ringelblum diary, Kermisz solved his dilemma by inserting the missing fragments on special yellow pages in a volume of *Yad Vashem Studies*, thus calling the attention of specialists to his treasure while still not allowing a revised edition of the stunted English translation ten years after it had appeared. What would now be done with the diary of Adam Czerniakow? To my mind, that diary was likely to be of even greater importance than the writing of the ghetto historian, because Czerniakow had been chairman of the Jewish Council of the Warsaw ghetto.

"If you have a diary by Czerniakow," I said slowly, deliberately, "then you should publish it in the United States." Oh no, not so fast, Kermisz answered. The diary was an extremely complicated text, he said, and required commentary by experts before it could be published. And in what language, I asked, would the diary appear? In Hebrew, of course, Kermisz answered.

I was already familiar with the argument that I was to hear for another twenty-five years—"We Israelis have the expertise; you Americans have the money"—but for the moment I could do nothing. I was leaving Jerusalem, not really sure I would ever return. Yet I could not forget this conversation after my departure. I had never seen such a document. Whatever its contents, it was bound to answer many questions. What was it like to be a ghetto leader? What sort of individual was Czerniakow? The diary was his private record, the scarcest kind of account altogether.

Several years passed before I learned that the diary had been published in an obscure Polish journal—the same publication of the Jewish Historical Institute in Warsaw that had printed the censored diary of Ringelblum. Since the original Czerniakow diary was in Polish, one had only to make sure that the transcription was complete and correct before using it for any purpose. Then I discovered there were two Hebrew editions, and that one of them contained the facsimiles of Czerniakow's handwritten pages next to the Hebrew translation. With a magnifying glass, one could discern the Polish words.

Although I could not undertake a translation into English myself—Polish was yet another important language I had not studied—I had a colleague, Stanislaw Staron, who came from Poland. It was he who had brought me a copy of the Polish journal after one of his visits to Warsaw. I looked at the format of the diary. Virtually every entry began with a notation about the weather. Clearly this piece of literature would not be a best-seller. It was a Pepys kind of diary, Staron announced. I was undeterred. This document had to be translated, studied, and explained, and Stanislaw Staron was the ideal man to accomplish these tasks.

Stan, as he liked to be called, was a highly sophisticated man. His field was political theory, and for his dissertation topic he had written on the Neo-Thomist thought of Jacques Maritain. When I read his dissertation I was taken by its lucidity. For the first time I became fascinated with a manuscript about theories that I would under no circumstances have examined myself. Staron was absorbed by their structure, symmetry, and balance, though he admitted to me that his analysis of Maritain had taken too long. "I should have chosen a simpler topic," he said to me. "Like what?" I asked. "Like 'Freedom,' for instance," he answered.

Staron, however, was also a man of the world, with an understanding of the world. He liked to ski, a sport I never appreciated at all. He lived in Scotland, where he had begun to admire British culture, but he remained the quintessential Pole and a hopeless romantic who never married. Once he met Bronia Klibanski, with whom he was completely enchanted. "Raul," he said, "it is a pity you cannot hear for yourself what beautiful Polish she speaks." Stan was in uniform from the first day of the Second World War to the last. He did not wish to be praised, and so, in describing him, one must recite only the simplest facts of his wartime life, which began with the German invasion of Poland and his capture. He escaped—"It was easy," since many Poles had accomplished this feat—and was brought by a Polish underground organization via Hungary, Yugoslavia, and Italy to France, where he joined a Polish division. After the German offensive in the west had broken through the Maginot Line, and British forces had retreated to Dunkirk, the officers and men of his division were told: Every man for himself! Staron and several thousand other Poles streamed to the French port La Rochelle (from which I had left Europe a year earlier in peace). On a blacked-out unarmed troopship they sailed for England, and Stan Staron spent the next few weeks as an artillery officer with something like Napoleonic cannon on the Scottish coast awaiting the Germans. Three years and eighteen practice parachute jumps later, Staron was on the Continent again. When the war ended he was fighting in the Netherlands. Like many Poles in his position, he could not go home, and after pursuing his academic studies in Scotland and the United States, he eventually came to Vermont. Here he devoted himself mainly to investigating Communist Poland's political institutions, particularly the relations of church and state. Always he was hemmed in by his own self-limiting rules. One must not write about this or about that. One must not be a traitor to Poland. One must not and must not.

I broached the question of the Czerniakow diary to him. It was an ideal venture, I argued, knowing that he would never write more than his well-crafted articles about the Polish political system. Yet he would not touch the text without my participation. Very well, we would work together. I already knew of microfilms containing records of the German city and ghetto administrations in Warsaw, which would be invaluable for our introduction, the notes, and an appendix. These films, made by the Jewish Historical Institute in Warsaw, had been delivered to Yad Vashem in exchange for a typewritten copy of the diary. It was that copy from which the Warsaw institute had printed the Polish text.

I also knew of an editor who would be interested in our project. In 1970 Benton Arnovitz, who worked at Macmillan, had written a blind letter to me, asking whether I would be interested in undertaking a study of half-Jews under the Nazi regime. The subject, I replied, was very important, but

I could not exploit it beyond the stage I had already reached in my book. Then, with an unfailing scent of what had to be written, he suggested Jewish councils. I replied that to my knowledge, Isaiah Trunk had prepared a manuscript on that subject in Yiddish, and that it was languishing in his drawer. Arnovitz published this pathbreaking study in English translation. It was not a popular work, but it received an American Book Award. Arnovitz later explained that the publication of such a heavy book had been possible because Macmillan "owed him one." "How so?" I inquired. Arnovitz pointed out that Macmillan was the publisher of the memoirs of Albert Speer, the man who had been in charge of Germany's armaments production during the Second World War. Trunk's work served to redress the political balance. Obviously, however, Trunk was no match for Speer in the book market, and Arnovitz was still interested in any manageable manuscript I could deliver. At this point I mentioned the Czerniakow diary, even though the diary assuredly would not be a fount of major profits.

Benton Arnovitz was a man of strong convictions. He had served in the United States Army as a reserve officer, eventually with the rank of lieutenant colonel, and he was not loathe to use the word "honor." He was also one of the best editors I ever had. His knowledge of books, my subject, and the market, was matched by his concern for authors and their expectations. He had a strong aversion for the city of New York, which is the capital of the American publishing industry, and when he moved, just to be away from the metropolis, we moved our contract with him, to Chilton of Philadelphia, a house known for automobile repair manuals, and then to Stein and Day of Briarcliff Manor, which filed for bankruptcy while the diary was still in print.

When I had suggested the diary to Benton Arnovitz, I considered it to be in the public domain. That was not the view of Yad Vashem, which asserted a copyright to the document. At one point a publisher engaged by Yad Vashem demanded that Arnovitz suspend publication "as promptly as possible." Then the two publishing houses agreed to cooperate, but with provisos, dictated by Yad Vashem, one of which, as summarized by Arnovitz, stated: "Hilberg's footnotes must be factual, identified as his, and under no circumstances can be evaluative." When Yad Vashem's publisher decided not to be involved in the project anymore, Arnovitz invited Yad Vashem to join us. Thus the cover of our edition of the Czerniakow diary featured Kermisz as one of the editors, and his separate introduction was included as well. All this required the good offices of Herman Wouk, the novelist, and Yehuda Bauer of the Hebrew University, as well as the dedication of Benton Arnovitz.

Our cooperation with Yad Vashem was remarkably smooth. I especially appreciated the work of Yad Vashem's specialists in identifying numerous Jewish personalities, many of them obscure, whom Czerniakow had mentioned in his entries. All the notes were merged and distilled to their essence. There was resistance in Yad Vashem in only one small matter. Benton Arnovitz wanted illustrations, and the archives of Yad Vashem did not wish to furnish any photograph showing Jews in factories working for the Germans. It was not a totally insignificant omission, considering Czerniakow's daily efforts to increase production in the ghetto.

By the mid-1970s the chairman of Yad Vashem was Yitzhak Arad, a former partisan in Belorussia and a retired general of the Israeli army, who also held a doctorate and who had written several valuable books, one of which, about Vilna, I used as a text in my course. Arad struck me as intelligent, plain-speaking, and purpose-oriented. Unfortunately I could not always deal with him personally. When an opportunity arose later to publish the diary in Germany, the vice-chairman, Reuven Dafni, was incensed that I had responded to the inquiry without deferring to Yad Vashem. In a "how-dare-you" kind of letter, he reiterated the assertion that "Yad Vashem had full copy rights" to the diary. I had never met Dafni, and not realizing that I was addressing a ranking diplomat deserving of all the courtesies due such a person, lectured him about copyright and taunted him with the question whether Yad Vashem's acquisition of the manuscript was the sort of transaction that could sustain a claim to ownership. I withdrew from the German edition, which was eventually published by Beck without my name and without explanatory apparatus save for a minimal introduction by Yisrael Gutman and a handful of notes. But I wished to impress upon Dafni that, whereas Yad Vashem had possession of Czerniakow's original notebooks, one of which was still missing, it had yet to show that the property had been acquired from someone whose ownership of the book was indisputable.

The "chain of custody," as lawyers refer to a document passed from hand to hand, troubled me from the beginning, and I repeatedly demanded that, so far as known, the successive possessors of the diary be identified in print. Josef

Kermisz had been evasive about this matter in conversation, but in his introduction he disclosed that in 1964 the Israeli embassy in Canada had purchased the diary from a woman, Rosalia Pietkewicz, and that she in turn had bought it from an unknown source in 1959. Stanislaw Staron, who traveled to Canada frequently, had already talked with someone who remembered reading about the transaction in the newspapers. But who was Rosalia Pietkewicz? From whom did she obtain Czerniakow's notebooks? I looked for her address in telephone books—we even wrote to a priest with the same last name—but then we learned that once she had been Rosa Braun, that she was a Jewish woman who had hidden outside the ghetto, and that she had left Poland with the diary in the 1950s. Stan Staron even managed to interview her in Canada. "Well?" I asked after his return. "Did you find out how she got hold of the notebooks?" Staron, the gentleman, had been an able artillery officer, but he was no interrogator of women, and when Rosa Braun did not offer an explanation spontaneously, he did not press her for an answer. In Jerusalem, where I pursued my inquiry without letup, I was told that she had offered the notebooks to the embassy for $100,000, claiming risks and expenses she had incurred, and that after lengthy negotiations the embassy had offered $10,000, which she had accepted.

Although I wanted to learn all the details of the diary's fate, if only because they were a part of Czerniakow's biography and the ghetto's history, I was never in doubt that the notebooks were genuine. I needed no tests of paper or ink, and no samples of Czerniakow's prewar handwriting, because a reading of even half a page convinced me that no one could possibly have made up such a manuscript with its wealth of references to specific occurrences and people.

Staron invested his entire background and personality in the work of translation. He approached it like a consummate musician examining a score for the first time. He played this text with all his training and restraint. His translation was artless, unadorned, translucent. When I read it, page after page filled me with suspense. The diary became a place, a strange locality that I was entering for the first time. I was a voyeur, a ghost inside Czerniakow's office, unobserved, and the longer I inhabited that enclosure, the more I saw.

My first and foremost impression was that Czerniakow knew, even while Warsaw was still under German siege in September 1939, that he was living through a time when every moment was significant. This consciousness penetrates each of his entries. He recorded events perseveringly, scarcely ever omitting a day, no matter how crowded his schedule or how wearisome his experiences may have been, and his entries were always factual, as if he had split himself into two men: the leader of the largest Jewish community on the European continent in his official functions, and the detached observer in his writings. He was almost sixty when he became chairman of the Jewish Council, viewing the scene with the eyes of a mature man, and because he stood at the interface between the German overlords and the Jewish population his vantage point was unique. The ghetto wall marked a sharp separation between perpetrator and victim, but Czerniakow was like a bridge. With him I crossed the boundary, as he went out to hold his difficult official conversations with Germans and as he returned dejected to the Jewish world. I dwelled with him to grasp his struggle with problems of housing, food, starvation, disease, taxes, and police, and to observe him while he had to listen to the incessant wailing of Jewish women beseeching him for help outside his office door. On the day when the diary was published in the United States, I believed that we were opening this vista to a larger public. At that crucial moment Lucy Dawidowicz wrote her negative review in the *New York Times*, belittling the diary and for good measure dripping acid on me, Professor Staron, and the University of Vermont.

One surprise in the diary was going to interest very few readers. Czerniakow, representing a community of 400,000 people, had met only once with the governor of the Warsaw District, Ludwig Fischer. Similarly, he had recorded only one conversation with the Gestapo chief of the district, Walter Stamm. By contrast he would talk repeatedly to some SS sergeant, and several times he would meet with a German functionary so low in rank that only diligent research in microfilms enabled us to establish the fact that this individual was also one of the official overseers. What had Czerniakow been reduced to? For the welfare of his people he depended on appeals, explanations of needs, and arguments. And to whom could he direct his entreaties? Sometimes he did not even know who would listen to him when he made his rounds to talk to clerks and functionaries who were half his age. One scrutinizer of the diary, who also noticed the subordinate status of the individuals in the German control apparatus, was Albert Speer. The former Reich minister of war production, however, looked at the phenomenon from the opposite vantage point. What struck him was the sheer delegation of power over the largest ghetto in Europe to such petty underlings.

How did Czerniakow retain his composure? He ate his ghetto soup and looked at a reproduction of a Watteau on his wall. He also made jokes. Once, he referred to himself as the king of Croatia. Another time, visiting a Jewish asylum for mental patients, he was accosted by an inmate who asked him whether he was Czerniakow. No, came the reply, he was not. In the matter of a typhus epidemic, he likened the effectiveness of Jewish physicians to that of rabbis. I recall giving a talk to several hundred functionaries of Jewish organizations in San Francisco, and I thought that these men and women might like to hear about an organization man from another time and another place: Czerniakow. In my summary I recited some samples of Czerniakow's humor. The audience sat stunned and silent.

I spent about six years with Czerniakow. The more I delved into the diary, the more I discovered there. What was it that drew me to this man? He had a sense of honor, of not being allowed to desert his post. He soberly noted his foreboding about the Jewish fate. Without an intelligence organization of any kind, relying only on chance remarks by Germans, veiled newspaper accounts, and ever-present rumors, he anticipated the bitter end. When the deportations began, he wanted to save the Jewish orphans, and when he could not secure even their safety, he killed himself.

I was immersed in Czerniakow's life when Claude Lanzmann filmed me in Vermont. I told him about my work, and Lanzmann had me speak about the man and read from the diary. At the end, Lanzmann said to me, "You were Czerniakow."

The Triptych

IN THE SUMMER OF 1961 I spent a month in Europe, traveling from country to country, from city to city, and from museum to museum. In the museums I found silence. The sculptures were silent. The paintings were silent. I studied the portraits in particular: here a youth, there an old man, a cardinal, a pope, but also peasants and soldiers. All were mute and all were dead, but at the moment they were close to me. Why did I dwell in these museums? At the time I did not know, but now I realize that I was reaching for a new conception, that then and there I had found a model for a book I would write twenty-five years later, *Perpetrators Victims Bystanders*.

All my life I had been preoccupied with organizations. I constructed organization charts and charted the flow of decisions. Now I looked for the people: individuals and groups. The images were in my mind, and I wanted to paint them, in words of course, but in such a way that they would remain portraits, to be absorbed in an instant just like a canvas that is seen at a glance.

When the perceptive German historian Eberhard Jäckel reviewed the book in its German translation, he juxtaposed it with my first book. In this comparison he saw something highly unusual: I had written about the same subject, but I had produced a completely different work. In my earlier effort, he said, I had been influenced by my mentor Franz Neumann. If Neumann's *Behemoth* was the classic description of the German Nazi system, then *The Destruction of the European Jews* was the *Behemoth* of Jewry's annihilation. Now I had evolved from Neumann in that I dealt with individuals. Jäckel's observation was true. I *had* stepped out of Neumann's confines, but my departure was also an abandonment of political science. Although I still used what I knew about political systems, I had chosen a medium that was different from the traditional writing of political scientists. My focus was no longer the closed realm of the political decision-making apparatus. I was now posing a question that was at once smaller and larger than my previous quest—smaller, because people as such are not a bureaucratic colossus, and larger, because I wanted to encompass everyone who stood on stage during the Jewish catastrophe. I did not intend to omit any man or woman solely for his or her political insignificance. Adolf Hitler rated a chapter by himself, and other important players might receive at least a paragraph or sentence, but in the overall scheme I strove for parity, and now and then the smallest individual was given equal space.

Furthermore, the perpetrator was no longer the primary factor. Perpetrators, victims, and bystanders were arranged in three groups, and to each I gave much thought in my research and analysis. I kept these groups apart, drawing vertical lines between them, just as they had been separated from one another, physically and situationally, in their life-time. Yet they were linked, despite their distinct experiences, by the event in which they were all involved, and which they witnessed simultaneously. In this panorama the reader could select one chapter or another, in any order. For one reviewer, Jonathan Rosen in *New York Newsday*, this interchangeability, and my uniform style, created a "disturbing sense of sameness."

I was not the first to deal with ordinary people. Christopher Browning wrote a book about a German police battalion, *Ordinary Men*, which appeared in 1992. John Dickinson talked to 172 persons to recreate the fate of one obscure Jewish victim in Germany. This biography, *German and Jew*, was published by Quadrangle Books in 1967. In the film *Shoah*, Claude Lanzmann dealt with all three personae, and virtually all the individuals who appeared on the screen were small people, none more distinguished than professors and a few who were illiterate. Lanzmann even found most of his interviewees in small places, and these people and localities are shown in a nine-and-a-half-hour mosaic.

When I began to assemble my own cast of characters, I thought the undertaking would be relatively easy. After all, I had been gathering materials for three and a half decades. But it did not take long before I was back in the archives to search with an altogether different perspective for more court records, personnel files, and correspondence, in order that I might provide telling illustrations of different *kinds* of perpetrators, victims, and bystanders. It was not until I had finished the work, in fact not until after its publication, that I fully realized something else.

Most often novelists, journalists, and even historians look for an unusual or bizarre occurrence in a mundane setting, but I was doing the opposite. For me, the destruction of the Jews already was the setting, the irremovable reality, and within this extraordinary outburst I looked for all that was ordinary. I had done so from the beginning, when I dealt with everyday bureaucratic procedures, and now I was pursuing the same object as I examined the lives of people. In their daily routines, these individuals, like agencies, sought stability, particularly their own private equilibrium. It did not matter whether they were perpetrators, victims, or bystanders; they all manifested a need for continuity and balance.

Often enough I had been struck by images of such behavior. Christopher Browning relates in one of his essays that Herbert Andorfer, the Austrian who commanded the Semlin camp near Belgrade, played cards with Jewish women to while away the time, before he received orders to shove these acquaintances into a gas van. In a book of photographs of the Warsaw ghetto, there is a picture of the ghetto elite, in suits and dresses marked with a star, drinking alcoholic beverages. The female bartender leans over the counter to join a conversation of patrons; half-empty liquor bottles can be seen in the background. Yet another compilation of bourgeois scenes is a pictorial work edited by Gilles Perrault and the prominent French historian Pierre Azema, on Paris under the German occupation. There one can see a display of fashion designs by Jacques Fath, Nina Ricci, and Schiaparelli; a young crowd at a swimming pool; and a 1943 photograph of Jean-Paul Sartre sitting in the Café de Flore with a glass of wine, smoking a pipe. Such examples are legion.

The craving for the familiar, the habitual, the normal, emerged as a leitmotif wherever I looked. Psychologically this clinging was aimed at self-preservation, and its manifestations run like a thread through the upheaval. At a basic level they provide an explanation of how these groups managed to go on—the perpetrators with their ever more drastic activities, the victims with their progressive deprivations, the bystanders with the increasing ambiguity and ambivalence of their positions. When Sigmund Freud delivered a lecture about war during the first major conflagration of the twentieth century, he said that mankind needed a passing check from the burdens of civilization. What I began to note was the reverse side of the phenomenon: the adhesion to time-honored products of this civilization in the midst of unprecedented destruction.

In my untutored walks through museums I have been an eclectic. I was riveted to the violence of trench warfare as depicted by Otto Dix, and I was electrified by the luminosity of the fantasies painted by Paul Delvaux. Most of the time, however, I would gaze at masterpieces, known and unknown, of the Renaissance. Once, in the Louvre, I saw a sign: "This way to the Mona Lisa." A coil of people stood in front of that most famous of all paintings, and I, to avoid the crowd, decided not to join it. Glancing to my left, I spotted a quiet portrait that everyone bypassed. Astonished and transfixed, I wondered: Who was the lady in this picture? Who was its painter? Her name was thought to be Lucrezia Crivelli, and she was painted by Leonardo da Vinci.

To be sure, I am not Leonardo, but in the English-speaking world my book *Perpetrators Victims Bystanders* has been bypassed by several cognoscenti who had hailed *The Destruction of the European Jews*. Some American and British critics used words like "short," "petty components," and "a sketch map" in describing my latest work. Since that is all they could see, they rushed on, disappointed, searching for new creations elsewhere.

VII
Vienna

O N OCTOBER 24 AND 25, 1992, a little more than a month after the publication of *Perpetrators Victims Bystanders* and its review in the *New York Times*, I attended a conference in the Chicago area. All those who came, about eighty people, were teaching Holocaust courses in colleges and universities. The purpose of the meeting was to explore how such courses might be taught. I was one of the specialists invited to address the whole gathering.

I had looked forward to this event, hoping to see a display of books and to spend a few hours in a congenial atmosphere with a group of like-minded people. There was no book display, and one of the speakers, Yisrael Gutman of Yad Vashem, who had as yet not read my new book, attacked me with reference to *The Destruction of the European Jews*. After I had spoken about problems of teaching the subject, he asked for the floor again to attack me for what I had said in my talk. The presiding officer was in dread that I would wish to reply to Gutman, but I had no such desire. Despondent, drained, and exhausted, I wanted to banish the last six weeks together with this unforeseen denouement.

On the afternoon of the 25th I boarded a plane again. In

my seat I ceased to think. As the aircraft took off, the
ground fell away and so did the oppressive feeling that had
weighed me down. The flight was my escape. In the morning I would be in Frankfurt, my initial destination, where
the German translation of my new work had already appeared. It was to be the first departure of ten to Germany,
or Austria, The Netherlands, Belgium, France, and Italy in
the next three years.

During my brief European stays I spoke and gave interviews dozens of times. Almost all the interviewers were
knowledgeable. They were interested in the origins of my
formulations, and they plied me with questions which were
not only personal but also philosophical. Most of the reviews in the newspapers were written by erudite historians
and journalists. Moreover, some of these discussions were
longer and more detailed than their American counterparts.
The historian Hans Mommsen devoted what must have
been many hours to his analysis, which he wrote with exac-
titude and deep understanding. When I compared the initial German and Dutch reviews with those I had received in
the United States, I was struck by a clear dichotomy. To verify my impression I sent the German comments to Eric
Marder and asked him whether anyone would believe that
the Germans were reviewing the same book. He agreed: the
difference was startling, whether one looked at the quantity
of the German discussions or their quality. After this appraisal I shipped copies of the German commentary to my
American editor at HarperCollins, Aaron Asher, for conso-
lation, and to Eric Vigne at Gallimard, where the French
translation was still in progress, for encouragement. Vigne

sent me a postcard suggesting wryly that Germany needed the book.

I should have known that a work offered primarily to one readership may instead be embraced by another. There is a place as well as a time for books. Still, this development made me reflective. Once, in 1961, a host on a New York radio station asked me whether I boycotted Germany. Yes, I replied. For how long, the interviewer asked me, would I maintain my boycott? Until 1985, I replied unhesitatingly. "Now you sit with us, eat with us, talk with us," said my German editor, Walter Pehle, one late evening when I sat with him, his daughter, and his assistant, at an outdoor table of a Berlin restaurant. "Yes," I replied, thinking that I had found new associations and a new acceptance in a country I had boycotted for so long.

Walter Pehle grew up after the war. He earned his doctorate in history and by 1992 had brought out a veritable library of books about the Nazi period. He liked to travel, and on two or three occasions he accompanied me on lecture trips he had arranged for the promotion of my three-volume paperback and the new title, both of which his company, S. Fischer Verlag, had published. When I mentioned that the Austrians had not been very interested in my work and that I had not set foot in Vienna since 1976, when I pursued my railroad research in one of the court archives there, he made sure that I had a few interviews and a small speaking engagement in that city. He liked Vienna and met me there.

What was I searching for in Vienna? On previous stopovers, and particularly during my stay in 1976, I had retraced the steps of my childhood, taking the walks that I remembered from the 1930s. On all these occasions nothing had impressed me so much as the fact that visually Vienna was unchanged. I saw the same houses and the same stores. Only distances seemed smaller. When I had walked with my father through the major park of the XX. District, the Augarten, it had seemed immense. In 1976 I traversed it in fifteen minutes. The Vienna of my youth had shrunk into a smaller replica of what it had been. Why did I return one more time? What could I find there in 1992? Did I seek encounters? Did I want to hear voices? Did I hope to discover a mirror in which I could see myself as I had been? As I was now?

In the early morning of November 27 I flew to Vienna from Cologne. An interviewer met me at the airport. He told me that a thirty-five-year-old colleague, to whom he had mentioned the planned interview, had exclaimed, "What, again?" "It is the first time," my interviewer had answered him.

Walter Pehle confided in me that Austria was not the very best market for Fischer books about the Third Reich. I was not surprised to hear his statistics. The postwar Austrians had isolated and insulated themselves from history. The shortest *Who's Who* I had ever seen was a 1948 Austrian edition filled with skiers and opera singers. Since then Austria had played the neutrality sonata masterfully, cajoling and beckoning to the foreign tourist. Here I was, a visitor myself, savoring the incomparable Wiener Schnitzel, Strudel, and Topfenkuchen. I could not help admiring the Austrian pronunciation of the German language, which—with its cadence and clarity—can in and of itself be made into a demonstration of perfection. No wonder that Walter Pehle, open-eyed though he was, could be entranced.

"Let me show you my Vienna," I said to him, after he had joined me in the city. "Let me show you the Danube Canal, my old street, and the house I lived in with its stone steps, bereft of hot running water. Let me show you the hidden Vienna."

We walked along the canal to the XX. District. Pehle, who had a camera with him, photographed the Viennese mountains from a bridge. The scene was no longer that of my childhood. A massive tower designed by Hundertwasser intruded upon the view. On the Wallensteinstrasse, which is very short, we reached the old apartment house in a minute. "Here," I said, pointing to the cold-water spigot on the floor, but there were signs of indoor construction. We asked a tenant who walked down the stairs whether she had hot running water. She had. "Come," I said, as we approached the door of my old apartment. This time, fortified by his presence, I rang the bell. I really wanted to see the apartment, to test my memory of its size and layout, to look out the windows. Possibly some of our old furniture was still there. But no one answered. The name, Anna Gruber, was still on the door. Evidently her husband, who had given us the ultimatum on November 10, 1938, to leave the apartment, was dead. Conceivably he had not survived the war. She herself might in the meantime have become ill, and as we stood there she might have been in some hospital. She had certainly not taken an afternoon walk. A notice from one of the utilities was stuck in the door. "We came too late," I said to Walter Pehle. She had lived there for fifty-four years.

In the center of the city I had several more interviews in a coffee house. One of the interviewers, Evelyn Adunka, was exceptionally perceptive and insightful. She asked me about Neumann, Baron, and my father, and she quoted a paragraph from a private letter she had discovered in an archive. The letter was written on March 6, 1962, by H. G. Adler, the survivor of Theresienstadt, who was the author of the massive book about the ghetto. I had never met or corresponded with Adler, who had lived in England until his death in 1988. Reading that thirty-year-old letter, which like all of his books was written in German, I felt as though Adler had peered directly into the core of my being. This is what he said about me:

> To be noted is Hilberg's "The Destruction of European Jewry." Surely you have heard of this work. It is until now the most significant accomplishment in this topic area and it is not likely to be surpassed very soon, even though it is by far not yet the final portrayal. No one until now has seen and formulated the total horrible process so clearly. The number of small errors and omissions do not matter seriously, and so far as I can see, they can be extinguished in a new edition. What moves me in this book is the hopelessness of the author, who was born in 1926, and who came to the United States before the war, surely from Germany to which he returned at the end of the war with the US Army. In 1948 Hilberg began his work. Therefore he already has the

viewpoint of a generation, which does not feel itself affected directly, but which looked at these events from afar, bewildered, bitter and embittered, accusing and critical, not only vis-à-vis the Germans (how else?), but also the Jews and all the nations which looked on. At the end nothing remains but despair and doubt about everything, because for Hilberg there is only recognition, perhaps also a grasp, but certainly no understanding. . . .

Index

Index

BLACK and BLUE

BLACK and BLUE

THE REDD FOXX story

michael seth starr

APPLAUSE
THEATRE & CINEMA BOOKS

AN IMPRINT OF HAL LEONARD CORPORATION

Published in 2011 by Applause Theatre & Cinema Books
An Imprint of Hal Leonard Corporation
7777 West Bluemound Road
Milwaukee, WI 53213

Trade Book Division Editorial Offices
33 Plymouth St., Montclair, NJ 07042

Every reasonable effort has been made to contact copyright holders and secure permissions. Omissions can be remedied in future editions.

Printed in the United States of America

Book design by Michael Kellner

Library of Congress Cataloging-in-Publication Data
Starr, Michael, 1961-
  Black and blue : the Redd Foxx story / Michael Seth Starr.
    p. cm.
  Includes bibliographical references and index.
  ISBN 978-1-55783-754-7
1. Foxx, Redd, 1922-1991. 2. Comedians–United States–Biography. 3. Actors–United States–Biography. I. Title.
  PN2287.F634S73 2011
  792.702'8092-dc22
                              2011015999
www.applausebooks.com

contents

preface

Writing a biography is always a tricky proposition, even more so when the subject is a pop-culture icon like Redd Foxx. An author's challenge lies in trying to separate the real person from his or her ubiquitous alter-ego, in this case the bow-legged, chest-clutching *Sanford and Son* junkman Fred Sanford ("I'm comin' to join ya honey!").

Fred Sanford exists in that timeless television netherworld inhabited by the ghosts of Lucy Ricardo, Ralph Kramden, Maxwell Smart, Archie Bunker, Cosmo Kramer, and all the other indelible, frozen-in-time characters we've welcomed into our homes and hearts over the years. Television is an intimate medium. We *know* these people, or at least we like to think we do. Thanks to endless reruns, DVD boxed sets, and the Internet, we have access to these characters at the touch of a button or the tap of a keystroke—24/7 immediacy in this digital age. So we know what Fred Sanford will say, when he'll say it, when he'll fake (yet) another heart attack or spar with Aunt Esther or lambaste that "big dummy" son of his. It never gets old.

That's the easy part. The challenge for this (hopefully) unobtrusive narrator of Redd Foxx's life story is in giving you, the reader, a sense of the *man* behind Fred Sanford. Redd Foxx, after all, didn't just materialize on television from whole cloth. He was an "overnight sensation" at the age of forty-nine, a street-smart, natural-born comic who, through sheer talent, guile, and brimming self-confidence, overcame a life of poverty in the slums of Saint Louis to impact three entertainment genres: stand-up comedy, recorded nightclub comedy, and television.

Jon Sanford was born in 1922, and by the age of twenty-five, having changed his name to Redd Foxx, was already a veteran nightclub comic seasoned on the streets of Saint Louis, Chicago, and Harlem. There he lived a hardscrabble existence with his (literal) partner-in-crime, Malcolm Little, who was later to morph into the Nation of Islam leader Malcolm X. After years of toiling on the segregated blacks-only string of nightclubs dubbed the "Chitlin' Circuit"—part of that time with his comedy partner, Slappy White—Redd Foxx recorded *Laff of the Party*, the album that would become an underground classic, in a dingy Los Angeles nightclub for the princely sum of twenty-five dollars.

Released in 1956, *Laff of the Party* was the first of Redd's famous (or infamous, depending on who you asked) "party records." It was racy for its time, but not profane—Redd Foxx *never* swore onstage, at least not in those early days. The devil was in the details. *Laff of the Party* was, though, replete with Redd's double entendre, almost folksy storytelling, which he overlaid with sexually suggestive wordplay. The album set the table for the fifty-plus Redd Foxx party records released in subsequent years that would revolutionize (some say invent) the genre. Redd's party records sold anywhere from twenty to fifty million copies—under the counter, of course, and usually wrapped in the brown paper bag that was expected to somehow mute Redd Foxx's blue material just waiting to be slapped onto turntables across the country (and, yes, even *discreetly* in white suburbia).

But while he was selling millions of party records, Redd Foxx was still shielded from wider exposure to a mainstream (white) audience, both by the color of his skin and by his refusal to compromise and tone his act down a bit, a decision that kept him off television and scared away potential bookers. (Redd claimed to have auditioned for *The Steve Allen Show* and *The Ed Sullivan Show* in the late '50s with "clean" material, which got him absolutely nowhere.) He eventually climbed his way up the show-business ladder, breaking through in Las Vegas and New York, opening a fondly remembered (but poorly run) comedy club in Los Angeles and taking baby steps on the big screen with *Cotton Comes to Harlem*, leading to that first *Sanford and Son* episode that hit the airwaves in January 1972—and changed his life, and ours, forever.

The following pages will hopefully serve to guide you through the sixty-eight years of Redd Foxx's remarkable life, from birth to death—and all the good, the bad, and the ugly in-between. Say what you want about The Man, but he was *never* boring.

You won't find any psychoanalysis of Redd Foxx in *Black and Blue*, nor is this book written in his "voice"—two approaches I find both pretentious and presumptuous. I didn't know Redd Foxx, and I never had the chance to interview him. And even if I had had the opportunity for just one conversation with him, how could I ever *really* know what was in his heart and in his mind?

That's where Redd's close friends and associates enter the picture to help splice together the narrative of his life, one frame at a time. Unfortunately, many of Redd's oldest friends—Steve Trimble, LaWanda Page, Slappy White, Bardu Ali—are gone now. But each, in his or her own way, left behind their memories of Redd for posterity.

In writing this book, though, I was fortunate enough to interview many people who knew Redd Foxx in different phases of his life and career. Some knew him more intimately than others. But no matter how deep their connection was to this remarkable entertainer, I was struck, almost to a man and woman, by the depth of their emotions in their reminiscences and, in some cases, in their recalling long-forgotten memories and incidents they hadn't thought of since his death. Most of these people were highly emotional—there was a lot of laughter, a few tears and, for some, a note of awe in emphasizing Redd's powerful presence, even twenty years after his passing.

Dee Crawford and Anthony Major, both of whom ran Redd's production company in different decades—Dee in the 1970s and Anthony from the mid-1980s until Redd's death—spent hours reminiscing about "The Chief," as he was called by those in his inner circle. They both had a bird's-eye view into the Redd Foxx Traveling Circus that defined his life. And, as they quickly learned, running "The Chief's" company—Redd Foxx Productions and its many subsidiaries—meant more than paying the bills and negotiating contracts. It was an all-consuming, seven-days-a-week job in which they lived Redd's life with him, both professionally and personally, while dealing with the hangers-on and wannabes who seemed to come out of the woodwork looking for a handout. It could be completely chaotic, and it usually was. With Redd Foxx, there was no in-between.

In addition to Dee Crawford and Anthony Major, I would like to thank the following people who agreed to share their memories of Redd with me for this book: Mariann Alda, Dennis Burkley, Della Reese, Hugh Downs, Greg Antonacci, Paul Whitford, Stuart Sheslow, Raymond Allen, Mark Risman, Louis Pittman, Stan Lathan,

PREFACE

Norman Lear, George Schlatter, Bud Yorkin, Herb Schlosser, Saul Turteltaub, Fred Silverman, Beverly Harris, John Barbour, Al Marquis, Bob Einstein, Sammy Shore, Jamie Masada, Bernie Ornstein, Fred Houpe, Kathy Chase, Rick Kellard, Marguerite Ray, Gerald Wilson, George Wallace, Samuel Goldwyn Jr., Jimmy Scott, Ilunga Adell, Hal Williams, Kathleen Fearn Banks, Pamela Adlon, Guy Deiro, Lynn Hamilton, Jimmy Mulidore, Bob Greenberg, Bobby Schiffman, Tony Orlando, Howard Platt, Gregory Sierra, and Karime Harris.

Black and Blue: The Redd Foxx Story would never have become a reality without Michael Messina, who guided my previous book, *Hiding in Plain Sight: The Secret Life of Raymond Burr*, and who believed in the Redd Foxx project from the get-go, as did John Cerullo, Carol Flannery, Bernadette Malavarca, and the staff at Applause Books. I would also like to thank Norm Clarke, the terrific entertainment columnist at the *Las Vegas Review-Journal*, for helping to get the ball rolling, Trish Geran in Las Vegas, for making some early introductions, Kristine Krueger at the Margaret Herrick Library of the Academy of Motion Picture Arts & Sciences, the staff of the Chicago Public Library, Rose Mitchell, the Black Resource Center Librarian at the AC Bilbrew Library, a branch of the Los Angeles Public Library, Bryan Cornell at the Library of Congress, Albert Fisher, for giving me permission to access his recording of the Jump Swinging Six on *The Major Bowes Original Amateur Hour*, and for providing a terrific, mid-1960s photo of Redd on *The Merv Griffin Show*, Brad LaRosa at ABC, for getting me a copy of Barbara Walters' 1977 ABC interview with Redd and Joi Foxx, John Edward Hasse, Curator of American Music at the Smithsonian Institution, who had access to Frank Schiffman's detailed note cards on Foxx and White's appearances at the Apollo Theater, and Dolores Williams at St. Benedict the Moor, who provided vital information (registration dates, etc.) on Jon and Fred Sanford's time at the school. Chris Hund was a late, but valuable, addition in helping me track down photos; and also a big thank you to Patricia Bergamaschi for her top-flight transcription talents. I apologize ahead of time to anyone I may have overlooked. Please know that your contribution(s) to this book were vital.

Redd Foxx wasn't big news to the mainstream press until he became a star on *Sanford and Son*. Consequently, the country's larger newspapers and magazines wrote little about Redd in the years leading up to

1972. This wasn't the case in the African American community, where Redd was always a superstar, especially after he hit it big with *Laff of the Party* in 1956. He was covered extensively in the African American press, and I am indebted to many of those publications in helping me piece together Redd's pre-*Sanford and Son* career—particularly *Jet*, *Ebony*, *Black Stars*, the *Chicago Defender*, the *Baltimore Afro-American*, the *Washington African-American*, the *Los Angeles Sentinel*, and the *Amsterdam News*. Their archives provided valuable biographical and anecdotal information about Redd's life beginning in the mid-to-late 1940s. And Jake Austen, in *Roctober* magazine, did a Herculean job of mapping the trajectory of Redd's output of comedy albums through the years—no easy task, given all the knockoffs, compilations, and hit-or-miss release dates.

While this book is the first comprehensive biography of Redd Foxx, there have been several other books written about him—both during his lifetime and in the years after his death—that helped me in my research. I owe a huge debt of archival gratitude to the late Joe X Price, whose book, *Redd Foxx, B.S.*, published in 1979, is jam-packed with colorful anecdotes from Redd's cronies and from "The Chief" himself. It also includes valuable information on Redd's Place, his short-lived, yet influential, comedy club on La Cienega Boulevard in Los Angeles, which was a training ground for many up-and-comers, most notably Richard Pryor. The late Dempsey J. Travis, one of Redd's DuSable High School classmates, who later became a successful Chicago businessman, cobbled together *The Life and Times of Redd Foxx*, which included some interesting information on "Smiley" Sanford's days running with the 58th Street Gang in Chicago.

Other books I found very useful in researching Redd's life and career include, in no particular order, Richard Pryor's memoir, *Pryor Convictions*, Darryl Littleton's *Black Comedians on Black Comedy*, the memoirs of Johnny Otis, *Upside Your Head! Rhythm and Blues on Central Avenue*, Jack Schiffman's *Harlem Heyday* and *Uptown: The Story of Harlem's Apollo Theatre*, Mel Watkins' *On the Real Side: A History of African American Comedy*, Alan Rafkin's *Cue the Bunny on the Rainbow*, Teddy Reig's *Reminiscing in Tempo: The Life and Times of a Jazz Hustler*, *Ain't Nothing Like the Real Thing: How the Apollo Theater Shaped American Entertainment*, Christine Acham's *Revolution Televised: Prime Time and the Struggle for Black Power*, and Barbara J. Kukla's *Swing City: Newark Nightlife, 1925–50*, which helped fill in the blanks of Redd's life in Newark, New Jersey, in the 1940s.

I've saved my biggest thank you of all for my wife, Gail, and my daughter, Rachel. Their constant support and encouragement has never wavered. I love you both very much.

introduction

"I'll Be Back"

Dawn broke hot and hazy that fall Friday in 1991. It wasn't the typical October day in Southern California, where the blazing summer sun usually concedes to cooler fall temperatures. This was a different kind of day. The weather had turned harsh during the past week as the city of Los Angeles, along with the rest of the state, baked in the grip of an unprecedented heat wave. Temperatures the previous day had reached 107 degrees in downtown Los Angeles—a new record. And it wasn't much better today.

Inside the cavernous, air-conditioned Stage 31 on the Paramount lot in Hollywood, the cast and crew of the new CBS sitcom *The Royal Family* were preparing to rehearse a scene for that week's show, which would be taped the following night before a live audience. The mood on the set was business-like but friendly, with a touch of jocularity. Everyone was feeling good, and why not? *The Royal Family* had premiered three weeks before to mostly positive reviews and solid ratings, pleasing the suits at CBS—a vibe that trickled down to the cast and crew. The show had legs.

While assistant directors scurried around, sound men positioned their boom mikes, and episode director Shelley Jensen barked last-minute blocking instructions to the cast and crew, series star Redd Foxx was backstage, being interviewed for an episode of *Lifestyles of the Rich and Famous*. The irony wasn't lost on anyone, since Redd, while certainly still famous, was no longer rich, and hadn't been for some time. His profligate spending, failed business ventures, willingness to open his wallet to anyone who asked for a handout—and the long arm of the Internal Revenue Service—had seen to that. But *Lifestyles* host and executive producer Robin Leach—chronicler of the jet-setting crowd with his plummy "Champagne wishes and caviar dreams!" mantra—knew that *The Royal Family* marked an important baby step in Redd Foxx's comeback from the abyss of financial and professional ruin. It made for a good story.

Redd knew how much *The Royal Family* meant to him now. He didn't need any more reminders of how far his star had fallen, or how he was going to repay the millions he still owed to the IRS. It was somewhere in the neighborhood of $3 million, but who the hell really knew? Maybe it was more, maybe it was less. It didn't really matter anymore. The bastards had taken pretty much everything he owned—even ripped the gold watch Elvis Presley had given him right off his wrist—and now they were garnishing his *Royal Family* salary. Was there no end to the humiliation? Redd tried to laugh it off—passing a hat around at his live stage shows in Las Vegas, asking for help to pay his bills—but it hurt him deeply. Deep down he knew he had only himself to blame.

So he knew it was important to at least *pretend* to be interested in answering the questions posed to him by the *Lifestyles of the Rich and Famous* interviewer. Robin Leach's show was extremely popular in syndication, and the fact that they even wanted to interview Redd Foxx offered a glimmer of hope that better times were ahead. The show's staff spent that October morning trailing Redd around *The Royal Family* set as he made his rounds, its cameras capturing his potbelly, poking out of his blue paisley shirt. He looked cool in his large, tinted eyeglasses. There he was, joking with his cast mates and *The Royal Family* crew, and sharing a private conversation with young co-star Larenz Tate as he playfully flipped the baseball cap on Tate's head. Later, sitting in an upholstered chair, Redd rehearsed a scene on the show's set with his co-star and old friend, Della Reese. Della was nine years younger than Redd, yet understood what made her old friend tick, what stoked that combination of anger and pride that, after the last few years of financial ruin and public humiliation, had mellowed into a resigned humility that seeped from Redd's pores. Or so it seemed.

Backstage, as the *Lifestyles of the Rich and Famous* camera rolled for Redd's interview, he didn't look particularly happy. His weary expression was a stark contrast to the jaunty blue cap he wore as he sat before the harsh lights. The single camera captured his mien—drawn and tired, almost beaten-down. He appeared much older than his sixty-eight years. His croaking voice, so familiar to the millions of people who fell in love with Fred Sanford, sounded even more gravelly than usual, the ever-present cigarette on which he now dragged lending it an extra-low, scratchy timbre. And he was audibly short-of-breath, *harrumphing* in short spurts as he glumly answered the questions put to him by his *Lifestyles* television interviewer.

And then, with the *Lifestyles of the Rich and Famous* cameras rolling, as Redd was answering a question about his new cast mates, an unseen *Royal Family* production assistant suddenly interrupted him mid-sentence. He was told he was needed on the set to rehearse a scene in which his sitcom character, Al Royal, would pass through nonchalantly in the background, unnoticed by his wife, who was played by Della Reese. It was a job that could have been handled by anyone with a pulse. Did they really need Redd now, in the middle of an important interview? Couldn't it wait?

Remembering the incident almost twenty years later, Della Reese was still angry about that interruption. "It was not required at all," she said. "Redd was very polite. He felt embarrassed that this man, in the first place, spoke to him in front of these strangers [from *Lifestyles of the Rich and Famous*]."

But Redd also knew there was nothing he could do about it. Maybe back in his *Sanford and Son* heyday, but not now. There was too much water under the bridge. He knew he was on a short leash, knew that *The Royal Family* producers and the network watchdogs on the set held the upper hand now. They were all-too-aware of Redd's reputation for making trouble behind the scenes. He needed them now more than they needed him. It was a simple Hollywood equation. Do what we tell you, or take a hike. We'll find someone else. It doesn't matter that you're Redd Foxx, who once played Fred Sanford. It doesn't matter that you're Redd Foxx, who was once the highest-paid star on television. It doesn't matter that you're Redd Foxx who, once upon a time, single-handedly brought a network to its knees. That was twenty years ago. A lifetime in this business. This is now. What have you done for us lately?

"They were forever on Redd about something or other, in some respect," said Reese. "They wanted to be in charge of Redd, which nobody ever was going to be."

So Redd did what he was told, like an errant child being scolded by a parent or a teacher. Visibly embarrassed and *harrumphing* again in short staccato bursts, he shot daggers at the person who had interrupted his interview with *Lifestyles of the Rich and Famous*, as the show's camera continued to roll, capturing the awkward scene. "Boy, that ticks me off," Redd mumbled, removing his glasses and wiping them absent-mindedly. The man who had created one of the most indelible characters in television history, who turned Fred Sanford's "You big dummy!" and histrionic "heart attacks" into national comedic treasures, was reduced to a chastened, embarrassed network employee, mumbling an apology to his interviewer. "I'm sorry about the interruption. I'll be back," he said, getting up from his chair to head back to the set.

Within minutes he would collapse into unconsciousness.

Within hours, he was dead.

chapter one

_____

"Every Word He Said Was Funny"

Jon Elroy Sanford came kicking and screaming into the world on December 9, 1922. He was the second son of Fred Glenn Sanford and his wife, Mary Alma Hughes Sanford, who knew the instant the baby arrived just what she would call her new child. "That name just fell on my heart," she said, and, once her son was famous, she always made sure that everyone knew his name was "Jon," without the "h," although no one ever spelled it that way.

Fred and Mary Sanford were married five years before, in June 1917. A very proper photograph of the couple taken at the time shows Fred, with his soft features and receding, wavy hair, gazing lovingly at his new wife. He's dressed in a sharp suit and tie and is holding an expensive-looking hat. His bride is dressed more demurely, and is wearing a long black coat and gloves, clutching a purse to her waist with just the slightest hint of a smile on her broad face.

But the elegant air Fred and Mary exuded in that photograph belied their true situation. Their new baby, Jon, was born in his maternal grandmother's house, and spent many of his early days there with his big brother, Fred G. Sanford Jr. while Fred and Mary, always short on money, did what they could to scrape by. The family's Saint Louis neighborhood was, for all intents and purposes, a slum on the wrong side of the tracks. Fred, an electrician by trade, was good with his hands and worked odd jobs on the side. The money he did earn was barely enough to keep the family from a life of abject poverty. Some of the extra cash Fred earned came from his other sidelight as a hustler in the local pool halls, which occasionally put him in the company of celebrities passing through Saint Louis, including heavyweight boxing champ

1

Jack Johnson, whose gift of his boxing gloves to Fred would remain in the Sanford family for years to come.

"My folks worked regularly, and we had the equivalent of what other people had in the neighborhood," Jon Elroy would say later. "It would be wrong to say we were poverty stricken. I'd describe our condition as semi-destitute."

Jon Elroy's older brother, Fred G. Sanford Jr., was born four years before on October 8, 1918. He was bigger and burlier than Jon, with a much darker complexion and more pronounced features. Fred Jr. took after the Sanford side of the family, which included Fred Sr.'s great-grandfather who, according to family lore, was an African native who wore a size seventeen shoe. The physical distinctions between Fred Jr. and his younger brother Jon were stark; Jon, like his mother, had a copper complexion, with features that were finer and more delicate than his brother's. He had a boyish, innocent-looking face, with smiling eyes that were framed by a head of thick, curly, reddish hair. Jon was definitely more of a Hughes than a Sanford, at least in his appearance (Mary's grandmother was a full-blooded American Indian). "There's some white in the family, too," he would say. "You can tell by my complexion and thin lips that *somebody* got integrated somewhere along the line."

Despite their four-year difference in age, the Sanford brothers were extremely close. The family had experienced its share of tragedy and grieving—two girls born after Fred and before Jon had died in infancy. That made the bond between the brothers an extremely strong one as they covered each other's backs in their tough Saint Louis neighborhood, where fights were settled just as commonly with bricks as with fists. Jon wasn't particularly close to his father, but he idolized his big brother. Fred Jr. was also the more athletic of the two Sanford boys. He showed off a natural talent on the baseball field, or more correctly, the rough-hewn fields or scraggly, garbage-strewn lots in and around the neighborhood where the brothers played pick-up games. "He was one of the best first basemen ever," Jon recalled. Fred had the talent; all he needed was an outlet to blossom.

The tough times didn't get any easier when, in 1926, Fred Sr. walked out on his wife and two young sons, never to return. Four-year-old Jon would see his father only one more time in his life. "I remember an ice cream cone, two for a nickel. He bought my brother and I one," he said. "That's all I remember about him. That's true." The two boys didn't even realize the man buying them their ice cream was their father, until a neighbor told them who he was.

Mary, who worked as a domestic, was at her wit's end; with two young mouths to feed—and the family's main breadwinner, such as he'd been, no longer in the picture—she was desperate and running out of options. Chicago, a much bigger city than Saint Louis and only two hundred-and-sixty miles away, offered the hopes of a better-paying job, even for a domestic like Mary without any formal training in anything else. If Mary could make enough money there, she would be in a better position to support her two sons. So, several months after Fred Sr. abandoned the family, she decided to make the trip to Chicago alone, leaving Fred Jr. and Jon in the care of Mary's mother, who lived in a rickety, ramshackle wooden house on the other side of the city, several miles from the Sanford residence. Jon, even at his young age, knew it wasn't right for a mother to be leaving her two boys for a new life in a city that seemed so far away. The seeds of resentment and abandonment were planted, deep in his soul. For the rest of his life, Jon would tolerate Mary Sanford. But he would never really forgive her.

Life with Grandma Hughes wasn't any more secure than it had been with Mary around. Grandma Hughes, a widow who was in her seventies by now, wasn't keen on raising her two young, rambunctious grandsons by herself. She also didn't approve of Jon's habit of lying in bed, his head next to the radio, so he could listen to Fred Allen and "Myrt and Marge," while dreaming of entertaining people that same way some day. She was visibly relieved when, shortly after Fred and Jon's arrival, Mary hatched a plan to send her boys off to a school in Milwaukee, three hundred and thirty miles and two states removed from Grandma Hughes' wooden shack. The school, St. Benedict the Moor Mission, was an all-black Catholic school founded in 1908 by Captain Lincoln Charles Valle and his wife, Julia. They had been inspired by the success of the Black Catholic Lay Congress of 1889, a movement of more than one hundred black Catholic leaders whose mission was to improve religious education for black schoolchildren. St. Benedict had a total enrollment of about three hundred students, half of whom, like Fred and Jon, were boarders who paid twenty dollars a month to live on the big campus. According to the school's Registration Journal, Jon, six-and-a-half at the time, was enrolled first, on August 24, 1929. Fred followed five months later on January 2,

1930. Harold Washington, the future mayor of Chicago, was one of Jon's classmates.

"It was across the street from a brewery, and I can remember so well the smell of the beer from the brewery, and the smell of lilacs in a yard nearby," Jon said of St. Benedict. But the patient guidance of the Capuchin Franciscans, who ran the school, fell on deaf ears for the Sanford brothers, who, even in the best of times, didn't tolerate discipline very well. Jon, who had a sunny disposition and was a prankster, got along well with his classmates but acted out in class. His behavior was, for a time, indulged. School officials were sensitive to the fact that he was far away from home at so young an age, that he missed his mother and hadn't seen or heard from his father in two years. At night, Jon would often lie in his bed, imagining that the shadows of the tree branches outside his window were really animals. He literally scared the piss out of himself, wetting his bed several times over the imaginary beasts. But as he got a little older there were no soothing reassurances from his Franciscan guardians, only spankings over his uncontrollable "accidents."

Jon relied heavily on his older brother to allay his homesickness and to help get him through the days (and nights) of loneliness. Fred, like his kid brother, was something of a clown. His behavior as the class cutup made him very popular among his classmates at St. Benedict the Moor. Fred's behavior also ignited in young Jon the first spark of what it meant to be the center of attention—and he saw the warmth and acceptance that enveloped Fred when he made other people laugh. "I remember one time [Fred] came into the cafeteria and he was pulling an electric iron; he'd found an electric iron with the cord and that was his dog. He upset the whole dinner," Jon remembered. "He'd say, 'Come on, Buster,' that was his dog's name. Everybody cracked up, and when I saw him do that and get all that audience participation from the kids in the Catholic home, I wanted to be a part of that thing." In time, that would become a reality but, for now, Jon would have to tough it out at St. Benedict, battling his homesickness at night and, during the day, causing trouble for his teachers by acting out in class. He ended up lasting less than two years at the school, leaving St. Benedict in July 1931 when he was eight and taking a bus back to Grandma Hughes' house in Saint Louis. Fred managed to grind it out at St. Benedict a while longer, but eventually followed his little brother home nearly a year later.

Back in Saint Louis, Grandma Hughes enrolled Jon, now eight-and-a-half years old, in Banneker Elementary School, an all-black school located in the predominant black neighborhood known as "The Heights." The neighborhood was dotted with churches—the George Washington Carver Settlement House was nearby—and had an insular, homey feel. Originally called Colored School #5, the newly renamed Banneker Elementary School had just moved from its original location at Montgomery and Leffingwell streets to the Stoddard School Building at Lucas and Ewing, situated near Grandma Hughes' house.

But the change in schools, and the fact that he was living at home again—albeit with his aging grandmother—didn't change Jon's behavior in the classroom. Although he was quite verbal, he was an indifferent student, and remained something of a discipline problem. He was given to talking back to his teachers and causing trouble wherever and whenever he could. In his mind, he just didn't see the point of learning meaningless facts that were of absolutely no use to him on the mean streets of Saint Louis. "School meant nothing to me," he said. "Knowing that George Washington crossed the Delaware—how was that going to help me in a brick fight in Saint Louis?"

One of Jon's classmates at Banneker was LaWanda Page, who was two years older and would, many years later, play a much more important role in his life. "Sometimes if the teacher would get on him about something, he would try to jive," she recalled. "I remember he said, 'Miss Blue,' that was the teacher's name, 'Miss Blue, I love you.'" Outside of the schoolyard, Jon could be found hanging around with his buddies on Saint Louis street corners, where no one told him what to do and the only rule was to try to survive through one's wits and street smarts. He managed to get by, hustling to make a buck here and there. "After school I'd dig around the market for old cabbage leaves and half-rotten fruit and vegetables," he remembered. "During the day I sold newspapers and switched to doughnuts at night." Jon's tenure at Banneker Elementary was even shorter than his stay at St. Benedict. In 1932, he was expelled from the fifth grade for throwing a book at a teacher. Jon remembered the incident differently. In his version of the story, he was only protecting himself—throwing the book *back* at the teacher who'd thrown it at *him*. He didn't take any shit from anybody, especially authority figures.

Grandma Hughes was at her wit's end. Her ten-year-old grandson was running out of options in Saint Louis and was without a school to attend. Fred, who was now fourteen years old, rarely ever went to school and spent most of his time on the streets, up to no good. Desperate, Grandma Hughes shipped Jon away from Saint Louis once again. But this time it was a journey that would reunite him with his mother, who was still living in Chicago. It marked the first time in nearly four years that mother and son were living under the same roof. Since arriving in Chicago, Mary had found a steady job working as a domestic for the vice president of the Chicago White Sox, and Jon moved into her cramped, one-room apartment on the second floor of a row of flats at 5730 South Indiana Avenue, located on the city's South Side. The house was owed by an absentee landlord who lived in Chicago's wealthy Highland Park section.

Mary enrolled Jon in Carter Elementary School, where he settled in and finally managed to behave himself. But Mary's job didn't pay much and times were tough. Mother and son lived a hardscrabble existence trying to make ends meet while sharing a toilet with the five other families who lived on the same floor. They were together again, but didn't spend much time with each other. Mary worked long hours and Jon, when he wasn't in school, hung out on the street corner with his pals, making a quick buck here and there by running errands for people in the neighborhood. Their close proximity in that tiny apartment on South Indiana Avenue also failed to rekindle any latent emotional bond between Mary and Jon. He still nursed a grudge against his mother for leaving him and his brother with their grandmother. The situation was exacerbated by Jon's failure, or unwillingness, to understand that his mother couldn't provide for him in the manner he envisioned for himself when compared to that of his classmates at Carter Elementary. "I was so raggedy I was too ashamed to go and pick up my diploma when I got out," he said. "They mailed it to me."

Jon graduated from Carter Elementary to DuSable High School, which had just opened its doors on South Wabash Avenue in Chicago's Bronzeville neighborhood, nicknamed "The Black Metropolis" for its heavy influx of African Americans who had migrated from the Deep South to look for work in the big city. DuSable High, built to replace Wendell Phillips High School, which burned down in 1935, was named for Jean Baptiste Pointe du Sable, known in some quarters as "The Father of Chicago." DuSable, a Haitian fur trader, was the first non-native, and the first person of African descent, to settle in the Windy City—which meant absolutely nothing to a teenage Jon Sanford, who was only interested in chasing girls and hanging out with his new DuSable buddies.

And, with Jon's new school, came a new nickname.

"We called him 'Smiley,' because he always smiled, of course, and he was funny," said Steve Trimble, one of Jon's friends from Carter Elementary who moved with him to DuSable. "Every word he said was funny." Jon was also initiated into the 58th Street Gang, a notorious group of young thugs who got their name from hanging out in and around the Dixie Drugstore on Fifty-eighth Street and Prairie. The store was open all night, giving the gang a base from which they could strong-arm teenage newspaper carriers for their collection money and run roughshod over the neighborhood.

When they weren't bullying everyone else, the 58th Street Gang would amuse themselves by playing "the dozens," a game of verbal one-upsmanship that was rooted in African American culture and was particularly popular in urban areas, where groups would congregate on the street corner to play the game. Here's how it worked: two guys would stand face to face, insulting each other—usually picking on the other guy's mother and his family—with jibes that more often-than-not described cartoonish physical descriptions (think of Fred and Aunt Esther insulting each other on *Sanford and Son*). The two guys would ratchet-up their insults as well as the speed in which they were delivered, until one guy ran out of comebacks and gave up, admitting defeat. Jon soon developed a reputation as one of the best "dozens" players around. It was a street-smart skill he would later put to good use to shout down hecklers in nightclubs.

"He could talk about you, your mother, and other members of your family in derogatory language that would make you want to fight, run, or simply just cry," recalled schoolmate Dempsey Travis, who was a year ahead of Jon at DuSable. "He had a split personality like Dr. Jekyll and Mr. Hyde. Because during the day at school he was a very jolly person, whereas after school in the company of the 58th Street Gang he turned into a reincarnated devil."

But Jon also had an impish side that he mixed into his street repertoire. He would frequently walk home from DuSable with classmate Bennie Green, later to become a renowned trombone player who played with jazz legend Earl "Fatha" Hines, among others. On their way home from school, Jon and Bennie would often stop at a German bakery in the neighborhood and, while "Smiley" Sanford made the proprietor laugh, Bennie would be stealing cookies and cakes, hastily shoving them into his pants leg before making a quick escape.

But it was DuSable's music program, under the direction of Captain Walter Dyett, which would have a far more important influence on the newly christened "Smiley" Sanford. Dyett's music program had gained some renown throughout the Chicago area—even nationwide—for its originality, creativity, and spark.

Dyett, born in 1901 in St. Joseph, Missouri, spent his childhood moving around the country with his father, a reverend in the African Methodist Episcopal Church, and his mother, a musician. He studied the violin at Pasadena High School in Pasadena, California, graduating in 1917, and continued to play the violin after enrolling in the pre-med program at the University of California at Berkeley. He moved to Illinois in 1921 in order to continue his medical studies on a scholarship at Illinois School of Medicine. But Dyett soon found himself performing with local orchestras to help pay his family's medical bills, and he eventually left medical school to pursue his musical career full time, playing in vaudeville orchestras and even conducting an Army band (hence the "Captain"). Captain Dyett joined the faculty of Wendell Phillips High School in 1931 and quickly established himself as both a popular music teacher and the man responsible for the school's annual stage show, "Hi-Jinks," which showcased the musical talents of students including future stars Bo Diddley, Nat King Cole, Dinah Washington, and Jon's classmate, jazz pianist Dorothy Donegan. When DuSable opened in 1935, Dyett moved there as a teacher and took the Hi-Jinks show with him.

Jon always had a love for music and enjoyed singing, spending many nights crooning along with the radio to his personal favorites the Ink Spots and the Mills Brothers. But he'd never had the chance to express himself to a wider audience outside of singing to his friends for a laugh.

That all changed when he arrived at DuSable, where an atmosphere of possibilities prevailed and the music program, under Captain Dyett's guidance, played such an important role in student life. Jon and his new pals Steve Trimble, Lamont Ousley, and Pete Carter decided to start a band, but didn't have enough money to buy the expensive instruments needed for a more sophisticated setup. Instead, they formed a rudimentary washtub band they called the Four Bon Bons, with Pete playing acoustic guitar, Steve on washtub bass, and Jon and Lamont singing, dancing, and generally clowning around. The Four Bon Bons played on street corners wherever and whenever they could, earning a few nickels and dimes with their repertoire, which included songs by Jon's favorite groups, the Mills Brothers ("Dinah"), the Ink Spots ("If I Didn't Care"), and Austin Powell's "I Need You So." Steve and Smiley would sometimes switch roles, Smiley playing the washtub bass while Steve sang with Lamont. What they lacked in professional musical experience they more than compensated for in enthusiasm. "We played on the street corners and passed the hat," Steve Trimble recalled. "We played all over Fifty-eighth, Fifty-fifth, Fourty-seventh Streets and did very well. We even had a route on the north side blocking traffic—so much so that the police threatened to put us in jail." At the end of every gig, Jon would pass the hat around again, hoping for more donations. If the take was deemed successful, the Four Bon Bons would perform an encore, usually "Tiger Rag."

But the energy that "Smiley" Jon Sanford invested in the Four Bon Bons and, to a lesser extent, in the 58th Street Gang, didn't translate over to academia, and he showed the same lackadaisical attitude at DuSable that he'd exhibited in his previous stops at St. Benedict the Moor, Banneker Elementary, and Carter Elementary. He lasted exactly two semesters at DuSable and dropped out in 1938, just after he turned sixteen. As a high school dropout without a job, living a life on the streets of Chicago, his prospects were dim. Trying to make a living with his wits while staying out of trouble was about the best Jon ·could hope for. Even after he dropped out of DuSable he continued to work Chicago's street corners with the Four Bon Bons, who would become the Three Bon Bons when Pete, Lamont, and Steve performed in Captain Dyett's year-end Hi-Jinks show at DuSable. Jon now considered himself a professional musician, even though the Four Bon Bons had never been contracted to play at a "legitimate" gig. "I was working professionally, because I was making money," he said. "That separates amateur from professional. I was making money when I was thirteen [in] Saint Louis and Chicago both. I had my own band, a washtub band made out of scrap metal. [We played] on street corners. Made plenty of money, too."

Although Jon was no longer enrolled at DuSable, Captain Dyett made a special exemption and signed off on allowing him to join his Bon Bon band mates on stage in the school's auditorium for the Hi-Jinks show, which also included seventeen-year-old Dorothy Donegan on piano and Gene Ammons on sax. (Ammons found later success as a member of the Billy Eckstine and Woody Herman bands.) The Hi-Jinks show was a success; a picture of the Four Bon Bons taken on the DuSable stage in May of 1939, shows Jon, on the right, wearing a hat and a penciled-on moustache and kneeling by his washtub bass. On the far left, Lamont Ousley, also wearing a hat and what appears to be a wig, is caught in mid-flapper pose, kicking his leg in the air. To his left, Steve Trimble kneels by his own washtub bass while, taking center stage, Pete Carter smiles and strums his guitar.

The positive reaction they elicited from the enthusiastic DuSable audience convinced the Four Bon Bons they had the talent to take their act another step further. For some time, the guys had been talking amongst themselves about hopping a freight train to New York City, where they were sure that fame and fortune awaited them. Now they decided to finally pull the trigger. After a few more weeks of talking and planning, they left Chicago on the night of July 5, 1939, with Jon's brother Fred driving them to the train station on Sixty-sixth Street and South Park. Pete Carter, the fourth Bon Bon, decided to stay behind. Jon left the apartment without even bothering to say goodbye to his mother. There was no love lost between the two, at least as far as Jon was concerned. "I don't think I have ever gotten to know her," he said of Mary Sanford. "She is two or three different people from time to time. A great actress. I was never at home much, anyway."

The plan now was for Jon, Steve, and Lamont to surreptitiously slip into a freight car that was leaving the station under the cover of darkness and, hopefully, make it to New York without being discovered by the railroad cops who combed the cars looking for hobos and stowaways. Redd Foxx would later tell the story, time and again, of how he, Lamont Ousley and Steve Trimble slid down into an onion car and "cried all the way there." Whether that's true or not remains a matter of historical trivia; what is true is that the guys, who had less than a dollar between them, made it first to Buffalo—where they stole some loaves of bread and a few cans of pork and beans—then hopped on another freight car, in the stifling July heat, to continue their journey south from Buffalo to New York City. After another day or so, they finally made it—not to New York, but to Weehawken, New Jersey, located just across the river from Manhattan. That's when their luck ran out, so close to the bright lights of the big city.

"A group of detectives chased us, and the other guys got caught and sent to the penitentiary," Redd recalled. "I didn't know that at the time." Steve Trimble said that he and Lamont Ousley were caught by the railroad cops, who accused the teens of breaking into a nearby nursing home. They threw the bedraggled pair into the county jail for thirty days. "They framed us," he said. Jon, meanwhile, managed to elude the detectives "because I could run pretty fast." He scurried down to the water's edge and jumped onto a small tugboat that was heading across the river to Manhattan. He had only one destination in mind. "As we got closer to Manhattan I saw it turn black and realized we were heading directly for Harlem," he said. "We docked at 125th Street."

chapter two

"The Funniest Dishwasher on This Earth"

Harlem during that summer of 1939 was a vibrant, bustling place. It was the epicenter of African American life in New York City, largely free of the urban blight that would later envelop the area in the post-war years. The area's boundaries were fuzzy—and changed frequently—but were generally considered to stretch from the Harlem River on Manhattan's East Side to the Hudson River on the West Side, and to encompass a forty-five-block radius from 110th to 155th Street. When Jon Sanford arrived in Harlem, the area was at the tail end of the so-called "Harlem Renaissance," a roughly twenty-year period of fruitful artistic and cultural endeavors and achievements that began in the 1920s and gave birth to an entertainment scene unrivaled in any of the city's other boroughs.

Harlem's inner neighborhoods had evolved through several ethnic identities. The heavy influx of Eastern European Jews at the end of the nineteenth century and the early twentieth century had given way, in the years following World War I, to the influx of Southern blacks, who arrived in New York City in search of work and a better paycheck. Harlem offered a more affordable place to live, and, by 1930, the area was 70 percent African American. Interspersed among its rows of jammed-in walkup apartment buildings and elegant brick townhouses were small churches, smoky jazz clubs, and family-run food and clothing stores.

Yet despite its overwhelmingly African American population, Harlem still wasn't immune to racism, which reared its ugly head in several entertainment venues. The Cotton Club, made famous by black bandleader Duke Ellington, was a whites-only establishment, as was Connie's Inn, where legendary black performers including Louis Armstrong, comedienne Moms Mabley, and tap dancer Peg Leg Bates were frequent headliners. But the locals had a few of their own swingin' venues, and the Savoy Ballroom, located between 140th and 141st Streets on Lenox Avenue, and the Renaissance Ballroom and Casino on 138th Street, were filled to capacity nearly every night. Even those clubs paled in comparison to Harlem's crown jewel, the Apollo Theater, which was located on West 125th Street and launched the careers of everyone from Ella Fitzgerald to Billie Holiday. It was also a regular stop for vaudeville favorites Stepin Fetchit, Pigmeat Markham, and comedian Dusty Fletcher (of "Open the Door, Richard!" fame).

On their train ride from Chicago to Weehawken, Jon, Steve, and Lamont had agreed that, if any of them were caught or were accidentally separated, they would eventually meet up at an apartment house on West 138th Street in Harlem, near the Renaissance Ballroom. Jon was alone now, without any money, but at least he'd finally made it to New York. Later, when he was the famous television star Redd Foxx, he never talked about what he did during the time that Steve and Lamont were in jail, or how he managed to support himself, or even where he lived—most likely on rooftops, using discarded newspapers as bedding. But he somehow managed to eke out an existence. He would later tell stories of skipping out on dinner checks, particularly at Chinese restaurants, and stealing milk and bread to keep himself going until his two pals arrived on the scene. But without even knowing where Steve and Lamont *were*, it was a dicey proposition.

Finally, towards the end of July, after serving about two weeks of their thirty-day sentence, Steve and Lamont were sprung from the Hudson County jail, crossed the Hudson River and showed up at the apartment house on West 138th Street. Without wasting much time, the Chicago Bon Bons—Jon, Steve, and Lamont—recruited three other guys from the neighborhood, whose names are lost to history, and discarded the group's old name. The newly renamed Jump Swinging Six were a washtub band not much different from the Four Bon Bons. As they had done in Chicago, Jon, Lamont, and Steve, together with their three cohorts, took to the Harlem streets (and now the subways, too), playing their washtub repertoire, tap-dancing, clowning around, and hoping for donations. "For a while we did pretty well with the group," Redd remembered. "We'd play on street corners and in subways, passing the hat, and we'd make as much as fifty dollars a night each," he added with atypical modesty. "Pretty well" was an understatement; the Jump Swinging Six had enough confidence in themselves, and in the act, to audition for and to win a coveted spot on the *Major Bowes Original Amateur Hour*, the popular coast-to-coast radio show that showcased amateur performers of every description. Each week, Major Bowes would ask his twenty-seven million listeners around the country (including a different "honor city" each week) to phone in and vote for their favorite acts.

Major Bowes was the *American Idol* of its day. The hugely popular Top Ten hit was earning its host, imperious, impatient Major Edward Bowes, over $1 million a year—an almost-unheard-of sum as the country continued to dig itself out of the Great Depression. The cultural impact of the show was huge; stories were told of people selling their homes in order to earn enough money to travel (by whatever means possible) to New York, for the slim chance that they would be picked to audition for the *Major Bowes* talent scouts. Over ten thousand people each week applied to audition for *Major Bowes*, with only five hundred to seven hundred acts actually earning that chance—and only fifteen acts appearing on the air, coast-to-coast, every Thursday night. In the summer of 1939, *Major Bowes* was airing on the CBS Radio Network from a studio in midtown Manhattan (it had begun its life on New York's WHN five years earlier in 1934). It was considered a launching pad to bigger and better things—especially for those acts that survived Major Bowes' obnoxious gong, which he banged to signal the end of an act he didn't like. Several years earlier, a gangly young singer named Frank Sinatra and his group, the Hoboken Four, garnered national acclaim after multiple, gong-free appearances on the *Original Amateur Hour*.

Jon, Steve, Lamont, and their three other Jump Swinging Six cronies somehow overcame the huge odds stacked against them and passed their *Major Bowes* audition. They made their national radio debut on Thursday, July 27, 1939, competing on the same bill as entertainer Jack Rodin ("washboard, spoons, flexotone, and bicycle pump"), a twelve-year-old "novelty singer" named Dick Chaplin, Carol Kane, "The Cowgirl Yodeler," violinist Roberta Liming, the Sid Garrison Sextet, and the Harmonic Jitterbug Trio, among others.

The Jump Swinging Six was placed ninth on the bill, and their performance was sandwiched between a five-minute promotional segment, in which Major Bowes pitched diesel trucks produced by Dodge, one of the show's four automobile sponsors, and singer Olga Stepanova. As the group waited nervously to go on stage (the show was aired before a live audience), Major Bowes stepped to the mike to introduce them.

"Now here's the Jump Swinging Six," Bowes said in introducing the group. "That's an awful title," he added with a note of typical disdain. "Call it instrumental, vocal, and debutees of Terpsichore." After stumbling over those words, Bowes then introduced the group, and an unidentified Jump Swinging Six member answered Bowes' questions in a barely audible, shy voice. (An existing recording of this broadcast confirms it was not "Smiley" Sanford who spoke for the group.)

> BOWES: "Do you boys work for a living?"
> GROUP MEMBER: "Garage, shoeshine, elevator, and
>   bellhop."
> BOWES: "You don't waste many words, do you?"
> GROUP MEMBER: "Two are married, four are single.
>   One of the lucky ones is me."
> BOWES: "Well, don't be so sure. You'll get married
>   someday."
> GROUP MEMBER: "Oh, I'm lucky because I am
>   married, and my wife, she's listening, too."
> BOWES *(impatiently)*: "Come on."

And, with that none-too-subtle prompt, the Jump Swinging Six launched into their version of the Tin Pan Alley hit, "The Sheik of Araby." Their five-minute rendition of the song was mostly scatted and was underscored by an acoustic guitar and a pulsating tom-tom drum. The act also included a bit of tap-dancing by one of the group's (unidentified) members, likely Lamont Ousley; in listening to a recording of the show, preserved for posterity in the Library of Congress, it's possible to hear the *clack clack clack* of tap-dancing shoes in the middle of the number. "Extraordinary dancer!" Bowes interjects in the middle of the tap-dancing routine.

But sudden stardom for the Jump Swinging Six wasn't in the cards that July night. At the end of the show, when Major Bowes announced the call-in votes, the group had tallied only 137 votes to finish second from the bottom, beating only singer Olga Stepanova (who received 125 votes). Baritone singer Joseph Hester, from the night's "honor city" of Waco, Texas, topped the bill with nearly 4,500 votes. Years later, after Redd Foxx became a household name, articles about the *Sanford and Son* star repeated the fiction that the Jump Swinging Six finished in second place on *Major Bowes* and earned themselves a week's engagement at the Apollo Theater. That never happened. But their poor showing on *Major Bowes* didn't dissuade the group, and they continued to perform on the streets and in the subways, confident that they had at least been good enough to appear on one of the country's biggest radio shows.

By day, Smiley Sanford and his cohorts worked the streets and continued to hone their act. By night, they explored Harlem's intoxicating club scene, usually hopping from venue to venue where everyone from Charlie Parker to Billy Eckstine to Louis Armstrong, along with a coterie of pretty young women, could often be seen. Jon found a second home at the Savoy Ballroom, which became his favorite nightspot. Years later he still fondly recalled his time spent in the swinging and sweaty joint. "Whenever I had the bread, I would spend all my time at the Savoy Ballroom on 140th and Lennox," he recalled. "The Savoy was very important because I found such a great relief in dancing, and I danced pretty good. I would hustle all day long, so I could get to the Savoy, meet some chicks and hear all the best bands."

For a young guy without much money, the Savoy was a godsend. It cost only fifty cents to get in, there were often several bands playing each night, and there was a pool hall below the main floor. What else could a guy want? "We saw some of the greatest bands in the world," Redd Foxx recalled more than thirty years later. "They had two bandstands, and usually they alternated two name bands, plus the Savoy Sultans, who were the house band. I think I paid seventy-five cents to see Erskine Hawkins' orchestra, the Jay McShann band with Charlie Parker in the sax section, and the Sultans. There was never anything like the Savoy before or since. Just imagine two thousand people dancing to that same beat—it was wild! Sometimes I'd be downstairs at the pool hall right under the ballroom, and you could see the floor sinking with the rhythm. Most of my life then was wrapped around the Savoy."

The good times for Jon Sanford and his buddies continued to pass by relatively leisurely until December 7, 1941, when the Japanese bombed Pearl Harbor and the United States entered World War II. "We kept going until the war broke up the group," Redd recalled. Steve Trimble enlisted in the service in the days following the attack on Pearl Harbor, and Lamont Ousley decided to head home to Chicago, effectively putting an end to the Jump Swinging Six.

Nineteen-year-old Jon Sanford, however, didn't share the patriotic fervor gripping the rest of the country. Life in Harlem, as difficult as it sometimes was, was still too good to give up for the chance to serve his country—or, worse yet, to be killed or injured overseas. He wasn't going to let a little thing like a World War cramp his style. That sense of style had, by now, earned "Smiley" Sanford a new nickname. His friends in Harlem had begun calling him "Foxy" Sanford, because of the sharp way in which he dressed and for his habit of romancing the ladies. Why leave all of that behind to go fight overseas? So, when his number came up and he was called to the local draft board in Harlem, "Foxy" Jon Sanford suddenly developed heart troubles that would have made his future television alter ego, Fred Sanford, proud. He was perfectly healthy, but pulled one of the oldest draft-dodging tricks in the book—and got away with it.

"I went to a draft board in Harlem. The doctor decided I had a heart condition, so I was rejected," he said later. "Those cats weren't hip yet to the soap deal. I had eaten a half bar of Octagon soap, which causes heart palpitations." So with the war raging overseas, and his hometown buddies out of the picture, "Foxy" Sanford strung together another washtub bass and hooked up with two guitar players to form an act whose name is lost to the dustbin of history. The trio managed to get a short gig at the Apollo, warming up Jimmie Lunceford's band, but they broke up shortly thereafter.

But the good times that Jon figured to awaited him in Harlem failed to materialize. There were plenty of girls who'd sleep with him—Jon always had a way with the ladies—but finding steady work turned out to be more difficult than he ever imagined. "It became just a fight for survival," he remembered. He ran through a succession of short-lived jobs, including stints wheeling dresses around in the garment district in midtown, and working as a busboy at the White Turkey Town House restaurant down in Greenwich Village. "And I like to starved to death waiting for my salary," he said. "I had me a couple of sleep-in chicks who gave me a helping hand—not whores, but girls who would spend their night off with me on Thursdays and bring me food. Man. I had me so much gefilte fish and bagels, I was Jewish before Sammy!"

Money was so tight that paying rent for a room, for any length of time, became nearly impossible; Jon's "accommodations" were often the rooftop of a building located at 707 St. Nicholas Avenue in Harlem, his "blanket" on cold winter nights consisted of newspapers he found scattered nearby. It was a miserable, hand-to-mouth existence. He was in only occasional contact with Mary Sanford back in Chicago and was too proud—and angry—to let his mother know how much he was struggling to get by. Still, she somehow found out about his plight and did what she could to lighten his load. "My mother knew about this, and one day on the mantel at the entrance of that building I saw a letter from her," he said. "She sent me five dollars for Christmas."

With steady work elusive and music, for the time being, not a part of his routine, Jon turned to crime in order to support himself. The petty thefts he'd pulled when he first arrived in Harlem—stealing milk, running out on restaurant checks—took a backseat now to more serious criminal acts. His rap sheet included an arrest for suspicion of armed robbery, which resulted in a prolonged stay in the dreaded Tombs jail complex in lower Manhattan. He would later insist it was a case of mistaken identity that landed him in the slammer.

"I wasn't guilty. I know that's what all cons say, but this is true," he said. "It was in the wintertime, and a couple of other kids and I were so hungry we went into a Chinese restaurant, ate, and ran out. The cops chased us. I turned a corner, slid on the ice into a parked car, and that's where they found me. They found the other guys around the corner in an elevator. At the time, there was a whole string of armed robberies going on in Harlem, and they said we were the ones that was sticking up all those Chinese restaurants."

Jon and his cohorts were sent to the Tombs to await trial—"just a bunch of kids, alongside some of the baddest group of folks I ever met, murderers and all kinds of people"—and were finally released after ninety days for lack of evidence. Another time, he was caught by a cop sleeping in the hallway of a building on 105th Street, an empty milk bottle in his hand and another empty milk bottle nearby. "I had just drank two quarts of milk that was delivered to the folks who lived there," he said. "I had to go to Riker's Island for five days. That place is like the Alcatraz of the East." He also served a stint in jail for marijuana possession after he was caught driving back into Manhattan without a driver's license, and in a car that was filled with pot he had harvested from a field in North Jersey. "It was hard to stay away from pot, knowing how much you could make with it," he said. "I was just using it for bartering, not peddling."

His drug use kicked in around this time. In the coming years, it would increase to eventually include copious amounts of cocaine, but, for now, he mainly smoked a lot of marijuana, which was relatively cheap to buy. For the most part, he stayed away from the "harder" stuff including cocaine, if only because he couldn't afford it, and heroin, the junkie's best friend, which was readily available in Harlem at the time and was a prime moneymaker for the local drug dealers. Ironically, it was on a visit back home to Saint Louis in 1945 that "Foxy" Sanford shot up for what proved, he claimed, to be the first and last time in his life. "I was watching the Buddy Johnson band that night, and one of the musicians laid some on me," he said. "Arthur Prysock made room for me on the band bus. I got back to New York and never got near junk again." Well, almost never. Back in Harlem, he was shooting pool one day and was on a hot streak, when two of his friends invited him to join them in some "good smack" in their place around the corner. When he was finished playing pool, he went to their apartment—where he found both of his pals laying on the bed, dead from an overdose. "From then on that was enough for me not to mess with no heroin," he said. "I can still see those two cats laying there backwards on the bed with their knees bent. If I'd of finished that pool game ten minutes sooner, I would have been just as dead as they was."

And then he met Malcolm.

Malcolm Little, who was two-and-a-half years younger than Jon Sanford, had taken a circuitous route to Harlem. He was born in Omaha, Nebraska in May 1925 and his father, a noted African American Baptist speaker, moved the family to Milwaukee, and then to Lansing, Michigan, when Malcolm was a small child. Like "Foxy" Sanford, Malcolm had a light complexion and reddish hair, the genetic byproduct of his Scottish maternal grandfather. And, like Jon, Malcolm grew up without a father figure; when he was six years old, his father was killed in what was ruled a car accident, though many in Lansing questioned whether Earl Little wasn't murdered for accusing a local white supremacist group, two years earlier, of trying to burn the family's house down.

In 1938, Malcolm's mother, Louise Little, suffered a nervous breakdown and was committed to a mental institution after being declared legally insane. Thirteen-year-old Malcolm and his ten siblings were sent to a series of foster homes around Michigan. Malcolm was a very good student and enjoyed school, but dropped out of the eighth grade after being told by a teacher that his desire to become a lawyer was "no realistic goal for a nigger." He moved to Boston's predominantly black Roxbury section, where he lived with his half-sister, Ella, and held a variety of jobs with the New Haven Railroad.

In 1943, when he was eighteen, Malcolm moved to New York, where he settled in Harlem and got a job working as a waiter at a Jimmy's Chicken Shack, which was located at 763 St. Nicholas Avenue, not far from Jon Sanford's rooftop sleeping quarters. Jimmy's, which was owned by bandleader Andy Kirk, was renowned not only for its fried chicken but for its celebrity clientele. It was a local hangout for notables including jazz piano great Art Tatum—who frequently held court in the front of the restaurant—and author Ralph Ellison, who, at that time, was working on his future classic, *Invisible Man*. "A jam-packed four-thirty a.m. crowd at Jimmy's Chicken Shack or Dickie Wells' might have such jam-session entertainment as Hazel Scott playing the piano for Billie Holiday singing the blues," Malcolm recalled. Jimmy's was also a landing place for Harlem newcomers looking for work—including future jazz great Charlie "Yardbird" Parker and Jon "Foxy" Sanford. It was at Jimmy's Chicken Shack, where Jon got a job washing dishes, that he met his new co-worker, Malcolm Little.

Jon and Malcolm became fast buddies and, before long, were nearly inseparable. They were both sharp dressers, were both lady-killers, and they physically resembled each other. Around Harlem, their similarities soon earned them nicknames, "Chicago Red" for Jon and "Detroit Red" for Malcolm (after their respective home states). ("Saint Louis Red" would have been more appropriate for Jon, but that sobriquet was already taken by a local stickup artist known to Malcolm Little, who later served hard time for attempted armed robbery on a train and for a jewelry heist gone awry.)

"He was a beautiful guy," Redd Foxx would say about Malcolm. "And we used to dress alike. You know then British tan was popular, you know we had British tan suits and those big colored shoes, you know, turned up at the toes. We were in New York, we were clean. I had long hair, a pompadour, with a ducktail in the back, we didn't call it that then."

More than twenty years later, when Malcolm Little had become the Nation of Islam leader Malcolm X, he paid tribute to his Harlem pal. "Chicago Red was the funniest dishwasher on this earth . . . who kept the kitchen crew in stitches," he wrote in *The Autobiography of Malcolm X*. "Now he's making his living being funny as a nationally known stage and nightclub comedian. I don't see any reason why old Chicago Red would mind me telling that he is Redd Foxx."

Redd Foxx would also look back fondly on those days running with Detroit Red in Harlem. "Malcolm was about the same color as me. You could hardly tell us apart," he said. "We both had those konks [hair-straightening] and our hair was red with a high pompadour and we had the zoot pants—just like the 'high drape pants' Billie Holiday used to sing about in her blues."

Redd confided to Anthony Major, who ran Redd Foxx Productions in the mid-1980s, that Malcolm was the only person Redd really trusted. "They used to rob places together and sleep on rooftops together. Redd said he knew [Malcolm] had his back, and he trusted him. If Redd was in a fight, he could turn his back and could know that Malcolm was gonna be on the other side, fighting with him."

When they couldn't afford a place to stay for the night, Jon would invite Malcolm up to his "humble abode" on the rooftop of 707 St. Nicholas Avenue. "We had about five hundred pounds of newspapers up there," he remembered. "Newspapers is some of the warmest stuff going on." Malcolm and Jon hung around and shot the shit in a pool hall across the street from the St. Nicholas Avenue building—not far from Jimmy's Chicken Shack—and before long they had turned the turf between 145th and 150th Streets into their personal playground, harkening back to Jon's days running with the 58th Street Gang in Chicago. "There was a bunch of guys in the neighborhood and it was ours, like a gang," Redd recalled. "When we got a job in Jimmy's Chicken Shack, we had all kinds of hustles going. It was the busiest joint uptown and we made a little extra bread upping the checks and so forth."

Malcolm, who would eventually spend six years in prison on a burglary charge, got into all sorts of criminal sidelines in Harlem. They were enterprises that would eventually drive a wedge into his friendship with "Foxy" Sanford. But, for a while, Jon often joined Malcolm in his illegal endeavors and even cooked up a few schemes himself. "Malcolm didn't have the showbiz talent so he didn't give a damn what he got into," he said. "He'd take on anything to get some dough. He was a little bit more aggressive, but I'd rather be sleeping with a broad and go somewhere [to a club] and do fifteen minutes of comedy."

One scheme that turned into a profitable side business for Jon and Malcolm involved them selling suits they had stolen from a dry cleaning business. A female employee there had the hots for "Chicago Red" and, one night, "accidentally" left the store window open. Jon and Malcolm slithered into the store under cover of darkness and stole around one hundred suits, which they then sold on the streets via the rooftop at 707 St. Nicholas Avenue. "We'd sell one or two of them a day off the roof," Redd recalled. "We never got caught for that. I guess that balanced out some of the stuff I had to pay for later that I didn't do."

The two buddies were also dealing marijuana, particularly to the musicians who played the Harlem nightclubs and were passing through town, looking for some action. Jon and Malcolm had reputations as savvy businessmen who'd carved a niche for themselves as well-known reefer dealers. "They hung around us 'cause they were shoveling pot," recalled John Williams, the husband of jazz pianist, composer and arranger Mary Lou Williams. "They were hustlers. Redd Foxx was more of a hustler than Malcolm X. He was something! He was down trying to sell marijuana to us. A lot of us used it."

Jon and Malcolm's pot dealing and crooked schemes were also a reminder that the insular world of Harlem was their entire universe. The war raging overseas in Europe and in the South Pacific, and the effect it was having on the home front, was the furthest thing from their minds. Jon had dodged the draft by eating a bar of soap, so he obviously wasn't interested in the bigger picture; Malcolm was too young to be drafted when war broke out. "What was going on in America wasn't on Malcolm's mind or mine," Redd recalled. "We weren't into that kind of bag. Not then. Harlem was our world. It was a place where we were fixed. Except for those jobs in the garment district, everything was happening uptown."

Even Malcolm, notwithstanding his later fame as Malcolm X, wasn't very much interested in politics at this stage of the game—unless it meant free food and a chance to meet some hot chicks.

"I remember one time Malcolm and I joined the Communist Party," Redd recalled. "Maybe not joined it, but signed something or other because they had white broads and food, and I hadn't had a broad in a year and hadn't had food in about two weeks." Jon and Malcolm, always on the prowl for food and sex (and not necessarily in that order), went to a Communist Party meeting that was being held on St. Nicholas Avenue, signed some papers, and were given a pile of Communist Party literature they were expected to digest. "You'd dance with the chicks, smell the perfume, and eat the sandwiches," Redd recalled. "You just couldn't avoid being part of things like that because there was food, man—stacked-high cake and lemonade, even boloney you could put in your pocket. I'd have joined the Ku Klux Klan if they'd had some sandwiches."

His talk of "white broads" was more of a boast than a fact, when it came to Jon Sanford's romances. While he might have occasionally slept with a white woman, especially during his days in Harlem, he preferred the company of black women. "I was always the one that wound up with the black chick," he said. "The light-skinned cats got the black women; when a white woman wants a black man she wants him real black; she wants some lips and some color to go along with it. Of course, there were some light-skinned cats who got white women, like Billy Daniels, who was an exception because of his show biz position. He used to come into the Chicken Shack and drink champagne out of chicks' shoes. Oh, he loved gray girls."

The friendship between Jon and Malcolm began to sour as the latter expanded his criminal activities in Harlem to pimping, drug dealing, and racketeering, leading him down a path that would result in his eventual incarceration (and his rebirth as Malcolm X). For Jon Sanford, who didn't take anything too seriously, having fun was more important than a life of hardcore crime. Running out on a check at a Chinese restaurant or stealing some suits was one thing; dealing hardcore drugs was some serious shit, and he wanted nothing to do with that. Once they parted in the mid-1940s and found fame in their respective careers, Redd Foxx and Malcolm X would reunite only once, in the early 1960s. For all intents and purposes, their friendship began and ended with their days together in Harlem.

chapter three

"Redd Foxx Looked Better on a Marquee"

Jon Sanford's break with Malcolm signaled not only the end of Chicago Red and Detroit Red but also the beginning of a new chapter in Jon's life. With World War II drawing to a close, he decided that it was time for a fresh start, to wipe the slate clean and emerge with a new identity. Maybe it would change his luck. He remained in Harlem after his split with Malcolm and resumed his tenuous life of hit-or-miss jobs, including a short stint as a sign painter. He still harbored dreams of becoming a professional singer and, never lacking in self-confidence, needed to find a catchy name that would light up the marquee once he hit the big time. His first choice was Red Fox, borrowing the "Red" from his previous nickname and adding the "Fox" because he was, after all, "Foxy" Sanford. But he decided that wasn't good enough.

"I didn't like Jon or Elroy so they called me 'Smiley.' In most of the black communities, a guy of my complexion, they would call 'Red,' so that was always with me," he said. "But I didn't like the reference to color, so I put another 'D' to change it from color. And Fox because of the animal. It has nothing to do with color." He also added another "X" to Fox. "I added the extra letters onto both names 'cause I figured 'Redd Foxx' looked better on a marquee than 'Red Fox.'"

With his prospects in Harlem looking bleak, the newly rechristened Redd Foxx caught a lucky break. In early 1945 he heard from his friend, singer Jo Ann Baker, that a club down in Baltimore called Gamby's was looking for an emcee. Gamby's was part of the "Chitlin' Circuit," a group of nightclubs scattered along the East Coast, in the Deep South and in the Midwest, which catered to a blacks-only clientele and employed only black performers, during a time in which segregation was still the rule rather than the exception. Although he had no experience as an emcee either introducing acts or providing the patter necessary between costume changes, etc., Redd decided to take the job. He drove down to Baltimore, where, on Baker's recommendation, he was hired at Gamby's and was thrust into the smoky, hostile world of a club emcee. And, as he soon discovered, his past experience playing "the dozens" back in Chicago, and his ability to trade barbs with the best of them, had nothing on the crowds he now faced night after night. "Baltimore was tough," he said. "No use in me lying; that was the toughest [town] on earth to work. I don't care who you were. If you were bad, and they thought so, you were going to know it. They wanted to hear something that they're used to down there on the docks, working on them ships and hauling all them big packages off."

Despite the tough crowds, and his inexperience as an emcee, Redd managed to hold his own, for the most part. Gamby's was a proving ground, not only for his interaction with a live audience but for planting the early seeds of what would, in time, become a polished comedy style notable for its studied improvisatory style. While Redd wasn't doing a set "routine" yet—that would come much later on—he was still expected to engage the Gamby's audience, and he discovered he had a natural affinity for off-the-cuff jokes and rapid-fire comebacks when defending himself against hecklers. "I had never done a night-club comedy routine before," he said. "Of course I knew a lot of the jokes, and had watched the best of them work, you know, fellows like Willie Bryant, Allen Drew, and others."

After only a short time at Gamby's, Redd developed a reputation as a "must-see" comic on the local circuit. "As a kid in Baltimore I would lie my way into Gamby's nightclub to hear Foxx because all the hip people had pegged him as the funniest dude to come down the pike," recalled *Baltimore Afro-American* writer Ralph Matthews. "He had not been in town long but the word was out: 'Dig Foxx!'"

A turning point for Redd's career in Baltimore came on the night that Captain Alexander Emerson, one of the cops feared most by the city's African American community, sauntered into Gamby's to catch Redd's show. Emerson ran Baltimore's vice squad with an iron fist and had a reputation among the city's black residents for paying especially close attention to them. He liked to bust numbers runners and pot smokers by using a sledgehammer to batter his way through the door.

Legend had it that he even had a black "rat" on the force that carried his sledgehammer for him "like a yassuh golf caddy."

On this particular night, Redd spied Emerson as soon as he entered Gamby's and wasted no time needling the hated cop from his perch on stage. "Folks, we have a celebrity in the house, none other than that stalwart crime fighter, Captain Emerson," he said. Then, taking "a long and sinister drag" on his ever-present cigarette, Redd blew a puff of smoke in Emerson's direction. "Forgive me, captain, I just wanted to smoke up all the evidence before you got any closer," he said. He then turned to a buddy in the audience. "George, you didn't flush your numbers down the toilet a minute too soon," he said. There was a long pause, then the entire joint burst into laughter. The red-faced Emerson walked out in total embarrassment.

During his short time at Gamby's, Redd also met singer Jimmy Scott, who was performing in the club at the time. They struck up a friendship that would last a lifetime. "Redd liked to party and Redd could be arrogant, but I loved his dirty drawers," Scott recalled in his autobiography, *Faith in Time*. "In the morning, he'd bang on my door shouting, 'Nigger, get up and get out of there. We need you and we love you and screw you!'" "Sometimes I just said, 'Oh, well, that's natural for Redd because, I mean, whatever went down he was going to get it straight. He wasn't going to wait until later. He was going to get it straight, *now*. That was Redd."

Scott, born and raised in Cleveland, was three years younger than Redd and had been dubbed "Little Jimmy" Scott by Lionel Hampton because of a genetic condition called Kallmann's syndrome, which stunted his growth, prevented him from reaching puberty, and left him with a falsetto voice. (He would grow another eight inches in his late thirties to reach the height of five feet, seven inches tall, but his voice never changed.)

Sixty-five years later, Scott, now eighty-four, could vividly recall Redd's effect on the crowd at Gamby's. "He was telling jokes and everybody was crazy about him," he remembered. "That was just his natural way. He would crack up the house. And he was cool with the women. They were crazy about him. He had a good set of ladies that ran after him."

When he met Redd at Gamby's, Scott was touring as the featured singer with Estelle "Caldonia" Young's "Caldonia Revue," which featured vocalists, comedians, and Caldonia's "exotic shake dancer" routine. The revue had just broken up, but "Mother," as Scott called Estelle, soldiered on as a single act, taking Jimmy along to Gamby's as her vocalist. At the time, former heavyweight boxer Joe Louis was also touring the area, meeting fans and signing autographs after his discharge from the Army. Redd, who was convinced that Jimmy Scott had the talent for bigger and better things, took him over to the Royal Theater to see Louis, who agreed that Jimmy was destined for stardom. "Redd did so much for so many people that he worked with," Jimmy said. "He really did. He was helpful in getting gigs for them all."

Redd and Joe Louis reached out to Ralph Cooper, the famous black actor, and persuaded him to call the emcee at Harlem's Baby Grand nightclub. "'This boy's gotta sing in the Big Apple,' Redd kept saying," Scott recalled. "So Ralph, who was hooked up with everyone in Harlem, arranged the date." Jimmy was booked for a week at the Baby Grand, which turned into a three-month gig that put his career on the fast track. "It almost became my new home gig," Jimmy said. "I helped a girl write her tune. . . . Regina Adams was her name. And while we were in New York, Redd came in the club and told me, 'Hey, man, you know your song is on the radio?' And I said, 'What song?' And Redd said, 'Man, they stole your song.' He was having a fit. He wanted to take [Adams] and spank her. And I laughed and said, 'Man forget that crap. Songs are songs and there are plenty of songs out there.'" Jimmy had written the melody for Adams' song, "Everybody's Somebody's Fool," and recorded it—but when the song was released, he wasn't credited as its singer or writer.

It looked for a while like Redd Foxx had engineered a genius move in choosing his new moniker. Back in Harlem in the summer of 1946, he managed to wangle an audition for Savoy Records, the noted jazz label started a few years earlier in Newark, New Jersey, by Herman Lubinsky, who ran the label—named after Harlem's Savoy Ballroom— from his former record shop on Market Street. Lubinsky was always on the prowl for new talent, but working for him was a double-edged sword that cut deeply into his stable of mostly African American artists. On the one hand, Lubinsky offered the chance to record for a growing jazz label and the promise of national exposure; on the other hand, he grossly underpaid his artists and was (quietly) despised by his roster of Savoy talent, which included Charlie Parker, Billy Eckstine, Sarah Vaughan, and Joe Turner.

Redd Foxx didn't much care how Herman Lubinsky treated his talent. The chance to record for Savoy Records was too good to pass up and was Redd's biggest break since his appearance on *Major Bowes* with the Jump Swinging Six seven years earlier. With his prospects not very bright, he wasn't about to let this chance slip through his fingers. So, on the morning of September 30, 1946, Redd traveled to the Savoy studio in Newark, New Jersey, where he was scheduled to record five tracks under the direction of Teddy Reig, the label's top producer. Reig had worked with Charlie Parker and Miles Davis (and later, in 1950, founded Royal Roost Records with Jack Hook). Redd would be backed in his one-day recording session by Savoy artists Kenny Watts and His Jumpin' Buddies, featuring Watts on piano, Les Millington on bass, Johnny Swann on trumpet, Arthur Herbert on drums, and Stafford "Pazzuza" Simon on tenor sax. Reig said that he hired Watts, who he knew from Brooklyn, for Redd's session because Watts often gave him rides into Manhattan.

Redd spent that day recording five tracks: "Let's Wiggle a Little Woogie," "Lucky Guy," "Fine Jelly Blues," "Redd Foxx Blues," and "Shame on You." While the tunes had a bluesy feel—this *was* Savoy Records, after all—they also had a humorous edge, which not only helped to turn the focus away from Redd's voice, which was serviceable at best, and hadn't yet developed its later gravelly growl, but also played off the hip attitude of "the funniest dishwasher on this earth." On "Fine Jelly Blues," a slow-moving number that begins with a sax intro by Pazuzza Simon, a boastful Redd sings about all the beautiful women he's tempted by.

> *Come here pretty baby, don't you try to stall.*
> *If you ain't got good jelly baby, please don't answer my call.*

"Shame on You," written by Teddy Reig, is more of an up-tempo, swinging number, underscored by Watts' jangly piano and Simon's bouncy sax riffs. The song finds its narrator, presumably up north, singing about a woman he's brought to town from down south, only to find she's fooling around with his best friend. Still, no matter what she does, he'll always love her nonetheless.

I brought you from Chattanooga, all the way up here,
Instead of acting right you kicked me in my rear.

"Redd Foxx Blues" finds Redd full of bluster about all of the women who 'never do nothin' but give her man the blues."

I'm gonna change my address, even give up my telephone.
I'm gonna do all that baby so you women will be leavin' me alone.

"Lucky Guy," the funniest of Redd's five Savoy tracks, is another up-beat number, underscored with Pazuzza Simon's snappy sax, in which Redd sings about his woman, who he knows will never go out and cheat on him because of her physical ailments. The song's lyrics and its comic, smirking tone would have been perfectly suited to future *Sanford and Son* junk dealer Fred Sanford, who would often scat out a few lines while cooking his son Lamont breakfast or dinner in their ramshackle Watts house.

I'm a lucky guy and I ain't gonna sing no blues.
My baby's got bad teeth bad feet can't even wear no shoes.

While Redd spent the better part of that day in Savoy's Market Street studio, singing about women, his life was about to imitate his art. Newark, in fact, held more for Redd than the promise of a recording contract. He'd met a woman named Evelyn Killibrew (sometimes spelled "Killebrew"), a Newark native who came into Redd's life under a dangerous set of circumstances and after a night of partying in Harlem at the Savoy Ballroom.

At the time they met, Redd, who always seemed to have a Ralph Kramden-type scheme going, was sharing a room in Harlem with a bus driver, selling booze out of their apartment to anyone who need-ed something to wet their whistle after the Savoy closed for the night. One of the musicians from the Savoy band brought Evelyn, who was making her first-ever visit to New York City, over to Redd's apartment. And it wasn't for the booze. "He was going to rape her," Redd said. "We had a big fight. I put him out, and she stayed there with me for protection, more or less, but five days later we were married."

Their whirlwind courtship, which began under the most unlikeliest of circumstances, took an even stranger U-turn. Evelyn's father, who ran a very successful dry cleaning business in Newark, wanted to make sure his daughter and his new son-in-law lived a respectable, middle-class life. In 1947, he moved the newly married couple into his big house in Newark, where he could keep an eye on Redd and make sure his daughter was well-provided for. It was the first time in more than eight years that Redd had lived anywhere but Harlem, notwithstanding a few brief trips back to Chicago and Saint Louis, and his stint working Gamby's in Baltimore. But Redd wasn't complaining, at first. "My father-in-law was so good [at supporting us that] pretty soon I didn't have to hustle," he said. "He was a Mason and got me in the Masons. Being away from New York, and having a fine wife, I felt I had something to look forward to and I began to become a respectable man."

But Redd's definition of "respectable" didn't mean that he'd given up his dream of launching a singing career. In October 1946, Savoy Records released the five singles recorded by Redd the month before. Label owner Herman Lubinsky took out a half-page ad in the October 26 edition of *Billboard* magazine to promote his new artists, "Cousin Joe's Brooklyn Blue Blowers" and its "companion smash hit!" Redd's "Let's Wiggle a Little Woogie" and "Lucky Guy" (labeled as Savoy 630), "by the sensationally great blues-boogie man, Redd Foxx."

But "sensationally great blues-boogie man, Redd Foxx" failed to live up to his advance billing. None of Redd's five Savoy tracks were reviewed by any of the industry's trade publications, including *Billboard* and *Variety*, and the singles failed to chart. But Lubinsky, to his credit, didn't completely give up on his new artist (who was living with Evelyn not too far from Savoy's Market Street headquarters). In the April 5, 1947, issue of *Billboard*, Lubinsky took out another big ad touting Savoy's roster of talent under the headline, "Savoy Parades the Blues!" The ad included "Really Redd Hot!" Redd Foxx and "A Special Double Header Boogie Woogie" featuring Redd's "Shame on You Boogie" backed with Pete Brown's "Back Talk Boogie." Later that month, Redd's contribution to the music world was limited to a single mention of "Fine Jelly Blues" (in very small type), which was listed under *Billboard's* "Race Records" heading.

Redd was getting restless. He'd spent nearly a decade in Harlem always on the move, always looking for the next hustle, the next job. The domestic life with Evelyn (and her father) in Newark was losing its luster. While it did seem to have a beneficial effect on his attitudes toward others—"I began to get tired of this whole idea of mistreating people, misusing them, stealing," he said—the housebound husband act was getting old.

Even though Evelyn's father did what he could to support his daughter and son-in-law, Redd insisted on finding work—which wasn't readily available in and around Newark (the dry cleaning business apparently was not to his liking). "It was hard to get work, and I hated sitting around idle," he said. He managed to scrape together a few gigs working the low-rent joints around Newark's Third Ward, in the Hill area—a largely working class, black section of the city—telling jokes for five bucks a night. For a while, he emceed at the more respectable Piccadilly Club, located at Peshine and Waverly Avenues, where his penchant for off-color humor earned him the nickname "Filthy Mouth" among the locals. At least they thought he had a catchy name; when Billie Holiday played the Piccadilly shortly thereafter, she was backed by a band that called themselves the "Redd Foxx Sextet." Carl "Tiny Prince" Brinson, who chronicled Newark's nightlife for fifty years in his magazine, *After Hours*, remembers that he was sent to retrieve Holiday from a private party and take her to the Piccadilly for her opening night. When he arrived to fetch Holiday, she was stoned and in no condition to be seen in public. Brinson remembers that it was Redd who kept the Piccadilly patrons amused "for a few hours" while they waited for Holiday to arrive (she never did, at least not on that night).

Newark might have been a dead end for Redd, but Baltimore was only three hours away, and several club owners there hadn't forgotten the young comic's impressive run at Gamby's, where he still appeared from time to time. While he was still living with Evelyn and her father, Redd returned to Baltimore to work a club date here and there, at Gamby's or places like the Avenue Café, which ran an ad for its October 1948 Halloween show trumpeting "Redd Foxx, Ace of Comic Emcees and His All Star Revue Featuring Peaches Webb" and "Sweet Songstress" Princess LaRae. "Gamby's is drawing good weekend crowds, offering faces well-known to strollers," noted the *Baltimore Afro-American*. "Baby Scruggs and her dance routines; songs by Oliver Travers, emcee; Maude Thomas, who delivers blues in a rocking manner that clicks; and the usual laughter that greets the unusual comic antics of Redd Foxx."

"REDD FOXX LOOKED BETTER ON A MARQUEE"

While Newark might not have held out much promise for Redd Foxx in terms of employment, the city offered up its bounty to him in other (illegal) ways. Redd already knew that that the fertile Northern New Jersey soil was a breeding ground for marijuana. Even his prior arrest for transporting a carload of weed over the Hudson River into Manhattan didn't stop him from, once again, trying his hand at gardening. He and Evelyn began growing marijuana in the backyard of the Newark home they shared with Evelyn's father, who had no idea what his daughter and son-in-law were up to. The details are lost to history, but someone dropped a dime on Redd and ratted him out to the cops—with the predictable result. His bust was big enough news to merit a mention in the *Baltimore Afro-American*. "Fellow entertainers often wondered how Jon Elroy Sanford, a small-time comedian, could afford to drive a Cadillac," the newspaper reported. "Last week they got their answer. Sanford, better known as Redd Foxx, was growing marijuana in his Newark, New Jersey, backyard. Federal agents found a quantity of reefers in his coat pocket and also in the Cadillac. Both he and his wife, Evelyn, are under $5,000 bail."

The couple was bailed out by Evelyn's father, who paid a hefty fine to get Redd and Evelyn off the hook and to avoid a lengthy jail sentence. Newark was a dead-end for Redd before the pot bust; now it was time to leave. He began taking almost daily trips across the river into Manhattan, where all roads inevitably led back to Harlem, and to St. Nicholas Avenue, where he met a young black comic named Melvin "Slappy" White.

Slappy, almost a year older than Redd, was working steadily in some of the smaller joints in Harlem but, compared to his new friend, was a seasoned pro. Born in Baltimore in September 1921, Slappy had some experience working the "Chitlin' Circuit." Like Redd, Slappy, who was then part of a dance team with Clarence Schelle, had appeared several years earlier on *The Major Bowes Original Amateur Hour*. He then segued into comedy, specializing in straight-ahead humor with an act constructed around old-style joke and storytelling with a bit of social commentary mixed in. He knew his audience. "We was so poor my uncle invented the limbo by slipping under the pay toilet," went one of Slappy's jokes. In another joke, he riffed on creation: "Jus' remember, if Adam had been born black, there'd be no woman. Can you imagine anyone taking a rib from a black?"

In Redd's estimation, Slappy was already a grizzled comedy performer. He'd been part of an act called "The Two Zephyrs," in which he teamed with comic Willie Lewis. They were good enough to win a rare (for blacks at that time) spot on television, appearing in 1949 on DuMont's *The Morey Amsterdam Show* (whose cast members included a pre-*Honeymooners* Art Carney and future pulp fiction author Jacqueline Susann). Early in their partnership, Slappy and Willie were written up in *Billboard* magazine as "colored boys" whose "comedy pantomime work of a crap game in slow motion is excellent." One of Willie Lewis's calling cards was to pull a floppy hat over his ears and drawl, "Ah was so tahred, ah wuz so lazy that ha couldn't even hoe in mah garden. Then ah took some of that there had-ee-call and now ah'm the best hoer in town." He also specialized in a trick in which a cane appeared to be glued to his fingers. But after Slappy and Willie went as far as they could with their act, they decided to call it a day and pursue solo careers.

At the time he met Redd Foxx, Slappy was married to singer Pearl Bailey. She, too, had toured the Chitlin' Circuit and was a show business veteran. But the couple's careers had been heading in different directions for some time now. Pearl, a rising star, had toured with the USO during World War II and was now living with Slappy in New York, where she was performing in nightclubs with A-listers including Cab Calloway and Duke Ellington. The year before, she made her debut on Broadway as "Butterfly" opposite two of the tap-dancing Nicholas Brothers (Harold and Fayard) in the Harold Arlen/Johnny Mercer musical "St. Louis Woman." Pearl's glitzy universe was far-removed from Slappy's world, which encompassed small gigs in smoky clubs no one really noticed (or cared about). Their careers were moving in different directions, and it was beginning to take its toll on their marriage, which was disintegrating by the time Redd Foxx entered the picture in 1947. Slappy's breakup with Pearl Bailey would set the stage for a love-hate relationship between Redd Foxx and Pearl that would rear its ugly head several times in the decades to come.

With his prospects in Newark at a dead end, and married life having lost much of its early luster, Redd began spending more and more time back in Harlem and with Slappy, often leaving Evelyn for days at a time, without much of an explanation, straining the couple's marriage to the breaking point. Slappy, who'd grown up on the streets of Baltimore, and Redd, with his streetwise mentality honed by years of hanging out on corners in Saint Louis, Chicago and Harlem, discovered they had a natural rapport with each other. Slappy's straight-man humor played nicely off Redd's more acerbic, quick-witted world view, punctuated by his lightning-quick ability to verbally cut someone down to size, like he'd done so many years before when playing "the dozens" with the 58th Street Gang in Chicago. Who knew those rapid-fire put-downs would serve him so well later in life?

With Slappy's marriage in its final death throes, and Redd's marriage to Evelyn heading down that same road, the two friends decided to combine their talents and form a comedy team. And why not? Slappy wasn't exactly setting the world on fire as a solo act, and Redd's musical aspirations were all-but-dead now that Herman Lubinsky had cancelled his contract with Savoy. Redd always thrived as the center of attention, and while he didn't have a scripted "act," per se, he was genuinely funny. His former co-workers at Jimmy's Chicken Shack (including Malcolm Little) could certainly attest to that. Slappy, who was more of a storyteller than a jokester, was content to play straight man to Redd's antics.

The new comedy team called themselves "Foxx and White," and put the word out that they were available for bookings. To draw audience attention away from their paucity of written material, Redd had his full head of reddish hair cut and styled into a bowl cut (think Moe Howard of the Three Stooges). It was a prop he and Slappy could use in the act. "When I took the hat off and showed my shaved head, those spooks laughed for five or six minutes," he recalled. The act would start with Redd and Slappy coming on stage:

REDD: I'm Redd.
SLAPPY: I'm White.
REDD: You're kidding!

But finding work wasn't easy. Finally, when "Foxx and White" managed to get booked into the Palace Theater on Broadway—their hoped-for "big break"—they generated nothing but flop-sweat. "Redd and I marched out onstage, confident and feeling real good," Slappy recalled. "The house was jammed. We had waited for this a long time. It was our opening, the first crack at the big time.

"So we took our bow, very low and very long, as usual. We stood there stooped over for what seemed to be a long, long time. And we heard nothing. Not a clap. Not a chuckle." This was that moment in the act where Redd would remove his hat, hoping the shock factor of his bowl haircut would have the audience in stitches. "I whispered to Redd, 'Okay, take off your hat!'" Slappy recalled. "He turned his head slightly to the left towards me, keeping his smile big for the audience, and whispered back, 'I did!' Silence. It took the smoke out of our chimneys real good."

Redd was characteristically more blunt in his assessment. "We died like dogs," he said. "The whole act bombed. That was my first and last time at the Palace."

With an unreceptive audience in New York, Redd and Slappy took their act on the road. Redd's marriage to Evelyn still existed, on paper, but for all intents and purposes it was over between them. The marriage survived for another few years until they were officially divorced in 1952, shortly before Redd's thirtieth birthday.

Once they hit the road, Redd and Slappy found more receptive audiences outside of New York, and their act picked up steam. They began to get steady bookings on the Chitlin' Circuit, and before too long impressed local theater owners with their ability to pack the house.

The Chitlin' Circuit took its name from "chitterlings" or "chitlins," which were stewed pigs intestines and were a common dietary staple in black households, especially in the South. The Circuit was formed in the late 1800s by the Theater Owners Booking Association (TOBA), an acronym which many black performers snidely referred to as "Tough on Black Asses" because of the circuit's low wages and brutal work schedule. For the most part, the Chitlin' Circuit offered steady employment for the better acts, but little chance to break into the mainstream (read: white) clubs. Among the many Chitlin' Circuit stops along the way, top acts could be expected to be booked into the Royal Peacock in Atlanta, Robert's Show Lounge, and Club DeLisa in Chicago, the Howard Theatre in Washington, D.C., the Ritz Theater in Jacksonville, Florida; and the Fox Theatre in Detroit. The Chitlin' Circuit spawned the likes of Mantan Moreland, Stepin Fetchit, Eddie Green, Dewey "Pigmeat" Markham, Ben Carter, and Jackie "Moms" Mabley. While some of these performers were able to break into big-time radio (Green appeared on *Duffy's Tavern*; Markham joined the *Andrews Sisters Eight-to-the-Bar Ranch* show), these were the exceptions among the many hundreds of talented performers forgotten through the passage of time.

Della Reese was one of the many performers who started out working the Chitlin' Circuit. "It wasn't that they were raggedy, dirty and lowdown. It was where they were, it was what they paid, it was the people that were there," she said. "It was a series of circumstances. Some of [the clubs] were very well equipped, but were not in the mainstream. You didn't get covered by the *Los Angeles Times* or the *New York Times* or any of that. It was like a backwater place to be. But it was a grooving place. Things were going on. People were happy and having fun in there."

Redd and Slappy traveled the Chitlin' Circuit and played most, if not all, of the better-known clubs (and even those that weren't as well-known). Redd, never one for understatement, insisted that he and his comedy partner were "as good as Dean Martin and Jerry Lewis." Whether that's a boast or a statement of fact is lost to history—there are no surviving recordings of Foxx and White to judge one way or another. Still, the fact that both men would later go on to successful solo comedy careers—in Redd's case one of historic proportions—lends a certain amount of credence to Redd's high opinion of Foxx and White.

Some indication of how Redd and Slappy went over with their audiences is found in the carefully organized notes of Apollo Theater co-owner Frank Schiffman. In 1934, Schiffman and Leo Brecher bought the Harlem landmark from Sidney Cohen, with Schiffman taking over as the theater's manager (his sons, Jack and Robert, helped him run the Apollo in the 1940s and '50s). In 1946, Frank Schiffman began keeping notes on each act that played the Apollo, typing his musings on small, five by eight inch index cards. Schiffman kept his note card system carefully organized, with each card listing the date of the act's opening night, how much each act was paid (down to the last cent) and Schiffman's personal critiques of the performers. When he retired in 1976, Schiffman had amassed a collection of more than one thousand, two hundred cards—including one on Foxx and White.

Schiffman's note card on Foxx and White lists the act as having made six appearances at the Apollo, with varying degrees of success, between 1950 and 1952. For their first appearance, they were paid $350, plus another $11.67 cents for an "xtra" show. "Corny. Can stand improvement. Do not repeat," Schiffman typed on his card. But he obviously didn't take his own advice, since Foxx and White appeared again on October 18, 1950, again for the same $350. "Satisfactory," was all that Schiffman typed on his card. Redd and Slappy returned to the Apollo five months later, on March 7, 1951, this time upping their fee to $375 but, in Schiffman's assessment, giving only a perfunctory performance: "Practically same routine. Some new material. Satisfactory."

Foxx and White's next Apollo appearance, on October 26, 1951, went over better with Schiffman, who increased their pay to $400. "Changed some of their material. Went over nicely," he typed on his card. The good vibes continued for Foxx and White's following engagement, seven months later, on May 23, 1952: "Some new material. Good comedy act," Schiffman noted. But only three months later, on August 22, 1952, just before Redd and Slappy joined Dinah Washington in Los Angeles, Schiffman was typing a different tune: "Worse (sic) routine they have ever gave (sic) us."

However good Foxx and White might have been as a comedy act, the unmovable hand of segregation made sure they would never break through to the "mainstream" clubs outside of the Chitlin' Circuit. And that really pissed Redd off. "Nobody wanted to hire us on a white job," he recalled. "The most we ever made was $450 a week for the two of us."

White comedy teams like Dean Martin and Jerry Lewis were getting huge exposure, not only in the country's top mainstream nightclubs but on the burgeoning medium of television, which was quickly overtaking radio as America's medium of choice. One three-minute spot on *The Ed Sullivan Show* or on Milton "Uncle Miltie" Berle's hugely popular *Texaco Star Theater*, even in those prehistoric days of television, could make a career. But those doors were closed to black comedy acts, at least those acts *not* of the Stepin Fetchit variety. "The white public's concept of black comedy was two white guys in plaid suits, shuffling about with a broom, and doing an act in blackface," Redd said. "A black stand-up comic couldn't find a job." Even the most famous black-oriented radio show, *Amos 'n' Andy*, was headlined by its two white creators, Free-man Gosden and Charles Correll, who played all the roles; they even donned blackface when, in 1930, RKO brought *Amos 'n' Andy* to the big screen in *Check and Double Check* (borrowing the title from one of the show's catchphrases). It wasn't until *Amos 'n' Andy* moved to television, in 1951, that black actors played all the roles (and were instructed to sound as much like Gosden and Correll as possible).

"REDD FOXX LOOKED BETTER ON A MARQUEE"

And if the Chitlin' Circuit was tough on the psyches of the black performers who resented its restrictions, both personally and professionally, the physical demands of traveling around the country, sometimes without a proper place to stay, didn't make life any easier. Many were the stories Redd would tell of how he was often booked into a local black theater—only to be forced to sleep in the train station or on a bus if the local "coloreds-only" hotel had no vacancy.

By the summer of 1952, circumstances were about to change for Foxx and White. Los Angeles beckoned—and with it the promise of a new beginning.

chapter four

"I Gave It to Them Funky"

Slappy White's marriage to Pearl Bailey might not have been one for the ages, but it did put him in the company of some very influential performers. One of Pearl's friends was jazz singer Dinah Washington who, in the summer of 1952, invited Redd and Slappy to be her opening act out in Los Angeles.

Foxx and White were, at the time, traveling with Washington's revue, and had opened for Dinah several times before, including a run at the Royal Theater in Baltimore. Washington was taking the show across the country to California, and wanted Redd and Slappy to join her there. It was the big break the comedy team was hoping for. Washington, who was affectionately called "The Queen" or "Miss D" by most of her close friends, was twenty-seven years old, at the top of her game, and married to the second of her eventual eight husbands. Her popularity, which began to climb after she joined Lionel Hampton's band in 1943, continued to skyrocket after she took her act solo, producing two big hits, "Baby Get Lost" and "Trouble in Mind." Washington was making big money now after hits like "Cold, Cold Heart" and "Mad About the Boy," and offered Redd and Slappy $1,000 a week to be her opening act in California. It was an offer they couldn't refuse, and was a chance for Foxx and White to be discovered by a West Coast audience after slogging through the Chitlin' Circuit. It sounded like a good deal.

Slappy recalled later that he and Redd had less than one hundred dollars to their names as they prepared to make the long cross-country trip. A chunk of that cash went into buying a chartreuse Oldsmobile convertible; they'd take turns driving, and figured it might take them a week before they reached Los Angeles and the good life in sunny California. But the Oldsmobile had seen better days, and there were mechanical problems from the outset; the car wheezed and rattled along Route 66 and lived just long enough to roll into Denver on a flat tire, carrying two dead-broke comedians wondering just how they would get to Los Angeles with empty pockets—and a car with three tires.

Slappy devised a plan to get the pair out of their jam. Luckily, they'd rolled into a black section of Denver, and would take advantage of their situation. The plan was for Redd to fake a terrible illness and force the unwitting gas station attendant to call for the nearest black doctor. More than likely, the doctor lived in a more upscale neighborhood, and could somehow be snookered out of some dough to pay for a new tire *and* fund the last leg of Foxx and White's journey to Los Angeles.

Redd sprang into action, moaning and groaning and holding his belly as Slappy got out of the car to inspect the flat tire. The plan worked like a charm; the gas station attendant put the call out for a doctor, and before too long Dr. Emmett Kincaid pulled into the gas station in his white Cadillac, took one look at Redd—still moaning and groaning—and decided he needed immediate medical attention. Dr. Kincaid loaded Redd and Slappy into his car and drove them back to his office. "As luck would have it, the good doctor took a liking to us, especially Redd with his mysterious disease that disappeared just as mysteriously, and he invited us back to his house for dinner," Slappy recalled. "The dinner was good, but it was the poker game afterwards that saved us."

Dr. Kincaid lived in a colonial-style mansion on the outskirts of Denver, and after introducing Redd and Slappy to his wife, Muriel— "She looked like something out of a 1940s Lena Horne Hollywood musical, wiggling around in one of them silky silver gowns," Slappy recalled—they sat down to a huge turkey dinner with all the trimmings (Redd's appetite having magically returned). The plan was for Slappy to talk Dr. Kincaid into a game of poker after dessert, giving Foxx and White a chance to hustle their way to a chunk of change. Their hearts sank, though, when Dr. Kincaid suggested a game of billiards—a game neither Redd nor Slappy played very well. But their moods brightened when the doctor, who'd been doubling over in laughter at every one of Redd's ripostes, agreed to play a few hands of poker. And, sweetening the deal, he invited four other friends to join the game—four more suckers to hustle. "All I could see was they looked like money," Slappy said of his and Redd's new poker buddies. "All of them wore business suits and ties, and they was all young enough so they wouldn't know a poker hustler when they seen one. Except maybe for the one white dude, who was the only one who didn't look like he just come from church."

Redd and Slappy bought one hundred dollars worth of chips apiece, explaining away their lack of cash to pay for the chips with a shaggy dog story about not being able to cash a substantial check while out on the road. After a few hours, Slappy had cleaned up on everyone else at the table, including Redd. By the time the game broke up at 2:00 a.m. it was too late for Redd and Slappy to return back to town for their car, so Dr. Kincaid invited them to spend the night. When they got up to their room, Slappy added up the kitty. They'd hustled $750—more than enough to pay for the new tire and continue on to Los Angeles.

The diversion with Dr. Kincaid and his unsuspecting poker pals turned out to be the lone highlight of Redd and Slappy's cross-country trip. They finally arrived in Los Angeles to join Dinah Washington, who was headlining at Frank Sebastian's Cotton Club in Culver City. The Cotton Club was one of the city's premiere jazz clubs catering to a black clientele, and was perhaps best known as the place where Louis "Satchmo" Armstrong was busted in 1931 for marijuana possession.

But from the get-go, Redd and Slappy's engagement with Washington didn't go as planned. Something just didn't seem right. The two men, who were expecting a more liberal attitude in Los Angeles, were put off by the city's overt racism and its segregation policies—no better than what Foxx and White had experienced back east. "California was a drag," Redd said. "We worked with Dinah, but about a month after we got out here, Slappy and I broke up. That was the end of our four years together."

The breakup, it turned out, was over money—and Redd's battered ego. At the end of their Cotton Club gig, it was Slappy who Dinah Washington asked to travel back east with her—and not Redd. Redd didn't count on his comedy partner accepting "Miss D's" offer, but Slappy was tired of California, and was eager to bolt the scene. He quickly accepted Washington's invitation—leaving Redd in the lurch, alone, and in dire financial straits in a city he didn't like. "Man, there just wasn't enough money for the two of us," Slappy said. Redd was pissed off at his erstwhile comedy partner, but there wasn't much he could do. Their messy breakup drove a wedge between Redd and Slappy. Time, and Redd's eventual success, would heal the rift. For Slappy, the move back east paid handsome dividends. He picked up steady work, and, after a short time, became Dinah Washington's regular emcee at her club dates.

Redd turned thirty years old that December. He was alone and nearly penniless in Los Angeles, and his prospects, sans Slappy White, were bleak. He didn't care much for L.A.'s segregated vibe, but he loved the climate, and he wasn't about to go back to the bitter cold of Harlem or Saint Louis or Chicago—where his mother and brother were still struggling to get by. While Redd, at least, had experienced a modicum of success, his revered older brother seemed to be a lost soul. Fred Sanford, blessed as he was with superb athletic ability, especially on the baseball diamond, had fallen in with a tough crowd in Chicago. He didn't have the resiliency or street smarts of Jon who, faced with equally tough obstacles in his own life, overcame them with ingenuity and moxie.

Around 1940, Mary Sanford had gotten Fred a tryout with the Chicago White Sox by pulling some strings with her boss, one of the team's vice presidents. It wasn't really a tryout for the White Sox, per se, since Major League Baseball was still segregated at the time, and Jackie Robinson wouldn't break the color barrier with the Brooklyn Dodgers for another seven years. The best that Fred could hope for would be to impress a Negro League team by showing off his skills in front of White Sox executives, which he failed to do. "He was the greatest third baseman that ever lived," Redd said of his brother with typically unapologetic hyperbole. "But they didn't really give him a chance. It was too early for a black man to make it in the majors. That hurt him till the day he died." Fred, who'd already been in trouble with the law, turned to a life of petty crime. He would spend the next two decades in and out of trouble in Chicago, serving a few stretches in jail and battling diabetes and a rare kidney condition that would eventually kill him at the age of forty-six.

Redd, meanwhile, needed to find work in Los Angeles. His month-long stint with Slappy at the Cotton Club wasn't long enough time to earn him any particular notice on the city's club circuit, and he was finding work more difficult now that he was a "single" act in a city that didn't exactly roll out the red carpet to young black comics. But one thing that Redd Foxx had going for him, especially when the chips were down, was his motor mouth and his self-confidence. With his gregarious nature, his likeability, and his sense of humor, he made friends easily, and before long had landed a job in the kitchen of the Club Alabam, a swingin' jazz joint located in the city's Central Avenue district.

The Alabam, which was owned by jazz drummer and bandleader Curtis Mosby, was a landing place for many black entertainers who were new to Los Angeles, and was a regular hangout for celebrities including Joe Louis, Ella Fitzgerald, Ethel Waters, and Billie Holiday. Next door to the Alabam was the Brownskin Café, which was owned and operated by Tila Ali. Her husband, Bardu Ali, and the Club Alabam's resident bandleader, Johnny Otis, would both play pivotal roles in Redd's career.

Redd's job in the Club Alabam kitchen didn't last long. Once management realized they had "the funniest dishwasher on this earth" in their midst, they moved Redd into the main room as a standup act. This was new territory for Redd; his only previous experience working a room as a solo act was at Gamby's in Baltimore—nearly a decade before—and his infrequent one-nighters, telling jokes for five bucks a night in seedy Newark joints during his marriage to Evelyn.

By now, Redd had ditched the silly bowl haircut he'd sported during the run of Foxx and White. And without Slappy as his straight man, he began taking his solo act at the Club Alabam in new directions. His stage patter had always been largely improvised, and would continue to be throughout the rest of his career. But unlike before, Redd now peppered his act with audience putdowns, which were usually aimed at his target's personal appearance—years before "the Merchant of Venom," Don Rickles, made a career out of audience putdowns. He chided female hecklers with lines like, "I didn't recognize your voice, but your lips look familiar," or "Black women have an advantage. They can have varicose veins and nobody can tell it." To a hostile audience, he would often fire back, "What did you come here for—revenge?" He used humor to poke fun at *verboten* topics, typically sex and bodily functions, which no mainstream comedian would ever think of discussing onstage in the prissy, straight-laced Eisenhower era. But while working the smaller, segregated clubs kept those "mainstream" doors closed for now, it also liberated Redd from the strictures of adhering to "acceptable" comedic norms. He could do his act without reproach—and his audience loved it.

Redd's stream-of-consciousness approach set him apart from the typical club comics of his day. Comedians in the mid-1950s would rattle off a series of jokes helter-skelter and maybe throw in a celebrity impersonation or two. Redd was a different comic beast. Many of his friends were jazz musicians, and he'd spent his years in clubs grooving to jazz riffs and immersing himself in their weed-scented lifestyle. What he did now was to cut and paste jazz's freeform vibe to his stage act, infusing his onstage patter and pacing with an almost anything-goes attitude. It pushed him toward a style that seemed leisurely and off-the-cuff as he strung together a loose mélange of comic stories, riffing on whatever seemed to pop into his head. And he used the language of the streets, since he felt that made him more identifiable and accessible to his black audience. "That's the humor I heard in the ghettos," he said. "They didn't pull no punches, and they didn't want to hear about Little Boy Blue and Cinderella. So I gave them what they wanted. I busted loose."

Redd's standup act at the Club Alabam went over well and was good enough to get him noticed elsewhere. His club dates in and around Los Angeles began to increase with frequency in 1953 and 1954. But money was still tight, and to help supplement his hit-or-miss club income, Redd began moonlighting as an assistant to Johnny Otis, the star DJ at KFOX radio in Long Beach.

Otis, who was almost exactly a year older than Redd, was only in his early thirties at the time, but was already a legend in the black community and in Los Angeles music circles. Born John Veliotes, he was the son of Greek immigrants and grew up in a largely black neighborhood in Berkeley, California. Heavily influenced by the black culture around him, John Veliotes changed his name to Johnny Otis in 1943, because he considered himself "black by persuasion."

A talented musician who played drums, piano, and vibraphone and fronted his own band, Otis became a leading figure in the Los Angeles music scene soon after moving to the city in the early 1940s. He first met Redd when he took his "Johnny Otis Show" to Baltimore's Royal Theatre in 1950, where Foxx and White shared the bill. Otis opened the popular Barrelhouse Club in Watts with Redd's future manager, Bardu Ali, in 1947, fronted the house band at the Club Alabam (where he was re-acquainted with Redd), and was responsible for discovering and nurturing talents including Esther "Little Esther" Phillips, Etta

James, and Big Jay McNeely. Otis produced and played drums on Big Mama Thornton's recording of "Hound Dog"—later to become one of Elvis Presley's biggest hits—and wrote and recorded "Willie and the Hand Jive," which shot to number nine on the pop charts in 1958. Redd's childhood friend, LaWanda Page, belonged to Otis's congregation at the Landmark Community Church in Los Angeles.

In the early fifties, Otis began hosting his daily rhythm-and-blues show on KFOX, which soon became one of the area's top-rated radio shows. According to local legend, a person could drive along the beach from Los Angeles to San Diego without switching on the car radio—but could still hear *The Johnny Otis Show* blaring from transistor radios dotting the beach and from cars passing by with their windows down. Among the show's biggest fans was future Beach Boys leader Brian Wilson, who was turned on to Otis by his younger brother, Carl.

Redd joined Otis around 1954, doing whatever needed to be done around the radio station and keeping Otis entertained while he was off the air. While Otis spun his R&B records, Redd would often amuse himself by doodling on a sketch pad. One of the drawings he sketched in the studio while working on *The Johnny Otis Show* was a "self-portrait," in which he dressed himself in a white dinner jacket, white shorts, red, knee-high socks, and black shoes. Redd kept the sketch, which would later become the cover for his first album, *Laff of the Party*.

In addition to his radio show and his work as a musician, Otis also hosted a weekly television show on KTTV, which featured musicians, comedians, and local acts, including Redd, on occasion. *The Johnny Otis Show* had its own cast of regulars, including a singing group called Three Tons of Joy, fronted by Marie Adams and her sisters, Sadie and Francine McKinley. "These were three rather large women singers," says author Nathaniel Mackey, who grew up in the area. "It was like a variety show. Redd Foxx appeared, I mean, a very sanitized Redd Foxx would come on and do comedy. But it was fun."

According to Johnny Otis biographer George Lipsitz, offstage Redd was "frequently sullen, grumpy, and morose"—completely opposite to the comedian who, on the air with Otis one night, told KFOX listeners that they shouldn't fear an attack from Russian troops, who would never be able to find a parking spot in Los Angeles. But Redd had a malicious side, and Otis was aghast one day when Redd ridiculed a friend so mercilessly that the guy broke down in tears.

Redd showed his more mean-spirited side in other ways. When Redd asked Otis if his mother, Mary, and her second husband, Harry Carson, could stay with Johnny, he agreed—and then couldn't get rid of the couple, who overstayed their welcome. When Otis asked Redd why he couldn't—or wouldn't—accommodate his own mother and stepfather, Redd told him that Harry Carson was okay, but that he felt differently about his own mother. "I can't stand that bitch," he said.

The money Redd made working for Johnny Otis helped him keep his head above water, but times were still tough. His nightclub work was sporadic at best and what work he did get didn't pay much, maybe twenty-five or fifty dollars for one or two shows a night. Redd made it tougher on himself, since he saved absolutely nothing of what he earned, compulsively spending his cash on women, booze, marijuana, and cocaine—using more of the white powder now than ever before. The profligate spending was a pattern he was destined to repeat, exacerbated later in his life once he became a millionaire. "I was doing so bad . . . making seventy five bucks a week," he said. "I got a raise and thought I was going great-guns making one hundred dollars! There was just nowhere to appear. I had to work where the broads got naked."

But Redd's spending was his Achilles heel in more ways than one, and wasn't just limited to his own hedonistic pleasures. He had a good heart below the wiseass demeanor and all the bravado, and was a sucker for anyone looking for a handout. He was always willing to help a friend, or even a casual acquaintance, with a few bucks—even if it meant emptying his pockets of what little cash he had.

Redd's luck took a turn for the better in the middle of 1954, when he was booked into the Oasis Club, a small, but popular, nightclub on Thirty-eighth and Western in the Crenshaw District of Los Angeles. The gig wouldn't make him a fortune, but it was steady work—every Saturday and Sunday night, two shows a night, at twenty-five bucks a pop. Word of Redd's "raw" act had spread after his stint at the Club Alabam, and the audiences who filtered into the Oasis each weekend night weren't disappointed. Redd's off-the-cuff double entendres and naughty verbal wordplay kept the place in stitches. His enthusiastic audiences literally howled with laughter as Redd talked playfully about subjects like farting and genital hygiene—subjects everyone could relate to but no one else dared to broach in public, let alone on the stage of a nightclub.

"I wasn't allowed to work in white places. . . . I couldn't even get into white clubs, let alone play them," he said. "So I had to work where the spooks were. And they don't want to hear no *Christian Science Monitor* stuff—they want nitty-gritty. So I gave it to them funky like they like it. There was always a double standard for comics in nightclubs. Black comics didn't get the big bookings, so they were allowed to be dirtier, expected to be."

It was earthy, scatological humor, told in the jazzy rhythm Redd heard on the streets of Saint Louis, Chicago, and Harlem and in the small-time clubs on the Chitlin' Circuit, where a sense of shared community bonded the performer with his audience. "Foxx removed the rural black dialect, molded the humor of these acts, and placed it within a contemporary urban context," said author Christine Acham. "His comedy was specifically created for black audiences and was not easily extricated from that context . . . His gravelly voice may have given him the down-home feel of Moms Mabley; however, he had the attitude of the 'Bad Nigger' of African American folklore."

This "Bad Nigger," though, spoke with his tongue planted firmly in his cheek. Redd's humor was rarely mean-spirited. His comebacks to hecklers were pointed, but funny. And while he wasn't overtly political, he still spoke directly to his black audience. "The president can end poverty by making rats as expensive as chinchilla," was one of his favorite lines. He would acknowledge the horrors of segregation but, at the same time, strike a vein of humor in the situation: "I don't even go down South. They found a Negro in Mississippi with six hundred pounds of chains wrapped around his body. Found him in the river. The sheriff viewed his remains and says, 'Just like one of them niggers, steal more chains than he can carry.'"

Politics wasn't Redd's bag. He focused, instead, on the interplay between men and women, on what was said and *wasn't* said between the sexes, subjects everyone could relate to. Unlike his white contemporary Lenny Bruce, Redd never used profanity, but specialized in playful sexual innuendo and double entendres. "He was the first of the *urban* black comics," said Quincy Jones, "and Dick Gregory and Flip Wilson and all the others who came later took from *him*."

Redd's growing reputation as an "X-rated" comedian derived from the taboo subjects he discussed but not from the language he used. His material was, in show-biz parlance, considered "blue," but he never,

ever uttered the word "fuck" or "shit," or "suck" on stage in those early days. In Redd Foxx-speak, "Fugg" and "Sugg" were much funnier, and he used the terms in his classic routine, "The New Fugg," with "Fugg" being a brand of soap and "Sugg" being a spot remover. The routine, which was included on Redd's first album, *Laff of the Party*, ended with this kicker: "And remember, ladies, if you can't Fugg it . . . you get the idea." It was snigger humor full of naughty wordplay, touching those raw nerves of sexual tension between men and women. "What's the difference between a pickpocket and a peeping Tom?" he would ask his audience. "A pickpocket snatches watches."

Meanwhile, several hundred miles up the coast, another young, verbally dexterous, white comic named Mort Sahl was making a name for himself in San Francisco, home of the Beat movement and an incubator for social experimentation. Sahl, armed on stage with that day's newspaper and dressed in his trademark V-neck sweater, riffed on foibles both domestic and international and was starting to gain some notoriety in the mainstream press. Those doors were closed to Redd, but he shared many of Sahl's comedic tics. Redd, of course, focused more on bodily odors and sexual peccadilloes than politics, but his bits were delivered with a similar veneer of streetwise savvy and insight. Redd regretted never finishing high school, and he compensated for his lack of a degree by becoming a voracious reader of books, magazines, and newspapers—all of which became fodder for his routines.

He was starting to create some buzz and to impress a lot of people in Los Angeles, including entrepreneur Dootsie Williams, the founder and president of Dooto Records, who heard about Redd's act and went to the Oasis one Saturday night to see for himself what all the fuss was about. Born Walter R. Williams Jr. in 1911—the nickname "Dootsie" came from a garbled interpretation of the Spanish word "Dulce"—he was a horn player by trade who worked predominantly on the West Coast. In 1949, he gave up performing and started Blue Records, which had some moderate success with a catalogue of blues records, R&B tracks, and raunchy songs like Billy Mitchell's "Song of the Woodpecker" (*He pecked and he pecked on my front door/Pecked 'til he made his pecker sore*).

Williams folded Blue Records in 1951 and changed the label's name to Dootone. The Dootone label issued mostly pop recordings (including two singles by violinist Johnny Creach, who would later find fame

as "Papa John" Creach) and had a big success in 1954 with "Earth An-
gel," recorded by the Doo Wop group the Penguins, which rose to number eight in the charts. In 1955, Williams changed the label's name to
Dooto Records (to avoid a lawsuit from Duo-Tone Records) and began
issuing a combination of "novelty" and R&B records. It was around
this time that Williams wandered into the Oasis to hear Redd's act. "I
listened to this guy, and he wasn't really obscene, just naughty by those
standards," he said. "But then, he was so outrageous in such a way
that nobody would ever think of putting him on record. But I thought,
'This guy can sell.' If he could shock and make such an impression that
people would fall out in the aisles on him, I said, 'This will sell.'"

Redd would do anything to make a quick buck, and was only too
happy to oblige Williams, who talked about recording his act. "While
I was in a club at Thirty-eighth and Western, a real popular place, a
black cat named Dootsie Williams came in and said, 'Why don't you
put this material on record. It might sell,'" he recalled. "It was a black
thing, in a sense, so I said I'd go ahead and record for my black brother,
because nobody else had offered me anything."

So Williams, armed with a tape recorder, sat in the Oasis Club
audience one night shortly thereafter and recorded Redd's act—without paying the comedian (and without Redd's knowledge). Williams
then took the recording to some "church people" he knew and played
them the tape. "They went crazy!" he said. "One lady says, 'I'm going back to Texas, can you make me a copy?' And so then I went back
to Redd Foxx and told him, I said, 'People would buy this. I'd like to
release it.' Redd said, 'Man, nobody's gonna take my act. If I record it
they won't want to see me live. No. No!'

"So the next day I see him and he's broke, and he says, 'Hey, what
was that you were saying last night about recording?' I said, 'I'll give
you twenty-five dollars if you just let me bring my recording set and
I'll record your whole act.' He says, 'Okay,' and the rest is history."
"History" also has a way of being rewritten—and sometimes blur-
ring the lines of reality. In later years, in various retellings of the story,
Williams offered Redd anywhere from twenty-five dollars to $100 or
even $125 to record his act at the Oasis. Whatever he paid him, it
turned out to be the biggest bargain of Dootsie Williams' life.

The recording was nice, but Redd figured it probably wouldn't
amount to much. And in the small-time club world, where promises

were made to be broken, who knew if Williams would ever release it? Besides, Redd had other things on his mind—particularly a shapely young singer named Betty Jeanne Harris.

chapter five

"The King of the Party Records"

Redd was smitten the first time he laid eyes on Betty Jeanne Harris, who was booked into the Oasis Club with her two sisters, Marcene and Beverly, in 1955. The singing Harris Sisters, who hailed from Oklahoma, were talented enough to land a contract with Capitol Records and, in 1955, had a minor hit with a perky tune called "Kissin' Bug." That same year, they charted with a Doo Wop-style tune called "We've Been Walking All Night" (also on Capitol). Like Redd, Marcene Harris, who was nicknamed "Dimples," had cut a few tracks for Savoy Records (in 1951) with a group called the Dimples Harris Trio (but not with her sisters). "Marcene, 'Dimples,' the little one, she had the talent," said Beverly Harris. "She taught us the songs, she put the show together, and we did it." The sisters' younger brother, Kent Harris, would become a songwriter of some renown, penning "Shoppin' for Clothes," which was a hit for the Coasters, and "Cops and Robbers," which Bo Diddley recorded in 1957.

Betty Jeanne had married businessman Milton Kelsey in the mid-1940s and the couple had a daughter they named Debraca, who was born in 1949. Jeanne and Milton Kelsey eventually divorced, and Debraca remained in the care of relatives while Jeanne, Beverly, and Marcene hit the road as the Harris Sisters. "We worked more classy clubs, more high-class things," Beverly said. "We had to be very careful where we worked. I was eighteen in those days. You had to be twenty-one [to work in the clubs], and that was a big problem at times." When the Harris Sisters were booked into the Oasis Club, Redd watched them from the audience, since he hadn't yet been hired as the club's comic and emcee. "I looked up there and I loved her," he said of his first

53

encounter with Betty Jeanne. "I was just in the background standing there wishing I had a job. But I finally got a job there. I stood outside until she left, and she left with another guy."

While it was love at first sight for Redd, Betty Jeanne wasn't particularly impressed with this guy who was hanging around backstage and flirting with her. For one thing, she didn't care for his brand of smutty humor. "I didn't like the jokes he was telling," she said. "At that time I thought they were awful." But Betty Jeanne wasn't aware of Redd's "foxy" way with the ladies; he could lay on the charm like nobody's business, and was rarely lacking for female companionship. It wasn't long before she fell under his spell. "I was young and handsome," he said. "A lot of girls go for a face rather than a job." "He would come in the dressing room and come in and kiss me while I was asleep," Betty Jeanne said. "But I didn't really like him at first. . . . But he said, 'I'm gonna marry you.'"

Once he hooked his bait, it was Redd who played hard-to-get. It was all part of the game. "I would see Redd backstage and he would never pay any attention to me," Betty Jeanne recalled. "For some reason, he would laugh and talk with my sisters. I didn't like him because he would be loud in the dressing room. Because the job me and my sisters had didn't pay much money, I also held a day job, and between shows I would sleep on a cot in the dressing room."

One day, Redd went back into the Harris Sisters' dressing room, where Betty Jeanne was lying on the cot, taking a nap. "I was cussing," he said. "Anyway, it was show business. I wasn't cussing to be nasty, it's just the way you talked. And she says, 'Who is that nasty guy?' She said to get him out of there. So that's the way we started."

"He was just chasing her down," Betty Jeanne's sister, Beverly, recalled. "One day, Betty Jeanne drove me with her to where Redd lived and she paid his rent, because he couldn't afford his rent that month. And I found that pretty strange, but I said nothing. So I knew then that she liked him too. So that was it."

Redd and Betty Jeanne embarked on a whirlwind romance and, one week later, they were married in Las Vegas. Beverly said she was "totally shocked" when the couple ran off to tie the knot. "But I was happy because he was a nice guy at that time, very friendly," she said of Redd. "My parents did not care for him, though—they thought he was too nasty. They didn't like his jokes—he was kind of nasty, poor taste for those years with bad words and stuff, and my parents definitely did not like him. We came from a family that didn't curse or say anything bad or wrong or degrading at all—and he was just the opposite. But I found him very funny. I just laughed."

The newly married couple returned to Los Angeles, determined to tour together as an act. Betty Jeanne, who now sometimes billed herself as "Jean Vegas," would provide the music, backed by Redd's standup comedy. Their marriage meant the end of the Harris Sisters, but not the end of Marcene or Beverly's singing careers. Marcene would continue to record for the next decade, sometimes billed as "Dimples" Harris (on singles including "This I Do Believe" and "If You'll Be True") and other times as "Marcene" Harris ("A Song To You," "Work It Out," and "I Just Don't Understand"). Beverly, meanwhile, had a short stint singing with the Platters, filling in for the group's only female member, Zola Taylor, for a few weeks in New York in 1959. She would play a different role in Redd's life further down the road.

But the end of the Harris Sisters also meant new beginnings for Redd and Jeanne. And that included Jeanne's daughter, Debraca. Redd always had a soft spot for children, and now that he and Jeanne were settled in, Debraca came to live with her mother and new stepfather in Los Angeles. Shortly thereafter, Redd agreed to adopt Debraca, and her name was legally changed to Debraca Foxx.

In the meantime, Dootsie Williams had proven to be a man of his word. In early 1956, Dooto Records released *Laff of the Party, Volume 1*, which featured Redd's self-caricature on the cover (the sketch he'd drawn while working for Johnny Otis). The back of the album jacket featured a black-and-white photograph of Redd, with closely cropped hair and a thin moustache, mugging for the camera. Alongside Redd's photo were a few paragraphs of hyperbole-laced liner notes, which began:

> "The Funniest Man in the World," is what they say of Redd Foxx and in hearing the contents of this album you will agree. In these recordings, which were made at actual performances at theaters nightclubs and parties, you hear Redd's unequaled sense of humor along with carloads of hysterical laughter that is hilarious proof of this rare genius.

Laff of the Party, Volume 1 is a slapdash collection of bits and pieces of Redd's act, backed by raucous laughter (and the occasional shouted comment) from his Oasis Club audience, which sometimes sounds like a packed house and other times like only a handful of cackling customers. The record, about thirty-seven minutes long, is short on production values—about what you'd expect to hear, aurally, from a reel-to-reel tape recorder in a small nightclub. It's divided into eight tracks, four on each side. The tracks on Side One are "Backward Conscious," "The Sneezes," "Song Plugging," and "The New Soap"; Side Two has "The Honeymooners," "The Politician," "The Jackasses," and "The Race Track."

Judging *Laff of the Party, Volume 1* by the standards of the times, it comes across as risqué, but the beauty of Redd Foxx's humor lies in his clever wordplay. There is no profanity on *Laff of the Party, Volume 1*, but there are plenty of double entendres sprinkled throughout Redd's four-to-five-minute-long monologues. Sometimes the wordplay catches Redd's audience off-guard, and their laughter is a beat behind as they struggle to keep up with his rapid-fire delivery, to digest the verbal volley he's just lobbed at them. At other times, Redd's Oasis Club audience is right there with him, almost giddy with anticipation as he winds up and gets ready to lob his next zinger.

The record begins (somewhat abruptly, without any introduction) with "Backward Conscious," in which Redd riffs on how some words spelled backwards have other meanings. "Did you know 'motel' spelled backward was 'letom'?" On "The Sneezes," constructed loosely around different types of sneezes ("The confessional sneeze: 'Ah Chew!'"), Redd segues into cigarette smoking with a smutty twist: "Do you know that out of four hundred, forty-six doctors that switched to Camels, only two of 'em went back to women?"

"Song Plugging" is a takeoff on the old show-biz practice of selling, or "plugging," sheet music or different acts to stores and record labels. But there's a Foxx-ian twist when Redd talks about all his success "plugging" in New York City: "Pieces like Laura, Marie, Margie. Those were good pieces. I plugged all those pieces, I plugged 'em all. I plugged that Old Gray Mare, but she ain't what she used to be."

In one of the record's most memorable tracks, "The New Soap," Redd talks to housewives in the audience about a new cleaning product called "Fugg": "Suppose your husband works on a dirty job, in a coal mine, on a truck, in a garage . . . when he comes home all dirty and nasty, when he opens the door and walks into the house, tell him to go

Fugg himself." Redd then segues into Garbage Can Week. "Bend over and look in your can . . . you have to check your can. Your neighbor could be using your can and you don't know what your neighbor might be putting in it. I suggested you Fugg your can or let someone Fugg it for you." In "The New Soap" kicker, Redd talks about Fugg's companion product, a detergent called Sugg. "So remember, folks, wherever you go and whatever you do, if you can't Fugg it . . . you get the idea."

He continues the smutty wordplay on "The Politician," adopting the hectoring tone of a politician in telling the women in the audience to be careful of casting their votes: "As long as you split like you are, the men will always be on top." On "The Jackasses," he reminisces about the time everyone in his town got their own jackass, including his preacher and the preacher's wife. "The preacher's wife had the biggest ass in town. I know because I rode her big ass all the time. It was the biggest ass I've ever been on. You ought to see the muscles in her big ass; sometimes her ass would sweat and I'd slip right off her sweaty ass. Because I had no saddle, you see."

Laff of the Party, Volume 1 concludes with "The Race Track," a bit that Dootsie Williams would cut-and-splice onto several of Redd's future Dooto releases. The scenario here is a horse race at Santa Anita between Cold Towel, Pussy Willow, and My Dick—with Redd narrating the race in a staccato voice—"My Dick slipped and fell!"—before the kicker: "I never saw My Dick run before. What a race! The winner by half an inch is My Dick!"

Meanwhile, Redd and Betty Jeanne bought a 1936 Plymouth and hit the road in search of work. *Laff of the Party, Volume 1* was hitting the record stores—an added bonus for Redd, who could promote himself on the strength of his first album. But while club owners were more willing to book him now, and the gigs (with Jeanne in tow) were starting to fall into place, it was a bittersweet time. Like other black performers, Redd was growing increasingly frustrated by the doors that *weren't* open to him. While he was working more regularly now, the "mainstream" clubs were still off-limits. Segregation was alive and well. The Chitlin' Circuit was thriving.

What that meant, for a performer like Redd Foxx, was lower pay and less of a chance for major exposure. The "white" mainstream clubs paid more and attracted the powerful show-business types who could make a career with one phone call to a powerful newspaper or magazine columnist like Walter Winchell, Dorothy Kilgallen, or Hedda Hopper. And the big mainstream clubs offered the chance that maybe, just maybe, you'd be "discovered" by a talent scout or producer and offered the Big Kahuna—a shot on a coast-to-coast television show. What were the chances of *that* happening if you were a black performer?

Even A-list black stars like Sammy Davis Jr., Louis Armstrong, and Nat King Cole felt the sting of segregation. Sure, they were welcome to come to Las Vegas to entertain the high rollers, and were paid good money to do so. But Las Vegas, despite its reputation for glitz and glamour and its "anything goes" attitude, wasn't any less suffocating in its prejudice than the rest of segregated America. Black performers like Davis and Armstrong weren't allowed to stay in the hotels in which they worked, and were forced to stay in blacks-only boarding houses on the city's Westside district or, later, at the Moulin Rouge, Sin City's first integrated hotel/casino located in West Las Vegas (which opened in 1955). And once they arrived to work at a hotel or a club, a black entertainer had to enter through a side entrance or, even more humiliating, through the kitchen.

Black entertainers performing on the Strip in Las Vegas weren't allowed into any of the hotels' main showrooms, casinos, rooms or restaurants. In 1953, the Last Frontier Hotel drained its entire pool after singer and actress Dorothy Dandridge deliberately dipped her foot into the water. It wasn't until 1955 that Nat King Cole became the first black entertainer to stay in a "white" Las Vegas hotel (the Sands), but he was the exception. Most of the other big hotels on the Strip remained segregated until the end of the decade.

"There was a black color line in Vegas," recalled George Schlatter, who managed nightclubs in Las Vegas and in Hollywood, including Ciro's on the Sunset Strip. He would later create *Laugh-In* for NBC (and would direct Redd in *Norman, Is That You?*). "Black people couldn't get in the hotel. They couldn't stand in the hotel. They couldn't come in and see the shows. When I booked Sammy [Davis Jr.] into the Frontier after his eye accident, I said to [owner Jake Kozloff], 'You're going to have to let black people come and see the show. If you don't, Sammy's going to go to the Sands.' So we booked Sammy—nobody played Vegas for more than ten days and Sammy was booked for six weeks. Because he had worked for me at Ciro's, Sammy and I were very close. He opened at the Frontier and it just ignited everything."

"I could perform in Vegas, but I could not eat there, sleep there, or gamble there," said Della Reese. "I lived in a place called 'The Dustbowl' and it was named accurately because there was not a piece of pavement on the ground. It was dusty. If it hadn't been for a black doctor and his wife, who came from Chicago and built around five houses, we would have been starring on the Strip and sleeping in a dirty Holiday Inn."

It was a double-edged sword for those black entertainers, particularly comedians, who did manage to get a shot on television. They were expected to replicate their Chitlin' Circuit acts for mainstream America rather than being given the chance to stretch and prove they could do something different. *Amos 'n' Andy* had transitioned to television in 1951, with an all-black cast replacing the radio original's white actors. Still, many in the black community objected. The powerful NAACP (National Association for the Advancement of Colored People) took offense to the show's perpetuation of black stereotypes, even while, in theory, it strove to portray its characters as more upwardly mobile. (Criminals who appeared on *Amos 'n' Andy* were usually white.) Letters of complaint were written to the show-business bible, *Variety*, and the NAACP's charge was taken up by various liberal organizations, including the American Jewish Committee, who deemed the show "regressive."

While it was difficult for a black performer to get a shot on a mainstream television show, the inevitable backlash—especially in the South, still governed by Jim Crow laws—didn't make it much easier for the networks or the show's hosts. Ed Sullivan, in particular, frequently featured black entertainers on *The Ed Sullivan Show*. Peg Leg Bates, Ella Fitzgerald, Eartha Kitt, Sammy Davis Jr., and Redd's fellow Chitlin' Circuit comedians, Dewey "Pigmeat" Markham ("Heyeah come da judge") and Tim Moore, were all guests on Sullivan's popular Sunday-night showcase. Sullivan received a lot of hate mail from white viewers labeling him a "nigger lover," but he stuck to his beliefs and his admiration for black entertainers, and never caved in to the pressure.

There were a few television shows in the mid-1950s headlined by black entertainers, but these were regional—*Happy Pappy* on Chicago's WENR and *The Hadda Brooks Show* on KLAC in Los Angeles. When, in 1956, Nat King Cole became the first black star to headline his own network show on NBC, sponsors fled in droves, worried that their sponsorship of Cole's show would affect sales in the South. George Schlatter, who had just joined NBC at the time, remembered how difficult it was in that heated racial climate. "The first thing I did [at NBC] was get them to buy the Nat King Cole series," he said. "When they canceled [the show] because they couldn't sell it, because the sponsors wouldn't continue to carry it in the South, we sold it to Rheingold Beer, and Rheingold Beer took a real hit on it. But they were the ones who sponsored it and had gotten it on the air." Cole took the news hard. "Madison Avenue is afraid of the dark," he said after his show was cancelled.

The odds were stacked astronomically high against comics like Redd Foxx and Moms Mabley making it onto network television. They "worked dirty" and, conversely, couldn't be trusted to tone down their material on the national stage (or so the thinking went). Redd's brashness and self-confidence didn't deter him from trying, though. He claimed to have auditioned for a spot on *The Steve Allen Show* in the late '50s, only to be shown the door by what he thought was subtle racism. Steve Allen, like Ed Sullivan, was a nurturer of talent, regardless of race, and had a special place in his heart for comedians. It would have been surprising, and totally out of character, if he personally had a hand in denying Redd a shot on his show because of his skin color.

"The material I did was the stuttering bit," Redd said shortly thereafter. "You know what they told me when they turned me down? They said they couldn't use me because it would offend all the members of their viewing audience who stutter. Asked them what about Joe Frisco or Roscoe Ates, who got their reputation affecting a stammer," he said of those white actors. "I didn't get the engagement. . . . Believe me, the door is closed and I don't see any hope in sight." He also claimed to have tried out for a spot on *The Ed Sullivan Show* and was told, "'stay off the South, white women, the Congo, and the President.' I asked them if I could do the Lord's Prayer."

Television might not have been beckoning Redd Foxx, but as he and wife Betty Jeanne crisscrossed the country in their battered 1936 Plymouth—Redd honing his standup act and "Jean Vegas" crooning the standards—Redd's album, *Laff of the Party*, slowly began to catch on. Dooto Records, no industry powerhouse by any stretch of the imagination, had a sales force strong enough to ensure that *Laff of the Party* was distributed nationwide, particularly in the urban areas. As word-of-mouth spread, the album found an unexpected life on college campuses, where students grooved to Redd's frank, anything-goes patter and anti-establishment attitude, and among black teenagers, as well. It also began to appear in "respectable" white record shops, which buried *Laff of the Party* behind other merchandise, or sold it under-the-counter (for those customers hip enough to ask). Redd's reputation for "working blue" was also a concern for record-shop owners, some of whom were leery of openly selling *Laff of the Party* for fear of running afoul of indecency laws.

Laff of the Party continued to sell strongly throughout the second half of 1956. Word-of-mouth spread, and urban record stores began reporting brisk sales of the album within a few months of its release. Word was also filtering back to Dooto Records owner Dootsie Williams that people were throwing "listening parties," where everyone would gather to drink and smoke and laugh as they listened, over and over again, to this "dirty" comic named Redd Foxx talk about "Fugg" and his preacher's wife's perspiring donkey ("sweaty ass" in Redd's vernacular). In the black community, *Laff of the Party* would often be spinning on the turntable at "rent parties," which were organized to pass the hat for rent money. "I had no idea the first album would sell like it did, because I had pretty bad material at that time," Redd said. "But the sales were fantastic."

The black press began referring to Redd as "The King of the Party Records." An underground star was born.

"Everybody bought the records," recalled Della Reese. "And a really good, fun night in the black community, and the white community, too, was, 'Come over, I have some Redd Foxx records and we'll listen and we'll laugh.' And he made you laugh. And he didn't have a problem with whatever was necessary, as he thought, to make you laugh."

To critic and author Mel Watkins, Redd's trailblazing party records were akin to the records issued by Okeh Records. In 1921, the Los Angeles–based company released what was believed to be the first catalogue of phonograph recordings "featuring music thought to appeal primarily to African Americans."

> The Redd Foxx albums, usually kept in the back of record collections, beyond sight of 'polite' Negro company, were seldom mentioned at racially mixed gatherings. An underground source of uncensored black humor, these early re-

corded examples of comic routines and monologues popular in black cabarets and the black stage circuit were among the first of their kind to be made available to the general public. Although at the time of their release they were considered more contraband than mere race records, the albums were essentially connected to the core of the unassimilated black community, as were the original Okeh releases of the Twenties.

With *Laff of the Party, Volume 1* selling briskly, Dootsie Williams released *Laff of the Party, Volume 2* in mid-1956. Like the original, it sported Redd's self-caricature on the cover and, on the back, included the same liner notes as *Volume 1*. The record had nine tracks (one more than *Volume 1*) and its sound was similar to *Volume 1*, with Redd's nightclub audience keeping up a non-stop stream of raucous laughter as Redd delivered his comic monologues on "The Two Oars," "The Brown Nosed Reindeer," "The Army," "The Pilot," "The Pregnant Woman," "The Lost Toupee," "The Preacher's Bicycle," "Breach of Promise," and "The Witch Doctor."

Despite his growing reputation as "The King of the Party Records," Redd still couldn't break into the mainstream clubs. The work was steadier now, and with the royalty checks starting to come in from the sales of his Dooto albums, he and Betty Jeanne were more financially secure. But the hoped-for "big break" didn't seem to be anywhere on the horizon, and the life of a club comic had its share of headaches. The tight-fisted club owners always seemed to have an excuse not to pay their headliners, or some reason to knock a couple of hundred bucks off the promised rate. Redd, like many of his peers, was burned one-too-many times, and began demanding to be paid in cash, up front, before venturing out on stage. It was a practice he continued for the rest of his nightclub career, even after earning millions as the star of *Sanford and Son*.

There were some highlights, though, as Redd and Betty Jeanne slogged their way through the nightclub circuit. In April 1958, Redd joined singer Fran Warren and dancers Coles & Atkins (Honi Coles and Cholly Atkins) at the Apollo as supporting acts for the Will Mastin Trio and its star attraction, Sammy Davis Jr. The following March, Redd opened for a successful run at Robert's Penthouse, one of the more upscale black clubs in Chicago. Joining him on the bill was

Betty Jeanne, working as "Jean Vegas," and singer Jo Ann Henderson. "Foxx, an ace comic, performs several times nightly with something different each time he appears," declared the *Chicago Daily Defender*. In April of 1959, Redd and jazz saxophonist James Moody were among the artists invited to back jazz great Sarah Vaughan at Chicago's Regal Theatre. Moody wrote his acclaimed flute composition, "Darben the Redd Foxx," in honor of his pal. That fall, Redd was playing the Royal Theatre in Baltimore when he was asked by his friend Red Garland, the noted jazz pianist who was touring with his trio, to be the best man at Garland's onstage wedding to Marie Adams (the couple met only three weeks before). Betty Jeanne served as the matron of honor.

Redd's party records continued to sell briskly, and Dootsie Williams was kicking his Dooto Records machine into high gear to capitalize on his biggest star. From 1956 to 1958, Dooto issued approximately twenty-five Redd Foxx party records of varying lengths (some were shorter EPs) and audio quality (ranging from muffled, poorly record-ed routines to crystal-clear sound). Some albums cannibalized mate-rial from earlier releases; others were slapped together and rushed to record stores with no rhyme or reason, sometimes even using the same covers (or covers that were changed only slightly). Dooto's helter-skelter release schedule created a tangled Redd Foxx record catalogue that's extremely difficult to track with any precision.

But Redd's records were selling like hotcakes now, and were start-ing to gain more traction among college students. More unexpectedly, Redd's comedy was crossing ethnic lines. Who couldn't laugh at sex and at Redd's riffs on its foibles and embarrassments? It was a univer-sal, color-blind selling point. Redd's records were also starting to find their way onto turntables in white households in upper-middle-class neighborhoods, although any "respectable" person would never admit to even *hearing* of Redd Foxx.

Redd's records were, for the most part, still sold under-the-counter, or were conveniently camouflaged, but Redd had cemented his reputa-tion as the "King of the Party Records." In early March 1958, Dootsie Williams presented Redd with his first gold record for having sold one million Dooto albums. A ceremony was held at the Oasis club, where it had all started with *Laff of the Party, Volume 1*. A beaming Redd Foxx accepted his gold record from Williams and posed for photographs with his old comedy partner Slappy White, singer LaVern Baker, and

Betty Jeanne. (Slappy and LaVern married three years later and were together for eight years, divorcing in 1969.)

Redd was now reaping handsome dividends, not only from the sales of his party records, but by his refusal to tone his act down. He never pandered to anyone, and his brash attitude and take-no-prisoners comedy style made him a hero in the African American community. Here was a comedian who spoke directly to *them*, in language they used with each other in their homes, and on the streets.

> Me and a lovely girl, we were both under the car, trying to see what was wrong, and a guy came by and looked under the car, he said, 'Hey, buddy! How far is the Old Red Log Inn?' I said, 'Go ahead and mind your own business!'

One night in 1961, singer Tony Orlando, who would later find mega-success with his group, Tony Orlando and Dawn, was in the audience watching Redd perform at the 20 Grand, a popular Detroit nightclub that also housed a studio for Detroit DJ Ernie Durham. "The 20 Grand held about three thousand people. It was a big, enormous dance club," Orlando recalled. "Acts would come in and lip sync to their songs, to promote their records, and there was a guy named Frantic Ernie Durham, who was a disc jockey. The background singers on stage that night were the Supremes. And I remember I was sixteen years old and I was coming out the door and Frantic Ernie says, 'You know who that is over there, man? It's the great Redd Foxx.' And there was Redd, walking into this room, and you would think, even in 1961, amongst African Americans, this was a God. He walked into that place and you would think Elvis walked in. I'll never forget that."

Redd's success selling albums for Dooto Records might have gone unnoticed in mainstream America, but the record industry sat up and paid attention. By 1959, with nearly thirty Dooto releases under his belt, Redd was being courted by bigger record companies who wanted a piece of the party-record action. "Some of the big companies have tried to get me to split from the little company I record for, saying they can offer more," he told the *Baltimore Afro-American*. "But, well, there's loyalty to consider. This fellow gave me my start and there are few enough colored record companies who can hold on to their properties, so I stick with him." They were words he would live to regret.

With the imprimatur of Redd's gold record came more opportunities. Television, for now, was still off-limits to the "blue" comedian who frightened network suits. They were convinced Redd Foxx couldn't be tamed for a nationwide audience. Redd was turning thirty-seven in December but still had never played any of the "upscale" clubs in New York City. He got his chance, and the hoped-for "big break," in the fall of 1959, when he was booked for a run at the Basin Street East, located on East Forty-eighth Street in Manhattan. It would be Redd's first appearance before a mainstream, white audience, and his first standup appearance outside the segregated confines of the Chitlin' Circuit. And, despite the usual Redd Foxx bluster and bravado, he was extremely nervous. "That was a powerhouse place at the time," he said. "I went in with Maynard Ferguson's orchestra and the Treniers. I was scared shitless because I didn't know how far I could go. I felt I couldn't say things like 'This is a great band. Look at those initials on the music stands, M.F.' By the time I'd think of what I was going to say, my timing would be off.

"On the third night, one of the Treniers said, 'Man, why don't you just do your thing, like you do wherever you go, and pump these people for all they're worth.' So it just happened that night Ethel Merman was in, and she was loud. I can't see people who don't respect another performer, regardless of what color they may be, so I really read her, and I read somebody else that bugged me. I came on strong, just opened up and let myself be Redd Foxx. I was in the men's room and I heard some cat on the phone saying, 'You get down here and catch this guy, he's the dirtiest son-of-a-bitch I ever heard!' Then he saw me and he nodded politely and said, 'Ah, hum, I enjoyed your show.'"

Steve Lawrence and his wife, Eydie Gorme, were also on the Basin Street East bill with Redd, and they pushed him to just be himself on stage. Shortly thereafter, on stage one night, Redd suddenly turned to an audience member who failed to applaud one of his jokes. "Better laugh now," he needled the man, "or I'll move into your neighborhood and lower the property values."

With a successful run at Basin Street East under his belt, other doors that were previously closed to Redd began to crack open—just a little. A movie career was the furthest thing from his mind, but, back in Los Angeles, Redd was hired as an extra for MGM's *All the Fine Young Cannibals*, a big-screen tearjerker starring Natalie Wood, her husband Robert Wagner, George Hamilton, and Pearl Bailey. Directed by

Michael Anderson, and reportedly based on the life of drug-addled jazz trumpeter Chet Baker, it was a silly, overly melodramatic story about a dirt-poor trumpet player with daddy issues named Chad Bixby (Wagner), who knocks up his dirt-poor girlfriend, Salome (Wood), then finds fame and fortune in New York with an alcoholic singer named Ruby (Bailey). Salome, meanwhile, marries Tony (Hamilton), a rich Yale college student who thinks Chad's baby is his own. The rest of the movie features a lot of histrionic *angst* as both Chad and Salome, who meet again in New York, discover their newfound riches won't bring them happiness—while Ruby slowly drinks herself to death.

Although Redd was unbilled in the movie, he appears in two scenes. In his first on-camera appearance, he's the honky tonk piano player named—what else?—Redd, who's tinkling the ivories (in a red shirt and jaunty cap) and dragging on a cigarette as Chad and Salome drop into the local saloon. Chad then shows off his trumpet chops while lamenting the loss of his daddy's affections. "Turn off that sick piano, Redd," the piano player is told by the saloon's manager. Redd is also seen at the end of the movie, among the mourners swaying in unison at Ruby's funeral. *All the Fine Young Cannibals* was released in September 1960 to mostly savage reviews and quickly sank from sight.

Three months later, several published reports noted that Redd could be seen with Ella Fitzgerald and Burl Ives in another movie, *Let No Man Write My Epitaph*. It made for a nice story, but it wasn't true. Redd wouldn't make another big-screen appearance for ten years.

In late September 1960, shortly after the release of *All the Fine Young Cannibals*, Redd announced that he'd signed a deal to appear at Gene Norman's Crescendo Club, a hip nightclub situated in the heart of Hollywood's Sunset Strip. Redd, who was following Lenny Bruce at the Crescendo, would share the bill with the Count Basie Band, blues singer Joe Williams, and promised "a swinger" of a time. Like his appearance the previous year at the Basin Street East in New York, Redd's Crescendo Club gig was a big step up the show business ladder from the blacks-only clubs he'd been working in Los Angeles for the past ten years. While he was glad to finally get a break in L.A., he was still bitter about his past failure to break the city's color barrier. "One club on the Strip where I was supposed to audition wouldn't even let me in; they had an all-white policy," Redd said. "So I kept working black clubs."

His opening at the Crescendo Club not only marked another step in Redd's growing acceptance among a crossover audience, but it was also the first time in several years that a black performer was invited to work the Strip—no mean feat. "The Crescendo engagement promises to be a historic one," noted the *Chicago Defender*. "Negro comedians, once a staple item in the entertainment stock, have all but disappeared. Foxx, Slappy White, and Nipsey Russell are, perhaps, the foremost young comedians of the day, but they are seldom seen or heard in the more fabled clubs."

Redd was asked to comment on his Crescendo engagement, and gave a stilted, atypical response. He sounded like he was reading from a press release—which he probably was. "This is an important break for me and for Negro comedy," he said. "I shall play this engagement always with the idea that it may lead to greater employment for all Negro comics."

chapter six

"It's Not Easy Out There"

The needle for black comedians was finally moving in the right direction. While older comedians like Redd Foxx, Timmie Rogers, and Slappy White were still finding it difficult to break through to a mainstream audience, a younger crop of black funnymen, led by Dick Gregory and Godfrey Cambridge, were making important inroads.

Gregory was ten years younger than Redd, and was also born in Saint Louis. He attended two years of college at Southern Illinois University before serving two years in the Army, where he won several talent shows for his joke-telling prowess. Gregory moved to Chicago in the late 1950s, and after getting fired from several jobs, including the post office (for making fun of his superiors), he turned to stand-up comedy, getting his big break at the Esquire Club in 1958. Unlike Redd's "blue" material, Gregory's act was topical and pointedly political, particularly when poking fun at the racial divide separating the country. Along with Cambridge, Gregory represented a new generation of black comedians unafraid to "tell it like it is"—and, in the process, to be accepted by a white audience finally waking up to the growing Civil Rights movement. Gregory even landed two Big Kahunas in show-business: a 1961 appearance on Jack Paar's *Tonight Show* and a four-page profile in the *New York Times*, headlined "A Negro Says It With Jokes," which included a passing mention of Redd:

> There are good Negro comics around today with Gregory's single-mindedness (some bitter or broad, others simply so oriented toward Negroes that their work takes on the nature of an ironic exclusivity), among them Redd Foxx, Nipsey

Russell, Slappy White, Dewey (Pigmeat) Markham, and Timmie Rogers. From time to time, they play for white audiences, but they earn their living mostly in Negro nightclubs and theatres.

Privately, Redd fumed at being ignored by the same establishment types who now embraced Gregory and Cambridge. Publicly, in the black press, he voiced his appreciation for Gregory's helping to nudge the "white" door open a bit for black comics. "If it had not been for Dick Gregory, we would still be playing the nickel joints," Redd said. "I don't tell racial jokes, but I have to take my hat off to Dick. He helped me a lot."

But Redd's own stubbornness continued to hold him back from reaching a bigger audience. It was noble, in some ways, but shortsighted in terms of his career goals. If he refused to clean up his act for the more "respectable" clubs, how could ever expect to get the better bookings? But, if he did sanitize his act, he'd be going against the very core of his comedic soul, the very essence of what he believed in, what helped him reach this point in his career.

"The King of the Party Records" was at a crossroads. Yet he still professed that he'd rather be true to himself than sell out to a phony image and pander to a white audience. "Working clean doesn't pay anything," he said. "If I do clean material, I'm just another Negro comedian. My forte is nightclubs. That's what I love, and they pay as much as anything else, maybe more. If I clean up I could do a couple of TV shows and then it's over. It's not easy out there."

He was much more at home in the smoky clubs, where he was in control and able to handle almost anything, including violent hecklers. In February 1961, working a room in Philadelphia, Redd mixed it up with a black Air Force sergeant and his wife, who were heckling Redd from their seats at the bar. The sergeant claimed that Redd insulted his wife, and challenged Redd to a fistfight. The challenge was accepted, but the sergeant's wife and others in the club short-circuited the brawl and Redd broke the tension. "If your lips were filled with quarters," he told the sergeant, "I could buy a farm with the lower lip and save the upper lip for social security."

Dootsie Williams, meanwhile, continued to ride the Redd Foxx gravy train. Dooto had other solid acts in its stable, including comedians

Allen Drew, Hattie Noel, and George Kirby and the Doo Wop act the Penguins. But Redd was still the label's best-known and best-selling act. In the five years between the first *Laff of the Party* album (there would be seven more) and *At Jazzville* in mid-1961, Dooto had released roughly thirty-five Redd Foxx albums, EPs, and compilations, some releases cannibalizing material from earlier records. Redd's party records were so popular they even spawned a lucrative bootleg market. In November 1961, police in Chicago busted a $1 million bootleg ring dealing mostly in Redd Foxx comedy albums. Dootsie Williams claimed the ring had illegally recorded fourteen Redd Foxx albums and seven of Redd's singles, selling over 200,000 copies of the pirated material to a (mostly) unsuspecting public.

But there was trouble brewing in Dootsie-ville. Redd felt that he was being cheated out of royalties for all the albums he'd sold on the Dooto label—some reports put the number at over ten million or more—and he claimed to have been paid only $11,000 in royalties since the first *Laff of the Party* album. Redd believed that Williams owed him about $350,000 in back royalty payments and, in May 1961, he filed a lawsuit in Santa Monica Superior Court against Williams and Dooto Records. Redd claimed that not only did Williams owe him the $350,000 in back royalties, but that he also never received any statements of earnings dating back to 1956. Redd's lawsuit also demanded that he have the right to inspect Dooto's books, to get an accounting of all his earnings over the past five years, and to have a receiver appointed for the company, in order to guard his financial interests. Redd also asked to be released from the last three years of the five-year Dooto contract extension he signed in 1958, which carried a two-year option. He also wanted all the masters of his albums and singles turned over to him.

"I just don't think I've been treated right," he said. "Anytime an artist can sell as many single records and albums as I have sold, and end up getting just $11,000 in royalties, then something is wrong. For quite some time I have been making an independent check of distributors across the nation, to see how my records have been selling, and what I found out was that I haven't been given an accurate accounting on my records' sales."

Dootsie Williams vehemently denied all of Redd's charges. He claimed that he'd paid his star comedian over $70,000 in royalties over the past five years, and said his company's "meticulous" bookkeeping and spotless reputation would prove his case. "He's just trying to break his contract now that we've built him up to the position where everybody wants him," Williams said. "We can prove our position. We've got cancelled checks in our files to prove that Foxx's royalties have been fully paid. To be frank about it, the charges made by Foxx mean nothing. Apparently he and his advisors want to break his iron-clad contract with us, and they're trying anything as an excuse for their own selfish interests."

As his case against Dooto Records dragged on in court, keeping lawyers on both sides of the battle busy, Redd turned his attention elsewhere. In July 1961, the "elfish redhead" was honored in Chicago by the Penthouse Players of Roberts' Show Club, a Windy City nightclub, for being "an inspiration to us who struggle for recognition." After being serenaded by singer Beatrice Williams (with "Red Is the Color of My True Love's Hair"), Redd was paid a surprise visit by his mother and several of his old 58th Street Gang buddies, including Lamont Ousley, Pete Carter, and Steve Trimble. He returned to Los Angeles in August to headline "Lon Fontaine's Cotton Club '62 Revue" at the Summit in Hollywood, getting a rare snarky review, this one from Joan Winchell in the *Los Angeles Times*: "distasteful and crude. Not recommended for those who don't appreciate cheap burlesque humor."

With Redd refusing to record any new material for Dooto Records while his lawsuit against the company dragged on, Dootsie Williams was forced to release a slew of rehashed Redd Foxx albums, some which included material that was deemed unsuitable for earlier releases. In 1962, Dooto released two Redd Foxx albums—*The New Fugg* and *Laff Along*—and two more albums in 1963, *Crack Up* and *Funny Stuff*. In the meantime, Williams kept up a steady drumbeat of criticism against Redd, who uncharacteristically didn't retaliate and kept his mouth shut, at least in print. In July 1962, over a year after Redd filed his lawsuit against Dooto, Williams gave an interview in which he criticized Redd—and his management.

"Foxx willingly signed his contract with us and, although he had made himself unavailable for recording a total of two years during the contractual period, we have paid his royalties on schedule, mailing checks to him when he was out of town," he said. "He has listened to poor advice and sought to break the contract by devious means.

"We have heard numerous reports of Foxx's derogatory statements about this company, yet we have never said less than that Foxx is, in our opinion, the world's greatest comedian. But that is beside the point. The point is this: our office is open six days a week and we are always available, yet not once has Foxx come to us with any complaint about his contract.

"His contract with us is now so seriously breached that he threatens his very career by listening to bad advice from those who want merely to use him and his great talent. One operator with whom Foxx has 'talked business' has a police record as long as your arm and is known throughout the trade as a shady operator."

Finally, in late September 1963, after nearly two-and-a-half years of back and forth accusations, the case was resolved—with Redd losing the battle. Judge John F. Aioso ruled in a Santa Monica courtroom that there had been no fraud on the part of Dooto Records, that Redd had not been underpaid on royalties owed to him, and that he had no reason not to perform for Dooto under the deal he'd signed in 1958. To add insult to injury, the court determined that Williams and Dooto had actually *overpaid* Redd Foxx to the tune of $18,000—and that Redd still owed Dooto Records $11,000. (Apparently Redd and his attorney, Burt Marks, knew about the overpayment and tried, unsuccessfully, to work out a deal months earlier in which Redd would drop his lawsuit for $25,000.)

Judge Aioso's ruling meant that Redd had to remain under contract to Dooto Records until September 14, 1967. Two years had been added to Redd's original Dooto extension, to compensate for the period in which he refused to record for Dooto since filing his lawsuit. Judge Aioso also ruled that Redd could not record for any other company while under contract to Dooto, and that Dooto would keep all the master recordings of Redd's albums and singles. For Redd, it was a loss on all legal fronts.

Dootsie Williams, though, took the high road in his court victory. "We recovered two years of over-payment to Foxx. Actually, we had overpaid him since 1956," he said. "We think Foxx is one of the greatest comedians we have under contract. Our other feeling is that we're glad he's found out that we've been perfectly honest and above reproach in every way. I don't see any reason why he should not resume recording for us." Redd, rarely at a loss for words, had no comment.

Williams, though, found trouble from other quarters. Dooto was also being sued for $200,000 by Rev. Martin Luther King Jr., who claimed one of his speeches, delivered at a Baptist church in Los Angeles, was being sold as Dooto's *Martin Luther King at Zion Hill* without his permission. King's Southern Christian Leadership Congress later obtained a court injunction barring Dooto from selling the album.

Redd was having better luck outside the courtroom. In October, a month after losing his case against Dooto, he opened for the first time in Las Vegas for a run at the Castaways, a brand-new hotel and casino located on the Strip just across the street from the Desert Inn. Headlining in Sin City was a big deal, but Redd knew he wasn't the star. Those guys worked the prestigious (and more lucrative) showroom. Redd was relegated to the Castaways lounge for a couple of post-midnight shows, where his nightly take depended on how many people showed up. Still, he'd busted down yet another barrier as he neared his forty-first birthday. Vegas was a big deal. Sharing the bill with Redd at the Castaways were Barry Ashton's Playmates of 1964, the Don Randi Trio, Dick Wells, and Peter Anthony. And while the Castaways didn't have the cachet of New York's Basin Street East or the Crescendo Club in Los Angeles—or even the big Las Vegas Strip palaces like the Sands or the Flamingo—it was an important step in Redd's evolution as a comic. Las Vegas was a place to be seen by high rollers and entertainment types flying in from L.A. to spend the weekend gambling and drinking. Who knew where that could lead?

All he had to do now was to prove he had the chops to make his mark.

"Redd Foxx, in his first Vegas appearance, clicked big with Castaways first-nighters, and word-of-mouth could well make him the sleeper of the season," wrote Forrest Duke in the *Las Vegas Review-Journal*. "On the strength of the Negro comedian's comedy albums, entertainment director Garwood Van booked Foxx to follow the successful engagement of bawdy storyteller-songstress Pearl Williams. Foxx has blue material which is more subtle than that of Miss Williams or Belle Barth, and most of his dialogue is new to the Strip . . . wisely, he doesn't concentrate on racial or off-color humor, but presents, in a casual style, a very funny and not-too-lengthy monologue."

Redd's successful run at the Castaways set the stage for bigger and better bookings. In February 1964, he opened at the Sugar Hill Club in San Francisco, raising his fee to $1,250 a week. Unbeknownst to Redd,

Hugh Downs, the co-host of NBC's *Today Show*, was in the Sugar Hill Club audience one night. Downs had caught Redd's act in Harlem and at the Castaways, and was a fan of his humor. "I had seen Foxx, who was indeed a toilet comic. His stuff was almost as filthy as Andrew Dice Clay [would be years later], but a lot funnier," Downs recalled. "The man had a terrific sense of humor, and this justified some of the depths to which he had to descend in material that could not be cleaned up and still remain humorous. Also, I liked his personality. He had, of course, his group that comprised his audience—they would follow him anywhere."

Downs thought that Redd deserved national exposure, and wanted to book him for a spot on the *Today Show*. It would be Redd's first appearance on national television, and convincing NBC officials that this bawdy nightclub comedian could behave himself on a live morning television show—and clean up his act—was more difficult than Downs envisioned. "I said I wanted to invite him on the *Today Show* for an interview. NBC officials were aghast," Downs said. "*Today* being live, it would be impossible to edit. I said I thought he could be trusted in a general audience situation—that he was sensitive enough to know the conditions under which he'd be broadcasting, and that he would not betray his friendship with me."

He didn't. Although Redd's 1964 appearance on the *Today Show* is lost to time—NBC, in those days, erased many of its videotapes so they could be re-used—he made a good impression. And he certainly wasn't dumb enough to sabotage his first shot at national television exposure by reverting to the language of his nightclub act. "I put him on the air and it worked," Downs said. "His humor was appropriate and his history was interesting."

Redd's appearance on the *Today Show* led to his second television appearance shortly thereafter on *The John Barbour Show*, which aired locally in Los Angeles. John Barbour, a Canadian-born comedian, met Redd for the first time the previous year in San Francisco. The two men were introduced to each other by Barbour's wife, Sarita—a singer in the Earl Hines Orchestra—and struck up a lifelong friendship. (Barbour would go on to host the hit NBC series *Real People* in the 1970s and also appeared in an episode of *Sanford and Son*.)

In 1964, Barbour was hired by Metromedia to host what he called "a sort of poor man's *Tonight Show*" on KTTV, replacing *The Donald O'Connor Show*. *The John Barbour Show* aired live, for ninety minutes, every Saturday night, and Redd was booked to appear with fellow guests Jack Carter, Rip Taylor, and Charo. "I knew all of Redd's material and I knew he could talk for hours and be clean and be funny," Barbour said. "He was filthy in a nightclub [setting], but he was filthy and funny. Redd had an enormous wit."

When he was introduced by Barbour, Redd entered from the wings wearing a pair of golf knickers—"so he looked funny"—and sat down to Barbour's left. "I thought he would be much more comfortable in a conversational situation," Barbour said. "I just thought he would be much more effective if he sat down and we just talked—and, of course, he killed."

One of Redd's routines at the time riffed on black power and white power in a typically apolitical way. "He said he didn't believe in black power or white power but in green power—if you had green power, you could buy the place where the blacks and whites were having their meetings," Barbour recalled. "Just on the spur-of-the-moment I said, 'Redd, why do you think money is colored green?' And without missing a beat he says, 'That's because Jews pick it before it gets ripe!' Well, I'm telling you, Jack Carter fell on the floor and the audience just went absolutely berserk," Barbour said. "It was the largest laugh on live television that I have ever heard in my life. The laughter went on for minutes and minutes and minutes. Redd just ad-libbed, and it was almost impossible to continue the show, because once it started back up again, Jack would reach into his pocket: 'Hey, Redd, green!'"

Having now appeared on a national morning television show, and a local nighttime television show, it was Redd's old friend, Bobby Schiffman, who was instrumental in getting Redd booked for his first appearance with Johnny Carson on *The Tonight Show*. Schiffman, the son of Apollo Theater owner Frank Schiffman, began working at the theater in 1950 (following in the footsteps of his older brother, Jack), and struck up a close friendship with Redd dating back to the early days of Foxx and White. One day, Redd was sitting in Bobby's office, bemoaning the fact that his television appearances were few and far between. "I admonished him," Schiffman said. "'You're a dumb son of a bitch. TV is a reality, but because you're such a blue comic, they will pass you by.' He said, 'There's not a damn thing I can do' and I said, 'If you promise me you won't embarrass me, I'll get you a TV show.' He said, 'Well, I don't believe you,' and I said, 'You got my word. I promise.'"

Schiffman didn't know a soul at *The Tonight Show*, but he called the show's production office and got *Tonight Show* bandleader Skitch Henderson on the phone. Henderson, who knew Frank Schiffman, said the show would "love" to have Redd as a guest, but that he was in a meeting and would have to call Bobby back. "I said to Foxx, 'If you embarrass me, I'll never forgive you.' The next day I got him booked on *The Tonight Show* and he did his routine about the stuttering paratroopers. He was an overnight sensation."

That's a bit of an overstatement, although Johnny Carson would welcome Redd back several more times in the years leading up to *Sanford and Son*—when Redd Foxx really *did* become an overnight sensation. Redd got off on the rush of a live audience. Like most stand-up comedians, he needed to feel the love and acceptance of his audience expressed through their laughter. On stage, no one judged him. On stage, he was his own man—take it or leave it. "TV is nice, but I love the applause. Nothing thrills me more than to hear hands clapping," he said. "Man, I'd get out of bed to do a show knowing that the applause is still going to be there. In fact, if my wife had hands as big as the state of Texas, that still wouldn't be enough. I like to know that I've made people happy, and telling jokes is one way." Betty Jeanne took a more introspective approach to Redd's love of live performing: "What my husband gets from a live nightclub audience can't be bought. That's love that comes from the people when they're laughing at your material and applauding for more. It's total acceptance, and even if it's only for the time he's on stage, a performer needs that the way a fish needs water."

And that was fine with Redd. For while his *Today Show* appearance proved that he could be "trusted" on national television, Redd's star didn't exactly rocket into the stratosphere after his fifteen minutes of morning television fame on NBC. There were no other television shows knocking down his door to book him, and he turned a deaf ear to people who told him he'd get more national exposure if he would just clean up his material. Dick Gregory, Godfrey Cambridge, and now Bill Cosby were making major inroads into "white" mainstream media. Cosby, in particular, was the rising star of the group. His reputation as a "clean" comic won him an appearance on Johnny Carson's *Tonight Show* in 1963, and he followed that up with his huge 1964 comedy album, *Bill Cosby Is a Very Funny Fellow. . . . Right!* Within a year, he was co-starring opposite Robert Culp on NBC's *I Spy* as the first black performer to co-star in a dramatic network television series. But that wasn't Redd's bag. He sneered at what he considered to be pandering to the white audience.

"There was always the question, 'Should Redd Foxx clean up his act?' I actually did it a couple of times. I started to believe all the crap about how it would keep me off the mass media. But . . . I hated the thought that I was selling out," he said. "I've always had the feeling you could say anything in a nightclub you wanted to because if there are any prudes or church people there, they brought themselves into that position, so they should be able to face what's happening."

Part of the Redd Foxx mythology that was perpetuated after his death was that his *Today Show* spot spawned a slew of television appearances for Redd on mid-1960s television sitcoms including *Here's Lucy*, *Green Acres*, *The Addams Family*, and *The Beverly Hillbillies*. It makes for a better story in chronicling Redd's rise through the ranks, but it's not true. Redd Foxx never appeared on any of the aforementioned shows, but an actor named John J. Fox, who sometimes used his nickname "Red"—and thus was billed as "Red Fox"—*did* appear on *Here's Lucy*, *Green Acres*, *The Addams Family*, and *The Beverly Hillbillies*. It wasn't until 1966 and early 1967 that Redd was booked for his first appearances on *The Merv Griffin Show* and *The Mike Douglas Show* (the first of his many appearances with Douglas). Television, for now, would have to wait.

So Redd returned to the club circuit, to the world he knew best. He played two sold-out shows at the Music Crossroads in Oakland, California in the summer of 1964 before returning to the Castaways in Las Vegas, where he was booked into the Samoa Room, sharing the bill with stripper Lili St. Cyr and the Hank Henry Revue. "Sophisticates will have a field day digging the humor of 'Bottoms Up' revue, back-to-back with the very funny standup comedy of Redd Foxx," *Variety* crowed. "Redd Foxx, Negro comic who was a tremendous hit on his first trip here several months ago, is in top form for this outing. He has a knack of describing bawdy situations with bawdy language, which because of the nonchalance of his delivery comes across with consistent hilarity rarely achieved by other comedians. Because of his apparent lack of resentment of the race problem he has his audience sympathetic and on his side from the beginning, laughing with him instead of at him."

Four months later, in February 1965, came news from Chicago that

Fred Sanford had died at the age of forty-six from a rare kidney disease and complications from diabetes. The big brother Redd had always looked up to never could stay out of trouble. While Redd traveled the country, honed his stand-up act and married twice, Fred remained in Chicago, in and out of trouble. His final three years were a blur of hospital visits and extended hospital stays. He died in Cook County Hospital, in his mother's arms. "I stayed out there two weeks with him, but I gave him my life," Mary Sanford said. "Never has there been a mother so faithful. I was there night and day." Fred, who died destitute, left behind no wife or children. "He was just a street urchin. He was on the street with no gainful employment, getting into trouble" said Redd's friend, Les Anglin. Redd flew back to Chicago for the funeral, which was held at St. Anselm's Catholic Church. Fred was buried at St. Mary's Cemetery. For the rest of his life, Redd would fly into Chicago, at least once each year, to visit his brother's grave. He also made a point of performing for free at jails and prisons around the country, to honor his brother's memory.

Redd brought his mother out to Los Angeles for a visit shortly after Fred's death, which had taken a noticeable toll on Mary Sanford. Redd, never very close to his mother, hadn't seen much of her after he moved to California with Slappy White in 1952. Mary's relationship with Betty Jeanne was also tense and fractious, putting that much more distance between son and mother. Mary's presence in Los Angeles now rekindled some of the old resentment Redd had toward the woman he felt had abandoned he and his brother when they needed her the most.

"When my brother died . . . she had two strokes on a train coming out here to California from my brother's death because we were the only two boys and I had never been around home too much so I was always like her only son," he said. "I get all of the love. I don't like that much love. It's hard to handle. It really is."

Redd didn't stick around Los Angeles for long and, in March 1965, about a month after Fred's death, he returned to Las Vegas to open a three-night gig at the Thunderbird Hotel on the Strip. It was his first time away from the Castaways and it was a lounge booking—again, not the main showroom—but word was spreading around town that Redd Foxx was a solid drawing card who could be counted on to keep the high rollers entertained. He was in.

Redd's live performances were the only way his audience could hear any of his new material. He still had two years to go on his court-enforced contract with Dooto Records, but neither he nor Dootsie Williams seemed too interested in trying to make the partnership work. Dooto issued only one Redd Foxx record in 1965, *Naughties But Goodies*, which proved to be Redd's last original Dooto release. For all intents and purposes, Redd's historic partnership with Dootsie Williams was over. In 1968, Dooto released one more Redd Foxx album, a back-catalogue job called *Adults Only*, which featured dated material.

Frank Sinatra now entered the picture. Sinatra had caught Redd's act in Las Vegas and was a fan. With Redd floundering on Dooto, Sinatra quickly jumped in, bought out Redd's contract and signed him to a deal on Loma Records, the R&B offshoot of Sinatra's Reprise Records (both labels were owned by Warner Bros).

"Frank Sinatra changed my whole recording scene," Redd said. "He saw me working one time and he actually rolled on the floor laughing. He said, 'I want to sign you up.' I told him I was all tied up, but he said, 'Don't you worry. I'll take care of it.' I don't know what happened, but somehow or other, a couple of days later I was free." Redd knew that, when it came to Sinatra, you didn't ask many questions.

Redd's association with Frank Sinatra paid off in other ways, too. Now carrying Ol' Blue Eyes' stamp of approval, better bookings quickly followed Redd's Loma Records deal. In August 1966, he opened with singer Ruth Wallis and fellow comic Ben Blue at the Aladdin Hotel and Casino on the Strip in Las Vegas. This time, though, he wasn't a lounge act, but a featured performer in the hotel's Bagdad Theatre, where Jackie Mason had just completed a twenty-week run. "Just Color Him Funny," blared an ad for the act in the *Las Vegas Review Journal*. Redd's show ran from 9:00 p.m. to midnight and again at 3:15 a.m., giving him time in-between shows to indulge his new obsession, Keno, an electronic gambling version of Bingo that held Redd in its grip until the day he died.

"He became quite a heavy gambler when he moved to Vegas and at the Aladdin Hotel, where he worked," said Redd's friend, John Barbour. "He used to bet thousands on Keno and they had a sign made up at the Keno station: 'Redd Foxx's Office.' He was totally obsessed with it. Sometimes he won a lot, but boy, he spent a fortune on it." His newfound passion was even noted in the black press. "Redd Foxx, some people swear, has won $45,000 playing Keno in Las Vegas in just six months time," blared a gossip item in the *Baltimore Afro-American.* "This rumor has caused people to follow him around . . . for between shows he heads straight to the Keno section, keeping on the move, for people trying to look over his shoulder to see what figures he marks. Redd himself swears he's 'way out' in the loss column, tho."

In October, Redd returned to the Aladdin on a bill with Billy Eckstine, again working the 9:00 p.m. to 12:15 a.m. show and, again, blowing thousands at the Keno table.

Two months later, in December 1966, Redd's first album for Sinatra's Loma label was released. *The Both Sides of Redd Foxx* didn't feature much "new" material per se, with Redd basically repeating earlier routines virtually verbatim, changing a line here and there (inserting Vietnam instead of World War II for example, into his standard "Foxx in the Army" routine). But for many people hearing Redd Foxx for the first time on a more established record label, the material was fresh— and the album sold fifteen thousand copies in thirty days. "Foxx, who is notorious for his blue material, has a relatively unexpurgated album . . . a funny display of the comedian's mimicry and quick wit," noted the *Los Angeles Times.*

December also brought the exciting news that Redd would make his prime-time television debut the following March, joining Dick Gregory, Godfrey Cambridge, Richard Pryor, George Kirby, Pigmeat Markham, and Moms Mabley in an ABC special called *100 Years of Laughter*, which would air as part of the network's *Stage 67* series. It would be narrated by Sidney Poitier, with singer Harry Belafonte serving as executive producer and also performing with Diahann Carroll. The special was billed as "a song-sketch-and-dance revue tracing the history and significance of Negro humor from the emancipation to the present."

The show's title was later changed to *A Time for Laughter: A Look at Negro Humor in America.* The special aired on March 28, 1967, and featured various sketches. In one, Godfrey Cambridge (who co-wrote the special) was paired with Moms Mabley and Broadway star Diana Sands in a sketch lampooning suburban social climbers (of all colors); in another sketch, impressionist George Kirby played all seven roles of a bunch of men congregating in a ghetto barbershop. "The ghetto talk moves into two other areas," noted the *Chicago Defender* critic. "In a pool hall we find Redd Foxx, longtime favorite of the circuit of nightclubs and theatres which play primarily to Negro audiences (and lately a guest on afternoon game shows) utilizing his zest for the language and the 'fast-talking hippie.' In a funeral parlor, young comedian Richard Pryor unsolemnly intones a satirical service that—like much of humor's spectrum—would be equally at home in any color scheme." Dick Gregory, who'd honed his political humor to a sharp point in the preceding turbulence of the Civil Rights fight, teamed with Harry Belafonte for a skit in which they're sitting in jail after a protest march, Gregory tossing cutting barbs at everything from President Lyndon Johnson to Red China.

A Time for Laughter provided a nice springboard for Redd's first full-length feature in *Ebony* magazine, which ran in the April 1967 issue under the headline, "Redd Foxx—Prince of Clowns." Written by long-time Foxx chronicler Louie Robinson, *Ebony's* West Coast editor, the five-page article offered up some interesting tidbits, including Redd's salary at the Aladdin ($4,000 a week, a figure Redd probably inflated a bit) and about his house in the Baldwin Hills section of Los Angeles ("$62,500," Robinson noted proudly) where he and Betty Jeanne "live with their seventeen-year-old daughter, Debraca, three dogs, a swimming pool, outdoor barbecue, and hammock" in a life of seemingly domestic bliss.

In May, Elvis Presley married his young bride Priscilla at the Aladdin. Redd had the honor of being the only show-business celebrity invited to the reception breakfast organized by Presley's manager, Col. Tom Parker, Redd's frequent gambling partner. Elvis had caught Redd's midnight show at the Aladdin several times and was a big fan. "It's the best thing that happened . . . to me," Redd quipped to a reporter at the reception breakfast. While Redd wasn't a part of Presley's inner circle by any stretch, "The King" showed his admiration as only he did—giving Redd a diamond-encrusted watch that never left Redd's wrist. In later years, Presley would also give Redd a huge necklace dripping with diamonds.

As part of Redd's record deal with Loma, he was allowed to issue releases on his own record label. So, in 1967, Redd formed two labels: Alma Records, named after his mother's maiden name, and M.F. Records, which played not only on Redd's "blue" reputation but on the last names of Redd and his attorney, Burt Marks. Redd's association with Sinatra was short-lived, and he ended up cutting only three albums for Loma: *The Both Sides of Redd Foxx*, *On the Loose*, and *Redd Foxx—Live in Las Vegas*, which was recorded at the Aladdin hotel. All three albums were released in 1967; when *On the Loose* and *Live in Las Vegas* sold poorly, Loma cut its ties with Redd. He was now free to issue his next string of record releases on his own labels, and he wasted no time. His first release on M.F. Records, *Laff Your Head Off*, hit stores in mid-1967 and was notable for being recorded in a place very close to Redd's heart: his new comedy club in downtown Los Angeles.

chapter seven

"Los Angeles Is a Rotten Town for Nightlife"

The Redd Foxx Club, which everyone just called Redd's Place, was located on La Cienega Boulevard in Los Angeles' Restaurant Row district. After working in so many dumps over the years, Redd's dream was to own his own place, where he wouldn't have to shake down the owner to get paid (in cash) or worry about someone skipping out with that night's take from the door. He wanted a place where could get up on stage and do his stand-up when he wanted to, with no language or content restrictions placed on him. He wanted a place where he could give other performers—not just comics—a place to work in an intimate, comfortable setting. He wanted a place where he could indulge his cocaine habit with fellow performers like Richard Pryor—and no one telling him he couldn't do otherwise. "I spent many nights when I felt as if we were in the coke Olympics," Pryor said of snorting the white stuff at Redd's Place with its owner.

More importantly, Redd wanted a place where his casual use of off-color language and "street talk" wouldn't get him thrown out or, worse yet, get him in trouble with the law. He'd seen how his friend Lenny Bruce, who Redd called "the great man," was treated for his use of on-stage profanity. Bruce's death the previous year was hastened by a descent into drug addiction, exacerbated by his legal troubles. Redd just wanted to have a good time, shoot the shit, and snort his coke among friends. Was that too much to ask?

"Ever get ejected out of a joint for saying 'shit'? I did. And that was a toilet, too," he told author Joe X Price. "I said it at the end of the first set. The owner didn't fire me right away; he just warned me not to leave the audience hanging with that word ringing in their ears. So the next set I opened with the word 'shit.' But that didn't please him, either. I got my ass ejected. That's why I had to have my own place, where no one could fire me no matter which four-letter word I used (or anyone who got up on stage would use)."

So, in March 1967, with the money coming in from his steady Las Vegas bookings and his other nightclub work, Redd plunked down $40,000 of his life savings to buy the old Slate Brothers Club, a small place on La Cienega. The club had been around for years, and was a destination for most up-and-coming acts; Frank Sinatra had "discovered" an acerbic comic named Don Rickles there in the late 1950s, and Lenny Bruce was a frequent headliner in the early 1960s. Redd didn't have any illusions about what he was getting himself into. As a veteran of the Los Angeles club scene, he knew how tough it was to make a go of it, especially in the city's restaurant district. But no one ever accused Redd Foxx of being a particularly shrewd businessman. "Los Angeles is a rotten town for nightlife. Everybody knows that," he said. "Everybody knew it in 1967, too, when I bought the joint. Everybody, that is, except me."

Redd turned to a member of his own family to help run the place, hiring Betty Jeanne's sister, Beverly Harris, to be the head waitress. It was also Beverly's job to hire the girls to work in the club. "We wore red patent-leather mini skirts and red boots," she said. "The place was small and long and cute with red tablecloths and red napkins. Every star you can name was there—Frank Sinatra, Joey Bishop, Peter Lawford, everybody. Bill Cosby was there constantly—we were so bored by him, by his act, but he was there constantly."

It was Redd's club, though, and he wouldn't let anyone forget that the poor kid from Saint Louis had worked his way up to own his own place. "I used to go to his club because I enjoyed Redd, I liked him," said George Schlatter. "So I'm there one night, and there's a guy in the club sitting ringside, a white guy. And every time Redd would go for a joke, the guy would top it. He was funny. The people are screaming now. Redd would top him, and it goes on and on. After a while, Redd finishes the show and comes over and stands right beside the table. And he says, 'Man, I want to tell you, you are one funny motherfucker. Every time I would tell a joke, son of a bitch, you were hitting the punchline before me.' And the guy says, 'What the hell, man. You're pissing on my table.' And Redd says, 'That's it. I'm gonna piss on you. Get outta here before I cut you.'" "He ran the club like a gangster, treating friends like relatives and enemies with scorn," said Richard Pryor. "People were beat up regularly."

In Redd's mind, his new club was a palace; Bill Cosby referred to it more acerbically (and probably more accurately) as "an aisle." Redd had the club renovated after he bought it, but that still couldn't hide the fact that Redd's Place wasn't any bigger than one of the larger walk-in closets in any of the houses in nearby Beverly Hills. "It was the Troc or the Grove or the Chez or any high-class spot you can name," Redd said. "At least that's what it was to me then."

When it was full to capacity, Redd's Place held about 150 people. It had seventy-five tables, each of which sat two people. The tables were crammed closely together on the plush pile carpeting—red, of course—in order to keep the atmosphere intimate. Customers entered the club from the front entrance on La Cienega and almost immediately were at the bar; the club's single dressing room, service bar, and bathrooms were located a long walk away in the back of the joint ("As long a hike as it is from here to Forest Lawn," quipped Slappy White). The main room was L-shaped; anyone sitting at the front table, located adjacent to the stage, risked being harassed by Redd if they dared to get up to use the rest room. (Redd's typical line to a woman who went to powder her nose: "Well, I'll talk loud so you'll be able to hear it while you're sitting down.") Redd eventually ripped out the front bar (it was too noisy), replaced it with tables, and moved the bar to the other side of the club.

Redd kept the lights low and always, *always*, had a Dinah Washington record playing over the sound system. "It was The Queen who brought me to California, and I will always thank her for that," he said. Once, Redd's friend Norma Miller, who was working at the club, decided she was tired of hearing non-stop Dinah Washington music, and incurred Redd's wrath by going into the back room and daring to lift the needle off the scratchy record to put something—anything—else on the turntable. Redd charged into the room, apoplectic, and when Norma complained about the scratchy records, Redd gave her one hundred dollars to walk down the street and buy a new batch of "The Queen's" albums.

The club became Redd's home away from home, and when he wasn't performing in Las Vegas or elsewhere, "The Boss," as everyone called him, would hang around Redd's Place, even if he wasn't sched-uled to go on that night. He could often be found sitting out in front of the club on La Cienega, holding court with young comics and staffers or simply bullshitting with passers-by. Comic Stu Gilliam recalls Redd once yelling to a passerby, "Come right in, this ain't no black place. Don't you worry about it, we'll see to it you get back to your neighbor-hood."

"Redd's Place became a kind of rallying point for a lot of the guys from New York, especially those of us who had worked the Chitlin' Circuit together and later moved out to the Coast," said Gilliam. One night, happy with the big turnout and pleased with his own on-stage performance, Redd dropped his pants and went outside, greeting the audience in his underwear as they left the club and thanking them for coming—Bill Cosby remembered—"just as casual as you like, as though there was nothing out of the ordinary about it."

"The audience was very hip, nightclub-comedy-oriented," Gilliam said. "And you would get the most in-order hecklers that you would ever run across. I mean, if a guy was going to bug you, he was right there where he was supposed to be to set up a line or whatever . . . and you're straining and squinting like hell to see, and by the time you finally focus in, you've got Richie Pryor and Flip Wilson, who snuck in through the back. And there are the two voices that you've been trying to shout down for the last fifteen or twenty minutes!"

The nights he was at the club, Redd would hang out until the wee hours of the morning with whomever was around, including Richard Pryor. In his autobiography, *Pryor Convictions*, Pryor remembered one long night and early morning spent with Redd, "battling each other for the attention of a sexy waitress, listening to jazz, and snorting cocaine by the spoonful." When Pryor asked Redd why he [Pryor] always want-ed more and more cocaine—even after a Redd's Place binge—Redd had a simple answer: "Because you're a junkie."

Redd gave his stepfather, Harry Carson, a job taking tickets at the door, and before long the old man developed a reputation as a stickler for anyone entering through the front door, making sure ev-eryone paid—on occasion even hassling that night's headliner if he didn't recognize him. Carson was an avid sportsman, who at one time traveled with boxing great Jack Johnson (Redd still had the pair of boxing gloves Johnson gave to his father years before). Even though Harry and Mary Sanford married in the 1950s, most people just assumed that Harry was Redd's natural father, so close was the physical resemblance between the two—down to Carson's squat build, reddish complexion, and his gravelly voice. "Redd used to call him the eighty-year-old hippie," Norma Miller recalled. "And he loved it. He was sharp and so spry, and he dressed the part, too. Like he always wore turtleneck sweaters and hung one of those big medallions around his neck."

Harry Carson became a beloved fixture at Redd's Place, but suffered a tragic fate several years later. One night, while Mary was gabbing on the phone, Harry decided to clean his fully loaded gun, a Colt Peacemaker he often showed off with pride. After cleaning the gun and putting all six bullets back into the gun's chamber, he was walking back toward his bedroom, Colt in hand, when he stumbled. The Colt fell to the floor, went off, and killed Harry instantly (cops later found a bullet lodged in the ceiling).

The timing of Harry's death couldn't have been worse. Redd was appearing (finally!) on *The Steve Allen Show* the night Harry was killed. Mary, who was hysterical, called Redd's manager, Bardu Ali, at the studio to tell him that Harry was dead. Ali waited until the next commercial break and ran up on stage to tell Redd that Harry had had an accident (but not that he was dead) and that Redd needed to rush back home. Steve Allen told Redd and Bardu that he would explain to his audience that Redd needed to leave, and that Redd could return to the show another time. "Steve Allen is a prince of a man," Ali said. Harry's death hit Redd hard. "Redd used to smoke marijuana, and when [Harry] died, he called and asked me if I would come down and sit around," said John Barbour. "About a dozen people sat around telling stories about [Harry]. And Redd smoked grass while he did that. They all smoked it." Redd accompanied Harry's body back to his hometown of Joliet, Illinois, where he was buried.

Once word began to spread throughout the Los Angeles club scene that Redd Foxx bought the old Slate Brothers place, many young comics, including Richard Pryor, began flocking there to sit at the feet of The Master. Pryor was eighteen years younger than Redd, but they shared common midwestern roots (Pryor was born in Peoria, Illinois and was raised in his grandmother's whorehouse—where his mother worked as a prostitute). Like Redd, Pryor's early ambitions were to become a musician; unlike Redd, once Pryor segued to stand-up comedy, he worked "clean" in the style of Bill Cosby, telling "neat little inoffensive chickenshit stories."

But Pryor had trouble reconciling his on-stage "plastic" act with his inner demons—something felt wrong, and, one night in September 1967, he walked out onto the Aladdin stage in his tuxedo and took one look at the middle-aged Las Vegas audience. "What the fuck am I doing here?!" he said into the microphone, and promptly walked off the stage. The Richard Pryor that reappeared on stage thereafter was hip, profane, and hysterically funny, channeling his anger into biting social commentary and peppering his delivery with the word "nigger," which he used liberally (it became Pryor's calling card, of sorts). He took his cue from Redd. "He was the epitome," Pryor said. "He was doing it all—being himself on stage, pulling no punches, a totally no-bullshit act. Wherever he worked, he was always Redd Foxx."

Pryor was a regular at Redd's Place whenever he was in town, both as Redd's friend and as a performer, and he recorded several comedy albums there. "I hung around there often," he said. "I loved it. I loved watching [Redd]. I loved getting on that stage and just tripping—ad-libbing new routines and so on." "Richard would walk in that club, and he'd blow Foxx away," said Bill Cosby. "He'd blow me away, with no problem. That was mainly because Richard was bringing in a new kind of language at that time—not really bringing it in, but using it and using it well."

Redd's Place catered mostly to young, urban comedians and musicians—George Kirby, Flip Wilson, Stu Gilliam, Scoey Mitchell—though it did have its "token" white comedian, Herb Eden. "Talk about intimate; actually the room was almost a living theater," Gilliam recalled. "Everything that went on was part of the show. I mean, the room was so small, you couldn't call out your drink order without it being heard all over. The place was a living stage, and a comic with his wits about him could stand there and do fifteen or twenty minutes just trying to slow them down long enough for him to tell one planned story or do one planned piece of material."

On paper, Redd's Place appeared to be the perfect set-up to make some cash. Rumors that Redd was simply fronting the club for white investors irked him to no end. He owned it outright—and would sink or swim on his own, thank you very much. But he couldn't be around the club all the time to watch his $40,000 investment, and some of the people he hired to work there—most notably the bartenders—started dipping their hands into a till that, more often than not, was more empty than full.

Business at Redd's Place was touch-and-go. Despite the club's reputation as a hip, happening hangout, its small size meant that a constantly packed house was needed just to break even. Redd was never the most astute businessman under normal circumstances, and he began to lose control over his club. He couldn't take charge if he wasn't there, and he made a habit of hiring staffers without adequate background checks. "He would hire a lot of his friends and later on he would find out they would be stealing from him, and I think that's what hurt him and upset him a lot," said his daughter, Debraca. And with his commitments in Vegas, where he was a regular headliner at the Aladdin, and his constant touring schedule, which kept him tied up for weeks on end, he just wasn't at Redd's Place enough. "Money is not green with Redd Foxx," said comedian Herb Eden. "In his hands it's transparent, it's invisible, it's disappearing and it has a couple of other qualities, too—slippery and flammable." Norma Miller put it more succinctly: "Money and him just ain't on the best of terms."

By the beginning of 1968, less than a year after he bought the club, Redd's Place had turned into a money pit. Bartenders and other staffers (including several managers) were siphoning off tips and stealing merchandise with alarming regularity. The sporadic crowds only exacerbated an already bad situation. Redd, no stranger to the rough-and-tumble milieu of the nightclub world, began carrying a gun to the club, a little black Derringer he would use to threaten unruly employees or defend himself against what seemed to be a constant element of danger lurking just outside the front door on La Cienega.

One night, between shows at the club, Redd grabbed Herb Eden and the two men went outside for a talk. Redd was hearing that one of his bartenders was stealing cash, and he wanted to know from Eden what was going on. As the two men talked, Eden noticed a car idling by the curb on La Cienega, with two big black men sitting inside. "Now the two black guys jump out of the car and really get on Redd's case," Eden recalled. "I don't know if he owes them money; I don't know the story at all (and, matter of fact, I never did find out). All I know is that they're after him."

The bigger of the two men pulled out a knife and waved it in the air.

"Where is it?!" he demanded, while Redd pretended not to know what "it" was. While the big guy with the knife continued to demand "it," Redd told him he had a heart condition, which caused him to urinate frequently. Turning his back to the wall and unzipping his fly, Redd turned back around—this time holding the black Derringer. "I don't have to pee no more, asshole! Now you better drop the knife and run!" he yelled, chasing the two guys down the street while their car continued to idle by the curb.

While the club's financial problems continued to drain Redd's bank account—and his nerves—his career away from La Cienega Boulevard was shifting into overdrive. In September 1967, he opened at The Village Gate in Greenwich Village on a rare trip back to New York. "For about an hour, Redd rattled off joke after joke, pausing only for liquid refreshment," wrote the *Amsterdam News'* Raymond Robinson. "Foxx hasn't changed much, if any. His material takes in everything in current events, but when the cigarette-puffing comedian is talking, things come out a little risqué and very, very funny."

He also began appearing more frequently on television. He was one of the celebrities tapped to appear on the syndicated game show, *The Hollywood Squares*, and was welcomed many times on *The Merv Griffin Show* and *The Mike Douglas Show*, where he would perform the more mainstream bits from his club routines. "A lot of you don't know that I'm a war veteran," he told Douglas' audience during one appearance, dragging on his ever-present cigarette. "I remember one battle we were in I backed up so far I bumped into a general. He said, 'Why are you running?' and I said, 'I'm running because I cannot fly.'" Later, when Douglas asked Redd if he was having trouble getting television bookings because of his material, Redd didn't miss a beat. "Why, no," he said, "but I noticed I haven't been here in two years." He continued to work steadily at the Aladdin in Vegas (always the late shows, usually 10:15 p.m. and 2:00 a.m.) and even won a court case against his old adversary Dootsie Williams, who was ordered to pay Redd $13,500 in back royalties after yet another protracted legal battle.

And, in the meantime, Redd hired his first business manager: a charismatic former musician named Bardu Ali.

The son of an Arab father and American mother, Bardu Ali was born in New Orleans in 1906. Passionately interested in music, he learned to play guitar, and by his early twenties was a noted jazz and rhythm-and-blues guitarist and singer. He moved to New York with his brother, a drummer, where he worked in bands fronted by Napoleon Zyas and Leroy Tibbs. Ali eventually became the front man for jazz drummer Chick Webb's band, and is credited by many with discovering Ella Fitzgerald (and convincing a reluctant Webb to hire her for the band). When Webb died, Ali formed his own band and moved to Los Angeles in 1940, where he met Johnny Otis (and, later, Redd). Ali and Otis formed a business partnership—they opened the Barrelhouse Club together in 1947—and Ali joined Otis's band. After splitting with Otis, Ali turned his focus to managing and promoting musical acts.

In 1968, Ali was managing tap dancer Harold Nicholas (of Nicholas Brothers fame) when he flew out to Los Angeles to meet with Redd in an effort to get Harold Nicholas booked into Redd's Place. Redd and Ali had known each other for years, and when comedian George Kirby walked into the club, extolling the virtues of having a good manager, Redd mentioned to Ali that he'd been looking for someone to manage his affairs. "So I said to Redd, 'You're looking at your manager now,'" Ali remembered, and the two men worked out an agreement. Ali put Redd, a profligate spender, on a strict weekly budget, including a household allowance for Betty Jeanne. Redd could borrow against the next week's allowance, which he did frequently during his years with Ali. The Redd-on-a-budget idea worked better in theory than in reality.

The new business partnership paid immediate dividends in more ways than one. Redd's first job under Ali's management, in late August 1968, was at the Top Hat, a club in Windsor, Canada (Ontario). After the show, Redd, Ali, and the club's manager went out for dinner. During the meal, Ali, who was eating liver, began choking; he turned all shades of green and blue until someone noticed he couldn't breathe. Redd grabbed a napkin, put it under Ali's chin, and yelled at him: "Puke, Bardu! Puke! You're dying!" Ali coughed up the liver, and forever after credited Redd with saving his life.

Shortly thereafter, Redd and Ali were in Atlanta for a club date, and were staying at the Regency Hyatt House, where there was a record convention. Henry Glover, who represented Starday King Records, which specialized mostly in country-and-western releases, approached them. Redd's recording contract with Warner Bros. had just expired, and Glover was interested in making an offer. (Starday was revamping its catalogue and would eventually add James Brown to its roster.) It was early in the morning, around 3 a.m., and Ali told Glover that Redd would sign for $20,000 cash. Glover, without batting an eyelash, told Ali that he'd get back to him after conferring with company president Hal Mehle. Mehle agreed to the deal, but Ali insisted on getting the $20,000 in the form of a cashier's check. It was delivered to his hotel room— by a man with an attaché case chained to his arm—a few weeks later while Redd was playing a Cincinnati nightclub called the Living Room (Starday King was, conveniently, headquartered in Cincinnati). Ali gave Redd the check and left his hotel room; when he returned, he noticed that Redd had chained the attaché case to a chair. "If somebody walks out of this hotel with the attaché case, no one's gonna say nothin' to him," he told Ali. "But if that bastard walks out of here with that chair on his head . . . " Redd ended up cutting five albums for Starday King.

As Redd's business manager, Bardu Ali was helpless to do much about the situation at Redd's Place. The club was losing money hand-over-fist through a lethal combination of insider stealing, Redd's financial ignorance, and half-full houses (even though hot comics, including Richard Pryor, continued to perform there). "He was a businessman, it was just the wrong business," said Redd's friend, George Schlatter. But one advantage Bardu Ali did have, in abundance, was an enviable roster of industry contacts—he knew just about everyone, or so it seemed, and he figured that if he could get Redd onto national television to talk about the club, and about its dire financial situation, it might spark an upsurge in business and help keep Redd's Place afloat.

So, in late December 1967, Ali approached Joey Bishop, who'd launched his much-ballyhooed talk show, *The Joey Bishop Show*, earlier that year on ABC. Although he was no longer close with fellow Rat Packer Frank Sinatra by this time, Bishop still had a considerable amount of show-business cachet, and his show was considered the first serious threat to Johnny Carson's late-night dominance. Unlike Carson, whose *Tonight Show* was based in New York, Bishop's show originated from Los Angeles, and Joey was a fan of Redd's, having caught his act several times at Redd's Place with his sidekick, Regis Philbin. Because Bishop had launched his show during one of Carson's periodic walkouts over money, *The Joey Bishop Show* started strongly. But that didn't last long; Carson returned shortly thereafter, and by late 1967 had reclaimed his late-night throne. Joey wasn't overly picky now when it came to booking his guests, and he liked Redd. It wasn't a hard sell for Ali.

Ali didn't tell Redd that he was going to see Bishop, fearing that Redd would tell him to fuck off, that he had his pride and didn't want to be turned into some kind of charity case on national television. But after Ali's visit to Bishop—who immediately agreed to put Redd on the very next night—there wasn't much time to argue about it. Besides, Ali told Redd, the publicity couldn't hurt. He had nothing to lose. Redd grudgingly agreed, and he and Ali showed up at *The Joey Bishop Show* studios the next day at 5:30 p.m. "I saw Redd and Bardu back in the guest star dressing room before we started shooting, and Redd was down, I could see it," Bishop said. "Sure, he tried to put on a happy front when he saw me—he shook my hand and smiled pleasantly enough—but it wasn't the old Redd Foxx. Something was bothering him, and I knew he hadn't been drinking."

Bishop's first guest that night was singer Tony Martin. After Martin performed several numbers, Redd was introduced, did a few minutes of stand-up, and was invited to sit on Bishop's couch next to Martin. Initially, everything seemed to be just fine. Redd fired off a few jokes about his recent gig at Caesar's Palace in Las Vegas—he was on the bill with Aretha Franklin, who was a no-show the first night—and then Joey asked him about Redd's Place. "How are you, Redd?" Bishop said. "I know I'm going out on a limb. I know you've helped a lot of people. I understand you're having trouble getting people to help you." "I own a club in Los Angeles, which is a good club with all the finest talent, but it's in trouble financially," Redd said, turning somber. "We like to call it the house that comedy built, but it's liable to be a tragedy before long.

"A tragedy because I may have to close it up," Redd continued. "And that would put a lot of fine young comedians and musicians out of work. But it'd be really rough on the comedians because, as you know, Joey, there ain't that many places where a comic can go and say anything he wants. There ain't that many . . ." and suddenly Redd's voice cracked. There was deathly silence in the studio, and the camera zoomed in on Redd's face. He was crying, with tears streaming down his cheeks. Bishop broke the silence. "I'm just choked up," he said. "Redd, I know what that club means to you, and I think everyone around the country who is tuned in to you now can see it, too." Redd raised his head, sighed, and composed himself. "The thing that I suppose bothers me more than any one thing is that a lot of folks think it's not my club," he said. "That I don't own Redd's Place. That I'm just fronting it for a bunch of white Mafia guys.

"Well, I do own it. It's mine," he said. "I don't know who I'm fronting for. There's nobody there but me. It's all the money I saved. And I don't intend to sell it, either, even if I have to ride it all the way down. Thank you, Joey, for letting me come on your show." And, with that, Redd got up and walked offstage. Bishop's house band, stunned by the emotional display, nearly forgot to play Redd's exit music as he strode off the stage.

It was high drama, and it worked. By the next day, Billy Eckstine, Sammy Davis Jr., Bill Cosby, and Lou Rawls were volunteering their services (for a reduced rate). Redd's Place was hopping, and the lines were out the door and snaking around the corner. For the first few weeks after Redd's meltdown on *The Joey Bishop Show*, there was often a forty-five-minute wait to get into the club. One night, Marlon Brando, Slim Pickens, Eartha Kitt, and Hazel Scott were in the audience. Redd told *Jet* magazine that he received a call from a millionaire in San Antonio, Texas, who volunteered to bankroll the club (that never happened). He added that a "national television executive" was interested in filming Redd at the club for a one-hour special (that also never happened). His crying jag on *The Joey Bishop Show* even earned Redd another television appearance when he was booked to appear on Woody Woodbury's syndicated talk show.

"Aesop's Fox, when he had lost his tail, wanted all his fellow foxes to cut off theirs," Leonard Feather wrote in the *Los Angeles Times*. "Redd Foxx, when he was in danger of losing his nightclub, realized that there was no percentage in trying to shut down all the other bistros. Instead, he made a recent appearance on the Joey Bishop TV show, talked about his economic woes, and met a heartwarming response. . . . On Friday, there were strong indications that the emergency was over. It was the first of two nights Billy Eckstine had agreed to work the room. He attracted an overflowing, friendly crowd . . . Bill Cosby jumped onstage and did fifteen hilarious minutes devoted exclusively to the subject of hair. ('I live in Beverly Hills but I still have to go to Watts to get a haircut.')"

"The stars came to Redd's rescue and everybody you could name was calling there to come to do a show, including the Platters, who I later joined," said Beverly Harris. "They all said, 'We wanna help Redd out' and we were just amazed. George Burns came every night and sat in the front row with two girls. Redd was a real popular guy."

Bill Cosby, who thought Redd's Place had a future and "loved" the club—particularly in light of its now-booming business—stepped up and bought a percentage stake in Redd's Place. With his fresh infusion of cash, Cosby improved the sound system and raised the cover charge from a dollar fifty to five dollars. And, much to Redd's displeasure, he plastered the club's walls with photos of black activists. He also had militant quotes framed and hung on the walls. The Foxx-Cosby partnership didn't last long.

Although Redd was on the road when Cosby moved in to run the club, Redd had given his new partner carte blanche to do what he wanted in order to boost the club's business—which was starting to slack off again once Redd's tearful appearance on *The Joey Bishop Show* began to fade into memory. "We tried everything. We had a six- to seven-thousand-dollar entertainment nut because we tried to make it the first club in the city to book two first-name artists at the same time—and three shows a night too," Cosby said. He booked Sarah Vaughan, Dizzy Gillespie, Carmen McRae, Della Reese, and Esther Phillips, among others, into the club, which helped a little. But it wasn't enough. "I think many people took a look at the marquee out front and, seeing the names, said to themselves, 'It must be a joke, and I'm not going to go in there,'" he said. Cosby also got a first-hand look at how the place operated in Redd's absence—or, more accurately, how it *didn't* operate. One night, while setting up the bar, Cosby noticed that there was no beer; when he alerted one of the staffers, they told him not to worry—they'd just run across the street to the supermarket and replenish the stock. No one had bothered to check ahead of time. Cosby also discovered what Redd already knew—that the club's majority owner was being ripped off by his employees to the tune of thousands. "I found there were several people who, because of Redd's involvement, were dipping into his little till," Cosby said. "Certain checks were cashed. Certain cash disappeared.

"I remember one night we took in around twenty-three hundred dollars. I was very happy about that, and I decided that I was going to go and buy some liquor," he said. "But before I could get to the bank, over half of it was gone. It got be very, very strange."

Redd, meanwhile, was irritated at Cosby for changing the club *too* much in his absence. "When Bill Cosby became active in operating my club in Hollywood last spring, he had all my pictures of show biz people taken down, and I came in and saw nothing on the wall but militant sayings, militant pictures; nobody on that wall was smiling," he said. "It affected me so bad I had them all taken down. Whatever happened to happiness? Being a comic, I have to look at it that way." Cosby backed out shortly thereafter for a variety of reasons, leaving Redd to flail about on his own.

While Redd's appearance on *The Joey Bishop Show* only helped his club in the short term, it did boost his television career. In between his gigs at the Aladdin and Mister Kelly's in Chicago, Redd was invited to appear on a prime-time special called *Soul*, which was produced by George Schlatter and aired in October 1968.

Earlier that year, Schlatter had successfully launched *Laugh-In* on NBC, and was producing *Soul* with his partner, Ed Friendly. Schlatter and Friendly originally intended on making *Soul* an all-black production—everyone from the stars to the staffers to the crew—but couldn't quite pull it off; there just wasn't enough black personnel in the unions to make that possible. Still, the special's director (Mark Warren), choreographer (Donald McKayle), musical director (H.B. Barnum), and graphics designer were black, while *Laugh-In* writer Digby Wolfe, who oversaw the script, culled the show's writers (Jeanne A. Taylor, Cal Wilson, and Larry L. Reed Jr.) from the Watts Writers Project, a group with which he was intimately involved.

"What the writers had to do was find a middle course, not to make it so the show would appeal just to the Negro community but so the Negro community would feel the program expresses some of their opinions," said the British-born Wolfe, who'd also written for *That Was the Week That Was*. "We're trying to let the white community in on black humor and to show that the black man can do something constructive," the writers said in a statement. "We're just saying it in an entertaining way."

Soul would be a mixture of black comedy and music. For the special's comedic elements, Schlatter and Friendly corralled Redd Foxx, George Kirby, Slappy White, and Nipsey Russell; Lou Rawls, Martha Reeves and the Vandellas, Joe Tex, the Chambers Brothers, Hines, Hines and Dad, and Leroy "Sloppy" Daniels rounded out the musical talent. "We're not trying to prove anything," Schlatter said of the special. "It's just that most of the humor today is really Negro-oriented. We felt there ought to be a platform for it." It spoke volumes about Redd's impact on the black community that Schlatter and Friendly included him as a cultural representative of black humor—even if he was still relatively unknown to network television audiences (read: white America).

The expectation was that *Soul* would be shot as a pilot for a possible network series; if the special proved popular enough, NBC could launch it as a midseason replacement in early 1969, or wait until the fall to include it on its prime-time schedule. There was talk at NBC that *Soul* could replace *The Phyllis Diller Show*, which was being cancelled by the network. The special was shot in color and utilized Schlatter's *Laugh-In* style of quick-cut blackout sketches—some only seconds in length—with the musical acts interspersed in between and a plethora of black go-go dancers. Rawls, who had a big hand in creating the special, functioned as the ostensible host.

Redd was featured in many of the sketches, sometimes solo but mostly in tandem with his old comedy partner, Slappy White.

> REDD *(holding a cigarette)*: What do you think of these
>   heart transplants?
> SLAPPY: Did you hear where they took the heart of a
>   Negro and put it in the body of a white man?
> REDD: I heard about that.
> SLAPPY: Not only did he live, he won a tap-dancing
>   concert in Harlem.
> REDD: And when he got home he had three welfare
>   checks waiting on him.
> SLAPPY: And a Cadillac with two notes due!

Another sketch poked fun at segregationist Alabama Governor George Wallace and his presidential campaign.

> SLAPPY: So what do you think of George Wallace running
>   for president?
> REDD: Here's what I think of it (makes a disgusted face).
>   You think Wallace should run again?
> SLAPPY: Yeah, and the next time I hope they catch him.

REDD: In Harlem.
SLAPPY: At night.
REDD: On a rooftop.
SLAPPY: With dark glasses on.
REDD: Eating a pig's foot.

In the hour-long show's only recurring sketch, Redd played a journalist questioning Slappy, who was playing the country's first black
Vice President. While some of the lines in this sketch would never fly
today—and were, in retrospect, insulting—it's important to remember
that they were written by black writers and reflected the tenor of the
times.

REDD: Mr. Vice President, where do you stand on
    unemployment?
SLAPPY: Right up front.
REDD: Why are you so anxious to get jobs for all Negroes?
    Don't you think it's important to see that white people
    have jobs, too?
SLAPPY: Don't no white people owe me no money.
REDD: Can you name three Negro holidays?
SLAPPY: Joe Louis's birthday, Jackie Robinson's birthday,
    and October 27—when the new Cadillacs come out.
REDD: The University of Mississippi just gave their first
    scholarship to a Negro athlete. What does he do?
SLAPPY: He's a javelin catcher.

Redd's finest moment in *Soul* came in a sketch in which Slappy asks
him what he thinks of the Grand Wizard of the Ku Klux Klan. Redd's
answer, delivered with a smile but underscored by smoldering resentment, is pure Redd Foxx—almost as if he was up on stage in Redd's
Place, riffing on current events: "I'd like to wish the Grand Wizard of
the Ku Klux Klan a five-car accident with no survivors, a slow ambulance with four flat tires and no spares, a junky doctor with an eight-
hundred-dollar-a-day habit with an orangutan on his back and a rusty
scalpel in his hand as he's operating on the Grand Wizard in the hospital that's burning down on top of the operating table and frozen fire
hydrants from Alabama to Nova Scotia—and if they ever thaw out,

muddy water in his coffin. Other than that, good luck, and may lightning strike him in the heart 374 times before some hungry possums chew through his expensive coffin for something strange to eat. Amen."

Soul aired on October 17, 1968, but Schlatter, who was hoping to sell the special as a series, wasn't taking any chances on its content, and previewed the series to one important group beforehand. "We had a screening for the [Black] Panthers," he said. "We brought everybody up from Watts to run it and they just loved it and the network was almost afraid because it was a pretty powerful reaction. Nobody had ever done it before; it was the first all-black variety show."

Soul generated "tons of mail," according to Rawls, and fairly decent reviews in the press. "Most of the comedy was naturally geared to the Negro predicament and poked fun at both themselves and the whites. . . . Putting it all together in a fast-paced mélange, the result was split about 50-50 between fair and good," noted the *Los Angeles Times*. "To succeed as a weekly show, however, *Soul* will need a sharper and more topical brand of wit."

But any hopes Schlatter had of selling *Soul* as a series—and, perhaps, giving Redd his first network television role—went up in smoke. "We ran it for NBC and . . . they didn't buy it as a series because, they said, if they bought that show—think back to 1969—they were afraid they could never cancel it," Schlatter said. "Because the Panthers and all that stuff was going on."

For Redd, though, *Soul* was terrific exposure, and he appeared on television more frequently, now that producers and network executives realized that, despite his "blue" act, Redd could and would behave himself on the national stage. "I can only remember one time being censored on television," Redd said. "On *The Merv Griffin Show* I told a story about this young couple that lives on a farm. The wife is going to a masquerade party dressed as a cow, and the husband is going as a bull. They are a little late so they cut across a field. Halfway across, a real bull sees them and starts to charge. The wife gets real scared. 'Look, Bill, here comes a bull, what shall we do?' And the guy says, 'I'm going to stand here and eat some grass; you'd better just brace yourself.' Do you know what they did? The bleeped out the word 'brace.' That made it sound dirtier than what I'd said."

The Merv Griffin Show was one of Redd's frequent stops; there were also visits to *The Mike Douglas Show* and the occasional chat with Johnny

Carson on *The Tonight Show*. In 1969, Redd also appeared on pal Della Reese's new syndicated talk show, *Della*, which Reese taped in Los Angeles with sidekick Sandy Baron. The show ended up running for only one season when many stations in the South refused to carry it (or, as Reese explained, "one executive told me they had a hard time finding sponsors because my gums were blue").

"I was doing the *Della* show and I insisted they have Redd on," Reese said. "And they were scared all the while that he was going to do something that was not apropos. And he came on and he was funny as he wanted to be. He didn't say one curse word. He didn't make one dirty gesture.

"They didn't give him credit for being an intelligent man, you see," she said. "What some people saw was a black man who told dirty jokes, like there was no more to him than that. That was his whole existence. That he was a black man who told dirty jokes. That was insulting—it was offensive to him and it was offensive to me."

Redd was also one of the real-life celebrities (including Norm Crosby, Peter Lawford, Xavier Cugat, Ray Charles, Frank Sinatra, Tony Martin, Charo, and Ike Turner) playing themselves in a two-part episode of the NBC drama, *The Name of The Game*. The episode, entitled "I Love You, Billy Baker," starred Sammy Davis Jr. (wearing a ridiculous wig and a big peace sign on his bare chest) as a superstar Las Vegas entertainer whose former dancer girlfriend is murdered.

Redd's appearances on television didn't always go as planned, and he wasn't always perfectly behaved. During an appearance on *The Dick Cavett Show*, the successor to *The Joey Bishop Show* on ABC, Redd incurred Cavett's wrath by mugging for the studio audience during Cavett's interview with conservative columnist James J. Kilpatrick. "Knock it off!" Cavett snarled at Redd, stunning the studio audience. "From a theatrical point of view," Cavett said later, "it was good."

While there wouldn't be any *Soul* television series for Redd, he did participate in "Soul Bowl '69," which was held in the Houston Astrodome in June 1969. Redd joined Aretha Franklin, Ray Charles, Sam and Dave, Percy Sledge, Jimmy Witherspoon, and Johnny "Guitar" Watson in the event, organized by Rev. C.L. Franklin (Aretha's father) to promote low-cost housing in the nation's ghettos. It was just one of many charitable events with which Redd would be associated. As time went on, he also performed regularly, free of charge, at prisons around the nation, usually around Christmas and on New Year's Eve. "What prisoners want to hear is what soldiers want to hear—what's happening on the street," Redd said. "They want to hear about women. They want to hear about home."

Redd's television exposure translated into better and better bookings. He was already an established presence in Las Vegas, where he appeared regularly at the Aladdin and, in the summer of 1969, Bardu Ali, booked him into the glitzy Caesar's Palace for a week-long gig opening for "Soul Sister" Aretha Franklin. Redd went on as scheduled at 10:00 p.m. opening night—"You couldn't get a matchstick in there," Ali remembered—but when the lights came up at the end of Redd's set, Aretha Franklin failed to materialize. After a few awkward minutes, a voice came over the room's loudspeaker, informing the audience that Franklin "was ill" and couldn't perform, and that the hotel would pick up the bill for everyone who'd attended the show (about 1,500 people).

Franklin managed to appear on stage for two shows before canceling the rest of her engagement due to what was later reported as a "bronchial and thyroid condition." Frank Sinatra filled in as the headliner for a few nights before Caesar's pulled the plug on the show. It was a disappointing turn of events for Redd, but it turned out to be serendipitous: he was booked into the Hilton—in the casino and not in the lounge—where he ended up staying for a year.

But the steady paychecks didn't seem to make much of a difference to Redd, who spent his money as soon as it came in. It was around this time that Redd was slapped with one of the first of what would be an almost cartoonish litany of lawsuits that dogged him until the day he died. This lawsuit, filed by Executive Car Leasing, a car rental company in Los Angeles, charged Redd with being behind on his monthly payments for a 1967 Cadillac convertible he'd leased in August of that year. The company was seeking over $850 dollars in back payments. The case was quickly settled—but Redd's future legal troubles wouldn't be so easy to dismiss.

As Redd's Las Vegas career began to pick up steam, the city in the desert became his second home. Not only could he feed his insatiable Keno addiction and chase women, but his twenty-plus years on the club circuit meant that he knew many of the entertainers who passed through Sin City. He especially enjoyed hanging out with jazz artists, many of whom he'd worked with over the years and considered friends.

They spoke the language of the streets and shared many of the same experiences—they understood each other without having to say too much. Redd loved the atmosphere.

When he was performing in Las Vegas, or just hanging out, Redd became friends with Jimmy Mulidore, the noted saxophonist who doubled as the musical director for the Hilton and the Flamingo hotels on the Strip. Mulidore—who'd worked with Red Norvo, Louie Bellson, Frank Sinatra, and others—was friendly with most of the jazz musicians who were working in town. "Redd was a tremendous jazz fan and, at the time, I had been associated with all the great legendary black jazz artists—Harry 'Sweets' Edison, who was a dear friend of Redd's—James Moody, Monk Montgomery, Bennie Green. We were playing with Redd, working with him and wherever we were, Redd was always around," Mulidore said. "He loved Miles Davis, Dizzy. It was like a scene. We hung out. Redd was just a great, great friend. He was always famous for working the Hilton and gambling away his paychecks on Keno. He played more Keno than you can imagine."

Mulidore would often invite Redd, Slappy White, and Billy Eckstine over to his house for dinner. Mulidore's friendship with Redd's continued after Redd became a famous television star. "My little son, Philip, was so engrossed with Redd from *Sanford and Son*, and when he walked in, Philip said, 'Mr. Foxx, how come you don't walk like Sanford?' And then Redd did his *Sanford and Son* walk and it was quite unique for him to take his time out to make my son happy with 'the walk.'"

Redd also incorporated his musician friends into his act. "Of course we would bring Redd out with his [*Sanford and Son*] theme," Mulidore said. "During the show, Redd would acknowledge something in his act, some of his funny lines, and he would pull one of the names from the guys, like, 'You know what I mean, Moody?' That kind of deal. He always kept us right in there and he would bring somebody up to play, just for thirty seconds. His participation with musicians was so unique that, when Redd was around, it was a happy time." Sometimes, it was "happy" for other reasons; Mulidore remembers walking into one of Redd's parties and watching him "get a round ball of cocaine and put it on the table and whoever wanted to indulge, fine. You're talking about $10,000 or $15,000 worth of cocaine. It's no secret that Redd did drugs."

The money problems, meanwhile, were beginning to pile up at

Redd's Place. Redd had been gone from the club for the good part of the past year-and-a-half, dropping in only sporadically in-between his aborted gig at Caesar's Palace and during his year-long run at the Hilton in Vegas. Bill Cosby, by this time, had seen enough of the behind-the-scenes shenanigans at Redd's Place and was thoroughly disgusted with the stealing and cheating.

The final straw for Cosby came one night in August 1970. He'd told the club's manager to bring in a vacuum cleaner, so the two of them could clean out the little house out in back of the club, which housed Redd's office. The manager, naturally, didn't bring the vacuum cleaner as requested, but Cosby decided to clean the office anyway— and when he lifted up the rug found an unpleasant surprise. "There were bills under there—bills that hadn't been paid, dozens of them," Cosby said. The club's manager said he didn't know who'd put the bills under the rug, but Cosby counted thirty-three unpaid bills—then found even more unpaid bills under the cushion of the dusty couch pushed up against one of the office walls. "It was just too much. There was no control. The wrong people were in the key spots," Cosby said. "It was too painful to see how Redd was getting hurt every time the place was open for business. He wasn't going to be back on TV crying again, but watching it happen was almost enough to make you cry.

"This was when I decided to pull out," Cosby said. "I figured they're going to keep doing all kinds of numbers on Redd, and it's going to go on and on, and he's just going to keep writing checks. It was like water on a red-hot frying pan. It was one of the toughest things I ever had to do when I told Redd I'd had enough. I felt like I was abandoning ship before the women and children. But I told him and we parted friends. The whole thing boils down to this: if you're going to own a nightclub, you'd better be there from nine at night until two in the morning. . . .That was what really brought Redd's Place down. He just wasn't there."

Redd agreed with Cosby, up to a point. But he surprisingly heaped much of the blame for the club's downfall not on his own lack of business acumen—and his absentee management—but on the black community. "I bought that place so I wouldn't have to travel. But it started going bad," he said. "I put on a show every night until I got a job in Las Vegas and I went to Las Vegas for two weeks and I stayed a year-and-a-half. I was gone, absentee ownership, and the place went down the tubes. I thought, how many blacks in California? Must be a million.

Well, I figured I could get a hundred [people] a night. Just one hundred out of all could have kept me open. But I couldn't get them to come out and support me.

"A lot of people can't get to Vegas but they could come up to La Cienega," he said. "You talk about a black brotherhood and they didn't show up. Couldn't understand it. I did a lot of advertising. I still owe the [*Los Angeles*] *Times* $10,000."

Betty Jeanne's sister, Beverly Harris, who was working as the club's head waitress, saw things a bit differently. Redd's employees weren't stealing from him, she said. "They weren't, but of course he would say that," she said. "When he would come to town he would go behind the bar and just reach in and take a handful [of cash] and put it in his pocket. The people there loved him and treated him wonderfully."

With Bill Cosby out of the picture, and Redd's Place losing money hand over fist, an act of serendipity—or was it?—solved Redd's problem. In December 1970, in the wee hours of a weekday morning, someone left a cigarette smoldering in that same dusty old couch in which Cosby found all those unpaid bills. The couch caught fire and burned the entire place down. "The way we heard it when we got back, nobody called the fire department till about 6:00 or 7:00 a.m. because nobody could see any fire from the street; the house burned first," said Bardu Ali. "Then it spread to the club itself facing La Cienega, but by then it was too late to save it."

But even with his dream nightclub literally going up in smoke, Redd was excited. And why not? He was up on the big screen, making his first major appearance in a Hollywood movie. And Bardu Ali was talking about a possible television project, something about a junkman living with his son. The future looked bright.

chapter eight

"Sanford and Son"

A movie career was never high on Redd Foxx's "to-do" list. Notwithstanding his unbilled 1960 appearance in *All the Fine Young Cannibals*, which was more happenstance than calculated plan, Hollywood wasn't exactly beating down Redd's door with offers to appear on the big screen. As the 1960s drew to a close, Redd, now forty-seven years old, could look back on the decade with some satisfaction. He was a major player in Las Vegas—no longer the lounge act but the big star working the big rooms—and for both the out-of-towners and the show-biz elite, catching Redd Foxx's late show at the Aladdin, Caesar's Palace, or the Hilton was what you did in Sin City. And while his career as a club owner lasted only three years, Redd's Place would be remembered for its singular vibe—and for helping to launch many young comedians on the road to stardom.

Television, at last, began to take notice of Redd Foxx, and his weepy turn on *The Joey Bishop Show*, exposed him to a national audience—some of whom might even have grudgingly admitted to owning his party records. The King of the Party Records was still churning out them out with regularity, and without having to battle Dootsie Williams for (real or imagined) unpaid royalties.

In the mid-to-late 1960s, most of Redd's album releases were on his own label, MF Records. Following the completion of Redd's deal with Frank Sinatra and Loma Records—their last collaboration, *Redd Foxx: Live in Las Vegas* was released in 1967—Redd began releasing a slew of albums on MF. The first release on his new label, *Laff Your Head Off*, came out that same year and was recorded at Redd's Place. (A sample from that album has Redd recounting how a white racist told him that he nursed at his colored mammy's breast. "You're lucky," Redd says. "I didn't get to a white one 'til I was twenty-two.") From 1967 through 1969, Redd released around fourteen albums on MF. Dooto Records, looking to cash in on Redd's popularity, re-entered the picture for a short time in 1969, issuing three Redd Foxx releases: *Jokes I Can't Tell on Television, Shed House Humor,* and *Favorite Party Jokes.* These albums contained no new material, since Redd hadn't recorded anything for Dooto in years. But Dootsie Williams, who still owned the rights to some of Redd's recordings, slapped together material and threw it into stores, figuring to sell what he could.

In 1969, when Bardu Ali approached Redd about appearing in a small supporting role in a movie called *Cotton Comes to Harlem,* Redd wasn't exactly enthralled by the idea. As usual with Redd, his reluctance wasn't so much the work itself, but the money being offered: he thought he was being low-balled by producer Samuel Goldwyn Jr. "I ain't working for no peanuts!" he told Ali, who did all he could to explain to Redd that doing the movie would pay off in the long run—giving Redd big-screen exposure that no amount of money could buy. Besides, who knew if there would ever be another offer like this? After some back-and-forth bickering in a New York hotel room, Redd agreed, and the *Cotton Comes to Harlem* deal was (grudgingly) signed, sealed, and delivered. It was the best decision Redd Foxx ever made.

Cotton Comes to Harlem marked the directorial debut of actor/playwright/activist Ossie Davis, who'd eulogized Redd's old Harlem buddy, Malcolm X, after the latter's assassination in 1965. The movie would be shot on location in Harlem, Redd's former stomping grounds, making the project a little more appealing to him. *Cotton* was based on the novel of the same name by Chester Himes, a black writer who was expelled from Ohio State University and later served eight years in prison for armed robbery before launching his writing career. Himes specialized in detective stories, pulp novels, and works built around the African American experience and the community's ongoing battles against racism. *Cotton Comes to Harlem* was the seventh in a series of eight novels that Himes wrote between 1957 and 1969 featuring wisecracking, tough-guy Harlem detectives Coffin Ed Johnson and Gravedigger Jones. Actor/comedian Godfrey Cambridge was hired to play Gravedigger Jones opposite Ossie Davis, who was working on the script with (white) writer Arnold Perl and was set to play Coffin Ed Johnson. But when producer

Samuel Goldwyn Jr. convinced Davis to direct the movie, Davis, in turn, hired veteran actor Raymond St. Jacques as his on-screen replacement.

"It was Ossie's first movie script, and when he got through it, I realized that he knew this world, this subject, so well and he understood humor, because he had a great sense of humor, a great wit," said Goldwyn. "I said, 'Well, how do you feel about directing the picture?' and he said, 'Are you out of your mind? Nobody is going to put real money in a picture that I direct.' He was a joy; he understood what it was about. He wasn't directing a movie, he was bringing a world that he understood."

Davis and Perl set the movie in the present time, but changed little else from Himes' novel. The movie revolves around Coffin and Grave-digger's search for $87,000 hidden in a bale of cotton by the scheming, charismatic black leader, "Reverend" Deke O'Malley (played by Calvin Lockhart). O'Malley, freshly sprung from prison, has collected the cash by selling certificates, at one-hundred bucks each, for his bogus "Back to Africa" trip aboard the Black Beauty—and now he's taken his act to Harlem to prey on the neighborhood residents. Coffin and Gravedigger are onto O'Malley's scheme, and wandering into the fray is Redd's character, Booker Washington Sims, better known to the locals as "Uncle Bud," a fast-talking Harlem junk dealer who lives in a shack on the East River. Uncle Bud becomes entwined in O'Malley's scheme and eventually ends up with the $87,000 bale of cotton through a series of farcical circumstances.

"He was cast because he *was* Uncle Bud," said Goldwyn. "I mean that seriously. He was perfect. I didn't know him, quite frankly, but when we were casting, Ossie [Davis] said, 'There is only one person to play this because he is Uncle Bud, and that's Redd Foxx.' And everybody agreed.

"My introduction to Redd Foxx was on the set," Goldwyn said. "I turned my back and there was this loud noise and clapping. It was Redd showing up for his first day of work, and the whole cast, as one, felt they were meeting a great celebrity."

To prepare for the role, Redd, who already had a mustache, grew a scraggly beard that, along with his hair, was tinted grey. His first appearance comes about eight minutes into the movie's opening scene, in which O'Malley arrives in Harlem (in his silver Rolls-Royce) to deliver his "Back to Africa" spiel to an adoring crowd. The pipe-smoking Uncle Bud, sloppily dressed in a ratty black jacket, grey pants, and a green knit ski cap, manages to wheedle a certificate to board the Black Beauty, for only twenty dollars, from one of O'Malley's busty helpers ("Please, ma'am, you don't want to break old Uncle Bud's heart, do ya? It's all I got in the world right now, give me a chance, please, ma'am.").

Redd reappears several times throughout the movie after O'Malley's bale of cotton is hijacked and proceeds to bounce around Harlem—including a stay in Uncle Bud's junkyard. Redd's big scene arrives around forty-five minutes into the movie, when he tries to sell the "genuine Mississippi cotton" to fellow junkman "Honest Abe" Goodman (played by Lou Jacobi), who agrees to buy the bale for twenty-five dollars. After Uncle Bud disappears, the movie's main characters assume that he's been killed for knowing too much about the $87,000 hidden inside the bale of cotton. But the movie ends with Uncle Bud, clad in African garb and wearing a Cheshire grin—and surrounded by three women (two of them topless)—narrating a video postcard to Coffin Ed and Gravedigger. "If you are still dragging the river looking for the body of old Uncle Bud and the $87,000, stop," he says in a voiceover. "I am now a retired gentleman raising cotton on my villa in Africa."

Cotton Comes to Harlem opened in May 1970 to mediocre reviews. Vincent Canby panned the movie in the *New York Times*, calling it a "conventional white movie that employs some terrible white stereotypes of black life." Several weeks later, though, Canby revised his opinion after watching the movie a second time in a quieter setting. The *Los Angeles Times* was a bit kinder in its assessment, dubbing *Cotton* "summerweight fare," and praising Redd's performance. "The pace is fast and there are some excellent performances, notably St. Jacques' as an intemperately angry cop, Lockhart's as the swindler, and nightclub comic Redd Foxx as an old junk scavenger who figures largely in the plot."

As is often the case, the public didn't really care *what* the critics thought. *Cotton Comes to Harlem* did strong business at the box office that summer. "We had more people when we opened in the theater than they had the opening day of the James Bond movie [*On Her Majesty's Secret Service*]," said Samuel Goldwyn Jr. "The line was all the way around the block. The picture just soared. I can imagine the feeling on the audience's part because it was filmed in Harlem with a lot of landmarks, the Apollo Theater being one, where Redd played many times, and I guess they were characters [the audience] could identify with and [had] a certain attitude they could identify with."

Cotton Comes to Harlem also had the distinction of being one of the first of what came to be called the "blaxploitation" movies of the 1970s, films that featured a mostly African American cast and catered to a largely urban black audience. The list eventually included *Sweet Sweetback's Baadasssss Song*, *Shaft*, *Super Fly* and *Blacula*, among many others.

But the blaxploitation movies were only one of the many seismic cultural shifts rocking America as the country began the new decade. The changes would, in a short span of time, alter the course of Redd Foxx's life and career.

As the 1970s began, the television networks finally began to rouse from their decades-long slumber, to gingerly sit up and take notice of the cultural earthquake shaking the country. The Civil Rights movement, which spawned the strongest societal shift of the 1960s, didn't initially have much of an impact on prime-time television. Specials like *A Time for Laughter* and George Schlatter's *Soul*, focusing on the African American experience in America—and both featuring Redd's comedy—were the exception rather than the rule. So was *Laugh-In* (another Schlatter production), which was considered politically naughty for its time but whose large ensemble cast featured only a handful of black performers (among them Stu Gilliam, Johnny Brown, Teresa Graves, and Chelsea Brown).

The biggest breakthrough had been Bill Cosby's role as spy Alexander Scott, working under cover as a tennis coach, in *I Spy*, which premiered on NBC in 1965. Cosby became the first African American to co-star in a network television series, and when *I Spy* ended its run in 1968, NBC continued to make cultural strides by casting Diahann Carroll in a new sitcom called *Julia*. In the series, which premiered in September 1968, Carroll starred as Julia Baker, a single mother (her fighter-pilot husband was killed in Vietnam) who worked as a nurse in a doctor's office and was raising her young son. It had been over a decade—since *Beulah*, *Amos 'n' Andy*, and *The Nat King Cole Show*—that a network dared build a series around an African American star. But it was a start.

It's fair to say that Redd Foxx, even more than Bill Cosby, Diahann Carroll, or NBC had more to do, indirectly, with the resurgence of blacks on prime-time television in the early 1970s. And that was due to his friendship with Flip Wilson.

Since the mid-1960s, Redd had been a mentor of sorts to Wilson, who was eleven years younger than his idol. Clerow Wilson was born in 1933 in Jersey City, New Jersey, as one of eighteen children, and spent his early life in a succession of foster homes and reform schools. It was in the Air Force, which he joined in 1949 (after lying about his age), that Clerow Wilson earned his nickname, "Flip," because his pals thought he was "flipping out" when he would break into stories he told in outrageous dialects. After being discharged from the service in 1954, Wilson worked as a bellhop at a San Francisco hotel, honing his comedy chops in the hotel's nightclub, and began touring as a stand-up act. He arrived on the New York club scene in the mid-'60s and was a frequent headliner and emcee at the Apollo Theater.

"Flip and the other young comedians used to go and watch Redd, and Flip had this . . . scientific way of looking at it. He would take a notebook, which he kept all his life, and study when people laughed and whether they were laughing at what he said or how he said it or what mannerisms he used," said Flip Wilson biographer Kathleen Fearn-Banks, who later worked closely with Redd as an NBC publicist on *Sanford and Son*. "Flip talked about going to the Apollo and just sitting in the back and watching Redd and taking notes. And then when he got the chance to work the Apollo, Redd saw him."

It was Redd, in fact, who gave Wilson his biggest boost. One night in 1965, when Redd was appearing as a guest on *The Tonight Show*, host Johnny Carson asked him who he thought was the funniest comedian in the business. "Flip Wilson," Redd said without hesitation. Carson booked Flip on *The Tonight Show* and that appearance, in turn, led to other television and nightclub work (including a prime-time special on NBC in 1968 and, that same year, a Grammy-winning comedy album, *Flip Wilson, You Devil You*).

When Redd opened Redd's Place on La Cienega, Wilson was a semi-regular, hanging out with Redd and breaking in new material—including a sassy, skirt-wearing character named Geraldine Jones (who had an unseen boyfriend named Killer). In 1970, NBC—continuing its tradition of breaking new ground for African Americans in prime time—gave Wilson his own show. *The Flip Wilson Show*, which premiered that September, was the first network variety show to be hosted by an African American performer and was an immediate hit, finishing as the second-most-watched television show its first season and repeating that feat again in its second season. Wilson's characters, including Geraldine and Reverend Leroy, became instant classics with their own catchphrases: "What you see is what you get!" (Geraldine) and "The Devil made me do it!" (Reverend Leroy).

Flip didn't forget about all the help Redd had given him over the years and returned the favor, inviting Redd onto *The Flip Wilson Show* a number of times during its four-year run. "There was a friendship, there was a rivalry and definitely a respect, a mutual respect," said Fearn-Banks. "And they also shared their love of marijuana. When I met Redd, he was in the dressing room and that's what the people did in the dressing room and they all loved it.

"But Redd was funnier in person than Flip or Richard Pryor or any of them," she said. "They worked at their craft and they could be funny, but in person and conversation, they weren't particularly funny. Flip could be funny occasionally—he tried jokes on you or something—but he was mostly a serious person. But Redd could come up with something from nowhere and you had to laugh at it."

The growing prevalence of black performers on television wasn't the only change occurring in the prime-time landscape. As the new decade began, the networks' mindset shifted to younger viewers, as the baby-boomer generation came of age and comprised the free-spending demographic craved by advertisers. The older, established variety shows, once a prime-time staple, began showing signs of age and ratings erosion. The younger generation was no longer interested in their parents favorites; Jackie Gleason, Red Skelton, Perry Como, and Ed Sullivan, once industry giants, all saw their television popularity wane as the '60s drew to a close. In 1970, CBS cancelled *The Jackie Gleason Show*; the era ended, for all intents and purposes, when the network pulled the plug on *The Ed Sullivan Show* a year later in June 1971.

America was ready for more edgy fare and Norman Lear was there to answer the call. Lear began his show-business career in the mid-1950s, writing first for Celeste Holm's CBS sitcom, *Honestly, Celeste!*—which was quickly cancelled—and then creating a half-hour series for Henry Fonda called *The Deputy*. In the 1960s Lear segued into movies, writing and producing *Divorce, American Style* and directing *Cold Turkey* before trying to convince ABC to air a pilot he'd written. Lear borrowed the premise for his new project from a hit British sitcom, *'Til Death Do Us Part*, which premiered on the BBC in 1965 and revolved around working-class, bigoted Alf Garnell (Warren Mitchell), his milquetoast wife, Else (Dandy Nichols) and his daughter Rita (Una Stubbs)—who was married to Mike (Antony Booth), a socialist and intellectual of sorts who clashed repeatedly with Alf.

ABC was afraid that Archie Bunker, Lear's version of Alf Garnell, was too controversial for Prime Time, and passed on the project. But the show, with relatively unknown Carroll O'Connor playing the bigoted, ultra-conservative Archie—a loading-dock worker who called his unemployed son-in-law a "Polak" and "meathead" and told his wife, Edith, to "stifle" herself—was picked up by CBS. The network was trying to break out of its perceived status as the "hayseed network" and had cancelled shows including *The Beverly Hillbillies* and *Green Acres*. Lear's pilot went through several title changes—*Justice for All*, *Those Were the Days*—until CBS settled on *All in the Family*, which was set in the blue-collar borough of Queens, New York. *All in the Family* premiered in January 1971 and didn't make much of an impact, but when it returned that fall, it became an overnight sensation and quickly shot to number one, averaging over twenty-one million viewers a week—nearly four million more viewers than *The Flip Wilson Show*.

Redd, meanwhile, couldn't have been further out of the loop regarding the revolution that was occurring in prime-time television. He and his manager, Bardu Ali, were working on the concept for a new television show that would feature Redd's prodigious cooking skills. Redd loved to cook and could often be found in the kitchen preparing something for his guests. He had an idea for a combination cooking and talk show in which he and Betty Jeanne would invite some of their celebrity friends over to the house to shoot some pool. After a bit of good-natured banter and discussion, Redd would then move into the kitchen to prepare a big meal, which he would then serve to his guests.

Redd was headlining at the Hilton in Las Vegas while he and Bardu Ali batted around ideas for the cooking show. Back in Los Angeles, Norman Lear and partner Bud Yorkin, flush with the success of *All in the Family*, were already on the prowl for another British sitcom they could adapt for American television.

They eventually landed on *Steptoe and Son*, which revolved around Cockney, semi-illiterate Albert Edward Ladysmith Steptoe—played by Wilfred Brambell, better known to American audiences as Paul McCartney's "clean" grandfather in *A Hard Day's Night*—and his son, Harold (Harry H. Corbett), who worked in the "rag and bone" trade (the British term for junk). The Steptoes, who lived on Oil Drum Lane in London's gritty Shepherd's Bush district, were constantly bickering with each other, and Harold's attitude toward his father often took on a tone of viciousness.

Steptoe and Son sprung from the fertile comedic minds of Ray Galton and Alan Simpson, who, in the mid-to-late 1950s, wrote *Hancock's Half Hour*. The show starred British comedian Tony Hancock and his side-kick, Sid James, and is regarded as one of the best sitcoms in British television history (*Hancock's Half Hour* also ran concurrently on radio for most of its television run). In 1961, spiraling into the abyss of alcoholism and afraid of being pigeonholed as a one-note sitcom star, Hancock initiated a much-publicized split from Galton and Simpson. His career never recovered, and he committed suicide seven years later while in Australia filming a hoped-for comeback sitcom ("Things just seemed to go too wrong too many times," he famously wrote on one of his two suicide notes.)

In 1962, Galton and Simpson's *Steptoe and Son*, premiered on the BBC and ran on-and-off until 1974. The show focused on the scheming Albert and the suffocating, vice-like grip he has on his son, Harold, who wants to better himself and escape from the junkyard for a more fulfilling life. But he can't bear to leave the old man—even though they spend most of their time sniping at each other. (Harold's admonishment to his father—"You dirty old man!"—became his catchphrase.)

Casting an Americanized version of *Steptoe and Son* proved to be more of a challenge than Lear and Yorkin bargained for. With Lear focusing most of his attention on *All in the Family*, Yorkin brought in sitcom veteran Aaron Ruben (*The Phil Silvers Show*, *The Andy Griffith Show*, *Gomer Pyle, U.S.M.C.*) to help develop *Steptoe*. The problem was, they just couldn't find the right combination of actors to play the bickering, yet loving, father and son—and they couldn't decide on the characters' ethnicity. Initially, the show was going to be set in New York. "Mainly, we had in mind Jewish or Italian actors, since most of the junk peddlers in New York are of that origin," Ruben said. "But we couldn't find the right characters—those wonderful old-timers are all gone, and you're not going to bring [Jimmy] Cagney out of retirement, either."

Yorkin and Ruben spent several months in mid-1971 shooting a few *Steptoe* pilots with different sets of actors. One version featured Lee Tracy and Aldo Ray as father and son; in another version, veteran stage actor Barnard Hughes played the Irish father and Paul Sorvino his son, who favored his mother's Italian heritage. Bardu Ali later claimed that Stepin Fetchit and Flip Wilson filmed a *Steptoe* pilot, but there's no record of that ever occurring. Yorkin and Ruben did approach Cleavon Little, who had a small role in *Cotton Comes to Harlem*, to gauge his interest in shooting a pilot. Little was interested, but had other commitments to fulfill, so he recommended someone he thought would be perfect for the role of the curmudgeonly father: Redd Foxx.

"We were either going to get Italian, Jewish, or Black … we tested a lot of people and we couldn't find anybody that I really thought was great, that could do it," Yorkin said. "We auditioned a lot of good actors but they just weren't built for that character. And then I caught *Cotton Comes to Harlem* and right away I said, 'There's the guy: Redd Foxx.'"

There he was, hiding in plain sight. Why hadn't anyone thought of it before? Redd was the perfect casting choice. Although Ruben's script for the *Steptoe* pilot was, in his words, written for a "faceless character"—giving the producers the option of plugging in whichever ethnic group they eventually decided upon—the role was tailor-made for Redd Foxx. His Uncle Bud character in *Cotton Comes to Harlem* was, after all, a junkman, and while Redd didn't have a son in real life, he could certainly mix it up with the best of them. A large part of his on stage persona was built on his audience banter and his lightning-quick zingers to hecklers, which harkened all the way back to Redd's teen days playing "the dozens" and one-upping his buddies in the 58th Street Gang. Even Redd's croaking, gravelly voice was perfect; hardened by years of cigarettes, booze, cocaine, and marijuana, it was the voice of a much older man. "Believe me, he lived hard," Yorkin said. "He was gray, and the way he walked on the show was pretty much the way he walked in real life. He had beaten himself up too much." That made the problem of Redd's age a relatively minor one; he was only forty-eight at the time, while Ruben's "faceless" father character was sixty-five. But it was nothing that some hair dye couldn't solve.

Redd, though, was still focused on his cooking show, and was in Las Vegas performing at the Hilton, far away from Hollywood. He knew nothing about what was going on behind-the-scenes after Yorkin and Rubin called Bardu Ali, asking him if Redd would be interested in shooting the *Steptoe* pilot. Without telling him about the offer, Ali called Redd's attorney, James Tolbert, and set up a three-way call with himself, Yorkin, and Tolbert to discuss the script. When Ali finally called him in Vegas to tell him about the offer, Redd was disappointed. What about the cooking show? Ali told him that, if this *Steptoe* project didn't work out, the cooking show would be their top priority. "That made him feel better," he said. "At least I thought it did."

Privately, though, Redd was thrilled at the prospect of starring in a network television show, and said as much when he flew to Los Angeles to meet Bud Yorkin. "He came in and I said, 'How would you like to do a television show?' He said he would love it," Yorkin recalled. He said, 'I've never been behind the doors of any of the different companies that were making movies, I've never seen none of it.' I said, 'Let me ask you a question. Are you willing to come up here, work with me? We'll do the show and we'll see if the network will pick it up. We're going to have to do the whole first show, you're going to have to memorize it, you'll have to learn it and then we're going to do it.

"I said, 'It's going to be two people that can't live with each other, and have to be together. They love each other but there are times they can't get together, like any father and son relationship. He said, 'I'll do anything, I'll take my teeth out if you want me to.'" And that's how it really started."

With Redd on board, Yorkin and Ruben needed to find his co-star. Bardu Ali later recalled that Ruben and Cleavon Little flew out to Redd's house in Las Vegas, so Little could read for the role of Redd's son. But that's likely an apocryphal story, since Little had already turned down the opportunity (before recommending Redd). Little *was* however, laterally involved in Yorkin and Norman Lear's decision to look in their own creative backyard and tap an actor named Demond Wilson to read for the role of the *Steptoe* son.

The twenty-four-year-old Wilson, a Vietnam veteran, was born Grady Demond Wilson in Valdosta, Georgia, and was already a show-biz veteran by the time he met Redd Foxx. He'd appeared in several Broadway and off-Broadway productions, and in a small role on the CBS series *Mission: Impossible*. In 1971, he co-starred in the movie *The Organization*; later that year, he and Cleavon Little were cast in an episode of *All in the Family* as a pair of burglars who break into Archie Bunker's house. Wilson's performance in that episode caught Yorkin and Lear's attention, and they dispatched Aaron Ruben to meet with Wilson in Los Angeles and offer him the chance to read for the role opposite Redd. "After learning about the series format, I was doubtful about my involvement in the project," Wilson said. "I thought about it long and hard and decided to take a chance. Redd and I thought we could grab some quick cash, plus notoriety, then move onto the next project."

So it was Aaron Ruben and Demond Wilson who, in fact, flew out to Las Vegas to meet with Redd. Ruben and Wilson were accompanied by Ruben's wife, actress Maureen Arthur, and the trio caught Redd's show at the Hilton. Afterwards, Redd, Wilson, and Ruben stayed up until the crack of dawn discussing the show and the script. "[Redd] liked the script, even though it wasn't for a black man," Ruben recalled. "He liked it because, as he says, it wasn't dishonest. I wanted him to add his own black flavor to the script—put in the juice. He was great, just the right touches."

The next day, after everyone caught up on some sleep, Bardu Ali met Wilson in his hotel lobby and brought him over to Redd's house. "I cooked dinner for everyone and we read the script and we just sort of hit it off in the very beginning," Redd said. "Some people, you meet them and you shake hands with them and from then on it's a lifelong thing. You get that sort of communication. That's the kind of personality [Wilson] had."

With their two principals in place, Yorkin, Lear, and Ruben's next step was to shoot the pilot. CBS had so much success with *All in the Family*, which was now the top-rated show on television, that Yorkin and Lear figured the network would jump at the chance to get the first look at the pair's next project (which still didn't have an official title). In August 1971, Redd and Demond Wilson began rehearsing a scene for the pilot at CBS' Fairfax Studio. But there was a problem: Yorkin and Lear couldn't get any network officials, particularly programming chief Fred Silverman, to come over and watch the rehearsals. "We were rehearsing *All in the Family* at CBS and any date I made for the CBS brass to see Redd Foxx in rehearsal, for some reason they couldn't make or they broke the date or whatever," Lear said. Said Yorkin: "We had a problem with Fred Silverman."

Silverman remembers the story a bit differently—and still rues the day he passed on the Yorkin and Lear pilot.

"It was one of the stupidest things I did at CBS," Silverman said thirty-seven years later. "We had *All in the Family* on the air and Bud and Norman came in with the idea, and it was called *Steptoe and Son*. They failed to mention that Redd Foxx was on it, or that it was going to be a black show.

They never said that. And they just described it and I said, 'Well, I don't understand, you are selling us a show we already have. I mean, we have *All in the Family* and this sounds like Archie and Meathead. What's the difference?' And there was silence. I said, 'We're not interested.' There was never any run-through, or never any talk of a run-through. It's one of the decisions I regretted for the next three or four years."

With CBS out of the picture, Yorkin set his sights on NBC and his old friend, Herb Schlosser, who was president of NBC's West Coast operations and was in a position to make programming decisions. It was Schlosser who, in 1967, had given George Schlatter the green light to produce and air NBC's prime-time special, *Soul*. While the special was never turned into the hoped-for weekly series, Schlosser was impressed with Redd's performance. "Redd played a reporter interviewing the first black Vice President of the United States and it was very funny," Schlosser said of one particular skit, in which Slappy White played the veep. "And I thought Redd was very funny . . . and I wanted to find something for Redd. I didn't have any great ideas . . . but I was viewing him as a television performer."

In fact, according to Schlosser, he had made the first deal for NBC to acquire *Steptoe and Son* from the BBC—a deal that did not involve Norman Lear or Bud Yorkin, he said. Schlosser, at the time, was heading up NBC's West Coast business affairs office. "We had committed to a pilot and I did the deal for an American version of *Steptoe and Son*," he said. "And the [pilot] had Lee Tracy and Aldo Ray in it. But it never got on the air. The head of programs on the East Coast was Mort Werner and I was on the West Coast. We both liked *Steptoe* but it just never got on [the air]. That's what happens, you know. A small percentage of the pilots you do actually become a series."

But Bud Yorkin wasn't going to let his *Steptoe and Son* pilot fall onto the scrap heap of television history. He believed in the show and, after seeing how Redd and Demond Wilson interacted in shooting that scene for CBS, he believed in his stars. ABC executives had passed on *All in the Family*, and lived to regret that decision for years. Yorkin wasn't going to let CBS' dismissive attitude kill his newest project.

So Yorkin called Herb Schlosser and told him he was doing an Americanized version of *Steptoe and Son*, with Redd Foxx in the lead role. "Well, when he said that, my ears perked up," Schlosser recalled, "because I was very familiar with the property, I knew exactly what it was and I was a big fan of Redd's." Schlosser wasn't so sure he could convince his East Coast counterpart, Mort Werner, to do another version of *Steptoe and Son* after the previous pilot (with Lee Tracy and Aldo Ray) hadn't worked out. "But I was on a mission," Schlosser said.

Yorkin's idea was to have Schlosser and Werner attend the taping of the *Steptoe* pilot, but there was one problem: since Redd and Demond Wilson were taping their scene at the CBS studios on Fairfax Avenue, how were Schlosser and Werner, executives from CBS arch-rival NBC, going to get into the studio to watch it?

"Herb said, 'I can't go to CBS' and I said, 'They'll never know,'" Yorkin recalled. "I said, 'I'll tell you how. You come in the back way, you come upstairs and it will be in the rehearsal hall.' He said, 'Well, I don't know' and I said, 'Come on, nobody's going to know, who gives a shit?'"

So NBC's two top executives, Herb Schlosser and Mort Werner, drove over to the CBS studios on Fairfax Avenue and entered enemy territory. The *All in the Family* cast was rehearsing just across the corridor from where Redd and Demond Wilson were going to tape their scene, and Yorkin had a brainstorm: why not have the entire *All in the Family* cast watch the taping? "I said, 'OK, you guys are going to sit and watch this with me' because I knew they hadn't seen it," Yorkin said. "All the crew and everything were there, because they were rehearsing and getting ready to tape the next day."

With the cast of *All in the Family*, Schlosser and Werner watching from the studio-audience grandstands, Redd and Demond walked in front of the cameras and did their scene together. It had been only four days since they'd met for the first time at Redd's house in Las Vegas. "The *All in the Family* cast fell on the floor," Yorkin said. "I've never heard guys laughing like that. It went on and on. So we finish this thing and Herb comes over and says, 'It was great, it was funny,' and he takes me over to the corner and says, 'You're on the air January 18th. I'll give you seventeen shows to start with.' And that's how it started."

Schlosser said Werner had a prediction as they were leaving the studio. "And as were walking out the door, and this is true, Mort Werner said, 'The guy who plays his son is going to be the star,'" Schlosser said. "He wouldn't give me Redd, but he meant it good-naturedly."

Now that NBC had committed to *Steptoe and Son*, the show needed a name change to make it more identifiable to an American television audience. When Redd told the writers that his real name was Jon Sanford, the problem was quickly solved. The new show would be called *Sanford and Son*, and, at Redd's insistence, the main character was rechristened Fred G. Sanford, in honor of Redd's late brother (Redd never forgave Fred Sr. for abandoning the family). Redd also suggested that Fred's thirty-two-year-old son should be named Lamont, after his childhood friend Lamont Ousley, one of the Four Bon Bons who, as runaways, rode the rails with young Jon Sanford to Weehawken, New Jersey in July 1939. Yorkin and Ruben agreed.

And now that the show's ethnicity had finally been decided upon, Yorkin and Ruben relocated the junkyard from New York City to South Central Los Angeles—specifically to Watts, the city's predominantly working-class black community and the scene of incendiary race riots in the summer of 1965.

Since the main set for *Sanford and Son*, where most of the show's action took place, would be the living room and kitchen of Fred and Lamont's house (at 9114 South Central Avenue), NBC carpenters constructed what would become one of the best-known and beloved interiors in television history: the junk-filled, cluttered living room, with stairs leading up to the (rarely seen) second floor, where the house's one bathroom—and the bedrooms of Fred and Lamont—were located. Off the living room, and through a swinging door, was the large kitchen, with a table in the center. Because of the quick turnaround time between Schlosser's series order and the show's debut, Yorkin and Ruben decided that, for the first part of its season (if it even lasted that long), *Sanford and Son* would use the original *Steptoe and Son* scripts. They would be tweaked here and there to fit the show's new father-and-son characters, and to and reflect an American sensibility and American vernacular.

Within days of its decision to add *Sanford and Son* to its midseason schedule, NBC leaked word to the press about its new series pickup. "Veteran black comedian Redd Foxx will star in an NBC-financed pilot-film of a series called *Sanford and Son*, a derivative of a British TV series called *Steptoe and Son*," Bob Williams wrote in the *New York Post*. "And the series will deal with the generation gap philosophies of a couple of garbage collectors. Does it sound impossible?" Two months later, in November 1971, the *New York Times* and the *Los Angeles Times* ran news stories about NBC's upcoming midseason schedule, pegging January 14, 1972, as the premiere date for *Sanford and Son*, which would replace *The D.A.* Fridays at 8:00 p.m.: "Redd Foxx stars as an aging black Los

Angeles junk dealer and Demond Wilson is his son and partner in the not-so-thriving business." (NBC also announced another midseason replacement, *Emergency* and confirmed that, along with *The D.A.* it was also dumping *Sarge*, *The Funny Side*, *The Partners*, and *The Good Life*.)

For Redd, it was a dream come true. All those years of struggle, of hard work on the Chitlin' Circuit, and working his way up the ladder to the bigger more "mainstream" clubs, had finally paid off. He'd be starring in a network television series, and even if it didn't last, at least he'd make a quick buck and gain some notoriety and visibility.

For his role as Fred Sanford, Redd grew a scraggly beard which, along with his reddish hair, was tinted gray. To emphasize sixty-five-year-old Fred Sanford's world-weariness and advancing age, Redd added a bow-legged shuffle to Fred's gait. Capturing Fred's voice was no problem; the combination of Redd's cigarette and marijuana habit and his cocaine use—seasoned by years of working smoke-filled nightclubs—gave him that sandpaper-on-sandpaper croak. Fred's voice alone aged the forty-nine-year-old Redd Foxx at least ten years. When *Sanford and Son* premiered, most people thought Redd really *was* sixty-five years old. But his real secret weapon, Redd said, could be found on his feet. "Just as soon as I put those big heavy shoes on and walk out there, I become Sanford—but not until then, not until I put my shoes on," he said. "I can put the rest of my outfit on, but if I don't have those shoes on, I don't walk like him, and I don't think like him." He also said he based Fred Sanford's emotional characteristics, in part, on his mother.

"Fred Sanford is Mary Sanford, who is my mother, but you can reverse personalities into male or female," Redd told Sammy Davis Jr. in a visit to Davis's talk show, *Sammy and Company*. "My mother would do the same thing that Fred [does] . . . she would have heart attacks when I was a kid, I remember. When she wanted something done she could hardly breathe—she had emphysema, she had cancer, she had lumbago, she had whooping cough."

As NBC's publicity machine shifted into high gear toward the end of 1971, Redd was dispatched for a series of interviews to promote *Sanford and Son* leading up to the show's premiere, still several weeks away. He was an unknown quantity to most television viewers, especially to white America, who considered him an X-rated comedian who recorded lots of underground party records. But to the majority of black Americans, Redd Foxx was a cultural institution. He knew that, which made him even more confident that America, specifically *black* America, was ready for his new show. "I anticipate we've got that audience going in," he said. "I know I've been waiting for something like this, for some kind of honest black comedy, for thirty-five years—all the years I've been in show business. And I figure that 22 million other black people have been waiting as long as I have."

To help get the *Sanford and Son* promotional ball rolling, NBC booked Redd for a mid-December appearance on *The Flip Wilson Show*. Wilson also talked up the show in a local Los Angeles television interview in which he said that *Sanford and Son* would be television's first "really black show" because it would have "black people acting and talking like black people really do. They'll be saying things the way black people normally say them. Like on some TV shows you might hear a black person saying, for instance, 'I am not going to do that.' Instead, he'd say it like this, 'I ain't gonna do dat. Not me!'"

In the meantime, Redd's manager, Bardu Ali, worked out a deal that allowed Redd to opt out of his contract at the Las Vegas Hilton so he could work on his new television series. In all the back-and-forth negotiations, *Sanford and Son* producer Bud Yorkin discovered that Redd—who often boasted in the press about a variety of topics—was embellishing his Las Vegas salary. He had, for instance, said on more than one occasion that he was earning $10,000 a week for doing two, forty-five-minutes shows a night at the Hilton. Yorkin, in negotiating Redd's *Sanford and Son* contract with Bardu Ali, discovered the real truth. "We paid him, when he came up [to read the script for the first time], what he got [in Las Vegas], and he was getting exactly $1,450 a week," Yorkin said. "He'd do his little monologue, talk a little bit and that was it." Whatever the case, Yorkin and Norman Lear agreed to pay Redd $7,500-per-episode for *Sanford and Son*—the same starting salary given to Carroll O'Connor on *All in the Family*. Once the deal was signed, sealed and delivered, Redd left Las Vegas and drove to Los Angeles to begin rehearsing for the first *Sanford and Son* taping.

Although he projected an air of extreme confidence and cockiness in press interviews leading up to the premiere of *Sanford and Son*, Redd was already anticipating a possible backlash in the African American community, based on Fred Sanford's less-than-glamorous occupation and his slovenly house in Watts. But he already had an answer for his critics. He always did. "I don't think that's a putdown," he said of making Fred and Lamont black junk dealers. "My granddad was a junk man in Saint Louis, so was my uncle and we were proud of them, owned their own business." He emphasized how *Sanford and Son* would be a different sort of black show, unlike Diahann Carroll's *Julia*, a series he had always detested—and which prompted some fierce criticism in the black community after its 1968 premiere on NBC.

"*Julia* was a putdown to black people because no nurse woman ever lived in an apartment like that and wore clothes like hers unless she had something going on the side. It was dishonest," Redd said. "We looked at kinescopes of the *Steptoes*. They were funny shows, what I could understand of that Cockney. Well, we're doing what you might call American Cockney—we're talking colored. Anyway, this show is not about the junk business. It's about an old faker of a father, a con man, a fox, who'll do anything to keep his son tied to him. He'll lie, cheat, fake heart attacks, do anything to keep his boy with him. It's not an English or a black thing—it's universal."

After several days of rehearsals, Redd Foxx and Demond Wilson went before the cameras on December 30, 1971, to shoot the first episode of *Sanford and Son* before a live audience on the NBC lot in Burbank. The episode, called "Crossed Swords," was written by Aaron Ruben (and adapted from an episode of *Steptoe and Son*, also called "Crossed Swords," written by Ray Galton and Alan Simpson).

The very first *Sanford and Son* episode established all the elements that would become so familiar and endearing to the show's fans—including Quincy Jones' funky, bass-and-harmonica-heavy theme music, "The Streetbeater." Bud Yorkin approached Jones shortly after he and Norman Lear bought the rights to *Steptoe and Son*. "He said, 'I'd like you to write the theme for it.' I said, 'Who's in it?' and he said, 'Redd Foxx.' I said, 'Man, you can't put Redd Foxx on national TV,'" Jones said. "I had worked with Redd thirty years before that at the Apollo. We used to do the Chitlin' Circuit. I used to write this music for him to come out. Yorkin said, 'No, it's gonna be a great show.' And it was. [Foxx] took his sense of humor and took it all the way to the top. I wrote that [song] in about twenty minutes, too. We had four musicians. Recorded it in about twenty minutes. Looking back, it's a trip."

In the opening credits of *Sanford and Son*—underscored by Jones' "The Streetbeater" —Fred is in the front of his beloved junkyard on a bright, sunny day, mopping his brow and positioning a fan in front of him before sitting down to read his newspaper under the shop's sign ("Sanford and Son Salvage. We buy and sell junk and antiques"). The camera then cuts to Lamont, who's driving a battered, 1951 red Ford pickup truck with the words "Sanford and Son Salvage. 2nd Hand Antiques. We Buy & Sell Junk," stenciled in white lettering on the driver's side door. Lamont pulls into the junkyard and drives toward the back of the shop, with Fred following the truck, ostensibly to help his son unload that day's haul.

The plot of that first episode revolves around a valuable porcelain figurine, which Lamont scammed from an "old white woman" while making his rounds looking for junk that he and his "pop," Fred, can sell out of their junkyard. Lamont and Fred take the figurine to a Beverly Hills antique shop, where the shop's owner offers them $850. Convinced he can get much more, Lamont decides to put the piece up for auction, where he manages to drive the price up to $1,300—until Fred, who's unaware that Lamont is artificially inflating the price, bids $2,000, and ends up winning the figurine. (The auctioneer is played by Robert Mandan, who would later go on to star in the hit ABC series, *Soap*.) Lamont is furious with Fred and vows to finally move out of the house and re-sell the figurine for lots of money. But his plan is thwarted when Fred—in a bid to keep his son from leaving him—purposely drops the figurine, which shatters, and then threatens to kill himself.

The episode is very funny and holds up today, over thirty-five years after it first aired. There are many "firsts" here that would become Redd's *Sanford and Son* trademarks: Fred picking through a tangled pile of reading glasses to find the right pair; his definition of "ugly" ("ain't nothin' on earth uglier than a ninety-year-old white woman"); his first fake "heart attack," where he clutches his chest; his first heavenward address to his dead wife ("You hear that, Elizabeth? I'm comin' to join you, honey!"); his comebacks to Lamont ("How would you like one 'cross your lips?" and the very first "You big dummy!"); and Fred clenching his hands and blaming his dropping the figurine on his *arthur-itis*.

"If you remember in that first show, how Fred lost everything because he screwed up on their bidding, well, when Fred got hurt, or his feelings got hurt, or he did something wrong, Redd was great in playing that character," said Bud Yorkin. "And you felt so sad for Fred; you wanted to pick him up and hold him. And that worked for us. Later on in that episode it was very dramatic and we worked very hard on that script. I said, 'You gotta memorize the whole thing, Redd, I don't care if it takes you all night, every night. I said, 'When we get into rehearsal, the third day, you don't carry that script.' And we did that show and he had that thing down. He memorized the whole goddamned show. I think we taped that show in forty minutes. Done. So he could memorize the script. Later on, he didn't."

"Crossed Swords" also gave a first glimpse into the show's underlying theme: that even though Fred and Lamont were constantly bickering with each other, their father-son bond was built on deep love and respect. That was really the message of *Sanford and Son*, and it would remain a constant thread throughout the series' long run, even in later years once the show's two stars began to act up and the storylines grew more outlandish. "A lot of whites just never stop to consider that black families are founded on love, were taught love, and weaned on love—love for people, and prayer, and religion," said Redd, addressing what he hoped was the show's message. "In America it's got to be black or white or red or egg or turnip . . . forget that. This is a human story and color has nothing to do with it. It's not a message show. A father loves his son and a son loves his father and that's the situation."

One element present in "Crossed Swords," and in several of the episodes that followed, was Lamont's nastiness toward Fred, which bordered on the physically abusive (as was Harold's relationship with his father, Albert, in *Steptoe and Son*). As the series progressed, Lamont's interactions with "Pop" softened noticeably, even when father and son were at odds with each other (as they often were).

Sanford and Son premiered on Friday, January 14, 1972, at 8:00 p.m. opposite *The Sonny and Cher Comedy Hour* on CBS and *The Brady Bunch* on ABC. NBC officials breathed a big sigh of relief the following day, when most of the critical reaction to the *Sanford and Son* premiere was positive—and, in some cases, absolutely glowing. "Veteran black comedian Redd Foxx . . . is superb, trying to hang on to the growing offspring with threats of heart attacks and suicide notes, while utterly destroying his dreams," critic Bob Williams wrote in the *New York Post*. "Desmond (sic) Wilson is ideally cast as the average bachelor trying to break out of junk."

"It's the funniest show to hit the air since *All in the Family's* debut," Cecil Smith wrote in the *Los Angeles Times*. "It's richly, humanly, roaringly funny in the genuine humor that comes out of character, not situations or gags. . . . The luxury [Aaron Ruben] does have is the immense depth of talent of Redd Foxx and young [Demond] Wilson. In black America, Foxx has long been one of the most admired of comedians: *Sanford* tells us why." The *New York Daily News* called *Sanford and Son* "a warm, funny show."

Three days later, influential *Los Angeles Times* gossip columnist Joyce Haber jumped on the Redd Foxx bandwagon. "If overnight ratings mean anything, Yorkin and Lear's new *Sanford and Son*, a half-hour comedy for NBC, looks to be the season's smash midseason replacement," she wrote. "And if my opinion means anything, it's a warm but stingingly hilarious, sharply written (by producer Aaron Ruben) and timed show which deserves that top honor."

Several weeks into the show's run, NBC announced that it was renewing *Sanford and Son* for the rest of the season, bringing the show's total order to fourteen episodes. It also meant *Sanford and Son* would return to NBC's Friday-night schedule in the fall for a second season (and its first full season), again at 8:00 p.m. "Niggas don't leave the house on Friday nights 'til they've watched *Sanford and Son*," Redd told Demond Wilson.

Sanford and Son, though, did have its critics—particularly in the black community. Some, like black *Soul* magazine columnist Walter Burrell, objected to the way Lamont treated his father in the show's early episodes. "To say that the younger man was disrespectful would be an understatement," he wrote. "He treated his father like a fool and it was not at all funny. How many black men treat their fathers like that? The relationship between the two men was degrading to the father and to the image of black fatherhood." Burrell, in blaming "white writers writing material for black actors," hit the nail squarely on the head. Both Redd and Demond Wilson, who were aware of how much *Sanford and Son* meant to the black community, also made their voices heard. They both criticized Aaron Ruben's early *Sanford and Son* scripts for Lamont's bullying attitude toward his father. To his credit, Ruben took the criticism to heart, softening Lamont's interactions with Fred, which made the father-son relationship a more believable (and loving) one and provided a warm, steady heartbeat for the series that was underscored by Redd's on-screen chemistry with Wilson.

Meanwhile, Redd's newfound television success meant a change on the home front. When he'd signed his three-year deal to perform in Las Vegas at the International (which changed over to the Hilton during his run), Redd and Betty Jeanne sold their place in the View Park section of Los Angeles and bought a spacious, ranch-style house on an acre of land in Las Vegas.

The house was in the city's Toluca Lake section in North Hollywood, down the street from Bob Hope and near the NBC studios. Debraca, now twenty-two and still single, moved in. The new place had a swimming pool and was spacious enough to accommodate the two-hundred-sixty-pound St. Bernard dog Redd brought over from Las Vegas (he would feed the dog left-over steak from the Hilton when he was working at the hotel). Redd was an animal lover and had a particular fondness for dogs, often keeping two or more hounds of different breeds around the house. Years later, when the Internal Revenue Service stripped him of nearly everything he owned, Redd begged the IRS officials not to take his dogs away. They were about the only possessions he had left to his name.

And now, with the sudden popularity of *Sanford and Son*, Redd got an up-close-and-personal look at the power of television. Almost overnight, he went from being an underground nightclub comedian to a household name. Within weeks of the show's debut, Fred Sanford was already being hailed as a classic television character along the lines of Lucille Ball's Lucy Ricardo, Carroll O'Connor's Archie Bunker, and Ralph Kramden, Jackie Gleason's blustery, bus-driving alter ego on *The Honeymooners*. "Redd became a star," said Bud Yorkin. "You have to realize that [coming] from nowhere, now he had people lined up to see the show. Every weekend, after we filmed, he went straight to the airport and went to Las Vegas and they mobbed him at the airport. This was a guy who was never well-known—I mean, he was known from any of us who knew he was a funny monologue guy—and all of the sudden he was a huge star."

The sudden thrust into the spotlight transformed Redd's celebrity status almost immediately. He earned his first-ever appearance on the cover of *Jet* magazine—"In the black community, this is the Bible," he said proudly—and, along with Demond Wilson and Aaron Ruben, was interviewed for a big Sunday feature in the *New York Times*, headlined "The Quick Redd Foxx Jumps Into a New Kettle of Fish." The feature (briefly) recounted Redd's life story, portrayed him as a teetotaler in love

Mary and Fred Sanford shortly after their wedding.

Sanford and brother: Jon Elroy and his older brother, Fred, looking dour for the camera, late 1920s.

"Smiley" Sanford, around ten years old.

Top: The Four Bon Bons, with Smiley Sanford (far right), rehearse for Captain Walter Dyett's "Hi-Jinks" show, DuSable High School, 1939.

Left: Redd's short-lived singing career encompassed five 78s, including *Lucky Guy*, produced by Teddy Reig and released by Savoy Records in 1946. (*Author's collection*)

Swingin': Working the club circuit, late 1940s. (*Digital Stock Planet*)

Redd and comedy partner Slappy White toured the segregated Chitlin' Circuit as Foxx and White, appearing often with musician Johnny Otis (to whom this photo is inscribed). Redd used his bowl haircut to get laughs. (*Johnny Otis Collection*)

The album that started it all. Redd sketched his self-portrait, used on the *Laff of the Party* co
while working as Johnny Otis's assistant at Long Beach radio station KFOX. (*Author's colle*

Redd and Betty Jeanne on
their wedding day. (*AP/
Wide World Photos*)

March 1958: Dootsie Williams presents Redd with his gold record for *Laff of the Party* at the Club Oasis. The smiles didn't last long.

That's Redd sitting at the piano in his (unbilled) appearance in *All the Fine Young Cannibals*, a sappy 1960 Hollywood melodrama starring Robert Wagner (blowing his trumpet) and Natalie Wood. (*Academy of Motion Picture Arts and Sciences*)

Top: Detroit Red and Chicago Red—now known as Malcolm X and Redd Foxx—get re-acquainted at Shabazz Restaurant in Harlem, summer 1962. (*Author's collection*)

Right: Fred Sanford, a gifted athlete, spent most of his adult life in and out of prison. He died in 1965 at the age of forty-six.

Publicity shot, early 1960s. (*Author's collection*)

The "King of the Party Records" with his bounty. (*Author's collection*)

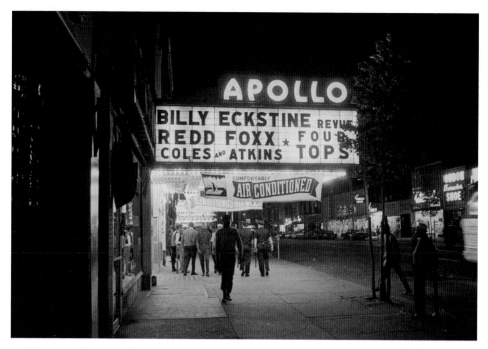

Redd was a frequent headliner at the Apollo Theater in Harlem, including this 1964 appearance with Billy Eckstine and the Four Tops. (*Corbis*)

Redd became a more familiar television presence in the mid-to-late 1960s and was a frequent guest on *The Merv Griffin Show* (with host Merv Griffin, left). (*Albert Fisher*)

with Las Vegas ("In Vegas, there's nothin' to do but gamble, drink, or have sex. I have two of 'em") and included his take on Fred Sanford ("a little bit of a Jewish mother"). In July, Redd and Demond Wilson graced the cover of *Jet's* sister publication, *Ebony* magazine. Both publications were owned by Jon Sanford's DuSable High School classmate, John Johnson.

But Redd wasn't about to let his "Jewish mother" television character get in the way of his real-life persona. And that included his stage act. *That* was sacred. *That's* what had brought him to the pinnacle. He hadn't spent nearly thirty years carving his reputation as the King of the Party Records (by some estimates, he'd sold anywhere from ten to twenty million albums by this point). And he wasn't about to throw his persona away now, just because he'd "cleaned up" for a network television series—the audience be damned if they didn't like it. Adults, he said time and again, should know better than to bring their kids to a live Redd Foxx nightclub appearance expecting to see Fred Sanford. *That's* who he really was. *That* was his identity. "Fred Sanford is just an infant in terms of working," he said. "I have to remind my in-person customers that Redd Foxx was around the nightclub circuit for twenty-six years before I turned into the old junkman."

So, in the wake of *Sanford and Son's* premiere, as the (mostly) positive reviews piled up and the show picked up even more ratings steam, Redd hit the stand-up circuit. In February 1972, he joined Louie Prima and the Four Seasons at the Newport in Miami Beach; in March, he returned to the Hilton in Las Vegas for two weeks, leading into Johnny Cash's much-anticipated engagement. NBC, looking to cash in on the *Sanford and Son* phenomenon, booked a series of traveling stage shows featuring Redd and Demond Wilson, who referred to each other on stage as "my son" and "my dad." Slappy White, Redd's old comedy partner, joined them. At Redd's insistence, Slappy guest-starred on an early episode of *Sanford and Son* as Fred's pal, Melvin (Slappy's real first name). Rounding out the *Sanford and Son* stage-show roster were singers Lynn Roman and Melba Liston and the Stovall Sisters.

In May, the stage show opened for a six-night run at the Mill Run Theater in Chicago. Redd's standard opening line in his live shows made it clear he wasn't about to play to his television alter ego. "Some people say I have a filthy mouth. I just want to clear that up," he would say. "That's a crock of shit!" Demond Wilson remembered that, at almost every live stage show, "the gasps from the audience were palpable." Chicago's respected black newspaper, the *Daily Defender*, liked the Mill Run show, but with a caveat: "Although he's paid his dues and certainly deserves every bit of the fame and fortune he is gathering," the paper said of Redd, "there's something queer about sitting among all those subdued Negroes trying to impress the white folks [who are laughing the hardest and longest]." In his monologue, Redd talked about "a nigger robbing a black man" and addressed the white audience members directly: "If you all didn't let me do what I'm doin', then I'd be out breakin' into your houses."

The *Sanford and Son* stage show quickly went downhill from there. One night in Dallas, the president of NBC came to the show and brought his kids with him. It was a big mistake. "The place was jammed with maybe 4,500 or 5,000 people," recalled Bud Yorkin. "And we didn't take any money. We didn't ask. We were the ones who came up with the idea and said [to Redd], 'Here's the chance to make some money,' but it was all done through Redd's people. I told Redd this would be great for him. He wanted to do a little monologue and I said okay. I said, 'Why don't we talk about it? and he said, 'You don't have to tell me how to do a monologue. People know me and love me.' I said, 'I'm only trying to help you, Redd, and you're already booked into three cities.'

"So he comes out and does his monologue and about halfway through, the [NBC] president and his kids get up and walk out. The whole fucking place started to walk out. I couldn't believe he had [that material] in his set. He never made the other cities. They all cancelled on him from the word that got out about that concert. They were all lined up for the summer. He could have made a fortune, and the next thing, he's cancelled."

In Demond Wilson's slightly different version of the story, the shows continued, but sometimes the outcome wasn't what anyone expected. "We played fair dates where blue-ribbon panels of good ole' boys with side arms tried to hold up our money, citing a breach-of-contract due to Redd's swearing." In some towns, promoters refused to pay at all, thinking they were getting crotchety-but-lovable Fred Sanford and not smutty nightclub comedian Redd Foxx. "Fuck that. I been Redd Foxx for over fifty years," Redd said. "I've only been Fred Sanford for two."

Even the *Sanford and Son* studio audience wasn't immune from Redd's live stage patter. He would often come out to "warm up" the audience before that night's taping. The "warmup" was a standard Hollywood practice, designed to get the studio audience revved up so they'd be sure to provide a booming laugh track once the cameras began to roll. Writer/director John Rich was at one *Sanford and Son* taping, representing Norman Lear and Bud Yorkin's Tandem Productions, when Redd came out to warm up the audience. Aaron Ruben had been pleading with Redd not to use any blue material in the warmup, since Ruben thought it created too much of a psychological credibility gap between Redd's real-life persona, and the audience's perception of Fred Sanford. Redd would have none of it. On this night, he launched into a routine in which a man and woman are deep into some heavy petting in a parked car. The woman gets so turned on she says to her partner, "Kiss me. Kiss me where it smells." After an "audible gasp" from the audience, Redd delivered the knockout punch: "So I took her to El Segundo."

Several months later, Redd dropped into Donte's nightclub in Los Angeles to perform some standup comedy in-between sets by the Louie Belson orchestra. The material was pure Redd Foxx, and when a woman walked out of the club in the middle of Redd's set, her small son in tow, Redd bellowed from the stage: "Don't blame me, ma'am. The sign outside says Redd Foxx, not Fred Sanford."

But all that was pure background noise for the commotion that Redd Foxx and *Sanford and Son* were creating in the television world. In April, only three months after the show's premiere, Redd earned his first Emmy Award nomination as Best Actor in a Comedy Series, joining fellow nominees Jack Klugman and Tony Randall (*The Odd Couple*) and Carroll O'Connor (*All in the Family*). *Sanford and Son* was nominated as Best Comedy Series along with *All in the Family*, *The Mary Tyler Moore Show*, and *The Odd Couple*. The Emmys aired in May, and while Redd and *Sanford and Son* didn't win, the nominations were a clear signal that the show was here to stay. *Sanford and Son* ended its first season averaging nearly sixteen million viewers over fourteen episodes, a remarkable number for a midseason replacement series. It finished sixth in total viewers in prime time, just behind ABC's *Movie of the Week* and roughly three-hundred thousand viewers ahead of seventh-place *Mannix*. *All in the Family* was the season's top-rated show, averaging over twenty-one million viewers.

Even *Life* magazine, that bastion of middle-American mores, weighed in with its assessment of the black junkman and his son. "It's an agreeable show, as sitcoms go, a cut above *Dick Van Dyke*, a cut below *Mary Tyler Moore*," it opined. "Redd Foxx is splendid as the junkman with dignity." It also sounded a cautionary note, one which would gain traction in the show's second season: "As with *Flip Wilson*, most of *Sanford and Son's* writers are white, despite all the jokes about Afros and chitlins. . . . Why not try young black writers like Ishmael Reed and Cecil Brown?"

Sanford and Son wrapped its first season on April 14, 1972. Those first fourteen episodes introduced many of the show's lasting iconic touchstones, chiefly Fred and Lamont's relationship, which formed the series' emotional and comedic foundation. It was clear from the very first episode that Fred and Lamont's bond was unbreakable, despite Lamont's (half-hearted) attempts to break away from Fred's clutches— and Fred's sly schemes to keep his son and partner-in-grime anchored to the junkyard at 9114 South Central. "He's a warm, lovable, saucy, dirty old man," Redd said of Fred, "who will stoop to anything, including faking a heart attack, to hang on to his thirty-two-year-old son."

Fred's frequent, comedically timed "heart attacks"—summoned from thin air—became a show-stopper, the moment in each episode eagerly anticipated by *Sanford and Son* fans. Whenever Fred was upset, usually because Lamont was threatening to fly the coop, he would suddenly clutch his chest, stagger back and forth a few steps and, looking up to the heavens, cry out to his sainted late wife: "It's the Big One, Elizabeth! I'm comin' to join ya, honey!" Sometimes, Fred would even set the scene for Elizabeth. 'I'm comin' to join ya, honey! And I'm holding a pistol!" Fred's "heart attacks" became the *Sanford and Son* calling card, taking their place in the pantheon of classic television moments like Lucy Ricardo's crying jags on *I Love Lucy*, Ralph Kramden's "Bang, zoom!" zingers to his wife, Alice, or Archie Bunker's oft-repeated admonishment to his "dingbat" wife, Edith, to "stifle yourself!" Fred's version of "stifle yourself!" was to call Lamont a "big dummy," and that, too, became a fan-favorite *Sanford and Son* catchphrase. Fred, who was allergic to any kind of serious work (excluding cooking Lamont's meals), also used his conveniently recurring *arthur-itis* to shirk any strenuous household duties. He would hold out his suddenly clawed hands to a dubious Lamont to prove his malady.

That first season of *Sanford and Son* also introduced some of the show's memorable recurring characters. Aaron Ruben, who wrote all but one episode of Season 1, used the first three shows to establish the relationship between Fred and Lamont. It wasn't until the fourth episode, "The Copper Caper," that viewers were introduced to hip beat cop Officer Smith ("Smitty") and his uptight, by-the-book white partner, Officer Swanhauser ("Swanny"), played respectively by Hal Williams and Noam Pitlik. Williams would remain a *Sanford and Son* cast member through the show's entire run; Pitlik left a few episodes into the second season and would go on to direct over one hundred episodes of the hit ABC sitcom, *Barney Miller*. Smitty and Swanny were friendly neighborhood cops; Smitty, who was black, spent much of his time translating Swanny's Joe Friday-type, machine-gun-cadence cop speak for a bewildered Fred. Slappy White's first appearance as Fred's old pal, Melvin, came in the ninth episode, "Coffins for Sale"; Melvin would re-appear three more times the first season and one time in the second season before vanishing forever from the *Sanford and Son* junkyard.

The tenth episode of the first season, "The Barracuda," introduced Fred's on-again, off-again love interest, Donna, a sophisticated, widowed nurse who, for reasons that were hard to figure out, put up with Fred's unpredictable behavior and was clearly in love with the older man. Donna was played by veteran actress Lynn Hamilton, who divided her time between *Sanford and Son* and a recurring role as Verdie Grant Foster on *The Waltons*. Hamilton, who was no prude, was still shocked at Redd's language when she arrived on the *Sanford and Son* set to begin the "table reads" of that week's show. (The "table read" was an exercise in which the entire cast read through the script before actual rehearsals.) "Redd could string together some words that you couldn't dream of. I mean, he put the 'd' in dirty," Hamilton said. "I was really embarrassed at sitting down for the table read, and there were about twenty-five people around and most of them were smiling in an embarrassed kind of way. But nobody said anything and I figured it wasn't my place to say anything. I would probably get fired if I had [said anything].

"So I decided that I would discreetly speak to the stage manager and excuse myself. So each time Redd would start that tirade of vulgarity, I would excuse myself to make a phone call or go to the ladies room or some such thing and I would leave the room. And, of course, after a while I think everybody knew what was happening, but no one said anything about it." Redd, though, took notice of Hamilton's frequent trips away from the table. "Gradually he stopped talking in a filthy way at the table read," she said. "I felt that was kind of a nice thing to do, because he obviously knew what I was doing and chose to stop. I felt he had a good soul."

He could also be extremely generous to Hamilton and his fellow co-stars. After taping each *Sanford and Son* episode, Redd would fly back to Las Vegas to spend the weekend, returning to the set for the Monday-morning table read—usually irritable and unprepared for the long day ahead. "We had a nine o'clock table read and of course he didn't want to be there, he wanted to sleep. And he was just miserable," Hamilton said. "So what he would do, instead of sitting down and getting it over with, he would tell jokes and have everybody laughing and waste the whole day, because he didn't want to rehearse. He never got used to the structure. The next day he would bring everybody gifts. I got a couple of diamonds that he gave me, a ruby necklace and diamond earrings. He was a complex, funny, sensitive, sad man."

He was now also a bona fide television star. Earlier that year, he'd won his first Golden Globe Award for *Sanford and Son*, beating out Alan Alda (*M*A*S*H*), Bill Cosby (*The New Bill Cosby Show*), Paul Lynde (*The Paul Lynde Show*), Carroll O'Connor (*All in the Family*) and Flip Wilson (*The Flip Wilson Show*). In September, Redd appeared, in character, on the cover of *Time* magazine under the headline "The New TV Season: Toppling Old Taboos." The cover featured photos of "Fred Sanford" (Redd), "Cousin Maude" (Bea Arthur, who was making her debut as Maude Findlay in the *All in the Family* spinoff, *Maude*), and "Archie Bunker" (*All in the Family* star Carroll O'Connor).

The accompanying six-page article focused on Norman Lear and Bud Yorkin, "The Team Behind Archie Bunker & Co.," comparing and contrasting their three network television shows—and each series' lead character. "The old man, played by Redd Foxx, has none of Archie's anger," the magazine wrote of Fred Sanford. "He is simply an engaging con artist who will resort to any ruse to keep his son from quitting the business and leaving home."

It also called *Sanford and Son*'s meteoric rise up the ratings ladder "one of the fastest ascents in TV history."

America was put on notice: Redd Foxx had arrived.

chapter nine

"The Godfather of Sitcom"

Sanford and Son returned for its second season on September 15, 1972, and proved to be no flash-in-the pan. The show quickly reclaimed its ratings mojo, and while *All in the Family* on CBS was still television's top-rated show, it now had some stiff competition from the NBC upstart. *Sanford and Son* was nipping at its heels, occasionally beating *All in the Family* for the week's most-watched television show. Bud Yorkin and Norman Lear's Tandem Productions was now packing television's most formidable one-two punch with shows on competing networks. And its third show, *Maude*, was off to a fast start on CBS. Tandem Productions was an industry powerhouse.

The viewing public continued its love affair with Fred Sanford and, by extension, with Redd Foxx. Never at a loss for words, his confidence at its peak, Redd attributed the show's success to the believability of its lead character—and to the way in which he played Fred Sanford. "He's not an idiot, even though he didn't have much education. But he's no Uncle Tom," he said. "He doesn't say 'y'all' and 'I is' and we're doing the shuffle bit. We aren't stereotypes and we don't act like stereotypes. Besides being truthful to black people, we are being truthful to all people. I play a widower, but I could be playing a Jewish mother.

"One black woman wrote to Demond Wilson and me and said she was disturbed because Sanford and Son had to be junkmen," he said. "This show has been running in England for ten years, and I bet no one ever wrote in and asked, 'How come you're showing white junkmen?' I wrote to this lady and I asked her, 'What do you want us to be? Black astronauts? Nuclear physicists? So we're junkmen—so what? We're honest. That's better than lying around on relief.'"

But not everyone in the black community was buying into the show. As *Sanford and Son* continued to score its weekly ratings triumphs, there were rumblings from some corners that Fred and Lamont were no more than updated *Amos 'n' Andy* characters, perpetuating black stereotypes to a massive television audience, including untold millions of white viewers.

Eugenia Collier, an author and teacher of Black Literature at the Community College of Baltimore, wrote an opinion piece for the *New York Times* slamming the show as a "white" creative vehicle pandering to America's worst black stereotypes. Under the headline "'Sanford and Son' Is White to the Core," Collier's lengthy essay labeled the show "insidious" and "dangerous," called out the show's white writing staff ("I have never *ever* encountered a believable black character created by a white American mind") and criticized the junkyard setting ("Now, how many black junkmen do you know? Well, there must be some, yes. But more typically, black men of limited education would be somewhere laboring for the white man"). She called Fred Sanford a "racist," "a liar," "narrow-minded" and "obnoxious"—before turning to Lamont ("he lets himself be completely dominated and manipulated by that selfish old man"). "Fred Sanford and his little boy Lamont, conceived by white minds and based upon a white value system, are not strong black men capable of achieving—or even understanding—liberation," Collier concluded. "They are merely two more American child-men."

But what Collier failed to note, or perhaps was unaware of, was that *Sanford and Son* did have several black writers, including Redd's close friend, Richard Pryor, and his writing partner, Paul Mooney. Pryor and Mooney co-wrote the third episode of the second season, "The Dowry" (in which Fred schemes to marry Lamont off to his cousin's stepdaughter, who has a $10,000 dowry); later that season, they contributed an episode called "Sanford and Son and Sister Makes Three" (in which Lamont wants to marry the daughter of Fred's old flame, Juanita, much to Fred's horror). Pryor and Mooney, though, worked on a freelance basis, which meant that Aaron Ruben and staff writer Gene Farmer were penning the bulk of the show's episodes—which were now all original scripts (no more *Steptoe and Son* remakes). So, early in the second season, Ruben reached across the country to hire Adell Stevenson as the show's first full-time black writer.

Stevenson was an actor and a playwright who was working in New York City with Joseph Papp's acclaimed Public Theater. His resume included acting in a 1969 play called *Five on the Black Hand Side*, which also featured Demond Wilson. A self-proclaimed "cultural nationalist," Adell Stevenson had just recently changed his birth name to Ilunga Adell, after visiting the Congo with his then-girlfriend. (His first few scripts for *Sanford and Son* were credited to Adell Stevenson; it was always Ilunga Adell thereafter.) "I'm a guy who got rid of his slave name because I wanted a name that reflected my African heritage," he said. When he returned to New York from Africa, Stevenson wrote a one-act play, *One: The 2 of Us*, which was produced by Joseph Papp. Papp had a knack for publicity and was generating lots of press for his Public Theater and its stable of writers (which included David Rabe and Jason Miller). The Sunday *New York Times* ran a feature story on Papp, which included a mention of Ilunga Adell. For Aaron Ruben, who had been looking for a black writer, it was perfect timing.

"Aaron Ruben reads the Sunday *New York Times* and sees these playwrights in the line-up. There are two black playwrights, myself and OyamO," Adell recalled. "Aaron was catching a lot of flack because he didn't have any black writers . . . and he says to himself, 'If they wrote for Papp, maybe they can write for us.'" Adell considered himself "a serious thespian," but those pretensions ended when Ruben offered him a one hundred-dollar-a-day expense account, a car, and the princely sum of two thousand dollars for each *Sanford and Son* script Adell wrote. For the time being, Adell remained in New York, mailing his *Sanford and Son* scripts to Los Angeles, then waiting for them to be mailed back for rewrites and edits based on notes and suggestions from Ruben and the other writers.

The absence of black writers on *Sanford and Son* certainly didn't go unnoticed by its two stars. In Redd's characteristically blunt words, working with Aaron Ruben meant having "to translate the scripts into spook," and teaching the white writers that their cultural divide wasn't a comfortable reality. "The writers are beginning to learn that black is another language," he said. It didn't matter to Redd Foxx that he was a newcomer to television working in his first network series; he wasn't shy about expressing his opinions when he found a line of dialogue objectionable—particularly if he felt it was demeaning or stereotypical. In one early *Sanford and Son* script, Fred referred to a "sapphire" ring.

Redd immediately objected. "In order to eliminate the word 'sapphire,' which you remember was a name in *Amos 'n' Andy*, I called it a 'red ruby,'" he said. "I just didn't want the word 'sapphire' on my show." He was usually more succinct. "I am not gonna eat watermelon on TV," he told one writer. "I don't [eat it] at home."

Redd was adamant that Fred, and the *Sanford and Son* universe surrounding him, reflect as much of an authentic black experience as possible within the framework of a half-hour network sitcom. The show had to be funny, of course, and Fred Sanford was often outlandish and often a buffoon—but his foibles fell within the context of his character, so the laughs were organic, and not insulting. Redd worked with the show's writers to insure there would be no cheap laughs at the characters' expense—particularly of a racial origin. "We sit around a table and I tell them . . . that this is essentially a black show reflecting black experiences, and to make it survive we have to keep it real," Redd said early in the show's run. When, in the first season of *Sanford and Son*, Fred used the word "nigger"—the first time the word was ever uttered on a network television show—it was only because Redd insisted on using it. "The first time I said 'nigger,' everybody in the studio was uptight about whether the public would accept it," he said. "I reminded them that I could hear it in another 'show' where it wasn't given a second thought: in any black home in the USA."

There were arguments on the set, but they were usually settled in Redd's favor, since he had a verbal agreement with Aaron Ruben, and the show's other writers, that he had the final say over anything he deemed offensive, either to himself or to the black community. "They would say that they didn't think something was offensive to black people. I knew it was, because it offended me," he said. Redd was particularly annoyed at what he felt were demeaning stereotypes on the show, "all these jokes about coffins, people rolling their eyeballs, girls dressed like damn fools in rummage sale outfits."

Redd was also instrumental in bringing in Stan Lathan as the first African American director on *Sanford and Son*. For months, Redd had been poking and prodding Aaron Ruben to bring in a black director, especially once Ruben hired Ilunga Adell for the show's writing staff. "He was making a lot of noise about not having an African American director, because he was feeling like there was this cultural gap from where he was coming from, and [from] where the directors they had were coming from," Lathan said. Ruben turned to Adell, who recommended Lathan, a veteran television director who was back in New York working on *Sesame Street*. Lathan also had big-screen experience, having directed Moms Mabley shortly before her death in the movie *Amazing Grace*, which co-starred Slappy White.

"It was a big deal that Redd had gotten them to hire a black director, and they all admired him [on the set] for that and appreciated him for that because it was a very symbolic move," Lathan said. "They would come around and watch rehearsals, and the first time I walked into the [NBC] commissary there was a huge stir among the black employees. I was immediately welcomed and made to feel it was something special. It was a huge event for the show's crew and staff, the experience of suddenly dealing with a black director who was under thirty and very skilled and aware of what he was doing."

After moving to Los Angeles a few months later, Ilunga Adell was asked by Aaron Ruben, on behalf of the show, to answer Eugenia Collier's scathing opinion piece on *Sanford and Son* that ran in the *New York Times*. Adell did what he was told, and reluctantly wrote a long response in which he defended the show, specifically citing two episodes he'd written, "Tooth or Consequences" (in which Fred insists on going to a white dentist) and "Lamont Goes African" (Lamont adopts an African name, wears African garb, etc.). "I did not want to do that," Adell said about his response to Collier. "I just got here from New York and I was settling in, learning how to become a TV writer . . . and I'm a little reluctant to do that because I don't want to get into an argument with my black sister on behalf of these white people."

But Adell's move to Los Angeles finally gave him the chance to meet Redd Foxx in person. "He was very down-to-earth and approachable," he said. "Also, he was the funniest motherfucker I ever met. You know how some people are always 'on'? He wasn't 'on.' He was just naturally funny. It was like he had a funny computer in his head and stuff just came out funny. And Redd Foxx was very intelligent; I really think he would have been a good dramatic actor."

Ilunga Adell and others working on *Sanford and Son* also got an up-close-and-personal look at Redd's behavior on the set, particularly his growing cocaine habit. Now that *Sanford and Son* was an established hit, Redd threw caution to the wind; he'd made it to the Big Time and he was in his element. No one was going to tell him what to do, or how to behave. They never had, and they never would. And that mantra extended to his cocaine use.

Earlier in his life, Redd's drug of choice was marijuana, with the occasional snort of cocaine. Smack (heroin) was much too scary, and he'd been an eyewitness to its deadly consequences. He still smoked reefer, but his cocaine use was increasing by the time he bought Redd's Place on La Cienega in 1967. Now, five years later, it was a full-blown habit. Redd made no secret of his jones for cocaine. He wore a very visible, very small, silver coke spoon on a chain around his neck, and would nonchalantly snort a few lines of the white stuff during *Sanford and Son* table reads. Aaron Ruben and the rest of the cast and crew were well-aware of Redd's prodigious drug habit. Ruben even assigned an assistant producer to monitor Redd; on show night, she would motion to her nose—a signal for Redd to check his nose and mustache for white powder just before he came out in front of the cameras.

But Redd's cocaine habit certainly wasn't unusual in 1970s Hollywood, where the white powder was the drug of choice and almost everyone, it seemed, was snorting the stuff. "It was rampant," recalled Kathleen Fearn-Banks, an NBC publicist who worked on *The Flip Wilson Show* before moving over to *Sanford and Son*. "It was almost like it wasn't illegal because it was there. And I knew who in the studio was providing it. It was just a common thing." The coke also helped Redd stay alert and focused, especially at those brutal Monday-morning table reads after a busy weekend of partying, gambling, and screwing in Las Vegas.

"Redd would snort cocaine at the table read," Adell said. "We would sit around a table and he would have cocaine in a little glass vial, and he would tap some out onto his thumbnail and snort it right there at the table, which was really a bold act. He wasn't trying to hide it. It was part of his routine every fifteen minutes, it seemed. He smoked weed and he drank. He had the constitution of a horse. He was a strong little motherfucker. He wasn't a big guy, but he was sturdy.

"Redd Foxx used a lot of cocaine. I was a pothead. I would jump over a pile of cocaine as tall as him to get to one good stick of pot," said Adell. "Redd gave me some cocaine and I couldn't even talk afterwards. It was like, damn! I stuck to weed. I know Redd smoked weed but he didn't smoke as much weed as I did—but I don't think Bob Marley smoked as much weed as I did."

There were two *Sanford and Son* table reads each week. The cast would read the next week's script first, take a break, then come back and read the script that would be taped that week. "In between the readings of the two scripts, all of the brothers would go to Redd Foxx's dressing room and get high," Adell said. "There would be a lot of people in Redd's dressing room on those breaks, and during other parts of the day, too." *Sanford and Son* director Alan Rafkin recalled that on Fridays, the day the show taped, Redd looked "like the godfather of sitcom" holding court in his dressing room and wearing nothing but his underwear while eating his dinner. "The parade included the mayor of Los Angeles, several musicians, and a steady parade of women. Redd loved the ladies. And I must say the ladies loved Redd."

Redd's drug use also meant that Bud Yorkin and Norman Lear couldn't get insurance on their star, since Redd refused to take a physical. It was standard operating procedure in Hollywood for studios like Tandem Productions to take out insurance policies on their stars, should something happen and they needed to recoup their financial losses for however many days of work were missed. "We could never get any insurance on him," Yorkin said. "He'd say, 'Nobody's going to look up my nose, nobody's going to look down my throat, I don't do that shit.' Why? Because he was taking too many things. You would know in a second he was taking drugs. That's why he wouldn't give in to them. We never had a dollar's worth of insurance [on Redd] during the whole show."

Alan Rafkin "adored" Redd, but recalled that working with such a temperamental man had its share of challenges on the set. "He was a man who openly did drugs and wore spoons around his neck as a show of allegiance to cocaine," Rafkin said. "As far as his work went, Redd was sometimes more like a testy child than a man. We'd call rehearsal for ten o'clock in the morning. It could be two o'clock in the afternoon before Redd came strolling in. When he finally did arrive, he might say, 'I was down in the parking lot. I couldn't get in the door. It was locked. I'm not kidding.' He would make up a story like a little child would. . . . With Redd, you never knew what was going to happen. It was a crapshoot. But as filthy-mouthed and drugged-out as Redd often was, deep down I always knew that there was a lot of good in him, too."

The drug use, though, never seemed to impact Redd's work on-camera. However much he fucked around during the table reads and during rehearsal—snorting coke, wasting time, and then apologizing to everyone by giving them gifts—he always knew his lines when it came time to shoot the show. At least he *pretended* to have memorized the script. "Oftentimes we wouldn't know what to expect from him during taping," said co-star Lynn Hamilton, who played Fred's on-again, off-again fiancée, Donna (aka "The Barracuda"). "But the man was a genius with comedy. He very seldom knew his lines and we were petrified because we never knew what he was going to say. At that time we taped before a live studio audience and it was like doing a stage play. Once you got started you were bound to continue . . . but sometimes he would get that little twinkle in his eye, and I knew that he didn't know what the next line was going to be.

"If you look very closely sometimes, I have a very petrified look on my face because I don't know what he's going to say—but, interestingly enough, what he would say was within the context of what Fred Sanford would have said, and [it] would continue to advance the plot. And sometimes his line was better than the lines that were written." It was Redd being Redd. And he was crazy like a fox.

Like many of his comedic predecessors, particularly Jackie Gleason, Redd believed in giving a minimal effort in rehearsals and saving his best for the live taping—when he could feed off the energy of the studio audience. Each *Sanford and Son* episode was shot twice before a live audience; there was a dress rehearsal, followed by the "real" show. "When we cut the show together we would use the best moments from either show," said *Sanford and Son* director Stan Lathan. "So Redd would even change his performance oftentimes between dress and air, and there were often two pretty good choices there about the way he might read a line or might respond to something. He would always be giving us something to work with. He was really special as a comedian."

Behind the scenes, Redd spared no one in the *Sanford and Son* cast or crew from his nonstop patter. His behavior could be offensive, childish, and mean-spirited. He couldn't turn it off the way some performers do—the loud, abrasive comic, for instance, who's quiet and morose offstage. What you saw was what you got, and the Redd Foxx traveling circus took no prisoners, including newcomers like Howard Platt. Platt joined *Sanford and Son* in its second season, playing Smitty's clueless partner, Officer Hopkins (or "Hoppy," as Fred called him). Hoppy tried his damndest to be hip but never quite pulled it off (unlike his predecessor, Officer Swanhauser, or "Swanny," who was a buttoned-down square).

While appearing on *Sanford and Son*, Howard Platt also had a recurring role as blowhard dentist Dr. Phil Newman on *The Bob Newhart Show*, which premiered in the fall of 1972 on CBS (the second season of *Sanford and Son*). The contrast between the two sets—and between the two stand-up comedians headlining their respective shows—couldn't have been starker, Platt said. "Redd would say things like, 'Fellas, smile if you like pussy,' and if there was ever a white woman there, he had to make a comment like that or he would say things like, 'You remember the first time you ever saw pussy? Looked like a tomahawk wound. Looked like Sammy Davis Jr. with his eye out.' I mean he was unbelievable.

"One time we were in the rest room together. I washed my hands and he said, 'Why do white people always wash their hands after they piss? Don't you wash your dick?'" After Redd was honored with a community service award by Los Angeles mayor Tom Bradley, he, Bradley, and Platt were standing in line to get some food. When Bradley asked Redd about the carrots (they were, in fact, sweet potatoes), Redd didn't waste a second to respond. "Nigger been mayor for two years and he forget what sweet potatoes look like!" he said to Platt. "And when there were crowds of people there after the show, they would let a certain number of them into the studio, and Redd would walk along and greet everybody and shake their hand and say, 'Good evening, madam, Good evening, sir, Good evening nigger.' Whenever there was a black guy, it was 'Good evening, nigger.' That was him."

He was raunchy, flirtatious, and downright smutty at times. In today's world, some of Redd's behavior, especially toward the women on the set, would have been tabloid fodder and potential sexual harassment lawsuits; in the 1970s, with NBC protecting its investment, Redd's behavior was laughed off and swept under the rug. And, in an industry dominated by men, it was accepted as the perks of a star doing as he pleased. It was standard show-biz operating procedure. And, really, how much has changed in today's Hollywood?

"There was a woman who worked on the show and who complained about him and she lost her job," said *Sanford and Son* publicist Kathleen Fearn-Banks. "Redd wasn't going anywhere. And so I think everybody kind of learned that you have to learn to live with this man, with his language. And he was quite a womanizer. I mean, he had this way of patting a woman on the back and in that one pat he could undo a bra strap through whatever clothes she was wearing. I mean, he was just doing it all over the studio. I started wearing leather clothes to work. But I only knew one person who actually hated him for it, and that was the woman who complained."

Redd's unfiltered, raw language and fuck-you attitude didn't just apply to the show's cast and crew. In late 1972, NBC announced that Lena Horne would guest-star on an episode of *Sanford and Son*. It was only appropriate, given Fred Sanford's oft-stated love and admiration for "The Horne," as he called her. She was the perfect female specimen in old Fred's eyes—and, apparently, in the eyes of his real-life alter ego. "Almost had a heart attack for real getting her on the show," Redd told the *Los Angeles Times*. "She's blacklisted, didn't you know? Why do you think you don't see her lately on television? She stood up and spoke out a little too loudly for black people to please certain folks and she got herself banned. Well, she's not banned on my show."

The episode was called "A Visit from Lena Horne" and it aired in January 1973. In the episode, Fred sees "The Horne's" car in the NBC parking lot while on a tour of the network's studios in Burbank with Lamont. One thing leads to another, and Fred eventually comes face-to-face with the woman of his dreams. Snaring Lena Horne for a rare television appearance was quite a coup for Bud Yorkin, Aaron Ruben, and NBC—but Redd almost screwed it up as soon as Horne appeared on the set. For starters, he arrived forty minutes late to the table read, keeping "The Horne" waiting. Bud Yorkin described the scene: "So in comes Redd. He sits down and says, 'Man, I'm sorry I'm late, but last night I had one of the most unbelievable experiences I ever had in my life.' By this time, everyone was shifting nervously in their seats. "He says, 'I was with one of the most beautiful, sexy women I've ever been with in my life. I want to tell you, my dick got as hard as a railroad spike' . . . and with that Lena Horne got up and said, 'You are the worst nigger I ever met!' and walks out."

Yorkin ran after Horne, and later paid a visit to her in her suite at the Beverly Hilton Hotel. Eventually, he talked her into returning to the *Sanford and Son* set. "She said, 'I'll tell you what. I'll come back if you talk to Redd Foxx and you tell him I don't want to talk to him. I don't want him to talk to me. I will say my lines and he says his lines. If I hear one dirty word, not only to me, but to anybody in that cast, I'm walking out. And I can assure you that I will do it. I'm not fooling around. I don't live that way. He does things that ruin our people. He has a dirty mind.'"

Yorkin went back to the set and read his star the riot act, explaining how much money NBC was spending to promote Horne's appearance on *Sanford and Son*, how big of a deal it was that she was appearing on the show, and how big the ratings would be once the episode aired. "And he came back and he didn't use one word: he didn't even use 'damn,'" Yorkin said. "They didn't talk, either. They played the scenes when she was there."

If Redd's boorish behavior was legendary, so too was his generosity. His gruff exterior masked a gentle heart. If you were a friend of Redd Foxx, you were a friend for life. But he was also a sucker for a sob story, willing to completely give his trust over to people he barely knew, to "brothers" and "sisters" and assorted hangers-on with a sob story and their hands out, looking for a quick buck from a television star with deep pockets. This was the same Redd Foxx, the same streetwise hustler who ran with "Detroit Red" in Harlem, who scratched and clawed his way up the show business ladder playing crappy nightclubs with crooked owners, who battled the stink of segregation—who carried a *gun*, for chrissakes. And he was a soft touch. Go figure.

To Dee Crawford, one of Redd's employees, he was "the Red Cross of the black race," always ready and willing to lend a helping hand with his open wallet. "Redd touched so many lives and helped an awful lot of people," she said. But that generosity came with a steep price and little return on his investment. Most of the people Redd helped never repaid him, and as his career rocketed into the stratosphere, and his pockets deepened with cash, the handouts, sometimes to total strangers, became more common. Redd's profligate spending and his willingness to throw a few bucks (or more) someone's way—without getting anything in return—created a vicious cycle that would come back to haunt him in later years.

Nowhere was Redd's generosity more evident than in his efforts to pull old pals from the Chitlin Circuit off the scrap heap of obscurity and into his television orbit. "He did look after his old friends," said *Sanford and Son* producer Saul Turteltaub. "He would come into the studio one day and some guy would walk in and Redd would say, 'Put him in the show, Turtle.' And we would put him in the show. There were a lot of guys from the old days . . . and they were all good. There was never any dead weight anywhere."

Once it became apparent early in its second season that *Sanford and*

Son would stick around for a while, Redd started reaching out to old show-biz pals and nightclub cronies and offering them roles on the show. Sometimes it was only a one-time situation with a few lines, or maybe no lines at all. Others, like the veteran Chitlin' Circuit comedy duo Leroy & Skillet—Leroy Daniels and Ernest Mayhand, who added LaWanda Page to their act in the 1960s—parlayed their initial *Sanford and Son* appearance into several return visits. "Most of my friends are in show business, and I help them as much as I can now that I'm in a position to do so," Redd said. "I went back fifteen years to get some of my friends to appear as guest performers. They're regarded as new faces in television. It's really unbelievable. Many of them lived right here in Los Angeles, and never had a shot at TV. Other people could have done something for them in the past and never did."

"A lot of people retired in show business and never thought they'd get a shot on TV," he told Sammy Davis Jr. in a visit to Davis' talk show, *Sammy and Company*. "There are good actors and actresses out there who would give a lung for just one shot, so I just find 'em and put 'em on, if they're good."

Redd convinced Bud Yorkin and Aaron Ruben to hire veteran comedian Don Bexley, with whom he'd toured the Chitlin' Circuit, to play Fred's best pal, Bubba—*Sanford and Son's* version of Ed Norton, Ralph Kramden's dimwitted sidekick on *The Honeymooners* (played by Art Carney). Bexley, who was sixty-two at the time and had never appeared on television, soon became a *Sanford and Son* regular and one of the show's best-loved characters. He showed off his understated comedy chops in a third-season episode called "The Blind Mellow Jelly Collection," in which Fred donates a collection of "Blind Mellow Jelly" jazz albums to a music library, then tries to get them back when he learns they're worth five hundred dollars. To pull off his ruse, Fred corrals Bubba into pretending that he's Blind Mellow Jelly's son ("I want my daddy's records!" "Junior" proclaims over and over). Once *Sanford and Son* ended its run, Bexley continued to play Bubba on *The Sanford Arms*, a short-lived *Sanford and Son* spinoff. It was sweet vindication for all those years toiling in crappy joints. "Bubba, Don Bexley, we worked all through Ohio and Pennsylvania when it was rough," Redd said.

"One day, NBC took a bus over to the South Side of Los Angeles and filled it up with Redd's cronies from the old days, and had them on the show as bums," said *Sanford and Son* publicist Kathleen Fearn-Banks. "A lot of people started [on *Sanford and Son*] who were his buddies. Raymond Allen, who played Aunt Esther's husband, was a buddy of Redd's."

But among Redd's circle of friends, it was LaWanda Page, Jon Sanford's elementary school classmate from Saint Louis, who really reaped the benefits of Redd Foxx's newfound television stardom.

Born Alberta Peal in 1920 in Cleveland, Page moved with her family to Saint Louis, where she spent her childhood (and was two years ahead of Jon Sanford at Banneker Elementary School). Like Redd Foxx, LaWanda Page began her career working small nightclubs, initially with a dance act. She called herself "The Bronze Goddess of Fire," and her act included fire-eating and a bit in which she lit cigarettes with her fingertips (a shtick she resurrected on an episode of *Sanford and Son*). Page later developed a standup act and worked the Chitlin' Circuit as a brash comic, often crossing paths with Redd through the years. Page followed in Redd's footsteps and recorded a few raunchy party albums for Laff Records in the late 1960s, then joined Leroy & Skillet's comedy act at the Brass Rail in Los Angeles.

In the fall of 1972, Redd called Page and offered her a small role on *Sanford and Son* as Fred's foil: his Bible-thumping sister-in-law, Aunt Esther. Page was asleep when Redd called and, thinking that he was kidding around, as he often did, hung up on him twice. When Redd said he'd come over and knock her teeth out if she didn't take him seriously, Page knew the offer was for real.

Aunt Esther made her first appearance in a second-season episode called "The Big Party," which was written by Aaron Ruben and Odie Hawkins. The plot revolved around Fred and Lamont's idea to throw a house party at the junkyard and charge admission, so they can raise some much-needed cash to stave off the bill collectors. Enter Aunt Esther, the sister of Fred's late, beloved wife, Elizabeth. Esther, with Bible in tow, wants to hold her Sunday-morning Bible meeting at Fred's house the morning after the big shindig. Fred and Esther's very first encounter set the stage for their classic verbal sparring:

> FRED TO ESTHER: "If I felt like you and looked like you, I'd go down to Forest Lawn Cemetery and hang around a while."

FRED TO ESTHER: "For years people going around
saying 'Black is Beautiful.' They took one look at your
family and said, 'Hold everything, Deirdre.'"
ESTHER: "We have inner beauty."
FRED: "You better put your liver where your face is."
ESTHER TO FRED: "If you lay one hand one me, I'll
unscrew your arm from your shoulder and beat your
brains out!"

In that same episode, viewers also heard what would become one of
Aunt Esther's two catchphrases. "You a heathen!" she shouts at Fred,
storming out of the house after their verbal jousting. In later episodes,
her warning to Fred to "Watch it, Sucka!" became another Aunt Esther
catchphrase, which *Sanford and Son* fans anticipated almost as eagerly
as one of Fred's chest-clutching "heart attacks." (Page released a 1973
comedy album, *Watch it, Sucka!* to cash in on her *Sanford and Son* popularity. The album sold millions and was certified gold.)

The role of Aunt Esther would cement Page's niche in television
history, but it was a role that came close to dying before it even began.
Unlike her friend Redd Foxx, LaWanda Page did not adapt naturally to
the rhythms and cadences of a sitcom script. Prior to *Sanford and Son*, she
had never appeared on television and, at the age of fifty-three, didn't
know how to dial down her sassy nightclub persona to fit the more
subtle confines of the small screen. When her first rehearsals proved
disastrous, the show's producers panicked; there were backstage arguments, and they wanted Page fired and sent back home (she'd flown
in from Saint Louis to audition for the role while caring for her sick
mother). Redd threatened to quit the show; it was his idea to bring Page
in, and he was damned if she was going to get fired—and make him
look foolish in the process.

He spent hours with Page off-camera, in his dressing room, going
over the script and giving her pointers on how to finesse the part of
Aunt Esther. "I hadn't seen Redd in a long time, and now there he was
a big star and I didn't want to let him down," she said. "The harder I
tried the more tense I got. They were going to let me go, but Redd said,
'No, you ain't gonna let her go. That's LaWanda and I *know* she can do
it. Just give me some time with her.' Honey, I went over to Redd's house
that Sunday and we went over that script and got it together. Redd told

me to let myself go and do it *my* way. And when we taped on Tuesday, that's just what I did. And, baby, it went over!"

Howard Platt sensed that Redd was tougher on Page than on his other old friends because he wanted her to succeed, to finally get the recognition he thought she deserved. "She was a sensational gal. I just loved her," Platt said. "Redd was so hard on her. One time, he got so pissed at her—and this was during a performance, between takes—that she passed out and fell on the sofa on the set. They brought down the curtain and revived her. He just wanted people that he brought on the show to be good. And she always was good, anyway."

Page was naturally funny, and she and Redd had obvious chemistry after their years of friendship and shared show-business background. She just had to learn to pace herself, to measure the give-and-take of a television script without stepping on Redd's lines. "I remember when she came onto the show," said Lynn Hamilton, who played Fred's love interest, Donna. "I had seen her as a comedienne in my neighborhood in Los Angeles, in a place called The Parisian Room, and she was a really funny lady. Redd felt she would be an asset to the show. And of course she had no [television] experience at all. And he went to bat for her. He felt that she could handle it if they would just give her a chance."

"They had a ball together on stage," Stan Lathan said of Redd and Page. "When we were in rehearsals, they would constantly be digging at each other. I had a great respect for the tradition they represented. I was no stranger to the fact that LaWanda and Don Bexley and [*Sanford and Son* guest star] Iron Jaw Wilson, what they represented for me, I felt really privileged to be hanging out with these people. I knew this was a moment in history that was not going to be here for long. I felt that."

On December 9, 1972, Redd turned fifty years old. He celebrated the half-century mark by joining Bob Hope on his latest USO Tour. It was a momentous tour for Hope, who'd been entertaining troops around the world since 1942. This would be his twenty-second and final Christmas tour, the last time he would be traveling to military bases in Southeast Asia, the Orient, and the South Pacific. In addition to Redd, the USO tour featured Miss World (Belinda Green), Los Angeles Rams quarterback Roman Gabriel, Fran Jeffries, Lola Falana, and juggler Rudy Cardenas. NBC cameras tagged along to record the best bits for Hope's annual prime-time special, set to air in January.

Even halfway around the world, Redd got a taste of just how popular *Sanford and Son* was less than a year since its premiere. "I ran into a *Sanford and Son* Seabees battalion in 'Nam," he said. "They even had the slogan stitched on their sleeves; 'We Deal in Fine Junk.' Their Jeeps were painted up and decorated to look like the *Sanford* truck. Fantastic," he said, shaking his head in disbelief.

But even a USO Tour with the venerable Bob Hope didn't stop Redd from doing his act his way. It was raw and uncensored, despite Hope pleading for Redd to tone it down for the soldiers. "Hope told me to take it easy on the tour. Soft pedal sex," he said. "When I soft-pedal sex, I eliminate ninety percent of my act. I think he's wrong. That last show on the aircraft carrier, I let go with my stuff and they loved it—they knew the real Redd Foxx was aboard." Redd knew his audience, knew that the soldiers, some of whom had been on the front lines, some of whom were injured, didn't want *anything* to be soft-pedaled. They'd been to hell and back. They wanted it real. "Soldiers are just like prisoners," he said. "What prisoners want to hear is what soldiers want to hear—what's happening on the street. They want to hear about women. They want to hear about home."

Redd left the USO tour a little early to fulfill a New Year's Eve commitment at the Valley Music Theater in Los Angeles; he also returned home a little lighter in the wallet after being robbed of four thousand dollars from his hotel room in Bangkok.

As the calendar year changed to 1973, Redd could look back on the biggest year of his life with a great deal of pride and satisfaction. Just twelve months earlier, he'd been a nightclub comic, "The King of the Party Records" who, through hard work and perseverance, was finally hitting it big in Las Vegas and appearing occasionally on television talk shows. Now, he was an internationally known celebrity and was the second-biggest star on television, earning the same per-episode paycheck as *All in the Family* top banana Carroll O'Connor—$7,500, a princely sum for a sitcom star in 1972.

In April 1973, the NAACP honored Redd with its "Entertainer of the Year" award. Even legendary actor James Cagney got into the act. Now seventy and living quietly in retirement, Cagney gave his first interview in twelve years to the *Los Angeles Times*, telling Charles Champlin that he watched a lot of television. "Now that Redd Foxx on *Sanford and Son*, he's amazing," Cagney said. "I love him."

To capitalize on the show's popularity, RCA put out a record album called, naturally, *Sanford and Son*, which included bits of dialogue from the show's first season (and also Quincy Jones' funky theme song, "The Streetbeater"). The record sold millions.

The money, though, was almost an afterthought. In typical fashion, Redd was spending hand-over-fist without giving it a second thought. He just didn't care. What came in went out just as quickly. He started amassing a collection of classic cars, lavished Betty Jeanne with expensive jewelry, sported custom-made clothes (and several red suits), and snorted cocaine with reckless abandon.

"I remember one day, Redd and Demond Wilson went out to lunch and both came back having bought a Mercedes for each of them," recalled Stan Lathan. "You knew if Redd was in the room, he was carrying probably a medicine bottle-full of cocaine, a switchblade, a pistol, and five thousand dollars in cash—or what looked like five thousand dollars in cash. He was known to have a fat roll at all times. That was Redd; he was a real kind of throwback to a time when, on the Chitlin' Circuit, you had to protect yourself, and I think there was some kind of thug left in him—certainly not a punk or a bully, but you knew that he was prepared to defend himself at any moment, even if he had to [do that] in a dressing room in Burbank."

One day, Redd dropped in to visit Tony Orlando, who was taping *The Tony Orlando and Dawn Show* at CBS. Redd told Orlando, who was dressed in a chicken outfit for a comedy sketch, that he looked "like hell," and pulled a packet of coke from his pocket. Orlando prided himself on being a straight arrow in a business riddled with drugs and drug abusers, but he was physically exhausted and at his wit's end. Redd told him that snorting a line or two would be "like drinking about fifteen cups of coffee." Orlando gave in, took a few snorts and felt great. That moment marked Orlando's downward spiral into a drug addiction that lasted for about a year.

Drugs weren't the only vice on which Redd spent his money. His love of Keno, a lottery-type game of chance he'd discovered in Vegas in the mid-'60s, was a full-blown obsession by now, fed by Redd's weekend jaunts to Vegas—trips he made even while taping *Sanford and Son*. "He was addicted to Keno," said Tony Orlando. "I would go to Vegas and I'd say, 'What are you doing tonight?' and he says, 'I've been playing Keno. I'll be in the Keno parlor.' He was loving that game, would be sitting there with pages and pages of Keno numbers. He would be in his dressing room, and the Keno girl would come to the dressing room. Walk in with the papers, you know? He'd write his numbers and give them to her and then look at the screen to see if his Keno numbers came up."

And now that he was a big television star, money was coming in from other, unexpected sources. In the 1960s, based on his popularity in the African American community, Redd appeared in several print advertisements for local beer companies, such as Ballantine's, in local black publications (including Baltimore). Now that he was a household name, Madison Avenue came calling. In 1973, Redd became a commercial spokesman for Teacher's Scotch Whiskey, appearing in a print advertisement with the tagline: "I told the scotch people I don't drink anymore. Then again, I don't drink any less, either." The full-page ad featured a photo montage of Redd's face on top, a picture of a Teacher's Scotch bottle on the bottom of the page and, in between, lots of Redd's jokes written in the form of a testimonial ("But seriously, there's a Redd Foxx nobody knows. And I wish they'd find him because he's been signing my name to a lot of checks").

The following year, Redd appeared in a national print advertisement for Colt 45 Malt Liquor ("If unique is what you seek"), smiling impishly into the camera and holding up a can of Colt 45. He followed that up with a television commercial for Colt 45 in which he drove a souped-up Dodge (with the words "Redd Sledd" stenciled on its side) over snowy, treacherous mountain terrain so he could deliver a case of Colt 45 to the cool-as-ice Colt 45 spokesman, seated at a table at the bottom of a cliff. Upon reaching his destination, Redd gets out, stumbles around a bit and clutches at his chest à la Fred Sanford, wipes his brow and utters his lines: "Sorry I'm late. I took the shortcut."

There were appearances on *Hollywood Squares*, daytime talk shows—Mike Douglas, Dinah Shore—a guest spot on *The Jacksons*, a CBS variety series headlined by the famous singing family, and even a visit to ABC's *The American Sportsman*, in which Redd and his pal from the Apollo Theater, Bobby Schiffman, went pheasant hunting in Pullman, Washington with series host Grits Gresham. "They needed somebody to work alongside Redd, so I contracted to get Flip Wilson," Schiffman said. "Flip agreed to do it, and then his mother passed away at the last minute, so he couldn't go. When Flip couldn't go, they put me in along with Redd to do the show. We had five days out there in the wild and had more goddamned fun because Redd couldn't hit a bullet in the ass with a paddle."

Schiffman also wanted Redd to host a syndicated television show that would showcase talent from the Apollo Theater, but Tandem Productions had exclusive rights to their *Sanford and Son* star and wouldn't allow him to work on another network. Several months later, Westinghouse approached Schiffman with a similar idea—a show to originate from The Apollo—and once again he went to Redd, who loved the idea but was prohibited from tackling the project because of his Tandem contract. The job went to comedian George Kirby, who hosted a television pilot that was never picked up for a series.

Redd's television work, bookended by his traveling back and forth to Las Vegas on the weekends, left him precious little time to write new material for his standup act. Redd Foxx comedy albums were still being released, with varying frequency, but they paled in comparison to his earlier work. Most of the albums released in the first flush of Redd's *Sanford and Son* fame were collections of older material, slapped together to capitalize on his emergence into the national spotlight. Even Doo-to Records, still being run by Redd's old nemesis, Dootsie Williams, continued to churn out cheap, sloppy releases like *Sanford and Foxx* and *Dirty Redd* featuring stale material, some of which dated back to the late 1950s. But Redd was just as guilty; his own company, MF Records, was spitting out albums (*Spice Can Be Nice*, *Elizabeth I'm Coming*) devoid of any new material.

But no one seemed to care. The Redd Foxx gravy train was rolling along—and there seemed to be no end in sight.

chapter ten

"The Way It Is, I'm Still in Slavery"

Sanford and Son ended its second season on March 16, 1973, as the second-most-popular show on television. NBC's juggernaut sitcom averaged nearly eighteen million viewers a week for the season, four million viewers behind first-place *All in the Family* but a comfortable two million viewers more than third-place *Hawaii Five-O*. Programming executives at the competing networks, including then-CBS programming chief Fred Silverman, tried everything they could think of to make a dent in *Sanford and Son's* viewing audience. Nothing worked. America, it seemed, just loved Fred Sanford too much.

"That show was monstrous," Silverman said. "The combination of *Sanford and Son* and *Chico and the Man* [at NBC] . . . it was probably the most successful period in the history of network television, and that one hour from eight to nine o'clock was the bane of my existence. It was like a brick wall. There was nothing we could put against it. We tried everything." Over the course of *Sanford and Son's* run, Silverman tried counter-programming several sitcoms to steal some of its thunder, including *Dirty Sally*, starring Jeannette Nolan, and *Colucci's Department*, starring James Coco. Both shows failed. Dramas didn't work either; a *Planet of the Apes* series, spun off from the popular big-screen movie series, bombed, as did *Khan!*, a private-eye series starring Khigh Dhiegh, who played Wo Fat on *Hawaii Five-O*. "There was a show Larry Gelbart wrote called *Roll Out* which was kind of a half-assed spin-off of *M*A*S*H* . . . so I'm not exaggerating when I say we must have put a dozen shows in that time period at CBS," Silverman said. "Nothing worked against *Sanford and Son*. It was just incredible."

In only two years on the air, Fred Sanford had morphed into a cultural institution. His chest-clutching antics ("Ya hear that Elizabeth? It's the Big One! I'm comin' to join ya, honey!") and his verbal battles with Aunt Esther ("I could stick your face in some dough and make some gorilla cookies!) were parts of the pop-culture landscape. And now Redd was reaping the rewards of his "overnight" ascent into the limelight. He was the focus of many magazine and newspaper features, which usually recounted his by-now-familiar story (struggling street performer works the Chitlin' Circuit, becomes "King of the Party Records" then hits it big on television) and he was generally credited with being the main reason for *Sanford and Son's* success.

"We probably don't have more than a couple of clowns in a century, and Redd Foxx was a clown," said Norman Lear, the show's co-creator. "I know he was considered a comedian. But the difference between a comedian and a clown, in my estimation, is that every square inch of a clown is funny. His knuckles are funny, his earlobes are funny; Redd could walk into a room and announce that your mother had died and get a laugh from you. He was inherently, innately funny in every part of his being. So we fell in love with that."

But, off-camera, Redd's life wasn't all laughs. Two years earlier, he'd been desperate to get on television; he would do anything to get that chance. And now that he had the success, and the fame that went along with it, he was paying a steep price. The *Sanford and Son* shooting schedule was a brutal, intense, five-days-a-week pressure-cooker; as the show's star, Redd carried a heavy load in each episode, and had to memorize many pages of script. His weekend forays to Las Vegas made his return to the studio on Monday morning all the more miserable— both for himself and for everyone else who had to deal with his cranky moods and unpredictability.

He was a night bird by nature, used to working smoky clubs and Las Vegas lounge shows into the late-night hours, and then partying until dawn, sleeping late, and repeating the cycle. *Sanford and Son* changed all that. And the cracks were beginning to show. "I come from a job where I had freedom. I worked ninety minutes a night, and I was through until the next night," he said, sounding the first notes of a growing bitterness. "Now, I have to convert and try to learn to sleep at night when I've been up at night all my life. I'll be sitting at home in the evening, and eleven o'clock comes, I get nervous. I want me a drink of Scotch, because all my life, around eleven, I already had a couple. After that kind of freedom for thirty-six years, I can't adjust to working seven days a week and being holed up in a rehearsal room with no windows. I haven't seen the birds in three years. When I get off, they've all gone to bed."

And with his success came the creeping feeling that he was being taken advantage of—that, as one of the biggest stars on television, he wasn't being respected or given his due. Redd not only felt that way toward NBC, for whom he was making millions, but also toward his bosses at Tandem Productions. Norman Lear and Bud Yorkin already had been through several contract squabbles with their biggest star, Carroll O'Connor, and the *All in the Family* patriarch was now the highest-paid star on television, reportedly earning upwards of $30,000 per-episode—on a show whose budget, according to Yorkin, was only $50,000 per-episode. But *Sanford and Son* was second only to *All in the Family* in popularity; now, its star, too, wanted *his* piece of the pie. Redd was earning $7,500 per episode, a pittance compared to what O'Connor was bringing home. Publicly, he inflated his salary, if only to save face. He also owned a seven percent stake in *Sanford and Son*. He thought he deserved more.

"I think part of the problem with Redd was that NBC didn't quite know what to do with him," recalled *Sanford and Son* director Alan Rafkin. "He was enormously talented and made a lot of money for the network. At one time he was the star of the highest-rated NBC sitcom on the air, yet he was also the only comedy star in the NBC stable who didn't have his own TV variety special. I always felt that he deserved a lot more credit than he got. . . . The respect just wasn't there."

In the spring of 1973, after *Sanford and Son* wrapped its second season, Redd started making noise in the press that he wouldn't return for the show's third season unless he got a big pay raise. He was, he said, getting paid "a pittance" by Tandem Productions, especially compared to O'Connor's salary. "I can make over $35,000 a week in Las Vegas," he said. "When they came after me to star in the television series, I had a contract at the time with the International Hotel in Las Vegas and that was torn up." The threat turned out to be short-lived; shortly thereafter, news broke that Redd had signed a new deal. "I wasn't worried about this contract," he said. "But that's all I can say about the deal. I take the fifth from here on out." His new *Sanford and Son* contract was believed to pay him around $10,000 per episode, a third of what O'Connor was making, and even less than what *The Little People* star

Brian Keith was earning—and Keith's show was ranked twenty-sixth that season. "We couldn't pay him any more than that in those days," Yorkin said of Redd's new salary. "He had the habit and all that stuff."

Redd, though, seemed content—for now. In addition to his raise, his brown-and-gold dressing room at NBC was refurbished with a complete bathroom, including a shower, and a new refrigerator. "My arguments were simple," Redd said. "I worked a long time to get out of those little places. It gives me a good feeling to walk in here, stretch out on the sofa or be able to get a cold drink out of my refrigerator." He also cited his precarious situation as the star of a prime-time show, and the notoriously fickle viewing public. "Hits aren't sure year after year," he said. "I could be off television in another couple of years. Besides, when you're in a hit your expenses go up. I have a secretary that does nothing but answer letters and send pictures to my fans. Some are even asking when I'm going to do a special."

Sanford and Son kicked off its third season in September 1973 without missing a beat, settling into its customary second-place position in the ratings behind *All in the Family*. But the good feelings didn't last long. In November, Redd and Slappy White were hit with a $300,000 lawsuit in Los Angeles Superior Court for allegedly beating and even threatening to shoot Joyce Witherspoon, the common-law wife of blues singer Jimmy Witherspoon. She claimed the incident occurred the previous May at Memory Lane, a nightclub in Central Los Angeles; Slappy, she said, made a degrading remark to her while she was chatting with Redd, and hit her when she didn't acknowledge him. Some others who were in the club at the time said that it was Redd who made the insulting remark to Joyce Witherspoon, who was there with her aunt. The official police report noted that she was "hit in the mouth with a clenched fist" by Slappy White. Her lawyer, Earl C. Broady Jr., claimed that Redd and Slappy were drunk at the time. Jimmy Witherspoon claimed it was Joyce who was "juiced" and who was trying to impress her aunt by "playing around" with Redd. He also accused Broady of being a "publicity hound."

Redd disappeared for a few days when the lawsuit hit the papers in mid-November, just after *Sanford and Son* knocked *All in the Family* off its perch to claim the top spot in the ratings for the week. Even Bud Yorkin claimed he didn't know his star's whereabouts. Redd resurfaced four days later, calling the office of *Los Angeles Times* columnist Joyce Haber to report he could be found at Shelley's Manne-Hole, a Los Angeles jazz club where he'd gone with Demond Wilson to see saxophonist Gerry Mulligan (at that time in a long-term relationship with actress Sandy Dennis). Redd enjoyed himself so much that he was booked at the Manne-Hole for a four-night engagement a few weeks later, opening for jazz great Charlie Mingus.

But even though the Joyce Witherspoon lawsuit quickly disappeared—it was probably settled out of court—Redd's very public aggressive behavior continued to raise eyebrows in Hollywood. Even though his mini contract dispute the previous spring was short-lived, Redd still thought he was being underpaid, and his resentment toward Bud Yorkin and Norman Lear simmered just beneath the surface. He also directed his anger toward NBC. Why, he wondered, did all of the network's big comedy stars get to host their own prime-time variety specials, while he was being ignored?

In December, Yorkin and Lear were honored in Hollywood by the National Television Academy with its "Man of the Year" award. It was a gala event, with many of the television industry's movers-and-shakers, including Redd Foxx, in attendance. But there were some noticeable absences, including *All in the Family* stars Carroll O'Connor and Rob Reiner. O'Connor claimed he was ill; Reiner said he had another commitment. Both actors were bickering with Yorkin and Lear over contractual issues. Trouble was in the air.

Earlier that night, in the festivities leading up to the event, Redd made an off-color remark to brassy *Maude* star Bea Arthur, who fired back with an insult of her own. Then, a little later in the evening, at the very moment that *Sanford and Son* producer Aaron Ruben was introducing Bud Yorkin, Redd made a show of noisily getting up from his seat to use the men's room—a none-too-subtle jab that drew a verbal reprimand from Henry Mancini. The famous composer grabbed Redd by his lapels and shook him, which pissed Redd off even more. The two men began shouting at each other and had to be physically separated before a fistfight broke out. The next day, when Yorkin approached Redd on the *Sanford and Son* set to calmly discuss the incident, Redd stalked off angrily, saying that he was entitled to some respect. His lawyer, James Tolbert, persuaded Redd to return to the set later that day. Things were getting dicey.

As the calendar turned to 1974, Redd's bickering with Yorkin was becoming more routine—and more personal. Redd began telling any-one and everyone on the *Sanford and Son* set that Yorkin's mere presence made him physically ill; he followed that up by plotting to have Yorkin, the show's executive producer, the man who was paying his salary, barred from the NBC lot in Burbank. Redd won this round; Yorkin arrived one Friday afternoon to attend the show's taping and was in-formed by the guard at the gate that he wasn't allowed inside. Fuming, he turned his car around and drove off. "Bud had such an annoying way of speaking, and Redd would break out in hives when [Yorkin] spoke," recalled *Sanford and Son* co-star Howard Platt. "One time, Redd pulled his shirt off and he was all red hives and he wouldn't listen to Bud anymore. He just couldn't stand what he was hearing coming out of his mouth. So Aaron Ruben suggested that maybe Bud shouldn't come to the set anymore—and he never did."

The cracks were also beginning to show in Redd's marriage. He and Betty Jeanne had been together for seventeen years now, longer than both of their first marriages combined. They'd been through thick and thin, through good times and bad. They had financial security after years of struggling, but that was overshadowed by a growing emo-tional gulf between them. Part of the problem was *Sanford and Son* itself. Redd complained about being exhausted from the rigors of shooting the show and having to memorize the script each week. It was a vicious cycle with no end in sight. "We never argued until I got this show," he said. "I come home sometimes and just raise hell to anybody, because I'll be so strained mentally." Once Friday rolled around, he usually took an NBC helicopter to Las Vegas, where he was on his own, away from Betty Jeanne, playing Keno, snorting cocaine, smoking dope, and chasing women.

Redd Foxx was never monogamous, even in the best of times with Betty Jeanne. The women were always ready, willing, and available, even more so once he became a household name. Redd partook with relish. One time, while on a *Sanford and Son* promotional tour, Demond Wilson was awakened by the hotel manager knocking on his door at 3:00 a.m. and asking him to come to the third floor, where Redd was staying. "I think you need to see this for yourself," the manager told Wilson. When they arrived on the scene, there was Redd—stark naked and banging on the door of one of the female singers on the tour. Wilson asked the hotel manager to fetch a bottle of Chivas Regal—Redd's favorite Scotch—then calmed his co-star down as they sat on the floor, drinking. Wilson took Redd back to his suite; the next morning he didn't remember a thing.

On another *Sanford and Son* tour, Redd and Wilson found themselves in Seattle for a one-night-only appearance. At around 6:00 in the evening, Redd's manager, Bardu Ali, called Wilson and told him that Redd wanted to see him in his suite, where there were "at least ten young women" sitting in the living room. One of the young women asked Wilson if she could go back to his room; it turned out she only wanted to talk about the television business, but when Redd found out, he was upset. "You took my woman!" he yelled at Wilson. "The girl you left with was my woman. I bought her a gold and diamond watch earlier today." Once they were back on the *Sanford and Son* set in Burbank, Redd never mentioned the incident again.

In public, Redd and Betty Jeanne said all the right things, but once in a while the façade would slip just a little. "For years while I did nothing but work the clubs I'd work late hours and be home all day long. We spent a lot of time together. Now I get home dog-tired, have to study my script for the next day and before I know it I'm falling asleep," Redd told the *New York Daily News* in July 1973. "It's still a good marriage but we've both been hurt by it. We always had such a good thing going for us." Betty Jeanne sounded a more optimistic tone, but alluded to problems in the marriage. "One must remember that when two people marry, it doesn't make them instant angels," she said in a magazine feature story on the couple. "Taking one another for granted is one of the most serious offenses."

Redd's crumbling marriage further exacerbated his problems with Bud Yorkin. (Redd's interactions with Norman Lear weren't as frequent, since Lear spent much of his time working on *All in the Family* and *Maude*, which was now another hit for the Tandem Productions empire). In mid-January 1974, Redd called to say that he couldn't come to work, blaming his absence on a variety of physical ailments including a skin rash—which, he claimed, was diagnosed as a nervous condition brought on by overwork. He also claimed to be suffering severe knee pain because of the bow-legged walk he adopted as Fred Sanford. "He came to me and said, 'I think I'm getting an ulcer and my doctor says my stomach. . . . I'm not getting enough sleep and I'm working too hard' and all that," Yorkin recalled. "I said, 'Well, go home, I'll cancel the show' and that's how it all started."

Sanford and Son still had six episodes left in its season, and couldn't afford to have its star miss any substantial shooting time. NBC managed to keep a lid on Redd's absence from the set, but as the days turned into weeks, word leaked out that there was trouble in River City between Redd Foxx, Bud Yorkin, and NBC.

By mid-February, rumors circulated that NBC was refusing to allow Redd to participate in a special about the Apollo Theater, and was also trying to put the kibosh on his being "roasted" at a fundraiser for the United Negro College Fund, which was scheduled for mid-March at the Beverly Hilton Hotel and would air on rival network ABC, with many of Redd's peers participating. There were reports that Redd had checked himself into a North Hollywood hospital to be treated for a mysterious ailment, possibly exhaustion. "Redd Foxx ailing?" blared a headline in the *Chicago Defender*. He wasn't.

What everyone in the industry knew, and what soon leaked out, was the truth: Redd was refusing to show up for work unless his newest contract demands were met. It was the classic Hollywood "sick-out," Redd Foxx-style. "He's much better but he's a long way from well," Redd's attorney, James Tolbert, told the press. "It's his nerves, as much as any physical problems. Redd's had a series of physical disabilities lately, but he's continued working through it all. It was just too much." Tolbert said that Redd even broke out in a rash while talking to the NBC doctors about *Sanford and Son*. "I've even been on the set when doctors had to come and extract pints of liquid from his knees," he said. "It's just been too much for him."

Redd even bailed on the United Negro College Fund "roast," claiming his illness made it impossible for him to attend. The show's organizers were forced to scramble to find a last-minute replacement. Billy Eckstine accepted the invitation and was duly honored.

Behind the scenes *at Sanford and Son*, Redd's absence threw the show into disarray. With six episodes still left to shoot for the third season, and his star nowhere to be found, Bud Yorkin sprang into action. He decided that Whitman Mayo, who had a recurring role as Fred's pal, Grady Wilson (Demond Wilson's birth name), would step in to act as the show's ostensible star until Redd's contract dispute was resolved, one way or another. It was a gamble—would *Sanford and Son* fans accept Mayo?—but was a risk Yorkin had to take. He had no other choice.

Through the first two seasons of *Sanford and Son*, the show's writers and producers tried to find a suitable sidekick for Fred, but weren't sold on either Melvin or Bubba, played respectively by Slappy White and Don Bexley. "For some reason the producers, they just ain't in love with none of these guys," Ilunga Adell said. "I thought Don Bexley, who I came to know on the show, was terrific . . . and I'm wondering, why don't these motherfuckers like him as much as I like him? I had no idea."

On Adell's recommendation, Whitman Mayo was flown out to Los Angeles, auditioned for the part of Grady, and won the role. The bumbling, sweet-natured Grady appeared for the first time in the fifth episode of season three, "This Little TV Went to Market," in which Fred buys a "hot" television set—which turns out to have been stolen from Grady.

Mayo, a New York City native, was only forty-three years old, but looked much older with his prematurely grey hair and matching grey beard. In the 1960s, the veteran actor, who'd also worked as a probation officer and a counselor for delinquent youths, established himself as part of New York's New Lafayette Theater, a Harlem-based repertory company producing works of African American writers. (It was there that he met Ilunga Adell.) "I was in a theatre troupe called the Black Magicians which was kind of like a workshop for the New Lafayette Theater," Adell recalled. "They had a smaller theater at another location that they let us use, so we worshipped them like gods and they treated us accordingly."

Once it became apparent that Redd wasn't returning to the set anytime soon, Fred's absence from the Watts junkyard had to somehow be explained. The show's writers concocted a storyline in which Fred had to return to his hometown of Saint Louis for a cousin's funeral. While he was away, he asked his best friend, Grady, to move into the house on 9114 South Central to care for Lamont until he returned. "That was a weird time when Redd Foxx wasn't there," Adell recalled. "It was another example of 'The show must go on,' but I also know they wanted Redd Foxx back. The shows [with Whitman Mayo] went well but, to me, there was a little something missing. Redd Foxx was a comedic genius. He really was."

Though Yorkin, Lear, Aaron Ruben, and NBC were anxious about how Redd's absence would affect *Sanford and Son,* their nerves were soothed when it became apparent that the show was still as strong as ever.

The first episode without Redd, "Lamont Goes Karate," aired on February 15, 1974, and was written by Ilunga Adell. In the opening scene, Grady, who's cooking Lamont's breakfast—which Fred did in many *Sanford and Son* episodes—takes a long-distance telephone call from (an unseen) Fred. The following week, Whitman Mayo took center stage for the first time in an episode entitled "Will the Real Fred Sanford Please Do Something?" Written by Aaron Ruben, the episode revolved around a case of mistaken identity, and a woman who thinks she's engaged to Grady. The episode was directed by Stan Lathan, who knew Mayo from their days working together at the New Lafayette Theatre in New York. "It was strange. It was awkward," Lathan said of the atmosphere on the set in Redd's absence. "Redd was a powerful personality and the set, in general, was all-about Redd."

The ratings for both episodes were terrific, and *Sanford and Son* continued to perform surprisingly well in subsequent weeks. Yorkin, Lear, and NBC now had the upper hand in dealing with Redd, and reports began appearing in the press that Tandem Productions wasn't really concerned about whether Redd Foxx ever returned. The show was doing fine without him, and Whitman Mayo would make a perfectly fine replacement. Yorkin and Lear were so pleased with Mayo's work that they guaranteed he would appear in at least ten out of thirteen episodes the following fall, if the show returned. "We got so mad," Yorkin said. "We were ready to replace Redd, between the two of us. I said, 'I'm not going through this shit every week with this guy saying he needs more money. How are we going to get these other shows going if we've got to have an argument every four weeks with this guy coming in and saying, 'I need more money'"?

Mayo, who was a gentle man by nature—and genuinely liked and cared for Redd—was caught in the middle. He took the high road when asked about the Redd Foxx contract dispute. "Most of my enjoyment is working with Redd Foxx. He's a beautiful, warm, sensitive, talented individual with an incredible sense of the stage," he said. "I'd like to see him do serious drama one day. He's used to doing stand-up comedy, which means you learn a routine and use it for years. Suddenly, he's faced with the pace of a TV series, and learning scripts every week, and this isn't easy to do. But Foxx, I'm convinced, can do anything. As for me, I just walk straight and try to hold up my own head."

On February 22, 1974, exactly a month after Redd's walkout, his attorney, James Tolbert, insisted that his client was ready to return to work. Redd, he said, was back in Los Angeles at his home in Toluca Lake after spending some time in Las Vegas, and in Acapulco at the Princess Hotel (where he dashed up on stage and did forty-five minutes of standup for the surprised audience). He'd also shaved off his Fred Sanford beard. "The rash is gone, his skin is smooth, and he looks twenty years younger," Tolbert said. "He wanted to go back to work this week, but was advised not to. The new target [date] is next week."

That never happened. "Next week" came and went and Redd remained AWOL from the NBC studios in Burbank. He and Tolbert leaked a story to the press that another, unnamed network was interested in Redd's services. "They're making a lot of bread off the brother and he's trying to do something about it. I believe another network is offering him more per week for the show than NBC," a "source" told the *Chicago Defender*. But Yorkin, Lear, and NBC weren't taking the bait.

In early March, Aaron Ruben stated publicly that he didn't expect Redd to return for the remainder of the season, and that the remaining episodes of *Sanford and Son* would be completed without its star. Several days later, Redd was invited to appear on *The Mike Douglas Show*, which was shooting a week's worth of shows in Las Vegas. He admitted that the reports about his "illness" forcing him to miss the show was "a lie," and told America what everyone else in Hollywood already knew: it was all about the money. Redd was making $10,000 per episode; he told Douglas he wanted to get what the person who was number one at NBC before him got—plus one dollar.

During the course of the *Mike Douglas Show* interview, Redd said he didn't want to revert to what he labeled "*Amos 'n' Andy*" and said he was treated "like a boy and not a man," adding that the atmosphere on the *Sanford and Son* set was like the Army—"You have to salute, almost," he said. "Nobody misses [the show] like I do," he told Douglas, dragging on a cigarette. "But if it's not right, if you can't do and give your best. . . . I got a good heart and I want it right for me once—and for the guy that follows me so he won't have to kick down too many doors to make it right for him."

Redd's on-air remarks to Douglas infuriated the executives at NBC who, up until that point, had given Redd the benefit of the doubt about his "illness"—even though they knew, deep down, that he wasn't really sick. "Until today, nobody could say Redd was not really sick," said a network spokesman. "All that has now changed. That changes the flavor of everything."

Redd now added another element to his unhappiness over his contract: he didn't like his working conditions on the NBC lot in Burbank—specifically the dressing room he inherited from Sammy Davis Jr. after Davis' 1973 series, *NBC Follies*, was cancelled. Redd complained that the dressing room didn't have a window. Bob Hope's dressing room down the hall had a window. Why couldn't Redd have a window? Yorkin, Lear, and NBC still refused to budge. The dispute reached a stalemate. Redd added further fuel to the fire when he said he'd turned down an offer of $50,000 to return for the season's final five shows. "If I have to work under those conditions, the money ain't worth being dead for," he said. "When people make a comment about my [dressing room] window . . . I have claustrophobia. I can only stay in an elevator three or four flights, have me a cigarette then keep going, so when I work in a place and there's no window, I go berserk. [But] I'm a rebel now, as far as people are concerned, but I'm not that way. I'm a nice guy until someone touches me."

In mid-March, with no resolution in sight, Redd held a press conference at his spacious home in Toluca Lake. Flanked by his attorney, James Tolbert, he now backtracked on the money issue, telling reporters that "twenty-five grand a week ain't bad. It's just that I don't even want it under these conditions, because I'll be rich and dead." He complained not only about the long hours on the set, but about how, after thirty-six years as a nightclub comedian, he was having enough trouble adjusting to his work schedule without "being holed up in a rehearsal hall with no windows and no skylight."

"It took me two years to get a dressing room and when they finally gave me one it was so small I could hardly get in there," he said. "Maybe those conditions are all right for an actor, but they're no good for me. When you're making as much money as I am, and you wake up in the morning and don't feel like going to work, you've got to be a damned fool or else conditions must be terrible."

He talked about having a "nervous condition" that caused him to break out in hives, resulting in four or five trips to the hospital; then he said he had undergone a physical, which showed that he had a bone spur on the "fifth cervical" on his spine, causing him terrible pain and deadening the feeling in his arm. For good measure, he threw in two torn cartilages in his knee—the result of Fred Sanford's bow-legged walk—and then attacked the show's writers for their racial insensitivity. "They had one show with a doctor who looked all disheveled, with ashes dropping down his clothes," he said. "Their whole conception of black people is absolutely ridiculous." He talked about the black actresses on the show being asked to sound like "Pearl Bailey or Ernestine Wade," said he was insulted that the show's casting directors hadn't even heard of Oscar nominee Juanita Moore, and was livid at the show's policy of pre-determined, five-minute bathroom breaks: "You just can't judge, 'Well, in forty-five minutes I'm going to the toilet for five minutes.' You go to the toilet when you have to go to the toilet."

Aaron Ruben, speaking on behalf of the show, fired back. "As for the working conditions, this is the same windowless hall everybody rehearses in at NBC, whether it's Bob Hope or whoever," he said. "The reason is to cut down on distractions. I don't know where he suddenly got the idea about the racial situation, because I made it clear from the start, three years ago, when we sat at the table and read scripts, that if there was anything that he or Demond Wilson thought might be offensive to the black community, all they had to do was speak up, without even giving their reasons, and we'd take it out."

Ruben noted that the *Sanford and Son* producers had even agreed to Redd's request to shoot three shows, then take a week off, giving Redd some room to breathe (most shows shot five or six shows before taking a week off). "This prolonged the season and made it more costly, but we did it for Redd," he said. "Everything was done to make him as comfortable as possible. His statement about the dressing room is inaccurate; NBC built one specially for him with a shower and plenty of office space."

NBC, meanwhile, made sure to let everyone know that *Sanford and Son*, which had been lagging behind *The Waltons* on CBS, was now back in second place (behind *All in the Family*) with Whitman Mayo at the helm. "The series seems to be alive and doing very well despite his absence," noted the *Los Angeles Times* in a story about Redd's walkout. That same story pointed out that NBC had received "an extra-large volume of telephone calls," most of them favorable, regarding Mayo's work in Redd's absence. Aaron Ruben was asked about the next season of *Sanford and Son* sans Redd Foxx. "It certainly must open up a lot of possibilities in our minds," he said.

Redd's Toluca Lake press conference failed to have its desired effect. Yorkin, Lear, and NBC still refused to budge on his contract demands. In mid-March, Redd was slated to open a weeklong engagement at The Apollo Theater, marking his first trip back to Harlem in quite some time. Accompanied by his attorney James Tolbert, his doctor and two bodyguards, he flew to New York to meet with NBC president Herb Schlosser (who'd been promoted from the network's West Coast office) just prior to the Apollo Theater gig.

After meeting with Schlosser, Redd held a press conference the day before his Apollo Theater opening (the bill also included Slappy White, singer Gloria Lynne, and the Little Steps dancers). He indicated that NBC had agreed to provide better working conditions and "better editing" of the *Sanford and Son* scripts. An NBC spokesman, when asked for a reaction, said Redd had a "very amicable" meeting with Schlosser, adding that the network "hoped" Redd would return—but said any final deal would have to be agreed to by Tandem Productions. Norman Lear told the *New York Post* that he and Bud Yorkin had no doubt Redd would return—that *Redd* had no doubt he would return—and that the entire salary dispute had "received more attention than it deserves." He attributed Redd's walkout to tensions stemming from the show's grueling production schedule.

Redd, though, was still sounding a combative tone. "All I want to do is have a piece of [*Sanford and Son*] for Redd, so old Redd has something for his family," he told the *New York Post*. "I been out there three years, I wrote eighty percent of the show, I had friends of mine that I put in the show, I think they should give me a piece . . . a quarter of the show is all I want. I think they got to agree that having seventy five percent of something is better than one hundred percent of nothin'. The way it is, I'm still in slavery."

He reasoned that he was bringing home only $7,000 of what he said was his $25,000 weekly paycheck, since he was in a ninety percent tax bracket and couldn't dump his money into a tax shelter. "But if I owned one-fourth of myself and had some capital gains, that would make a difference," he said. "My biggest concern right now is the fate of the fifteen people on my payroll. I've been criticized for making jobs for my people and some folks close to me call my employees hangers-on, hustlers, and pimps, but I call them friends. All of them needed work and I could afford it."

In another interview, he took a shot at the *Sanford and Son* writers among his many barbs aimed at the show and his bosses at NBC. "I've had to change the script many times to make black folks talk like black folks and not like niggers in slavery," he said. "I want the screen credits to give credit to the producer but add 'in association with Redd Foxx Inc.' I want some wardrobe changes, too. I don't want [guest star] Judy Pace on the show talking like a southern belle and dressed up like a prostitute."

After completing his run at the Apollo Theater, Redd flew down to Miami Beach for a show at the Fontainebleau Hotel—where, at one point, he shocked the audience by appearing to streak, buck-naked, across the stage (he was actually wearing body-hugging panty hose; a strobe light made it appear that he was nude).

Sanford and Son, meanwhile, wrapped its third season on March 29, 1974, with Whitman Mayo front-and-center in an episode titled "Hello Cousin Emma . . . . Goodbye Cousin Emma," (which revolved around an unwanted visit to the junkyard from Grady's cousin). Shooting on the fourth season of *Sanford and Son* was scheduled to begin at the end of April, with or without Redd Foxx—who was now joined in solidarity in his contract dispute by his co-star, Demond Wilson. When both men failed to show up for the first day of shooting, Yorkin and Lear finally had enough. Tandem Productions slapped Redd and Wilson each with a $10 million lawsuit in Los Angeles Superior Court for not showing up for rehearsals. They were also barred from making any public appearances until May 6. In its legal papers, Tandem claimed it had an agreement with Redd for the new season that would give him a "substantial" raise; Redd's lawyers countered that their client refused to accept Tandem's offer, and was asking for more money. Tandem did not offer Wilson a pay raise.

Redd said he planned to return to the show for its fourth season, but that, because of his bad back, he had to be in traction for a half-hour each day—meaning that changes would have to be made to his *Sanford and Son* shooting schedule. "But I hope to honor my other commitments, since they don't put such a strain on me," he said. And, he added, his personal physician, Dr. Lindberg Gallimore, would accompany him on all of his personal appearances.

Gallimore insisted that Redd was suffering from "nervous exhaustion," claustrophobia, and calcification between the fifth and sixth vertebra in his back, irritating the nerve. "This is why he has a problem turning to the left because of the pressure," Gallimore said. "Mild sedation and rest is what he needs, plus decrease of the stress situation under which he works. The amazing thing is that this man has tolerated this kind of stress as long as he has." For good measure, Gallimore added "tenderness of the skull" to Redd's physical ailments, "one of the first signs of reaction to stress," he added emphatically.

In the meantime, Redd's attorney, James Tolbert, was talking tough in the wake of Tandem's lawsuit. "Not only can Redd tough it out for the twenty weeks remaining on his contract, but he will launch an effective counter-attack when the $10 million suit Tandem has filed against him goes to trial, perhaps within ten months," he said. "Redd has been made out to be the villain, when all along he has just been asking for things he was promised when he started." Redd called the ruling "unconstitutional" and talked about taking the case to the U.S. Supreme Court. With a straight face, he said he just might even become a maitre d' at a Las Vegas nightclub, or move back to Chicago and work in a clothing store.

The first few weeks of May 1974 proved to be quite an eventful time in the life of Redd Foxx. In the midst of all his contract chaos and the Tandem Productions lawsuit, Redd—already dodging rumors that he was seen in London with a blond mystery woman—found the time to call *New York Post* columnist Earl Wilson to complain about Betty Jeanne. His wife, he said, went out and bought a $10,000 Mercedes Benz while he was out of town. "She has a Mercedes that isn't a year old yet and she buys a new one," he griped. "I don't think she should do that when her husband's away."

Less than a week later, under his birth name Jon Elroy Sanford, Redd filed for divorce from Betty Jeanne in Las Vegas after nearly eighteen years of marriage on grounds of incompatibility. Redd's attorney, Robert Reid, obtained a restraining order from a district judge blocking Betty Jeanne from "removing, hiding, or secreting" any property from their $150,000 house on Eastern Avenue in Las Vegas. The order also ordered Betty Jeanne to return "all monies, checks, specifically, $110,000 removed from bank accounts," or anything else earned by Redd.

Betty Jeanne responded a week later, suing for divorce in Los Angeles Superior Court and citing irreconcilable differences. She asked for alimony and a "division of community property," and told a reporter from *Jet* magazine that Redd had moved out of their Toluca Lake house the previous week. "There seems to be another woman involved," she said, but declined to elaborate because she and Redd were trying to "get back together." When that failed, she blamed Redd's fast lifestyle for leading to the breakup of their marriage. "A lot of it was the friends taking him to different places, keeping him out all night—from that, things would come up and it just got to be too much," she said. "So I decided it's best if we part. Redd said if I couldn't keep up with him to get an attorney—so I went and got an attorney."

The hits just kept on coming. On May 14, Tandem won an injunction against Redd in Los Angeles Superior Court. The ruling forbade him from working without the company's permission—part-and-parcel of its bigger lawsuit against Redd for not showing up to work. "I'm going home to Las Vegas and I may just retire," Redd said after learning about the injunction. "They have got me up against the wall, motherfuckers. I've had to cancel $300,000 in nightclubs and theater engagements because of the court order. They have put the squeeze on me." Redd claimed to have already spent $200,000 in attorney's fees in his fight against Yorkin and Lear. "I'm no nigger slave," he said, angrily. "I can't understand being sued for $10 million by someone who is trying to keep me from making $1 million." A day later, Tandem Productions agreed to let Redd fulfill his summer engagements, including a weeklong appearance at the Westbury Music fair in Long Island and a gig at Buddy's Place in Manhattan. The clouds appeared to be lifting. "I won't say it's settled yet, but we're talking, and that's a lot better than it used to be," said Redd's attorney, James Tolbert. "The suspension is good until July 3."

Demond Wilson, meanwhile, had buckled in his short-lived contract dispute. He was back on the *Sanford and Son* set, rehearsing for the show's fourth season. So much for solidarity.

And then, just like that, it was over. In late June, word broke that Redd had settled his contract differences with Tandem Productions—just as his NBC colleague, *Columbo* star Peter Falk, was suing *his* producer, Universal Studios, to break his contract and leave the show (claiming that Universal was behind in payment of his salary). Redd was scheduled to return to work on July 8 to begin shooting the fourth season of *Sanford and Son*. He'd missed five months and six shows of the third season, plus the first three shows of the fourth season. He was given a generous raise to $25,000 per episode for a twenty-four-episode season, which came out to $600,000 for the season. He was also given up to $5,000 for every *Sanford and Son* rerun and 25 percent of the producers' net profits. And he finally got that window in his new, super-sized dressing room, which featured all the amenities.

NBC, thrilled to have its star back, even threw in a personalized golf cart, which Redd used to tool around the studio lot in Burbank.

Behind the scenes, though, the IRS was nipping at Redd's heels, clamoring for back taxes he was accused of not paying. The pressure from the IRS forced Redd, and his accountants, to make a decision that would end up haunting the comedian years later.

"When he was on *Sanford and Son*, he would get a check and it would go to the bank and be cashed. He liked having cash," said one of Redd's friends. "He was a heavy gambler, of course, and the IRS was threatening to take his building. They were going to do all sorts of things. A deal was worked out between Tandem Productions and the taxing authorities and Redd, whereby Redd's rerun rights [to *Sanford and Son*] were purchased for $3 million. "But after all the taxes were paid Redd got just $300,000. So, from that time forward, part of his shtick was that they made him sell out for $300,000, that they were a bunch of crooks, but that wasn't the case. So he had a sort of resentfulness of authority."

The fourth season of *Sanford and Son* premiered on September 13, 1974. Redd's walkout had forced the show's producers to shoot three additional episodes around his absence and, once again, Whitman Mayo filled in as the show's star. But once Redd returned to the *Sanford and Son* set, it was decided to start the season with his first episode back, "The Surprise Party," in which Fred finally returned from his sojourn to Saint Louis—only to ruin the surprise party Lamont and Grady planned for him.

The new season brought other changes as well. Bud Yorkin, Redd's chief punching bag—both verbally and metaphorically—left the show after hammering out Redd's new deal with Tandem Productions. Yorkin's departure was bittersweet for Redd; it was Yorkin and Norman Lear, after all, who'd plucked a largely unknown nightclub comic from obscurity and turned Redd Foxx into a household name—and an extremely rich television star. But it was also Yorkin's day-to-day work on *Sanford and Son*, and his interactions with the show's increasingly unhappy star, that struck an adversarial tone into their relationship that, in the end, neither man could surmount.

The burden of producing *Sanford and Son* now fell to television veterans Saul Turteltaub and Bernie Orenstein, who were fresh off a run on ABC's *Love, American Style* when Norman Lear called, offering them the job of replacing Yorkin. "They knew that we got along with everybody because we had done shows with other actors who they said were 'difficult,'" said Orenstein. "But we went to the show and we got along with Redd perfectly."

The new producers jumped right into the fray, writing the script for Redd's return episode, "The Surprise Party," and girding themselves for trouble from their star. They were pleasantly surprised by a Redd Foxx who now seemed, for all intents and purposes, content. Or at least as content as Redd Foxx could ever be. "He came in and we did the show together and we became friendly beyond the show," Turteltaub said. "Redd had some medical problems and we looked after them and we saw that the doctors took care of him. There were a lot of things physically wrong with him and he would just grit through them and come in and do the show—and do it well."

Redd's divorce from Betty Jeanne, meanwhile, was taking an ugly turn. In August, a few weeks before *Sanford and Son* kicked off its fourth season, Redd was denied a summary judgment in his divorce case by a District Court judge in Las Vegas. Redd was petitioning the court to make his divorce from Betty Jeanne immediate and final, hoping they could settle their property issues at a later date. Redd told the court he'd moved out of the couple's Las Vegas home and was living in a hotel in Los Angeles. "We just don't get along," he said. "She wants to go out at night and I'm too tired." A month later, Betty Jeanne was awarded $10,000 a month for temporary support, and Redd was ordered by the same Las Vegas court to pay her $50,000 for preliminary attorney fees pending their formal divorce, which was scheduled for the end of October. Redd actually got off easy, since Betty Jeanne had asked for $25,000 a month in support and for $150,000 in attorney fees.

"The easiest thing I can say about *Sanford and Son* is that it broke up my marriage," he said afterward. "That was the man who broke it up. When I was away from home eight hours a day and came home tired and had to read the script and learn fifty pages late in life it was tough.

It was hard and I know my old lady suffered with me having to ignore her at times when I fell asleep after reading the script."

The couple was still battling in November, when they refused to acknowledge each other during a two-hour divorce hearing in Las Vegas. The judge, Keith Hayes, wasn't happy to hear that Betty Jeanne hadn't yet carried out court orders to return some personal items to Redd, including twelve Bert Williams comedy albums, a pair of boxing gloves given to Redd's father by the great heavyweight champ Jack Johnson, a scrapbook of sports events covering the years 1910 to 1970, and an expensive tape recorder—which Betty Jeanne claimed was stolen from her house.

Betty Jeanne, meanwhile, told the judge that Redd never produced the financial statements (tax returns, contracts, bank statements, payroll records, *Sanford and Son* royalty statements) that her attorneys needed in order to prepare their divorce case (translation: how much she would ask for). "My wife handled all of my business affairs," Redd said on the stand. "I never checked behind her for accuracy in handling my business. I don't have any records at all." It was an ominous sign. Their divorce battle dragged on for another year before a settlement was reached.

But it wasn't all doom and gloom. Los Angeles Mayor Tom Bradley declared October 28, 1974, "Redd Foxx Day" in the city, and Redd was feted in a gala celebration at the Shubert Theater, using the occasion to raise money for the tiny community of Taft, Oklahoma, which had named him as its honorary police chief. Guests included *Sanford and Son* co-star Demond Wilson, Freddie Prinze—just getting a taste of fame on his first season of *Chico and the Man*—Scatman Crothers, Slappy White, John Amos, Raymond St. Jacques, Ernest Borgnine, Sammy Davis Jr., and Rev. Jesse Jackson.

chapter eleven

"A Cross Between Disneyland and a Circus"

Redd's divorce from Betty Jeanne meant that his ex-wife would own a piece of Redd Foxx Productions, the company Redd founded a few years before after his initial flush of success on *Sanford and Son*. But that wasn't as enticing as it sounded, since nothing produced by Redd Foxx Productions was actually making much money. Redd ran his production business in much the same way he ran his former comedy club on La Cienega—badly. His DuSable High School classmate, Robert Johnson, was now a multi-millionaire thanks to his publishing empire, which included *Ebony* and *Jet* magazines and several spin-off publications, all catering to the African American community. Redd thought he could tap into that lucrative market.

He moved his growing staff into a four-story building, located at 933 North La Brea Avenue in Los Angeles. For the first year or so, Redd leased his office space from movie producer Bert Schneider (*Five Easy Pieces, Easy Rider*), then bought the building outright and moved his personal office suite to the top floor. The suite included plush carpeting, top-of-the-line office furniture and even a sauna; an elevator opened directly into Redd's offices. Redd Foxx Productions also occupied the floor directly below, which was patrolled by Redd's burly bodyguard, Barry Wright, who kept anyone who wasn't invited from getting into Redd's fourth-floor inner sanctum. Redd's company rented out the rest of the building, the side of which was emblazoned with REDD FOXX in huge letters and adorned with a caricature of a red fox.

"It was a decent building in a great location . . . and he didn't make a payment on it for all the years I was with him until it was finally sold at auction," said Redd's attorney, Paul Whitford, who entered "The

Chief's" orbit in late 1983. "It was interesting for me because when I went over [to Redd Foxx Productions] I was the only white face there. And [Redd's staff] was a little stand-offish, but it didn't take long where if any event happened, I was told to be there—933 North La Brea, or as Redd used to say, '933, the place to be.'"

Redd also moved his mother, Mary Carson—who was now in her early seventies, but still lively and spry—into Park La Brea, an apartment complex just down the street from his new office digs. "He wanted the best for her but that still wasn't close enough," said one of Redd's secretaries, Kathy Chase. "She was a block away and she still was down there [at 933 North La Brea] every day. He loved her. He just didn't like her whining over him. 'You got your hat, it's cold outside?' Redd would say, 'Please, please, I'm fine.' It was always like that. She said she was a metaphysician. And that she saw things and everything. She would always say she felt stuff and it would make [Redd] nervous. He was raised Catholic. He didn't need negative energy and things."

Mary would frequently fly to Las Vegas to see Redd perform, but it was never easy for those traveling with her, usually one of Redd's assistants. In later years, Florence Scott, a nurse's aide Redd hired to care for his aging mother, was her usual traveling companion. Mary would often throw temper tantrums when she left her apartment, in the airport, and in the hotel lobby once she arrived in Las Vegas. There always seemed to be a problem.

Redd's attitude toward his mother was ambivalent at best; he loved her, yet still held deep-seated resentment about the way he and his brother, Fred, were shuttled back and forth during their childhoods—from their grandmother's house to St. Benedict the Moor in Milwaukee then back to their grandmother's house, finally moving back in with their mother in Chicago only when they were teenagers.

"She is a reverend. Like a preacher. I don't think I have ever gotten to know her," he said. "She is two or three different people from time to time. A great actress." He was blunter in his feelings when talking to Les Anglin, a Chicago cop who became a close friend. "He would say, 'Man, how am I supposed to feel. I never knew her, knew nothing about her—my grandma raised me—and now that I get some money, here she comes.'"

Redd was more brusque in discussing his mother during an appearance on *Sammy and Company*, a short-lived talk show hosted by Sammy

Davis Jr.—indicating she was more interested in her son's money than in her son. "I don't like to say this about my mother. She called me one time, not less than a month ago, and said, 'Son, mama's not feeling so good and you haven't called me in two weeks.' I said, 'I'm gonna send some money over there this evening, ma.' 'You gonna send some money over this evening?!'" he said, imitating his mother's sudden perky demeanor. "'When you gonna send it by? Make sure you put it in an envelope, put it in an envelope so nobody steals it!'"

Television producer Stuart Sheslow, who grew close to Redd in subsequent years when they worked together on *Sanford* and *The Redd Foxx Comedy Hour*, said Redd "never forgave" his mother for being absent during much of his childhood. "He did not like her at all," Sheslow said. "He would never let her up to his apartment [at 933 La Brea] during the ten years I knew him. She was never allowed upstairs. He said he would never forgive her for leaving him and his brother in [St. Benedict the Moor]. He told me that when Al Capone visited Saint Louis and went to one of the clubs there, he spotted [Redd's mother] and took her back to Chicago with him. I don't know how much of that is the truth, but that's what he said.

"I always found his anger toward his mother to be much bigger," Sheslow said. "He didn't become a clown because of the [racial] injustice. He became a clown to mask the pain he was in. He did the cocaine because it was part of growing up the way he did, from being shifted from one side of the family to another, to an orphanage. He felt like cattle."

"When Mama Carson would come into the building and Redd knew she was there, he would break out in hives," said Redd's attorney, Paul Whitford. "She'd sit down in the lobby for maybe two hours. He supported her, but she nearly drove him crazy. I would come over to work in the office and she'd be sitting downstairs. I'd say, 'Mama Carson is downstairs' and they'd say, 'Oh, we know, Redd doesn't want to see her.'"

"The Chief," as everyone in the company called Redd, would drive to the Redd Foxx Productions offices in his Rolls Royce after rehearsing *Sanford and Son* on the NBC lot in Burbank. La Brea Avenue ran parallel to La Cienega Boulevard, the scene of Redd's previous business venture. Redd Foxx Productions paralleled Redd's Place in other ways, too. And none of them were good.

For starters, Redd had no business sense. Under the guise of Redd

Foxx Productions, he concocted a variety of get-rich-quick schemes, none of which succeeded. Early on, after he'd first established his company, Redd approached his *Sanford and Son* co-star, Demond Wilson (who he called "Demon"), about investing $25,000 in his brilliant idea for a "car velvetizing" business—which Redd said would revolutionize the industry and eliminate the need for people to wash their cars. The idea was to cover a car in velvet; once the velvet got dirty, all someone had to do was brush the dirt off. It was that simple.

What Redd didn't take into account was what happened to the velvet when it got wet, maybe in one of the infrequent-yet-torrential downpours that soaked the city of Los Angeles. Wilson passed on the offer to invest in the business, which Redd opened on Sunset Boulevard. It closed six months later. "It was called 'car flocking,'" said Redd's friend, John Barbour. "People would bring in their convertibles and then he covered the damn things with fur. I mean, what a ghetto business. He was an extremely bad businessman. He also never kept accounting records."

At one time or another, Redd Foxx Productions owned a record store (which was managed by Redd's daughter, Debraca), oversaw a stable of recording artists and stage acts, and sold hair care products and other beauty essentials. Redd hired chemists to work on ingredients for his hair-care line, which included a conditioner called "Napp Snapp" and an Afro comb called "Napp Snapper." He said he was inspired to start marketing his hair-care products years before, when, down on his luck and struggling to make ends meet, he would visit "a black dude" on Central Avenue in Los Angeles, who gave Redd food and took the time to talk to him. The "black dude" made konk, the slang term used to refer to the gel some African Americans used to straighten their hair (primarily in the 1940s and '50s). Redd promised his pal that if he ever made it big, he'd start his own cosmetics company and hire his friend as a vice-president—which is exactly what he did.

"Redd had such an inflated ego sometimes, it defied rationality," said Paul Whitford. "He was a little delusional when it came to his success and importance. His office building had a ground-floor retail space that wasn't being used, so he decided to sell his collection of items, open up a store, everything. He said, 'You know what? Tour buses will stop and let people off, they'll wanna go in there and look at it.' I never saw a customer in there.

"He also had like four or five of the *Sanford and Son* red pickup trucks and he also owned a Cadillac limousine that was painted fire-engine red—the tackiest thing I'd ever seen, except for him, it wasn't tacky. He could pull it off."

In July 1975, he opened the Celebrity Beauty Shop on Sunset Boulevard in Hollywood. Decorated completely in red (including its tiled floor and sinks), it featured an indoor pond stocked with Japanese carp and fancy, expensive, vibrating chairs. Redd threw a lavish, opening-night party that drew Richard Pryor, Marilyn McCoo, Billy Davis, Mayor Tom Bradley, Flip Wilson, LaWanda Page, Whitman Mayo, Redd's *Cotton Comes to Harlem* co-star Raymond St. Jacques, and former *Little Rascals* co-star Matthew "Stymie" Beard. Beard, an old friend, was trying to mount a comeback after years of battling drug addiction and homelessness. Redd was instrumental in helping Beard get back on track, and hired him for a few episodes of *Sanford and Son*.

To manage the Celebrity Beauty Shop—later renamed the Redd Foxx Hairstyling Salon—Redd hired John Barbour's wife, Sarita. But nothing with Redd Foxx was ever easy, and his questionable business practices led to weird occurrences—and, in time, questions from the Internal Revenue Service.

Sarita Barbour, was, her husband said, "incredibly close" to her boss. But she ended up leaving the beauty shop over what she felt was the "shady" atmosphere in and around the business. "She stayed with Redd until one day some guy came in with a brown box and said, 'This is for Mr. Foxx.' And nobody ever called him 'Mr. Foxx' and my wife got suspicious," John Barbour said. "He said, 'I'm going to leave this here for Mr. Foxx.' She said, 'No you're not, you're going to take it away' and he said, 'I had instructions to leave it.' So she handed him the box and led him out the door. She had the feeling that somebody was trying to set Redd up, and that's when she quit. She said, 'You know, Redd, what you do in your private life is your own business, but I have a child and a husband' and there was something shady about this so she left."

At one point, Redd asked Sarita to act as a co-signer on his bank account. She refused. "When my wife managed his beauty parlor she kept track of every single cent in that place," John Barbour said. "Redd had gotten in trouble a few times with the IRS, but an accountant came in, and thank God my wife had all those books and helped him out. Redd was absolutely terrible at that."

Sarita also got a glimpse into Redd's no-holds-barred personal life when an attractive young woman came into the beauty shop one day with her three young children in tow. She was there to see Redd, she said, whom she'd met in Detroit several weeks before under God only knows what circumstances. Redd never expected to see his conquest ever again, and told her he'd "set her up" if she ever came to Los Angeles. Well, now she was here, expecting a handout—or more. "Redd wouldn't come down to the beauty parlor to see her and she had a breakdown in front of my wife," Barbour said. "I'm sure a lot of that kind of stuff happened, but I guess Redd sometimes made these promises to people."

Redd was generous to a fault to people he trusted, which included many members of his office staff, and that led to problems when he began doling out cash without giving it a second thought. "I seen him just give people around his office three hundred, four hundred dollars, just for nothing," said LaWanda Page. "He'd say, 'Take it. Buy yourself a cigar or candy or something.'" Della Reese had also seen the extent to which Redd's generosity extended. "If you walked up to Redd and didn't have any money, he would stick his hand in his pocket and what he came up with he would give you," she said.

Redd's return to *Sanford and Son* in September 1974 helped the series reclaim its second-place spot behind *All in the Family*. His new television contract, with its ownership stipulations and bonuses, was earning him over $1 million a year now, and he spent like there was no tomorrow. His car collection grew to include a silver Mercedes 450SL, a Rolls Royce Corniche and a Panther, which was modeled after the original Jaguar SS 100. Always a clotheshorse, he now converted one bedroom of his house into a walk-in closet. He wore a huge pendant around his neck, which spelled out "FOXX" in diamonds. It was reportedly worth $100,000; Redd wore it constantly as his good-luck charm and never went onstage without it.

Although a chunk of his earnings went to Betty Jeanne in their divorce settlement, Redd wasted no time in expanding his production empire. In addition to his line of hair care products, the record store, the beauty shop, and various and sundry entertainment acts, he was now managing a professional boxer—no surprise, since he loved the fights almost as much as he loved Keno. One of Redd's boyhood classmates in Saint Louis, Bob Satterfield, fought as a heavyweight in the 1940s and '50s and was the ostensible subject of the 2007 movie, *Resurrecting the Champ*, starring Samuel L. Jackson. Redd claimed that heavyweight champ Archie Moore was a neighbor of the Sanfords in Saint Louis.

In the late 1950s, Redd applied for, and was granted, a boxing manager's license, which he'd never used until he saw heavyweight Fred Houpe in a 1973 bout in Oakland, California. "I could see he was good, and after he won on a third round TKO, I went back and found out that he needed help, financially," Redd said. "I don't talk about it, but I help a lot of young brothers and sisters who need it. That is my main interest in helping this young man. I'll help him all I can, and be at ringside when possible."

Houpe and his wife had moved to Los Angeles in 1973. Shortly thereafter, Haywood Jones, who was vice president of Redd's cosmetics company, DDER Manufacturing, introduced his mutual friends Houpe and Redd on the set of *Sanford and Son*. When Houpe won the Golden Gloves championship in Los Angeles, Redd decided to help the twenty-three-year-old fighter turn pro and manage his career. Redd nicknamed Houpe "Young Sanford" and took the boxer under his wing. "He was just like an old pop," Houpe said. "He paid my rent and gave me food to eat. He treated me like that because I was used to respecting the older people. And he'd lost a brother named Fred Sanford, so that sort of binded him with me."

Redd made good on his word to help Fred Houpe's career any way he could. "He kept my name in the news," Houpe said. "He let me fight any way I wanted, and every time I fought, he would have some big star come to my fight. He would have Richard Pryor, Flip Wilson, and all his friends on the show come to my fights." After Houpe's boxing career ended, Redd gave him a job as a security guard at the Redd Foxx Productions building on La Brea. When Houpe eventually divorced his wife, Redd got *her* a job chauffeuring his mother to see his shows in Las Vegas.

Redd's generosity was legendary and knew no bounds; he was good at giving handouts—sometimes to total strangers with a prefabricated sob story—but not so good in demanding to be repaid for his generosity. People took advantage, and the crowd of hangers-on seemed to grow exponentially with Redd's bank account. There was the trusted inner circle, which included, among others, bodyguard Barry Wright—

a giant-of-a-man—and Prince Spencer, who succeeded Bardu Ali as Redd's *de facto* manager/Guy Friday.

Prince, who was five years older than Redd, was an old friend and a fellow Chitlin' Circuit veteran. He'd been a longtime member of the Four Step Brothers, a popular dance team that appeared alongside Bob Hope in the 1953 movie *Here Come the Girls* and were featured on *The Ed Sullivan Show* and *The Jack Benny Show* in the '50s. Now, with his dancing career over, Prince dedicated himself to the care and feeding of Redd Foxx. He would remain a loyal and trusted friend and confidante until the day Redd died.

Dee Crawford also entered into Redd's orbit around this time. Crawford, the wife of Los Angeles Dodgers star Willie Crawford, was working as a successful real estate agent, and was the first African American real estate agent hired by Coldwell Banker in Beverly Hills. One day, she got a call from a friend, the president of Redd Foxx Productions, asking her if she could help "The Chief" find a house. When she met Redd in person, he told Crawford he wanted a house "where I can see the water," and which would be far enough away from Hollywood to grant him a safe haven. Crawford found a place for about $2 million in a gated community in North Ridge, around twenty-five minutes outside of Hollywood. Redd was impressed.

Shortly thereafter, Dee, who was still working for Coldwell Banker, helped Redd buy his Redd Foxx Productions building on La Brea Avenue. A short time later, when she helped Redd seal a deal with scriptwriter Max Keller—"I think they handed Redd a check for $100,000 or $200,000 in about an hour," she said—Redd offered her the job of running Redd Foxx Productions. "He just started hounding me to come and run his company," she said. "And after long talks with my husband, Willie, I said okay—with the stipulation that I could continue to sell real estate."

Redd agreed to Crawford's stipulation. But, as she soon discovered, being the president of Redd Foxx Productions, and trying to untangle its muddled financial tentacles—while dealing with the assorted hangers-on, wannabes, and shady characters—was a full-time job. "So I started to run his company, and by that I mean weeding everybody out, getting all the yes-men and the leeches out," Crawford said. "He wanted me to be the bad cop and he wanted to be the good cop. You couldn't get to Redd Foxx without going through me. He said, 'You gotta help me say no. I can't keep doing what I'm doing. Everybody's got their hand in my pocket. And everybody around me is stealing.' So I became the bad guy."

Crawford's forthright manner alienated some of her employees, but she needed to rule with an iron fist if the company had any hope of succeeding. She was especially busy helping Redd deal with the "talent" that came to the building on La Brea hoping to be signed by Redd Foxx Productions. It was, she said, a non-stop revolving door in a circus-like atmosphere—reminiscent of the anything-goes milieu fostered by the Beatles during their short-lived foray into management in the early days of Apple Records.

"Just about everybody across the country called us, everybody that needed a hand, everybody that wanted a chance, everybody that wanted to be on TV," Crawford said. "The men, the women, the comedians—everybody who thought they had an ounce of talent came to Redd Foxx Productions. It was almost a cross between Disneyland and a circus. I used to say we were Miami Beach, Las Vegas Boulevard, San Juan, Puerto Rico, and the Comedy Store all in one building. I called Redd's friends 'the Hookers, the Hos, and the Homies.' If you could picture a circus with all the performers in a room about one hundred feet by one hundred feet, all doing their thing, that was Redd Foxx Productions and that was Redd's life.

"Each day was a new circus," she said. "Redd may show up with some girl that he saw on Central Avenue on one arm and a model on the other arm. It was everybody with a script, everybody with a punch line, everybody with a story." The cocaine also flowed freely in the office, only adding to the frenetic atmosphere. "It was just something Redd did from the time he got up until the time he closed his eyes," Crawford said. "I mean, everybody did cocaine back then. And you'd go into Redd's office and . . . I would play like I didn't even see it. It was no secret that Redd had a cocaine problem. He just loved it."

Part of Crawford's duties also included overseeing Redd's ongoing business ventures, none of which ever made any money—and all of which, eventually, failed. "It just wasn't the right time," she said of products like Napp Snapp and Napp Snapper. "How do you compete with Johnson Products out of Chicago? Who could compete with them? But I think that Redd was so spread out in so many different directions. And he was making so much money that every other check went to the IRS.

He was, in some instances, averaging $100,000 a week." Redd often walked around with a briefcase containing $50,000 in cash and checks "that he forgot he had until I reminded him or asked him for them," Crawford said.

Not all of that money came from *Sanford and Son*. Redd continued performing in Las Vegas at the Hilton, where he was reportedly pulling down $75,000 a week. With the revamped *Sanford and Son* shooting schedule giving him a week off between shows, he continued to travel to Vegas for three to four days at a time—often with Kathy Chase, who'd been hired as his secretary.

But mixed in with the nonstop sideshow that was Redd Foxx Productions was "The Chief's" generosity, and his willingness to give anyone a chance. Redd Foxx Productions signed several musical acts, including Milk 'N Honey and a musical group called Janice. Redd also backed a theatrical musical called *Selma*, which celebrated the life of Rev. Martin Luther King Jr. and recounted the Civil Rights struggles of the 1950s and '60s. The show opened in Los Angeles in 1975 and toured the country for two years, with a cast including legendary R&B singer Ruth Brown as Mahalia Jackson.

Redd first met Ruth Brown years before in Virginia. Then, in the early '50s, when he was struggling to make a name for himself on the club circuit, their paths crossed once again. Brown, who was, by then, known as "Little Miss Rhythm," was at the top of her game as an Atlantic Records recording artist. She was performing at the Fillmore West in San Francisco when Redd, nearly destitute, knocked on her hotel room door in San Francisco, begging Brown to help him out. She told Redd to take whatever he needed, and he grabbed four hundred and fifty dollars in cash, which was enough to pay for a plane ticket back East, where he was hoping to find more work.

Redd never forgot Brown's generosity, and when they met again in the mid-'70s—their professional and financial situations now reversed—Redd invited Ruth to California, where he got her a role on *Sanford and Son* then hired her for *Selma*. "He's helped so many people, but he doesn't want publicity about that," the play's writer and star, Tommy Butler, said when Redd decided to back *Selma*. "I've been in his office and seen his kindnesses to people. There's a lot to Redd Foxx that most people don't know a thing about. Even though he's been up front with the money, he's let me own my own property."

Thanks, in large part, to Redd Foxx opening the doors for her return to the entertainment world, Brown's acting roles grew. After *Sanford and Son* and *Selma*, she snared roles in television (*Hello, Larry* and *Checking In*), movies (*Hairspray*) and on the Broadway stage (*Amen Corner* and *Black and Blue*, for which she won a Tony Award and a Grammy Award for the soundtrack album). "Redd brought me back," she said. Ruth Brown wasn't an isolated case among Redd's show-business friends, many of whom he treated like family.

There was the time when Della Reese was in Las Vegas, trying to return home to Detroit because she wasn't working and didn't have any money. "I went to see Redd," she said. "Not to ask him for anything, I just needed a laugh because everything was going to hell in a bucket. I'm sitting in his dressing room and the man who owns the club comes in. And Redd says, 'I don't feel good at all and I don't know if I'm going to be able to do the show because I feel so bad.' And he put on this act of feeling bad. He said, 'Maybe I can get Della to do to the show for me. Dell's been working here in Vegas and the people like her. Call the piano player in here.' And the piano player and I went over several blues numbers and a couple of standards and Redd turned to me and said, 'Dell, will you do this show for me? I'll do the second show because that's not until 12:00 and, by then, I should be okay.' He didn't have to do that. I wasn't his mother or his sister or his woman."

Redd was also known for his generosity in helping hard-luck cases, even for people he didn't know. That included former baseball player Lou "Sweet Lou" Johnson, who'd fallen on hard times after retiring in 1969. Johnson had played for the Dodgers in the mid-1960s with Willie Crawford, Dee's husband. He called the Redd Foxx Productions office one day, asked to speak to Dee, and told her he was living out of his car. With Redd's permission, Dee hired "Sweet Lou" as a security guard for Redd Foxx Productions. "He became an instant hit with Redd," she said, and even appeared on a few of Redd's later television shows. That, in turn, led to a job with the Dodgers in their community relations department—where "Sweet Lou" still works today.

In the summer of 1974, Redd gave $10,000 to the community of Taft, Oklahoma, where he was named honorary police chief. "He was looking for an all-black community to help so he took the job," said Taft mayor Lelia Foley. (Redd's pals Flip Wilson and Sammy Davis Jr. were honorary police chiefs in Boley and Langston, respectively, two other all-black towns in Oklahoma.)

Redd announced his plans to build a museum and a swimming pool in Taft, and was sworn into office in late October, casually dressed in bleached jeans and a denim jacket. The following year, he donated two police cars (one white, one blue) to Taft—but not before having his likeness painted on the cars, both of which identified him as the town's police chief. He added that he wouldn't mind if the town changed its name to "Reddfoxxville" to honor its benefactor.

Meanwhile, in late November 1974, Redd was honored for his forty years in show business with "The Redd Foxx Anniversary Show," held at the Shubert Theatre in the ABC Entertainment Center in Holly-wood. It was a gala affair, with Sammy Davis Jr. and Rev. Jesse Jackson in attendance. Redd announced he was using the shindig to help raise part of the $22,000 needed to build the pool in Taft (the nearest swimming pool was twenty miles away). Four days later, he presented a $10,000 check to the town so it could start construction on the pool.

But, as frequently happened in the world of Redd Foxx, things in Taft started to go south. In December, citing a "leg injury," Redd failed to show up for the town's Christmas celebrations, but he did send his bodyguard, Barry Wright, and another employee to distribute over 170 turkeys to Taft residents. The following April, after Lelia Foley was reelected the town's mayor, she vowed to "oust" Redd as Taft's police chief, charging that votes [for Redd] had been bought. She also asked federal and state officials to investigate "accusations of alleged election irregularities involving an aide to Foxx and the Taft postmaster." "There are now individuals here and outsiders who want to control Taft," Foley said. Whatever was done behind the scenes, the brouhaha blew over quickly. The following Christmas, Redd gave the Taft police force a patrol car and donated $4,000 to the town, throwing in three hundred turkeys for good measure. Yet his *modus operandi* didn't change; he said he was "ill" and couldn't attend the holiday ceremonies.

With the money coming in from *Sanford and Son* and from his night-club and Las Vegas appearances, Redd's recording career had taken a back seat for some time now. The genre that was instrumental in launching him forward to national prominence was now a distant thought; "The King of the Party Records" no longer paid much attention to that aspect of his career. The Redd Foxx albums that were released between 1973 and 1975 by Redd's own label, MF Records, were sporadic, sloppy, and slapdash—reheated platters served cold, without any effort or enthusiasm.

It seemed that pattern would change in the spring of 1975, when Redd was approached by Bob Greenberg, the vice president of Atlantic Records. Atlantic wasn't doing much with comedy albums in the 1970s—it was known more as the home of rock acts including Led Zeppelin and Genesis—but Greenberg thought that Redd's fame, and his popularity, would move some product. "That was my feeling," he said over thirty-five years later. "Redd's show was in the Top Three at that point and I was watching it all the time. And, of course, I knew the act in Vegas was so raunchy, but I felt that he could sell. I was star-struck in those days—and Redd was a star."

Redd's management team negotiated with Greenberg for six months and, in November 1975, and agreement was reached. Atlantic Records and Redd Foxx jointly announced their new "long-term" recording deal for a series of comedy albums. Henry Allen, Atlantic's senior vice president, said the company had outbid a dozen other labels to snare Redd's services; the new album was being rushed into production in order to be in the stores by early December, just in time for the Christmas holidays.

The new deal, though, didn't mean Redd would record any new material. He told Bob Greenberg that between *Sanford and Son* and his live gigs he just didn't have the time. "He said, 'Why don't you and my lawyer go into the studio—I'll give you all the tapes, pick out what you want and record this record," Greenberg recalled. "So I turn around and I go in and we made a record, which turned out to be very funny, as far as I was concerned." The material Greenberg chose was culled from one of Redd's live performances at the Apollo Theater, a raucous affair that captured Redd at the top of his game, bantering with the audience, one-upping hecklers ("rest your lips because you got a long night ahead of you") and giving an overall riotous performance: "When I was a kid, funky didn't have anything to do with music! Funky was grandma's bloomers. Funky was grandpa's long drawers, with the nicotine stain in the back when he had sneezed and got snuff in 'em—that was funky!"

Redd insisted on calling the album *You Gotta Wash Your Ass*. He borrowed the title from one of his standup bits in which Redd, as only he could, had some fatherly advice for couples in love: "If you're here today with someone you love, be considerate of your mate. Care. Worry about their feelings. The most important thing you must do in a romance or love affair—when you love someone, you got to wash your ass! I don't mean your whole ass, I mean your ass *hole!*"

The album cover for *You Gotta Wash Your Ass* was shot in a Burbank car wash and featured Redd, sporting a shaved head, holding up a horse's tail and making a disgusted, twisted, grimacing, *that smells like shit* kind-of-face. The words "You Gotta Wash Your Ass" were stenciled over the horse's rear end. When Bob Greenberg showed the cover art to the suits at Warner Elektra Atlantic, the distribution arm of Atlantic Records, the shit really did hit the fan. "The head of WEA called me up and said, 'Bob, you gotta be kidding me. I don't know how the hell we're going to be able to get this into the [record] racks. I mean, like I'm sure [retail store] E.J. Korvettes is not going to carry this record.' But the bottom line is, the record did sell. We sold pretty good with it." *You Gotta Wash Your Ass* ended up reaching number 87 on the Billboard LP charts. It was Redd's last time charting with a comedy album.

Redd turned fifty-three on December 9 and, for all his fame, money, women, and cocaine, he seemed restless and bored. He had everything he ever wanted, yet it still wasn't bringing him any sense of happiness or accomplishment. The "illnesses" that afflicted him during his *Sanford and Son* walkout were becoming a reality now. He suffered from knee pain and almost constant back pain. The previous April, he'd spent several days in a Los Angeles hospital being treated for a pinched nerve in his back. He had his daily cocaine and marijuana habit, and continued to be a heavy cigarette smoker. His breathing was becoming noticeably more labored, his familiar growling voice sounding raspier than ever.

To break up the monotony, he began shaving his head, which created extra work for *Sanford and Son* makeup man Harry Blake, who had to fit Redd with a wig to ensure Fred Sanford retained his gray-haired look for each episode. "I got tired of being the same old dude all the time," Redd said. "I was beginning to feel like the old man in *Sanford and Son*. This makes me feel new and different. Now I can give all the chicks a real treat."

Sanford and Son was still garnering solid ratings in its fifth season, but, like Fred Sanford, it was starting to show signs of wear and tear. In previous years, the show constantly nipped at the heels of *All in the Family*, sometimes even beating television's top-rated show on any given week.

Now, it was finishing further back in the pack, behind fellow sitcoms *Laverne & Shirley*, *Maude*, and *Phyllis*. In its fourth season, *Sanford and Son* averaged over twenty million viewers each week. Now, a season later, it was averaging seventeen million viewers each week. Its slip was showing.

In December, shortly after his fifty-third birthday, Redd went public in the *National Enquirer* by revealing that he'd been in a nearly two-year relationship with a twenty-eight-year-old Philippine woman who called herself Jacinta. They had reportedly been living together for over eighteen months, which meant their romance began shortly after Redd's divorce from Betty Jeanne. "We're homebodies," Redd said. "That's why we've never become a gossip item. Jacinta's only aim is to please me, her man. She's not a pushy women's lib type. I've been living in a dream world—having my every whim catered to."

Redd and Jacinta said they met in Hawaii in early 1974 while Redd was on vacation in the islands; she told Redd she wanted to be an actress, and he told her to call him if and when she ever got to Los Angeles. She arrived there two weeks later. "I love her," Redd said. "Jacinta was so soft and understanding she made me forget my hurt" after his breakup with Betty Jeanne. Apparently the couple's love for each other did not last. Jacinta was never heard from again.

As the calendar turned to 1976, Fred Sanford and, by extension, Redd Foxx, were still iconic pop-culture figures. In January, Redd earned his fourth consecutive Golden Globe nomination as Best Actor in a Sitcom. But he sounded a dour tone that same month in a lengthy feature in *Sepia* magazine under the headline, "Redd Foxx: TV's Unhappy Millionaire." The accompanying article painted a portrait of a man who was at turns truculent, defiant, sad, resigned, and bitter. It wasn't pretty.

"He has been plagued by domestic troubles that wrecked his marriage. He is continually bickering with his TV producers, trying to get even more money. He constantly complains of physical ailments. He drowns some of his unhappiness in drink and keeps himself occupied… and adding more to his bank coffers . . .by working in nightclubs and theater dates when he does not need a penny of the money he earns."

In the article, Redd sounded off on a variety of subjects, including sex—"I don't see no color when it comes to the women. My only requirement is that they come before I do. It's better that way. . . . I can take care of six or seven women at a time"—and then proceeded to make an offer to the article's writer, Shirley Norman: "How would you like a little sex? Look at all the handsome dudes in my entourage. Pick the one you want."

He also took a shot at Bill Cosby, his short-lived partner in Redd's Place. "A few years ago I could have used a spot on one of Bill Cosby's shows—even just a onetime guest spot. But it didn't happen. Now, well . . ." Norman went on to describe her subject as "ornery and ungracious," and even turned her nose up at the way he flicked the ashes from his cigar, describing it as "a typical obscene gesture he likes to use." Though Redd now owned a quarter of *Sanford and Son*, he was still bitter about his battles with Tandem Productions and NBC. "Why can't a black man get a piece of his show? You know what I was? A tuxedo slave— they sent a limousine for me and patted me on the hair and goosed me at parties and expected me to be a happy black buck."

But the "tuxedo slave" was taking a giant step toward getting revenge against NBC. And it came from an unlikely source.

Fred Silverman, who had tried—and failed—to topple *Sanford and Son* while he was at CBS, was named president of ABC Entertainment in 1975. But even at his new network, Silverman wasn't having any more luck against *Sanford and Son*, which was now followed on NBC's Friday-night lineup by the equally popular *Chico and the Man*.

In the fall of 1975, ABC premiered Jack Webb's one-hour drama, *Mobile One* (starring Jackie Cooper) from 8:00 to 9:00 p.m. The show was up against NBC's sitcom juggernaut of *Sanford and Son, Chico and the Man,* and *M*A*S*H*, which aired at 8:30 p.m. on CBS. *Mobile One,* which revolved around a mobile television newsgathering unit, lasted eleven episodes—but that was still better than *Kodiak*, which ABC threw up against *Sanford and Son* the year before and which was cancelled after one low-rated episode.

Silverman figured that, if he couldn't beat Redd Foxx, why not try luring him to ABC? Redd still had another year to go on his NBC contract, which meant another full season of *Sanford and Son*. If Silverman was successful in getting Redd over to ABC, the network would have to wait until the fall of 1977, at the earliest, to put its newest star on the air. It was a gamble Silverman was willing to take.

In late 1975, Fred Silverman put out feelers to Redd's management team. One of Redd's biggest gripes since hitting it big on *Sanford and Son* was NBC's reluctance to give him a prime-time variety special and a development deal, which would allow him to produce other shows. He would even be happy, he said, with the occasional offer to host *The Tonight Show* in Johnny Carson's absence, but the offer was never forthcoming. Sure, Redd was the "star" of a *Dean Martin Celebrity Roast* in 1974—where Joey Bishop, John Barbour, Slappy White, and Nipsey Russell took their best shots—but that was Dean Martin's show. With *his* name in the title.

What Redd wanted was his own variety showcase, something to indicate NBC's appreciation of and confidence in one of its biggest stars—a way of saying "thank you" for turning Fred Sanford into a cultural icon. Redd waited and waited for a variety show, griped about it in the press during his contract squabbles, but it never happened. Shit, even that arrogant windbag Howard Cosell—*Howard Cosell*—was hosting a Saturday-night variety show on ABC—the network now run by Fred Silverman.

Silverman was offering Redd the Holy Grail: the chance to host a prime-time variety show, which would air weekly. And, to sweeten the pot, he threw in a production deal that would give Redd the opportunity to develop shows for ABC. One of Redd's many complaints about NBC was that it never offered him the chance to develop his own show(s), although he did own a piece of the short-lived *Sanford and Son* spin-off, *Grady*, which aired for twelve episodes before being cancelled in March 1976. Redd also had some creative input into the show, in which Whitman Mayo's Grady Wilson moved out of Watts and into his daughter's house in the Los Angeles suburb of Westwood. Redd's cameo appearance as Fred Sanford in the show's second episode failed to ignite much interest. Mayo returned to *Sanford and Son* after his show was cancelled.

For Silverman, stealing Redd away from NBC was a no-brainer, and was his top priority. "He was a major star. He was very, very popular. And he was the star of a major show on NBC," he said. "There was no *Sanford and Son* without Redd Foxx, or so they learned after he left. We took a shot at a new variety show which I desperately wanted to introduce. We had done *Donny & Marie* and there was room for another variety hour, and Redd Foxx, before he did *Sanford and Son*, was a variety artist. He played Vegas, although you know the act had to be adapted to television. We couldn't put his nightclub act on TV or they would shut us down. So I thought it was a good idea."

Silverman sensed that his timing was right. Redd was getting bored with *Sanford and Son* and the show was showing signs of age, with some tired scripts and silly plotlines (Fred and Lamont become landlords of an apartment house; Fred goes into show business to force his brother-in-law out of the house). The ratings were still good but those, too, weren't what they once were. The writing was on the wall.

Bud Yorkin later claimed that he'd had enough of Redd by this time. He was ready to let him go. "I really didn't want to do another year," he said. "We had five years [of *Sanford and Son*] and we had enough of him. But I thought, what the hell, *All in the Family* is going on another year and everybody thought, it's only fair. I didn't want to do it, go another year, but we'll raise the money for him because now *Sanford and Son* is a big hit and we're getting more money from the network and he's getting more money. But no, this dumb fuck decided that he wanted to host a show. He wanted to be Ed Sullivan, he could do all that shit. But he was the wrong guy to play a host. What is he going to say to somebody?"

On April 8, 1976, ABC dropped its show-business bombshell, announcing that it had signed Redd Foxx to a "multi-million dollar contract" as a performer and a producer, starting in the fall of 1977. Redd's producing output would fall under Ef-Oh-Ex-Ex Productions, a division of Redd Foxx Productions. "He is a consummate entertainer whose creativity and versatility have yet to be fully tapped on television," ABC president Frederick Pierce and Fred Silverman said in a joint statement. "We are also very pleased by the production prospects offered by his company for a future series."

Silverman later likened the production end of Redd's deal to Lucille Ball's production deal at CBS (she contributed *December Bride*). Snaring Redd was the first of a two-pronged ABC talent raid on NBC; the network was also trying to lure *Today Show* co-host Barbara Walters to join Harry Reasoner on its nightly newscast. It soon won that chase, too.

"I changed networks because of the initials ABC—A Big Contract," Redd joked. Several days later, he invited a group of reporters to his big house on Mulholland Drive in the Hollywood Hills to talk about his new ABC deal—and used the opportunity to take some swipes at NBC. "I flew to New York two years ago to suggest some ideas to NBC and get a little development money," he said, referring to his meeting with Herb Schlosser in the midst of his contentious 1974 walkout. "They said they'd get right back to me, but they haven't yet. I could have had two babies by now."

NBC officials fired back that the network didn't really care for any of Redd's ideas, and vice versa, and that it wasn't for a lack of trying. Once again, Redd voiced his dissatisfaction that NBC never gave him a prime-time special. "They never asked me to do a special; that holds me back, because I don't get a chance to prove that I can put together a show as good as anyone else's," he said. "I just don't understand why they didn't recognize what they had. . . . I never got a chance to host *The Tonight Show* like everybody else in the business. I asked for a chance to produce, but they wouldn't let me. I wanted to grow but they wouldn't let me."

Redd wasn't shy about who "they" were. He linked NBC's reluctance to show him the proper respect with (what he felt was) subtle racism. "These things happen to you and you wonder why, and you hate to think it has anything to do with prejudice," he said. "But it's all around, man, it *has* to be. If people can't see racism in the Emmy awards, then they ought to open their eyes, because I haven't noticed any black nominations lately."

NBC's senior vice president, Dave Tebet, took the high road in commenting on Redd's imminent departure. "I spoke to Redd last night, and even though his pursuits are different than ours we are still friends and wish him well," he said. "We're also happy that he'll be with *Sanford and Son* for another year." Be that as it may, NBC wasted no time in milking Redd's final year with the network. Shortly after Redd went public with his ABC deal, NBC announced it would give viewers a double dose of *Sanford and Son* each week—a *Best of Sanford and Son* airing on Wednesdays, followed by that season's repeats on Friday night. The network would be sure to get its money's worth before Redd flew the coop.

NBC's post-Redd Foxx attack plan was to build a revamped show around Demond Wilson, explaining Fred's absence by having him "move out of town." When Wilson balked at the money he was offered to stay on *Sanford and Son*, NBC and Bud Yorkin called his bluff and cut him loose. Even Redd couldn't believe that Wilson turned down NBC's offer of $25,000-per-episode to continue on the show—or that he asked for an $85,000 silver Rolls Royce as a token for signing a long-term deal. "Some people 'go Hollywood' awfully fast," Redd said.

Bud Yorkin was now talking about developing a new *Sanford and Son*-type show using many of the series' supporting characters. That show,

The Sanford Arms, centered on the rooming house Fred and Lamont bought in the penultimate season of *Sanford and Son*. The basic plotline of *The Sanford Arms* had Fred and Lamont moving to Arizona and selling their house at 9114 South Central to Fred's army buddy, Phil Wheeler, played by Theodore Wilson (who had a small role in *Cotton Comes to Harlem*). Phil lived in the house and ran the rooming house. LaWanda Page, Don Bexley, and Whitman Mayo returned for the new series, which premiered in September 1977 to abysmal ratings and was cancelled after four episodes. Call it Redd Foxx's final "fuck you" to NBC.

Redd's life was changing in other ways. His divorce from Betty Jeanne had grown bitter and contentious, and the couple was barely speaking to each other by now. Redd claimed the divorce cost him $300,000 in attorney's fees alone, and that it was wiping him out financially, but his own profligate spending and his casual attitude toward paying his taxes wasn't helping matters.

Redd and Betty Jeanne's enmity spilled over to a battle over the wedding of their daughter, Debraca, who married Los Angeles businessman Ralph Russell in June 1975. Redd thought the $40,000 that Betty Jeanne was spending on the wedding, which was held at the Beverly Wilshire Hotel—with four hundred and fifty guests, live doves, and a string orchestra—was outlandishly expensive (since most of it was money she'd won in their divorce). He made matters worse by not bothering to show up for the ceremony. But it wasn't just the cost that bothered him; Betty Jeanne left Redd's name off the wedding invitations. Debraca's uncle, Kent Harris, Betty Jeanne's younger brother, gave her away. "I felt we should spend less money and give those kids maybe $20,000 in cash," Redd said afterward. "What a good start we could have given them."

Redd wasn't at his daughter's wedding on her big day, but, in the meantime, he'd also met someone special. She was a Korean cocktail waitress named Yun Chi Chung. Redd called her "Joi," and they met in front of the Hilton Hotel in Las Vegas, shortly after Joi, who was married and divorced in Korea, arrived in Las Vegas. Joi knew about *Sanford and Son*, which was shown on Korean television, but she had no idea that the man she was flirting with—who was much younger than Fred Sanford and without the old man's arthritic shuffle—was the actor who portrayed him.

Although she'd learned English grammar as a student in Korea, Joi wasn't too conversant in English, and she and Redd communicated, at first, by smiling at each other. "I met him in the hallway, like greeting each other when I got off work, you know?" she said. She was thirty-three, twenty years younger than Redd, and their friendship eventually blossomed into a romance over the next two years.

But Redd continued to see other women—including one person Dee Crawford described as his "hope-to-die girlfriend," who often traveled with Redd—and he dallied with whomever else struck his fancy. "Redd was a womanizer," Crawford said. "He was macho, he was kind, he was a player, he was a player-hater, he was a pimp. A gangsta. He was a comedian. Oh, man, I could just see him pimping through the office right now with that little walk."

Now that he was divorced and no longer had to keep up the appearance of being the happily married husband, Redd partied and slept around with reckless abandon. "I remember going up there to Redd's house on Mulholland and there were a lot of young black women there," said *Sanford and Son* writer Ilunga Adell. "I remember thinking that they were young. They were like twenty-one or twenty-two and one of them apparently had gone out with Redd before, because he knows her and is talking to her. But she's brought three or four of her little friends with her and all of them are going out with Redd.

"He had a Rolls Royce and they're all getting into his car. Now, the one who had gone out with Redd before assumed she's going to ride in the front seat beside him and he takes one of her friends and says, 'No, *you* ride up here beside me.' Like he's designating her as his 'date' for the night. Well, the one that knew him from before looked a little upset and the newly chosen shotgun rider also looked a little surprised and uncomfortable, like, 'I don't know if I signed on for this. I don't know if I want to be added to the harem or not.' Anyway, she sits her ass in the front seat and they drive off.

"What happened after that, I don't know, but it was just another moment in the life of a TV star."

chapter twelve

"Like Hearing Zircon Scratch Glass"

With his final season of *Sanford and Son* looming on the horizon, Redd decided he was a big enough star by now to give the movies another try. Despite all his success on television, six years had passed since he played Uncle Bud in *Cotton Comes to Harlem*, and Hollywood wasn't exactly inundating Redd with offers. There was the occasional hoped-for movie project—producer Max Keller approached Redd in the mid-1970s with an offer to star in a movie—but, for whatever reason, these never came to fruition. It was difficult to gauge whether the lack of movie offers was due to Redd's tainted reputation in Hollywood, especially after his contract squabbles with NBC, or whether he was being pigeonholed as a one-dimensional television performer. But a "reputation," and whatever that implied, was almost a given when it came to performers. And it certainly hadn't stopped Redd's troubled and drug-addicted protégé, Richard Pryor, from making movies.

Redd's stab at movie stardom took a hopeful turn in early 1976, when *Laugh-In* creator George Schlatter offered him the co-starring role in *Norman, Is That You?*, a film adaptation of a short-lived 1970 Broadway comedy. Schlatter reportedly offered the role to George C. Scott, then decided to take the movie in a different direction when Scott turned the project down. It would be a reunion of sorts; Schlatter, an old acquaintance, had directed Redd in the 1968 NBC television special, *Soul*. And Redd's co-star would be Pearl Bailey, Slappy White's ex-wife, whose relationship with Redd stretched back to the late 1940s. Bailey also knew Schlatter from his days working in Las Vegas and at Ciro's nightclub in Los Angeles.

With Redd Foxx and Pearl Bailey signed to play the leads, *Norman, Is*

That You? would have to be re-written. For starters, the original Broadway farce, written by Ron Clark and Sam Bobrick and directed by the legendary George Abbott, starred Lou Jacobi and Maureen Stapleton as Ben and Beatrice Chambers, a married Jewish couple (he's a dry cleaner) who've hit a rough patch in their relationship. When Beatrice runs off with Ben's brother, Ben, distraught, decides to visit their son, Norman, in New York—and discovers, much to his horror, that Norman (played by Martin Huston) is gay and living with another man, Garson Hobart (Walter Willison). When Beatrice eventually shows up in New York—after being dumped by Ben's brother—she also learns the truth about Norman and is equally upset. Ben and Beatrice eventually accept Norman's lifestyle and, when he's drafted into the Army, invite Garson to live with them. All ends happily ever after.

Norman, Is That You?, which was considered the first play to openly explore the topic of homosexuality, opened in Broadway's Lyceum Theatre on February 19, 1970, to mostly scathing reviews and closed after only twelve performances. The following year it found a second life in Paris with Arthur Lesser's production, which begat similar revivals in regional theater companies around the United States, including a twenty-six-week run in Las Vegas and an interracial adaptation staged by the Ebony Showcase Theater in Los Angeles. (The Ebony Showcase was co-founded by Nick Stewart, who played Lightnin' on *Amos 'n' Andy*. Its production of *Norman, Is That You?* ran for over five years.)

In 1970, George Schlatter had bought the rights to *Norman, Is That You?*, convinced it would make a fun movie. "But I couldn't sell it," he said. His luck took a serendipitous turn when Sherry Lansing, a one-time dancer on Schlatter's *Laugh-In*, became the head of production at MGM Studios and gave the project the green light.

Redd hoped the movie would expose him to an international audience, since *Norman* had proven so popular in many different countries since its initial (and extremely short) Broadway run. "Already most of the world knows the story of *Norman*, and I thought it could be an international picture which could be dubbed in different languages and Redd Foxx could be known around the world," he said. "*Sanford and Son* doesn't go everywhere, and neither do my party records. I think a movie like this would be world famous, world renowned."

Schlatter was given only a $1 million budget to shoot his movie—measly by Hollywood standards—which meant he would have to cut corners after paying Redd, Pearl Bailey, and co-stars Michael Warren and Dennis Dugan, who were playing the now-interracial couple of Norman and Garson. In order to save money, Schlatter decided to shoot the movie on videotape, rather than the more expensive film stock, which didn't endear him to the technicians on the MGM lot in Culver City, where the movie was being filmed. "They really resented having videotape even *come* to the lot," he said. "And then, not only did I shoot on videotape on the lot, but I edited in the Thalberg building. They almost went into shock. They were not unsupportive, but the technicians were not crazy to have it there."

Schlatter was also working on a quick turnaround time, and scheduled only three days of rehearsals before the twelve-day shoot commenced on Stage 22. He was used to a frenzied shooting schedule from his days on *Laugh-In*, when he often taped over two hundred pages of script a week in just two-and-a-half days. Filming got underway that summer, with a planned September release date. There was no time to waste.

The movie version of *Norman, Is That You?* was written by Ron Clark, Sam Bobrick, and Schlatter, who tweaked the script here and there to differentiate it from its Broadway predecessor—and to accommodate the casting of Redd Foxx and Pearl Bailey. Ben Chambers, Redd's character, was now an ex-Marine who ran his dry-cleaning business in Tucson, Arizona. Bailey played Beatrice, who runs off to Ensenada for a fling with Ben's brother. In the play, Ben visits Norman in New York; in Schlatter's movie version, Ben flies out to Los Angeles, where he discovers that his son, Norman (Warren), is living with his white lover, Garson (Dugan). The rest of the movie hewed closely to the play.

The atmosphere on the set, especially between Redd and Pearl Bailey, was tense from the get-go. Bailey arrived on Stage 22 tired and irritable, having just returned from a trip overseas in her role as a goodwill ambassador for the United Nations. She was scheduled to leave in another four days for yet another trip, this time to the Middle East and Africa. And neither she nor Redd were thrilled with the prospect of working with each other. Their thirty-year relationship had experienced its share of ups and downs, dating back to Pearl's marriage to Slappy White during the years Foxx and White were touring the Chitlin' Circuit as a comedy team. Redd felt that Pearl, who was already a big star then, didn't do enough to promote her then-husband's act; Pearl thought that Redd was uncouth, and she didn't appreciate his blue humor. "I didn't know this, but Redd had always been trying to jump on Pearl, and always wanted Pearl to help the act, which she never did," Schlatter said. "She was a big star, but she didn't help the act that much. Pearl and Redd fought. This was a movie by itself, almost."

The trouble started when Redd arrived for the first day of shooting in his red convertible, with his vanity license plate that read "NIGGER." "Pearl said, 'That's a terrible word!' and Redd said, 'What's the matter, big mama? I'm a nigger, you're a nigger, we're all niggers,'" Schlatter recalled. "And she said, 'Redd, I go over to Africa and I go into the villages and I go into the straw huts and they sit on the mud floor and we talk about life and love and getting along and be-ing together. Africa is important.' And he says, 'Pearl, listen big mama, there ain't no nigger living in a grass hut on a mud floor that means shit to me, so Africa can kiss my dick.' Well, now, she goes into her trailer and he goes into his trailer and I'm now running out of time."

Schlatter was directing his first movie, which he was also co-produc-ing. Time was money. He implored Pearl and Redd to call a truce for the sake of the movie, and they agreed to put their differences aside. But it didn't last long. "So Pearl said, 'George is right, Redd. We gotta learn to get along. Let me show you something,'" Schlatter said. "She said, 'These are my cards—I am an ambassador, this is my card to the White House, here's my card to the CIA, here's my card to the Senate, here's my card to Congress.' And Redd dropped a roll of hundred-dollar bills on the floor and he says, 'Excuse me, mama, I dropped my cards—this will get me in the front door, where that bullshit won't get your big fat black ass past the kitchen.' Well, now, the fight was on again."

Their bickering continued over the course of Pearl's four-day shoot-ing schedule. In one scene between Ben and Beatrice, Redd ad-libbed a line, throwing Pearl into a rage. She stormed off the set screaming: "Next time, I'm going to work with Burton!" When she returned, she pushed Redd away with a brusque, "Away from me, old man." Turning to Schlatter, she said, "I've had five heart attacks, nearly died—I had to come back to this?" Redd defended himself. "Sure I improvised the line," he said. "It was such a warm thing to say. I'm creative and add things. She thinks I'm showing her up." When Pearl interrupted Redd in his dressing room during an interview he was giving to a newspaper reporter—"Redd, get out here and do your work," she said—he snapped at her: "I ain't going nowhere. There's a man here talking to me. No respect," he said, shaking his head.

Redd's off-screen habits also made the shoot challenging for Schlatter. "Any time we had to stop to re-light, Redd would say, 'Okay, George, while you're doing that, I'm gonna go into my trailer and work on my lines,'" Schlatter said. "I said, Redd, don't go in there,' because anytime he went into his trailer, when he came out, he had either snorted some coke, had a joint, sniffed some brandy or got a blow job. Any one of those noticeably changed his speech pattern, so the shots wouldn't match." Schlatter also noticed that Redd had trouble remembering his lines, which made it necessary to place cue cards all over the set. "He would look up on the ceiling and there was a cue card there. And then I would put one behind the sofa. He would turn around the room, look in different directions and read the words," Schlatter said. "It was all eventually done on cue cards because he couldn't remember anything."

By the end of their four days together, Redd and Pearl seemed to reach a truce. Pearl even had some very nice things to say about her old friend and sometime-adversary. "This is a great thing for Redd's career," she said. "He's never gotten the chance and he should have. He's a rare talent." She added that she thought it was an "insult" that Redd never won an Emmy Award for *Sanford and Son*: "He should have had an award. You cannot have the top comedy show and not win as the top funny man in it. Inside that can hurt, whether a person says it or not."

If shooting the movie was difficult enough for Schlatter, getting his star to promote *Norman, Is That You?* proved to be nearly impossible. As with everything else in the working world of Redd Foxx, it boiled down to money. MGM wanted Redd to do a promotional tour. He said he would be glad to do it—for $25,000 a day. "I said, 'Redd, why? You got ten percent of the movie,'" Schlatter said. "He said, 'Bullshit, I don't have ten percent of the movie; they have ninety percent of *my* movie. I'm not going to put my black ass on some white airplane to promote a movie that they own ninety percent of.' So he would not do any promotion. So that's what hurt it a lot."

That's one interpretation of why *Norman, Is That You?* failed at the box office. But the critics, with or without a Redd Foxx promotional tour, weren't cutting the movie any slack when it was released in late September. New York's *Amsterdam News* gave the movie, and Redd, a positive review—then again, it referred to *Norman, Is That You?* as "a Broadway comedy hit," so its judgment was a little skewed—but for the most part, the movie was savaged. "It is possible to imagine *Norman, Is That You?* on television some rainy afternoon seen through the rising steam of a pile of ironing, and with the sound turned all the way down," wrote *New York Times* critic Richard Eder. "Otherwise— unless customers sneak ironing-boards and tubs of wet wash into the Criterion, Apollo and other theaters. . . . *Norman* is hard to imagine, let alone see." Eder described Redd as "a capable performer" and directed most of his criticism of the movie at Schlatter.

The *Los Angeles Times* was no less tough on Schlatter's movie—"we can now gaze in wonder and mixed emotions at the arrival of the first television [show] made for the movies"—but spared its two stars. "Foxx was an inevitable choice for the father, and the sarcasms and the pale blue jokes are perfectly suited to his image and his style, delivered here as if to a live audience as usual. The wife, who shows up late, is not much more than a walk-on, but Pearl Bailey makes it a stride-on and enhances it with her own strong and vivid personality."

It was clear that *Norman, Is That You?* would fail, both at the box office and at capitalizing on Redd's popularity. The movie was released just as Redd's final season of *Sanford and Son* premiered with a two-part episode that found Fred and Lamont attending a convention of junk-men in Hawaii, where they unwittingly get mixed up with three professional jewel thieves. The episode was an excuse to take the show to Hawaii and for Redd (as Fred) to clown around on the beach, showing off his hula moves in several scenes.

Back home, the situation wasn't so sunny. In October 1976, Redd was sued for $48,000 in Manhattan Supreme Court by television consultant Paul Klein. According to Klein, he'd been hired the previous January to help Redd promote his career. Redd promised to pay Klein over $2,000 a month in salary, which Klein said he never received. Two months later, in December, Redd was in the news again when Haywood Jones, a vice president of Redd's cosmetics company, DDER Manufacturing, Inc., accused Redd of punching him in the eye and pulling a .22-caliber Derringer "from his waistband" after the two men argued over a check. The Los Angeles District Attorney's office said it was launching an investigation. It would take nearly two-and-a-half years to be resolved.

On December 30, 1976, eight days after he turned fifty-four, Redd and his girlfriend, Joi took out a marriage license in Las Vegas. While Redd's close friends didn't doubt he was in love with Joi, he didn't seem too thrilled by making it official with his third marriage. When asked by the clerk if he wanted a marriage license, Redd responded accordingly. "I don't, but I think she does," he said, only half-jokingly. Later, when he and Joi were stopped by reporters outside, Redd was asked where he met his future wife, who was twenty years his junior. "I just opened my wallet and there she was," he said. It wasn't exactly a ringing endorsement of married life.

But the very next day, Redd and Joi were married on the stage of the Thunderbird Hotel in Las Vegas, where Redd was headlining a string of holiday shows. It was a double-ring ceremony attended by about fifty invited guests. Clark County District Judge Michael Wendell officiated over the ceremony, which was held under a floral canopy. Joi, wearing a traditional white wedding dress with a white carnation adorning her veil, was given away by her brother, John Hyun, a general contractor from Los Angeles. Joi's girlhood friend from Korea, Kathy, served as her maid of honor. Redd looked dapper in a tuxedo and wore a matching white carnation in his lapel. The buffet reception was held in the hotel's Cardinal Room, and a few hours later Redd was back on stage for his midnight show. He called Joi up from the audience so they could ring in 1977 together, and Redd announced the couple would go on their honeymoon in Hawaii in a few months.

Joi moved into Redd's ranch-style house in Las Vegas, which she quickly adorned with Korean furniture, including cushions, a low table used for afternoon tea (complete with elbow mats) and custom-made, century-old cabinets she imported with the permission of the Korean government. Redd promised things would be different with his third wife, even if he had to change his diet a little to accommodate Joi's home cooking, which included squid and octopus. "This is my third wife and *I'm* making the adjustment," he told *Jet* magazine. I had the first two [wives] make adjustments and now I'm trying to make some." Redd seemed particularly taken with Joi's jaw line, and her talent for painting ("I can't believe the way her touch is, you know?"). He considered himself a fellow artist, dating back to his self-portrait that graced the cover of *Laff of the Party*, his breakthrough party record. For years he carried around a sketchpad, even when he was on the road, and would relax by drawing friends, family members, and fellow celebrities, mostly by using crayons and chalks.

With Redd's run on *Sanford and Son* scheduled to end in late March, there was still time for one last insult from NBC in the form of a wedding present sent to Redd by network president Robert Howard. On the surface, it appeared innocent enough: two bottles of expensive liquor, a common wedding gift from an employer to his employee. But Redd saw it differently. He interpreted Howard's gesture as a vindictive, passive-aggressive, final fuck you parting gift from NBC. Why? Well, he'd given up drinking the year before, or so he said. Network officials knew he was on the wagon, but wanted to send a message. "Talk about dirty tricks," Redd said. "Some of those fuckers will stoop to anything. Nobody I've met at ABC is that low."

Not only was the booze an insult, but couldn't they have at least sent a more *expensive* insult? Redd was convinced the liquor paled in comparison to what other NBC stars received when they were married. "No way they send two bottles of booze to Johnny Carson or anyone else that got married," Redd said. "And I bet you I was low on the totem pole. That was like a kick in the face to me. I mean, is that a great wedding present for the star of a network? I'd like to find out if it isn't prejudice, what is it that makes a man belittle you so small to send two bottles of booze to your home for your wedding gift." There was only one problem, though: Redd conveniently omitted one important fact. Along with the booze, Robert Howard sent him a painting worth $7,000 as a thank you gift from NBC.

In mid-January 1977, Redd and Joi flew to Washington, D.C. for President Jimmy Carter's inaugural ball at the Kennedy Center for the Performing Arts. Redd was invited to perform, along with *Chico and the Man* stars Jack Albertson and Freddie Prinze, *Saturday Night Live* troupers Chevy Chase and Dan Aykroyd, Elton John, Linda Ronstadt, John Wayne, Bette Davis, Mike Nichols and Elaine May, and Leonard Bernstein, among many others. CBS taped the two-and-a-half-hour shindig for a prime-time special called *Inaugural Eve Gala Performance*.

In March, ABC announced that *The Redd Foxx Comedy Hour* (sometimes referred to as *The Redd Foxx Show*) would premiere in the fall, airing Thursday nights in the plum 10:00 p.m. timeslot. ABC, confident in Redd's ability to draw viewers, scheduled his show as the final piece of its solid prime-time lineup of *Welcome Back, Kotter, What's*

Happening!!, *Barney Miller,* and *Carter Country* (a freshman sitcom playing off the new White House occupants and their Southern roots). *The Redd Foxx Comedy Hour*, though, would face stiff competition—it was up against *Barnaby Jones*, the Buddy Ebsen detective series that was scoring big ratings for CBS.

Sanford and Son went out with a whimper on March 25, 1977. The once-powerful sitcom, which used to battle *All in the Family* for prime-time supremacy, had stumbled badly in its sixth and final season. It finished the season ranked twenty-seventh out of the top thirty prime-time shows, averaging around fourteen-and-a- half million viewers— just behind *Good Times* on CBS (a spin-off from Norman Lear's *Maude*) and ahead of ABC's *Friday Night Movie*. After nearly one hundred and thirty-five episodes, the show's writers were obviously struggling to come up with fresh storylines, and they pulled out all the stops in the final season. In one episode, Fred enters a Redd Foxx look-alike contest and meets his superstar hero (sort of) face-to-face; in another episode, Fred, Lamont and Bubba visit NBC's *The Gong Show*. In the show's penultimate episode, "Fred Sings the Blues," blues legend B.B. King dropped by for dinner at the junkyard.

There was nothing extraordinary about the final *Sanford and Son* episode to set it apart from any other typical episode from the previous six seasons. In "School Daze," Fred and Bubba secretly attend night classes so they can earn their high school diplomas; when Fred's (white) teacher, Doris, shows up at the junkyard to help Fred study, Lamont, his pal Rollo, Aunt Esther, and Donna assume that Fred has fallen in love with Doris, and has abandoned Donna (his longtime girlfriend who stuck with him despite their many ups-and-downs).

By late May, ABC was already promoting *The Redd Foxx Comedy Hour*, and the network arranged for Redd to be introduced to its viewers in a splashy, prime-time interview special hosted by Barbara Walters— the *other* big star Fred Silverman poached from NBC the previous year. Walters also sat down for separate interviews with Bob Hope and Bing Crosby.

The Barbara Walters Special gave viewers a peek into Redd's private world, which seemed at turns exotic and strange. Walters conducted the interview in Redd's chartreuse-colored house high in the Hollywood Hills, an expansive, two-story residence with a large swimming pool in the backyard and a view of the Pacific Ocean. It was one of the four houses Redd owned, including the place in Las Vegas and a house in Saint Louis. He wouldn't fess up to Walters where his other "quiet" residence was located.

Redd sported a shaved head and a dapper gray mustache for the interview. He wore an all-white ensemble, including white shoes, with his shirt unbuttoned just enough to show off the huge diamond pendant hanging around his neck and his familiar Fred Sanford paunch peeking out over his waistband. The interview opened with Redd in his den, playing a washtub bass and retelling the story of jumping on a freight train in 1939 with Lamont Ousley and Steve Trimble and arriving in New York. "I was the funny one in the group," he said. "I got into comedy because I was the funny-looking one. All the good-looking guys are somewhere else now."

The house was lavishly furnished inside. Walters noted that Redd chose all the furniture and decorations himself (including a blue baby-grand piano). Figurines of ceramic red foxes were on display in nearly every room, and one large room was devoted solely to Redd's huge wardrobe (which included, naturally, a shirt adorned with red foxes). The second floor housed the just-completed art studio Redd built for Joi, where she did all her painting, and down the hall was the couple's bedroom. Their bed, designed by Redd, was on a platform (three steps up) and was surrounded by a motorized green curtain, which could be open or shut electronically. Directly above the bed was a mirrored ceiling, and on one of the walls, just above Joi's imported chest of drawers, was a glass enclosure in which live macaque monkeys cavorted and looked down on their human counterparts. The house, in fact, was a veritable menagerie; in addition to the macaques, Redd and Joi had sixteen dogs, several birds (in cages), large fish tanks, and a pond stocked with a variety of exotic fish.

Walters sat down for a quick backyard interview with Redd and Joi, in which they recounted how they met, then sung a love song they'd written to each other while on trip to Boulder Dam. Redd and Walters then repaired to Redd's combination pool hall/bar/movie theatre, which had a billiard table, a fireplace, a movie screen, and a row of chairs from the Apollo Theater. Walters tried to get Redd to talk about his childhood, especially his father, but he was reticent, answering her questions curtly and without much emotion. He opened up a little more when the subject turned to Malcolm X and their days running together in Harlem. "We were in New York, we were clean," Redd said. "I mean we thought [we were]. I had long hair, a pompadour, with a duck tail in the back, but we didn't call it that then." Walters asked Redd how he felt when Malcolm was assassinated. "I felt a deep hurt inside, you know like I still feel bad about it, because I knew him so well from his early beginnings. And I saw what led him into what he was into, you know, even to go to jail. He was doing things you have to when you don't have anything. You know, you're forced to do something."

They talked a little about Redd's standup career, and how they first met on the set of *The Today Show* in 1964, when Redd made his first national television appearance. "I came down to see you, we all came down to see you," Walters said. "Our producer had said, 'There's a sensationally funny man.' I must say, you were the dirtiest act I've ever seen, but I hadn't seen too many like that. However, you were also terribly funny."

The conversation turned to money. Walters noted that Redd owned thirteen cars and a racehorse, in addition to the beauty shop and his houses. "Are you afraid of spending too much and ending up with nothing?" she asked him, rather prophetically. "I wouldn't care if I wound up with nothing, because only those that never had anything worry about it," he said. "So I always say starving to death is simple—all you have to do is go home and wait."

They touched on Redd's contract squabbles with NBC, most notably the 1974 "window in the dressing room" incident, which was all anyone seemed to remember from the kerfuffle. Walters noted that Bob Hope never demanded a window in *his* dressing room. "Well, maybe Bob doesn't have claustrophobia," Redd fired back. "I've got to have freedom for my eyeballs, because, you know, that controls what my body feels. You know, they have facilities there to build stages . . . then they certainly can make me a window. It's not asking too much as the star of the network. Is that asking too much when they give other people organs and automobiles and have their homes wired? I never got any of that."

If ABC was hoping that Redd's prime-time interview with Barbara Walters would make him a happy camper, it wasn't long before problems arose. Just one week after the Walters interview aired, Redd approached the ABC brass and asked for another $100,000 per show, "to make up for what I'm losing by not playing Vegas." It was a familiar refrain from the NBC days. By July, ABC president Fred Silverman was forced to publicly deny that he was having any problems with Redd, calling him "a pussycat" and alluding to the fact that ABC caved in to Redd's demands for that extra $100,000 per show. To sweeten the pot, ABC gave Redd the title of executive producer on *The Redd Foxx Comedy Hour*. He would now earn additional profits from the show on top of his regular salary.

As the summer progressed, rumors started to swirl that Redd was giving ABC censors the jitters with the material he was green lighting for his new show. Al Schneider, the head of ABC's broadcast standards, insisted that only one sketch had "disturbed" him so far, but he refused to discuss it any further. One Hollywood wag, meanwhile, summed it up thusly: "When you take the hells and damns away from Redd, you reduce him to a cute mute."

The job of producing *The Redd Foxx Comedy Hour*—and dealing with the show's star, for better or worse—fell to Bob Einstein and Allan Blye. Einstein, thirty-five, was the older brother of comedian Albert Brooks and the son of radio and film comedian Harry "Parkyakarkus" Einstein (who dropped dead in Milton Berle's lap at a Friar's Club roast for Lucille Ball and Desi Arnaz). Einstein won an Emmy writing for *The Smothers Brothers Comedy Hour*, which Blye co-produced (Rob Reiner and Steve Martin also wrote for the show).

After working on *The Smothers Brothers Comedy Hour*, Blye, forty, went on to co-produce *The Sonny & Cher Comedy Hour* and *The Sonny Comedy Revue*; his resume also included co-creating the sitcom *That's My Mama* and, along with Einstein, writing for Dick Van Dyke's short-lived show, *Van Dyke and Company* (Einstein was also in the cast). Einstein and Blye teamed up to form a producing team, and were signed by ABC to a three-year development deal. Shortly thereafter, network president Fred Silverman approached them about working with Redd on his new show, which, at that point, was still in its infancy stage.

"Supposedly the deal that Fred made with us was we only did what we wanted to do," Einstein said. "He wouldn't force anything on us. And the first call we get is, 'I got a chance to get Redd Foxx away from *Sanford and Son* and you can do his variety show.' We said no and hung up. It was so ridiculous, the thought of it. Fred said, 'Please?' and we said, okay, we'll have a meeting." It was a meeting that, over thirty years later, Einstein recalled with bemusement.

"So we go to the meeting at Redd's office and he comes up the stairs and he's kind of in a bad mood," Einstein said. "And he goes into a revolving bookcase and disappears, like Charlie Chan, and he comes back out with white shit all over his lip and says, 'How are you doing, Blynstein!' He didn't know Allan but he knew me, so he made us into one name. So I said, 'Redd, you got white shit all over your lip' and he said, 'I know it, it always happens when I have sugar doughnuts for breakfast.' So he says to us, 'I got a great idea. I want to do a variety show in Harlem.' I said, 'Boy, that's a really good idea, but I don't live in Harlem and I don't know that it would be really good for us to move there. That's going to be great.' So we thank him and leave.

"Three weeks later [Fred] Silverman calls us back and says, 'Look, he realizes he made a mistake. He'll do anything you want, just meet him at his house.' He lived off Mulholland Drive in Beverly Hills. We come down a long driveway and big guy, like 6'4" or 6'5" meets us and says, 'The Chief will see you now.' So we go in and Redd says, 'I'll do anything you want. I just want it to be funny, I want it to be great. You'll use some of my people.'"

Einstein and Blye noticed that Redd had a closed-circuit camera system in his house, which monitored who was coming down the long driveway. In the middle of their meeting, Slappy White arrived at the house. "Outside the windows of this house, I see four dogs that look like part dogs and part horses—they are the biggest things I've ever seen in my fucking life and they're just pacing the yard," Einstein said. "And Slappy comes down and says, 'I gotta talk to you, Chief'—they all called Redd 'Chief'—and Redd says, 'I'm having a meeting with my producers, Blynstein, right now. Go down and wait for me in the pool house.' Slappy says, 'What about your dogs?' and Redd says, 'Motherfucker, I've known you how long, thirty years? My dogs ever touched you?' and Slappy shrugged his shoulders. And then we watched the dogs chasing Slappy White around the yard and he dives into the pool with his clothes on. And Redd made no attempt to save him! Redd just said, 'Goddamn, they *did* go after him!' And we went right back to the meeting."

Despite the wild, circus-like atmosphere surrounding Redd Foxx, which he fostered and seemed to thrive on, he was focused on proving NBC wrong—and on making *The Redd Foxx Comedy Hour* a success for his new network. Fred Silverman was confident his two producers could make the show work, which is why he felt comfortable persuading them to join forces with Redd. "Blye and Einstein were first-class producers. We didn't put Redd in the hands of a couple of shlockmeisters," Silverman said. "I mean, these guys really had a good sense of style and they were both really good comedy writers." The producers spent that summer working with Redd on the direction of his new show, trying to come up with innovative ideas.

"Let me tell you what he did—he trusted us," Einstein said. "He let us do it. He worked his ass off. He had such a bad reputation at *Sanford and Son*, about not showing up, not wanting to work and problems and all this stuff. He said that since this was his own show, that he would cooperate." In Einstein's view, Redd felt differently this time around, especially about his two producers. "I spent time with him at his house. So if you spend time to get to know someone and they respect your sense of humor and the two of you are able to really laugh, it's a whole different ballgame. I don't think Redd wanted to fuck us over because he knew how hard we were working to make this happen and this was *his* show. It was a different ballgame."

In Redd's world, though, the word "cooperate" took on a different meaning. One day, during rehearsals, the show was running short, so Einstein asked Redd to go out and talk to the studio audience. *The Redd Foxx Comedy Hour* was shot on the CBS lot adjacent to the Farmer's Market in the Fairfax district of Los Angeles; the majority of the studio audience was comprised of people from the Farmer's Market who were given free tickets to watch a taping. "So I said, 'Can you go out and just talk to the audience?' He said, 'Sure,' and whenever he said 'Sure' to me, I realized, oh, fuck, this is going to be a problem," Einstein recalled. "He comes out and says, 'How you doin' everybody?' And they all cheer. He says, 'How many people washed their assholes this evening?' And now there's silence, purses are snapping. He says, 'They got all kinds of flavor douches on the market: strawberry, raspberry, persimmon. I told my wife about it. With my luck, she came back with tuna.' And he looks at me and says, 'Is that enough?' I said, 'Yeah, great, thank you so much.'"

Redd, though, really was serious about his executive-producer title on *The Redd Foxx Comedy Hour*. Einstein and Blye ran the day-to-day operations and oversaw the cast and crew, but Redd had the final say. On everything. "Redd insisted they use so many of his people," said

Dee Crawford, who was nearing the end of her stint as the president of Redd Foxx Productions in the run-up to the ABC show. "Redd called the final shots. Redd ad-libbed almost every line. Nobody could write for Redd. They'd write it, but he ad-libbed because it was never what he wanted to say."

True to his word, Redd hired old friends Slappy White and Iron Jaw Wilson for the show. (Iron Jaw's talent, in his heyday, was to lift entire tables and other heavy objects with his mouth; by the time *The Redd Foxx Comedy Hour* came around, he settled for holding a table in his mouth while spinning around, seated.) A featured segment on the show, "Redd's Corner," featured Redd interacting with comedians from his Chitlin' Circuit days. The cast was rounded out by veteran actor Billy Barty, Hal Smith (who played Otis the drunk on *The Andy Griffith Show*), comedian Bill Saluga (aka Raymond "You Doesn't Have to Call Me" Johnson), and newcomer JoMarie Payton, who would play the role of Redd's comic foil in the sketches (with LaWanda Page busy on *The Sanford Arms*).

As part of Redd's deal with ABC, the network gave him $250,000, with the stipulation that the money would be used by Redd to produce a show for ABC under one of his production banners (Eff-Oh-Ex-Ex Productions or Redd Foxx Productions). And now that he finally had the power to develop programming, Redd began to corral a stable of talent for his planned projects, including Pat Morita, who played Ah Chew on *Sanford and Son* and Arnold on *Happy Days* and comedian Reynaldo Rey. For his first project for ABC, Redd signed his old friend, comedian/impressionist George Kirby, to star in a show called *Big George Diamond*.

In late 1976, *Big George Diamond* was scheduled to begin shooting at the Dunes Hotel in Las Vegas, but soon ran into problems. Redd blamed the white producer ABC put in charge of the Kirby project. "Before, I couldn't be there and George's comedy series pilot got out of hand," he told *Jet* magazine. "I wanted one dude and [ABC] wanted somebody else and I went for it. Anyway, the dude came in like he was running a plantation. All the niggers hated him but they wouldn't call me and tell me because he had told them, 'If you call Redd, you're fired!' How's he gonna fire somebody I hired? But he had them fooled—just like slavery again." Kirby himself put the final nail in the coffin of *Big George Diamond* when he was arrested in May 1977, in Las Vegas, for selling over a pound of heroin, valued at $26,000, to a federal undercover agent. Kirby was released on bond; later that year he was sentenced to ten years in a federal prison (he was paroled after three-and-a-half years).

There were more problems in June, when syndicated columnist Marilyn Beck reported that Redd's business empire "could be going down the tubes unless a miracle occurs soon." The company, Beck reported, recently fired twelve staffers, one of whom told her that Redd Foxx Productions and its subsidiaries were operating on a "skeletal" staff and that he was owed four weeks' back pay. "They're hoping Redd will be sending money in from his nightclub tour to help cover back payroll," the unnamed employee said. Asked to respond, Barbara Perry, the president of Eff-Oh-Ex-Ex Productions, said the company was "working and functioning as usual—and [we] intend to keep doing so." Addressing the staff cuts, Perry brushed it off. "Companies do change employees from time to time," she said.

Beck, throwing more fuel on the fire, also noted in her column that *The Redd Foxx Comedy Hour* still didn't have a format and/or a production team, "and no real notion established as to how Redd Foxx will meet the challenge of making the successful transition from playing a scripted role on *Sanford and Son* to being the host of a weekly, hour-long show." An ABC official said he expected shooting on the show to begin within a month. "Foxx wants to put in as many of his ideas as possible," he said.

The chaotic world over at 933 North La Brea, the headquarters of Redd Foxx Productions, made the thought of actually producing *anything* difficult to fathom. "If we started a day at nine o'clock or ten o'clock in the office, and there was no taping and Redd showed up in the office, there were thirty people waiting to see him and thirty people with their hand out," said Dee Crawford. "He took care of those people [They had] a song, a play, a script, an opening line, a punch line, a TV show, a bit from Vegas, a skit for the show. It was actors, singers, dancers, comedians, the Unknown Comic, Iron Jaw Wilson standing there holding chairs. Reynaldo Rey begging for a chance and driving me nuts. Women. It was trying to get meetings done and this done and airlines and travel. That little cosmetics company."

Redd took it all in stride. And he was loyal to a fault. If he wasn't handing out cash to stragglers, wannabes, and hangers-on, he was doing favors for old friends. In September, Richard Pryor's comedy-variety series premiered on NBC, and was quickly cancelled after four controversial episodes. Pryor complained vehemently about NBC's interference, even before the show began. (This included NBC censoring a bit in which Pryor said he wouldn't compromise his comedy style for television—when the camera cut away, he appeared to be naked, with his genitals removed. He was, in actuality, wearing a body stocking, as Redd had done when he "streaked" across the stage during his *Sanford and Son* walkout.) "Richard said, 'Man, I don't know what I'm gonna do' after his show was cancelled," Crawford said. "And Redd said, "Come on down here and do my show. We'll get you going again.'"

Redd might not have been getting any actual deals done, but he was having a good time that summer. He was snorting coke and screwing women left and right, apparently unbeknownst to Joi, his bride of six months. He did what he wanted to do, whenever the spirit moved him. Those were Redd's Rules. He was the boss, and fuck everyone else if they didn't like it. He'd paid his dues and would do it *his* way. The women were plentiful and willing, and Redd was ready for anything—any time, any place.

That included the very first day of taping on *The Redd Foxx Comedy Hour.* The show's set featured a stage with big block letters spelling out "REDD," with the letters then turning over into a tenement setting, where Redd was supposed to enter through a door. But when the show's announcer gave his elaborate introduction—"Ladies and gentleman, Redd Foxx!"—there was no Redd. Nothing. Nada. The studio audience stirred in their seats.

"So we do all that, this big introduction, and there's no Redd," Einstein said. "I stop tape. Now he loves to screw, and a little grass and a little coke would be a great day. So I knock on his door and I hear, 'What!' And I open the door and the girl who does his hair is on top of him. He's sitting in the chair and she's over him, so I see her face and body and her skirt is over him. And I say, 'Redd!' And from under the skirt I hear, 'What?!' I say, 'We're on camera.' And he says to me, 'Can't a man relax?!'"

And he was acting—always acting—rarely ever letting his guard down even to intimates including Dee Crawford. "We were taping [*The Redd Foxx Comedy Hour*] the day Elvis Presley died and I said to Redd, 'Geez, Elvis just died' and he broke down on his knees like he was in church and he was crying and I said, 'Are you okay?' And he said,

'Damn! There goes my free watch every year!" I thought he was having a nervous breakdown and he was just doing his act."

"Think of his life. This is not a guy who came from a comfortable upbringing and had a few mishaps and had a lot of shots and all this shit—this was almost a slave mentality where he had to struggle and try to convince people," said Bob Einstein. "Then he finally makes it at fifty and he has so much money all of the sudden. And when you're stoned and coked up and shit, it's very confusing. How do you handle it? He was fifty-five when he did our show—he looked eighty-five. That was a *life*."

Redd played by his own rules and existed in his own universe, where the truth was what he said it was—and no questions asked. "Redd liked to get out of rehearsal when he could, if he could," said Einstein. "I had one call from Vegas. He made everyone under him a vice president or general manager, so they were always above you, even if you were an executive producer. So I get a call from Dee [Crawford]. I said, 'Where is Redd?' and she said, 'He had a massive heart attack over the weekend.' 'My god, is he alright?' 'Well, we think he's going to be.' I said, 'Does the press know?' She said, 'No, he said don't tell the press.' I said, 'Will he be coming back?' She said, 'Yeah, he'll be there tomorrow.' So he told her to tell us it was a massive heart attack rather than a cold, or I don't want to fucking come in, or something else like that. That was so far over-the-top.

"And there was the drug use, of course," Einstein said. "It was grass and coke. And one week he gave up coke because he was having heart palpitations and he turned into such a Jekyll and Hyde at the end of the week I said, 'Go back on it. You're impossible to deal with.' He was stoned basically all day long because he would do grass to relax and coke to get him up."

The Redd Foxx Comedy Hour premiered on September 15, 1977, with an opening sketch featuring Queen Elizabeth and President Jimmy Carter—or reasonable facsimiles thereof—attending the opening of Redd's new show. "If a peanut farmer can be President, succeeding a football player who was President, doesn't it follow in logical progression that a dirty old man could have his own show?" Redd asked his audience. He added that he was invited to do the same type of show he did in his nightclub act. "But after the censors got through with it, the only thing I can do on stage is smoke . . . cigarettes."

There were references aplenty to *Sanford and Son*. After the faux Queen Elizabeth delivers a speech welcoming the start of the television season—and pointing out that *Sanford and Son* was a spin-off from Britain's own *Steptoe and Son*—Redd gives one of his patented, "This is the Big One, Elizabeth!" heart attacks. To drive the point home that Redd was back on television, LaWanda Page guest-starred in a risqué skit set in a massage parlor (with Redd doing one of his patented sourpuss faces when he looks up to see that his masseuse, Tandra the Tigress, isn't what he expected). There were jokes about Redd's past behavior on NBC (he refuses to come out "until I get a window") and a segment called "Redd Foxx Black History" which recounted how Yuma, Arizona got its name.

The critical reaction was generally positive. "This Allan Blye-Bob Einstein concoction is a funny outing for the white-haired old curmudgeon from *Sanford & Son* (sic), now in a dinner jacket and surrounded by dancing girls," opined the *Los Angeles Times*. "It's generally an easygoing hour with Foxx handily in charge, his comic timing as impeccable as ever."

"The blue is gone, the black remains and Redd Foxx has himself one very funny, very special show," wrote the *New York Post*. "This show looks like a winner." Even the staid *New York Times* was impressed: "Relaxed and amiable, the veteran comedian has surrounded himself with an attractive format and generally first-rate material." The *New York Daily News*, however, struck a disappointed note: "He's not the same funny man he was as Fred Sanford." Most critics took exception to Redd's warbling Cole Porter's "You'd Be So Easy to Love" near the end of the show ("like hearing zircon scratch glass," one wag wrote).

The show got off to a strong start in the ratings, and some belated controversy stemming from a skit in its second week helped to keep *The Redd Foxx Comedy Hour* in the headlines.

In late October, James and Pauline Fawcett, the parents of former *Charlie's Angels* star Farrah Fawcett, sued ABC. The Fawcetts said they were libeled in a sketch from the September 22 episode of *The Redd Foxx Comedy Hour* in which Redd and an actress played Fawcett's parents—each wearing blonde wigs resembling Farrah's famous hairstyle (known as the "Farrah Flip")—while answering questions about negotiating to bring their daughter home for Christmas. The family's dog and parrot also wore Farrah wigs. The real Fawcetts claimed the spoof held them up to ridicule and was "untrue, degrading, malicious, humiliating, embarrassing, libelous, and slanderous." They wanted $7 million in damages, a retraction, and an on-air apology from ABC.

Redd was livid. The lawsuit was frivolous, he said, and ABC wanted him to make the on-air apology, which he was refusing to do (the network denied asking him to do so). "Satire is satire," he said. "We did 'General Custard' three weeks ago—am I supposed to look for all the Custards to show up and make me apologize? She's in the public like everybody else in show business. What would happen to satire, what would happen to television, if you couldn't poke fun at people." He had a point. "What's Bob Hope been doing all these years, with presidents on down. And Don Rickles, with everybody who crosses his mind? What's the world coming to?"

But there was more to Redd's anger than being asked to make an on-air apology. He was pissed off that ABC, and his union, were hanging him out to dry, and weren't coming to his defense. He threatened to quit *The Redd Foxx Comedy Hour*, and went so far as to tell the *Los Angeles Times*, which reached him in his dressing room on the CBS lot, that he was leaving the show. "I'm just here closing up so that I can get my check," he said. "Because if I don't finish this after working four days [this week] already, then I won't be able to get my money."

He also said he was concerned, after all the problems at NBC, that he was being made to look like a villain—again. "No one's standing up for me," he said. "I'll be glad to come back if they give me some kind of protection against that kind of thing, because I'm tired of being a target. That's all I want." The situation blew over when ABC agreed to never again joke about Farrah Fawcett's hairstyle. Her parents dropped their lawsuit. A source close to Redd told *Soul* magazine that Redd wasn't ever *really* angry—that it was all a publicity stunt to goose the show's ratings. "I think he did it just to get people to watch the show that night," said the source.

If it was all a publicity stunt, it worked, at least for a while. "Farrahgate" gave *The Redd Foxx Comedy Hour* a ratings jolt, but by November the bloom had worn off the rose and the show slipped to fifty-second place in the ratings. There were whispers that ABC was getting ready to pull the plug, and one network official said he couldn't figure out why the show's ratings were "up and down." Redd seemed to adopt a philosophical tone and hoped for the best. "I'm down, but it's not a terminal case," he said. "I'm in some pretty good company when you consider the company I'm keeping—*Carol Burnett, Maude,* and *Police Woman,* all of whom bombed out in the last Nielsen numbers."

Bob Einstein and Allan Blye, backed by ABC, decided the show needed an extra boost of star power, and lined up Milton Berle, Bill Cosby, Suzanne Somers, and Red Buttons as guest stars. One of Redd's heroes, boxing legend Joe Louis—who was nearly sixty-five years old and weary from his battles with ring opponents, racism, and the IRS— also came on the show. Louis appeared during Redd's opening mono- logue. Dutifully following the script, he wound up to "punch" Redd in the face in reaction to an "offensive" comment made by the host. It was all played for laughs, but Louis's haymaker unintentionally caught Redd flush in the face, knocking him down. The champ could still pack a punch. "Redd gets up with a knife—he pulled a switchblade out of his coat. He pulled a knife on Joe Louis because it was the funniest thing you could ever do," Einstein said. "You know, this was an old man, an old champion, who had no idea what he just did. The audience went crazy."

When it was Berle's turn to visit *The Redd Foxx Comedy Hour,* every- thing went smoothly on the air. Backstage, it was a different story. Berle, who was notorious for his didactic and overbearing manner during re- hearsals—even on shows *not* bearing his name—was practicing the old pie-in-the-face routine with Redd when things got out of hand. Bob Einstein, who was supervising the rehearsal, couldn't believe what he saw next. "Berle is all over Redd, 'Rip my shirt!' Redd says, 'This is fucking rehearsal. I'm not going to rip your shirt.' Berle says, 'Rip it!' And he gets Redd crazy. Redd cuts his tie, rips his shirt and shreds his pants down to his shoes. Berle, who's standing there in stained shorts, says to Redd, 'Those were not my rip-away pants.' Redd shredded his mohair slacks right off him!"

But the infusion of star power didn't help the show, and by the end of November *The Redd Foxx Comedy Hour* was on life support. A report in the *New York Times* mentioned undefined "production difficulties" that were said to be plaguing the show, but didn't elaborate any further. The reality was that the money that ABC was pumping into the show— and the way it was being spent—was a big part of the problem. When co-producers Bob Einstein and Allan Blye signed on to the show, they made sure they were not responsible for spending any of the network's money. That end of things was being handled by Redd Foxx Productions—which was always a risky proposition.

"We did a 'Best Of' show, and Redd was given money to pay the dancers," Einstein said. "So the money was paid to the dancers, and all of the sudden I'm getting calls from the choreographer saying, 'Our dancers haven't been paid, there was $9,000 due to them, can you call Redd?' So I called him and I said, 'Did you get $9,000 for the dancers?' 'Yeah, I did.' I said, 'Where is it?' He said, 'I put in the damndest hot tub, you gotta come out here and see it. It's all oak.' I said, 'But the money goes to the dancers' and he said, 'Nah, they don't need it. That's fine.' So we had to go to small claims court."

Redd couldn't accept the fact that the show bearing his name was being tuned out. How could America not love Redd Foxx? He convinced himself that viewership for *The Redd Foxx Comedy Hour* was being undercounted by Nielsen, the company that measured television ratings. Nielsen, he said, wasn't putting enough of its electronic measurement boxes into African American households. He implored readers of *Jet* magazine, published by his boyhood friend Robert Johnson, to launch a write-in campaign to Nielsen. "Tell 'em Foxx wants the black vote because Nielsen can't give me the ratings that I'm supposed to get and I want the networks to know how important the black TV viewer is," he said. "If there are thirty million blacks I got at least half of them, so that's fifteen million. If you get fifteen million viewers, you can stay on TV."

The show's woes continued. In December, ABC announced it was taking *The Redd Foxx Comedy Hour* off its weekly schedule, but that the series would continue to air on a "semi-regular" basis for the rest of the season. That same month, Redd celebrated his fifty-fifth birthday in Hollywood, with a big bash at the Los Angeles Playboy Club hosted by Hugh Hefner. Raymond St. Jacques, Flip Wilson, Billy Eckstine, Smokey Robinson, Brock Peters, Pat Morita, and Shirley Jones all turned out for the shindig. Slappy White and Prince Spencer were there of course, as was Whitman Mayo, who'd filled in so admirably for Redd during his *Sanford and Son* contract squabbles and who was fresh from guest-starring on *The Sanford Arms*, NBC's short-lived (two months) answer to *Sanford and Son*. Redd and Joi sat at the head table with Hefner.

ABC officially pulled the plug on *The Redd Foxx Comedy Hour* in February. Eighteen out of the twenty-one shows the network ordered had been completed (seventeen had aired). ABC officials said their decision to cancel the show was reached by mutual consent with Redd. Both sides agreed his time would be better spent working on a series pilot for the network's fall schedule, possibly produced by Einstein and Blye.

The decision to cancel *The Redd Foxx Comedy Hour* was bittersweet for network president Fred Silverman. He'd hired Redd away from NBC and made him the highest-paid star on television, with the intention of destroying *Sanford and Son* once and for all. Mission accomplished. He also thought that, in Redd Foxx, he was getting a proven television star who could draw a sizeable audience. That didn't quite work out as planned.

"They mounted a good show but, ultimately, a variety show like that, which is a star-dominated show, depends on the appeal of the star," Silverman said. "And Redd Foxx on ABC just wasn't strong enough. Maybe had he done that show on NBC or CBS it would have been a different situation. The people who tuned in to ABC were used to a certain kind of show. That was the network of *Donny & Marie* and *Starsky* and *Hutch* and *Charlie's Angels* and *Happy Days* and *Three's Company*. Redd Foxx just didn't fit." Sy Amlen, vice president of ABC Entertainment, had a simpler explanation for Redd's failure: "To most viewers, Redd Foxx is Fred Sanford. The moment you take him out of that role it's like Superman encountering Krypton—he loses his strength."

If there were any good feelings left between Redd and ABC in the wake of the show's cancellation, those slowly evaporated over the following months. Redd still had over a year to go on his ABC contract, and with the network paying him $5 million a year, it wasn't about to let him just walk away from his deal. He might not have his show anymore, but ABC would be sure to keep him working, while waiting for the sitcom he was supposedly developing for them. In April 1978, two months after *The Redd Foxx Comedy Hour*'s cancellation, Redd hosted *The Redd Foxx Special*, which ABC aired in late-night (Redd's guests included Slappy White, Red Buttons, Lorne Greene, and Rip Taylor). In July, Redd appeared as a guest on *The Krofft Comedy Hour*, a summer replacement show on ABC.

But there was still no sign of the pilot on which Redd was supposed to be working, and in September 1978, ABC sued its erstwhile star for $5 million in Los Angeles Superior Court for failing to deliver the promised project. The network was also seeking an injunction barring

Redd from working for anyone other than ABC, saying that it advanced $250,000 to Eff-Oh-Ex-Ex Productions, Redd Foxx Productions, and Redd Foxx Enterprises to produce *The Redd Foxx Comedy Pilot* by April 3, 1978. The pilot was never shot. ABC alleged that it suffered $350,000 in damages; it also added another $60,000 to the lawsuit to recoup its losses based on Redd's failure to deliver the George Kirby pilot, *Big George Diamond*.

Redd fired back at ABC, charging that the network didn't promote *The Redd Foxx Comedy Hour* or advertise it in the black press (a strange allegation, since both *Jet* and *Ebony* magazines devoted several big articles to the show). He asked PUSH president Jesse Jackson to serve as a mediator in the lawsuit. Jackson agreed to get involved, and after he met with George Reeves, the network's senior vice president of entertainment, ABC agreed to drop its lawsuit. It still held out a slim hope that Redd would eventually deliver a sitcom pilot before his contract was due to expire the following September.

"Redd has been protesting against roles that could be perceived as degrading to black people, and using a stereotyped kind of black woman," Jackson said. "He simply wanted to move on to another level of presentation. There appeared to be some resistance to that. He was concerned that he, as the producer, was fundamentally determining the punch lines, the content, and the conception of the program. So now what they [ABC] have done is given Redd absolute free rein to produce the show and to determine who his producers and writers will be. He was told only to operate within the budget and he has agreed to do that." Reeves put it more bluntly after his meeting with Jackson: "We agreed in principle that Redd would come back to work for ABC and do his pilot that we have agreed to under his contract and always wanted him to do."

With his television career on hold for now, Redd returned to what he did best—his live standup act. He was back on NBC briefly in the spring as a guest on *Happy Birthday, Bob*, which feted comedian Bob Hope on his seventy-fifth birthday. In March, Redd opened at the Silverbird Hotel and Casino in Las Vegas (formerly the Thunderbird Hotel), where he had a scary moment when an over-enthusiastic fan rushed the stage and lunged at Redd while reaching for something in his jacket. Redd had his back to the man, but heard the commotion and quickly grabbed a heavy metal cup that was nearby, swung around, and crowned the guy with a roundhouse punch, knocking him to the floor. The unidentified man, who was drunk and (it was later discovered) had no weapon, was never charged, and Redd continued with his show. "I'm not going to be another Martin Luther King Jr.," he said afterward. "I'll strike first." While his stint at the Silverbird got off to an inauspicious start, Redd liked the hotel, and agreed to let the fledgling cable network HBO tape his act there for *On Location: Redd Foxx*, which aired in late 1978.

But Redd Foxx was never far from trouble or lawsuits, and his past track record proved no different once he began his run at the Silverbird Hotel. He was accused of verbally harassing a very young waitress in the hotel's coffee shop, and narrowly avoided having the daylights beaten out of him by the young girl's enraged father. A lawsuit followed shortly thereafter.

"The father was going to head down to the Silverbird Hotel to beat the crap out of Redd Foxx, who always had bodyguards around him, so I knew it wasn't a good idea," said Al Marquis, the attorney hired by the young woman's family. "The only way I could talk [the father] out of going was to agree to file a lawsuit." The family alleged that the young woman, named Cheryl, was working at the Silverbird's restaurant one Sunday morning when she heard someone calling her name. Marquis said that's when the trouble started. "And there's Redd Foxx sitting there and he says, 'What's your name? Cheryl? Is that like Cherry? If I had that name I'd never go hungry.' She goes over to the side station to deliver some dishes and as she walked by him he grabs her arm and says, 'This is the one I want.'

"She said, 'I don't like the way you spoke to me. It's not appropriate.' He said, 'What's with you, you fucking bitch? Why are you all high and mighty?' At that stage he gets really angry and proceeds to do his X-rated show in front of her and all the customers, calling her a 'fucking bitch' and 'fucking cunt' and 'you oughta go fuck yourself because no one else will.'

"When he kept it up she had to run from the restaurant, crying, and that's why her dad was so mad. We filed a lawsuit for intentional, emotional distress. It turned out that after this event Cheryl was afraid to go to work, was afraid Redd Foxx would walk in again. Some of the other black employees thought she had done something bad, that she did something to incite [Redd]. She was afraid to stay home alone at night."

The case ended up going to trial. According to Marquis, Redd's attorney, and the judge hearing the case, were "old hunting buddies." Redd denied everything and said it was the young girl who'd yelled at him. The judge eventually threw the case out. "He said using the word 'cherry' could be used as a compliment," Marquis said. The case dragged on for another five years, and when Marquis eventually won his appeal, and a re-trial was scheduled, Redd settled with the family out of court for $25,000. "Right about then Redd was in financial trouble and living in Vegas," Marquis said. "I think he paid it out of his pocket."

In July, after his initial run at the Silverbird, Redd opened for a limited run in New York at Lincoln Center's Avery Fisher Hall, backed by singer Jean Carn. He then announced plans to produce a stage revue at the Silverbird called "Red, Hot & Foxxy," which premiered that fall. Della Reese, who was signed to a three-week deal at $21,000 per week, headlined the show's opening night, which featured a variety of acts including Leroy "Sloppy" Daniels, the Nicholas Brothers (Harold and Fayard), impressionist Johnny Dark, and a bevy of topless showgirls. Gerald Wilson, Redd's musical director on *The Redd Foxx Comedy Hour*, reprised that role at the Silverbird. Opening night was a big enough deal to draw LaWanda Page, *Good Times* star Esther Rolle, Gladys Knight, and Redd's former manager, Bardu Ali. Redd didn't appear in the show, but came up on stage after the finale to acknowledge the standing ovation.

But the good times didn't last long, and by late October, less than a month after it opened, "Red, Hot & Foxxy" was shut down after Redd got into a dispute with the Silverbird's new general manager, Obie Oberlander. To no one's surprise, the rift was over money. Redd locked horns with Oberlander, who closed the show after balking at Redd's demands that he be paid $75,000 a week to headline "Red, Hot & Foxxy" after Della Reese's three-week engagement ended. Oberlander thought Redd's salary demands were ludicrous; he was especially outraged since Redd only offered himself as a headliner after he failed to land an A-list act to replace Della Reese. The hotel, which was footing the cost of the show, was shelling out $65,000 per week in production costs alone—and another $10,000 per week to advertise "Red, Hot & Foxxy" on four (pink) billboards in Los Angeles and six billboards in Las Vegas. There was no way it could afford the $75,000-a-week Redd was demanding on top of all its other "Red, Hot & Foxxy" expenses.

"I'm making $30,000 for three shows, three nights," Redd said, referring to a separate deal he had to perform at the Silverbird. "They wanted me to do fifteen ['Red, Hot & Foxxy'] shows for $21,000. But it's horseshit. I just can't take somebody else's salary, hard as I've worked." Oberlander was angry enough to lock the members of the "Red, Hot & Foxxy" troupe out of their Silverbird hotel rooms. "I stuck with that hotel for two years, loaning them my name trying to help them out," Redd said. "And now that they've almost completed renovations they started all this stuff." The show never re-opened.

There was more trouble that summer when Redd flew to Bogue Chitto, Alabama to attend a music festival. It was part of a statewide "Redd Foxx Day" in his honor, but the celebration turned into a nightmare when stories began circulating that Joi Foxx was getting threatening phone calls in the couple's hotel room, and that Redd was being harassed by the local cops. "All kinds of things went wrong," said one eyewitness. "The limousine service wouldn't pick up LaWanda Page and Whitman Mayo from the airport; some of the luggage was stolen from the airport; the sound equipment wouldn't work; Redd's wife was getting threatening phone calls in the hotel." The final insult came when Redd, who was supposed to receive an award from Alabama Governor Fob James, got a phone call just five hours before the event and was told, "If you can't come now, forget it."

Redd and Joi celebrated their second anniversary in January 1979 with a bash at the Landmark Hotel and Casino in Las Vegas. "There were a lot of people who predicted that we wouldn't make it," Redd told the assembled guests. "The prophets of doom were wrong and tonight I am a very happy man." There was more good news when, shortly thereafter, Redd announced plans to star in his long-awaited ABC pilot.

It was called *My Buddy* and was written by *Sanford and Son* associate producer Norman Hopps (Redd was given an executive-producer credit). The plot revolved around Woodrow "Buddy" Johnson (Redd), a garrulous San Francisco bartender who owns Buddy's Bar, the popular local watering hole. One of Buddy's steadiest customers and closest friends is Mr. Worth, the billionaire owner of Worth Enterprises, who shared his deepest secrets with Buddy over the years, as customers sometimes do with their trusted bartender. When Mr. Worth dies suddenly, Buddy is invited to the reading of his will—only to learn that he's been made chairman of Worth Enterprises, much to the chagrin of Worth's sister, Catherine (Pamela Mason). Slappy White and Marvin Brody played Buddy's fellow bartenders.

In the midst of what seemed to be some positive vibes for a change, Redd found himself on the receiving end of yet another lawsuit. This one dated back to December 1976, when Haywood Jones, vice president of one of Redd's companies, DDER, accused his boss of pistol-whipping him and pulling a .22-caliber Derringer on him after a dispute over a check. Jones sued Redd for nearly $41,000 and Redd was served with papers on the set of *Sanford and Son* in February 1977. In the span of the nearly two years since then, Redd had asked for three continuances in the case, requesting four times that the case be dropped. All of his requests were denied. Redd then appealed the decision, but never paid any of the appellate fees, nor did his attorney request a transcript of the proceedings. Finally, in November 1978, his appeal was dismissed outright. But Redd wasn't through, yet. Five months later, he was requesting a fourth continuance and, by this time, Judge Ronald Swearinger had seen enough. He granted Haywood Jones his judgment against Redd, who was ordered to pay his former employee $40,600 in damages.

Then, in May of 1979—in the midst of taping the *My Buddy* pilot for ABC—Redd ran afoul of the Internal Revenue Service. The agency placed a lien on nearly $250,000 of Redd's assets, alleging that he'd never bothered to pay his 1977 income taxes. The IRS lien didn't come as a surprise; Redd had been battling the agency since at least 1977, when it first demanded he pay nearly $1.5 million in overdue income tax (plus interest and penalties). He ignored them. Around the same time, the state of California demanded that Redd cough up $700,000 in franchise taxes. He ignored them, too. He also ignored the various creditors who were lining up to collect payment in the neighborhood of nearly $900,000. It was only the start of a long and contentious relationship that lasted until Redd's death—and thereafter.

"He would file his returns but not include a payment," said Mark Risman, one of Redd's Las Vegas-based tax attorneys. "So it wasn't tax fraud, because he declared his income [but] he just never paid his taxes for what was close to a fifteen-year period. He was never in any criminal trouble because he filed." According to one of Redd's later accountants, Louis Pittman, Redd owed at least $300,000 to the IRS each year dating back to the early days of *Sanford and Son*. It wasn't that Redd was stupid and didn't know what he was getting himself into. He simply didn't give a shit, and had the same "fuck you" attitude toward the IRS that he had toward other symbols of authority.

"He certainly was aware of the problems and it just surprised me that he continued filing every year without doing anything about it," Risman said. "And I never got a straight answer out of him of why he didn't do something or what his involvement was." But he knew what he was doing. One day on the set of *The Redd Foxx Comedy Hour*, Redd was chatting with Bob Einstein. "He said to me that he won money in Vegas gambling, and bought two Mercedes for a fortune," Einstein recalled. "I said, 'Well, what did they take out in taxes?' He said, 'Fuck that.' You figure he must know something I don't know."

As his tax woes mounted, Redd cooked up what he figured was a surefire scheme to get the government off his back. In the summer and early fall of 1979, after being socked with yet another multi-million-dollar tax bill from the IRS, he embarked on a worldwide, USO-type tour of U.S. army bases and military facilities. "He decides that if he performs around the world at all the army bases and it costs them $50,000 for his performance, he can turn around and send the bill to the U.S. government and he'll be clean," said Redd's friend, Stuart Sheslow. "So Redd books a world tour and he plays everywhere, even Diego Garcia, and he sends the government a bill. He sends a bill like you would write on a piece of paper: 'You owe me $3 million. I owe you $3 million. We're even.' And the government writes back to him, 'Thank you so much for your service to your country, we're sure the troops enjoyed it, but you still owe us $3 million.' Redd went crazy. 'How could they do this to me!?' So he went around the world, charging everybody $50,000 and sends the government a bill. That's how he thought. He was not a brilliant businessman."

ABC aired the long-awaited Redd Foxx pilot, *My Buddy*, in July 1979, and the show sank without a trace. With Redd's ABC contract set to expire in September, ABC finally cut him lose, severing all ties with Redd and his various production companies. He was a free agent now, and was considering his options.

With the IRS still on his back, and no other television offers coming down the pike, NBC extended an olive branch to its former *Sanford and Son* star and offered Redd a guest-starring role on *Diff'rent Strokes*, a successful sitcom starring a heralded, ten-year-old actor named Gary Coleman as the younger of two orphaned black brothers from Harlem who are adopted by a wealthy, white Park Avenue businessman (played by Conrad Bain). Redd agreed to appear on the show in a two-part episode in which he would play a con man named Jethro Simpson, who was trying to wrangle legal custody of the two young boys. NBC executives talked about offering Redd a recurring role on the series if his guest-starring role was deemed successful. But they never got the chance to find out. Redd failed to show up for the taping of his *Diff'rent Strokes* episodes, claiming that he was ill. Lightning struck twice when NBC hurriedly called in Whitman Mayo, who'd replaced Redd during his prolonged contract squabble on *Sanford and Son*, as a last-minute replacement.

(Redd eventually made amends to the show in his own way, at least to *Diff'rent Strokes* co-star Todd Bridges. One day, he passed Bridges in the studio hallway and noticed Bridges holding a motorcycle helmet, a Christmas gift from the show's producers. When Redd asked Bridges what *else* he'd received for Christmas from the producers—figuring they'd also given him a motorcycle to go along with the helmet—he was pissed to find out Bridges had only gotten the helmet. "That's stupid," Redd hissed. A week later, he came back to the studio, pushing a gas-operated three-wheeled motorbike. "I bought you something," he said to Bridges.)

Redd's relationship with ABC wasn't the only short-term deal that ended for him that fall. In October 1979, Joi Foxx filed for divorce in Los Angeles after less than two years of marriage. She was asking for $5 million in the settlement and she wasn't taking anything for granted, hiring pit-bull attorney Marvin Mitchelson to represent her. (Mitchelson was famous for representing Michele Marvin in her "palimony" live-in lover case against actor Lee Marvin.) Joi claimed in her divorce petition that Redd hit her with a gun and refused to let her eat her native (Korean) food. "Shortly after we were married, he got mad and pointed a gun at me," she said. "Redd would argue with me and start slamming doors, yelling all the while, threatening me, grabbing me, even in front of guests." She said that, the previous August, she'd been sick for a few days and wanted to eat some Korean food—which triggered Redd's rage. "He refused to let me go to a friend's residence to eat," she said. "He started yelling at me and hit me over the left eye with his fist. I suffered a terrible headache."

"There was a little bit of activity on Redd's part, so [in addition] we asked for a restraining order so there wouldn't be any violence," Mitchelson said. "Actually, they both were beating on each other a little bit, I think." Joi was alleging $10 million in community property, including real estate, eight cars, and royalties and residuals from *Sanford and Son*. She was also asking for $20,000 a month in temporary alimony. "I got used to living in a certain style and must maintain my standard of living," she said. "Is that so unreasonable?" She also claimed that she'd caught Redd with another woman.

Redd then counter-sued for divorce in Las Vegas, listing "incompatibility" as the reason for the action and asking that the case be tried in Nevada. He claimed Joi set fire to their home in Las Vegas and that he had to report the incident to the police. Redd also said that Joi went to the home of a friend, Preston Hale, threw something through the window to get into the house and, once inside, shred some of his clothing—and then threatened to kill both Redd and Hale. A few months later, Redd was sounding a more contrite note. "Oh, I can't say anything against the woman. She's a great lady. It's just incompatibility. If I can give up neck bones and black-eyed peas, she can give up kim chee," he said, referring to the Korean dish of garlic, cabbage, and peppers. "See, I gave up neck bones and black-eyed peas for her because she couldn't cook them." The case dragged on for another two years.

Behind the scenes, Redd's career was about to take another unexpected turn.

chapter thirteen

"I'd Do Anything for Money"

In 1978, Fred Silverman, Redd's old boss at ABC, jumped to NBC to become the network's president and CEO, completing his triumvirate of having now worked at all three networks. Silverman's three-year run at ABC was rife with success, *The Redd Foxx Comedy Hour* notwithstanding, and in the incestuous world of television, he'd come full circle. In 1976, he'd lured Redd Foxx to ABC and brought NBC to its knees by finally plunging a dagger into the heart of *Sanford and Son*. Now, three years later, he was trying to save NBC, the very network he'd vanquished. And, once again, Redd Foxx figured into Silverman's equation.

But in the three years since Redd left NBC, his star had fallen dramatically. Silverman knew that, but figured that if he could re-capture just a bit of the old Redd Foxx magic, it would be a boon to NBC, which was in the doldrums and struggling for viewers. "It went from feast to famine," Silverman said. "At NBC, we desperately needed shows that got an audience. The hell with the demographics."

In the fall of 1979, while Redd was in the midst of his divorce battle with Joi, Silverman reached out to initiate a meeting. He was well aware of Redd's notoriety, and had only to look as far as his failure to show up for his guest-starring role on *Diff'rent Strokes* as proof that this tiger hadn't changed his stripes. But Silverman threw caution to the wind and figured it was worth the trouble returning "Fred Sanford" to his rightful place on television. And Redd needed the work. The divorce from Joi was bound to hit him hard in the pocketbook, and Redd figured he needed $100,000 a month just to keep going. The IRS, meanwhile, was still breathing down his neck and dunning half of his wages, and he had a prodigious cocaine habit and multiple hangers-on to support. He was still paying alimony to Betty Jeanne and owed thousands of dollars to the attorneys fighting his various lawsuits. His losses at keno, which he played constantly when he was in Las Vegas, exacerbated his financial abyss. "I'd do anything for money," he said. "And I always follow Fred Silverman around."

But Silverman wasn't only offering Redd the chance to return to NBC, to where it all started seven years earlier. With a new decade just around the corner, he was offering Redd Foxx a second chance at recapturing the old Fred Sanford magic, to bring the crusty Watts junk-man into the 1980s to a new generation of television viewers. Could Redd turn the television clock back to 1972?

The show was called *Sanford* and, in late December, NBC announced it had struck a deal with Redd to star in the series and reprise his role as Fred Sanford. This time around, though, he would get a significant raise to $75,000 per episode, with his salary rising to $100,000 a week if the show ran beyond its original thirteen-episode order. *Sanford* was set to premiere on NBC at the end of February 1980, and the similarities with *Sanford and Son* didn't end with the new show's shortened name. Although *Sanford* would air on Saturday night—unlike its predecessor's familiar Friday-night timeslot—gruff Fred Sanford (and his "bad heart") would still be living in the house at 9114 South Central in Watts. And Fred hadn't changed much in the three years since *Sanford and Son* left the airwaves. He was a little paunchier now, but still walked with his bow-legged gait, still had the scraggly gray beard and gray hair. There were other reminders of *Sanford and Son*, including the new show's theme music—once again composed by Quincy Jones—and its producers, Tandem Productions (though neither Bud Yorkin or Norman Lear were involved). Mort Lachman, who'd produced *All in the Family* for Tandem, would handle those chores on *Sanford*.

But there were also changes. Demond Wilson had moved on, and there would be no Lamont living with Fred (Lamont's absence was explained by his new job on the Alaskan pipeline). Fred's live-in companion at the junkyard was now Cal Pettie (Dennis Burkley), a bearded, burly, good-natured white Southern redneck who worked with Lamont on the pipeline. Sent by Lamont to check up on his "Pop" in Los Angeles, Cal ends up moving in with the crotchety junk dealer.

Fred also had a new love this time around. With Donna ("The Barracuda") apparently a distant memory, Fred now focused his affections on Evelyn Lewis, a wealthy and refined Beverly Hills widow who, for some reason, returns Fred's affections and finds him irresistible. *Sanford's* humor was built around Fred's interactions with Cal, and the opposites-attract, fish-out-of-water humor of Fred's life with Evelyn in Beverly Hills. Marguerite Ray, who played Evelyn, knew Redd slightly after appearing in two episodes of *Sanford and Son*. She won the job only after Redd approved of her (many actresses competed for the role). "Mort [Lachman] told me that the concept they wanted for the show was something like [comic strip characters] 'Maggie and Jiggs,' a blousy, fat lady who dominated the man and stuff, and they were really at odds with Redd about that," said Ray. "Redd had a totally different concept for Evelyn, and he told them he would walk unless they went with his concept, which was me. He had a concept about women and he was very particular about ladies. He wanted ladies around him."

The *Sanford* cast included former *Sanford and Son* semi-regular Nathaniel Taylor, who returned as Lamont's cool-cat friend Rollo, who was now working for Fred. Percy Rodriguez and Suzanne Stone played Evelyn's (snobby) brother and daughter, respectively, while Cathy Cooper was hired to play the Aunt Esther-ish role of Clara, Evelyn's no-nonsense maid who tangled with Fred.

Redd, as was his wont with strangers, treated his new co-star Dennis Burkley a bit coolly upon their first meeting; their rapport, and trust, deepened after a few drinks in Burkley's dressing room. Burkley knew that he was hired, in part, due to his size (he weighed close to three-hundred pounds at the time), and he was still a bit sensitive about his girth. But that didn't stop the *Sanford* writers from repeatedly using Cal's burliness as a punchline. "Basically the writers loved anything that was obvious, like a fat joke, that was easy for them, so there would be a lot of fat jokes in the script," Burkley said. "After Redd and I got to be closer, basically he just said to me, 'If there's something you don't like, just let me know and it won't be in there.' So if there was a joke, a bad joke, he would look over at me and kind of raise his eyebrows, like he wasn't crazy about it and how did I feel about it? And if I just went, you know—the slightest shake of the head 'no'—it was gone. He would say, 'I don't want to say that about him' and it was gone. Because he had the ultimate power on those scripts."

Redd's behavior on the *Sanford* set was no different than it had been during his first stint at NBC. "When I was offered the show, I said to the producer, 'I hear Redd has a cocaine problem.' And he said, 'He doesn't have a problem, he does coke and he shares.' And I thought, 'Okay, that's more information than I needed,'" said Burkley. "But really, honest to God, I don't think it ever affected his work at all. It would be like you or I taking an aspirin to keep our heart going." One day, during a rehearsal, Redd appeared on the set with white powder all over his face. "He looked like Al Jolson," Burkley said.

Redd's cocaine use was the rule rather than the exception. Cocaine use in Hollywood at that time was rampant; it was an accepted part of the industry, with many people, both in front of and behind the cameras—including some network executives—partaking freely. Stuart Sheslow, who was an NBC executive at the time, remembered a square box, filled with cocaine, that was available to anyone on the *Sanford* set. "I wasn't a big fan of cocaine. It was certainly prevalent in the dressing room, which was ridiculous," he said. "Redd said, 'You white guys get high from it. I just level off so I can function.'" Dennis Burkley remembers NBC executives, looking to get high, "always asking me, you know, 'Where is the blow?' And I would say, 'I don't know what you're talking about,' because it was none of their damn business."

Redd snorted coke in his dressing room, where he was always surrounded by his close buddies and assorted hangers-on, and clowned around during rehearsals. But he was always prepared when it was show time. The great clowns always are. "Redd hated to rehearse. He was kind of lazy, for lack of a better term," Burkley said. "I don't think he liked to work except to do the show, and of course he knew that character pretty well, so he didn't have to rehearse five days a week. I thought, 'Well, this guy is very professional, he is not going to know what he's doing and when we do the show, I'll get the laughs because he didn't even know his lines.' And then, come Friday, he knew every bit of comedy that can be bled out of that script. It was like magic, like, where has this cat been all week?"

Sanford premiered on March 15, 1980, to mixed reviews and middling ratings. "Fred Sanford is back and you wonder why," opined the *Los Angeles Times*. "Redd Foxx's portrayal of the irascible, gravel-voiced junkman had worn so thin the last time out that tonight's debut of *Sanford* seems a bit too much, too soon. . . . *Sanford* rises and falls on Foxx and his bagful of one-liners, which hit about fifty percent of the time. His timing is impeccable. The material a good deal less so."

Holding court onstage at Redd's Place, 1967. (*AP/Wide World Photos*)

Redd visits *The Flip Wilson Show* (1970). Wilson (left) credited Redd with getting him his big break on *The Tonight Show*. (*Photofest*)

Wiley Harlem junkman Uncle Bud tries to pull a fast one on Calhoun (J.D. Cannon) in *Cotton Comes to Harlem*. (*Author's collection*)

The classic BBC sitcom *Steptoe and Son*, with Wilfrid Brambell (left) and Harry Corbett morphed into . . . (*Author's collection*)

. . . Sanford and Son, starring Redd and Demond Wilson. (*NBCU Photobank*)

Redd's sudden rise to fame opened many doors, including a 1972 USO tour of Vietnam with Bob Hope. (*Carl Villanueva*)

"Five across your lips!": Redd's childhood friend LaWanda Page found late-in-life fame as Fred's nemesis, Aunt Esther, on *Sanford and Son*. (*NBCU Photobank*)

Redd found work on *Sanford and Son* for many old friends and colleagues. Slappy White appeared in season one as Fred's pal Melvin. (*Photofest*)

March, 1974: During his walkout from *Sanford and Son*, Redd used this appearance on *The Mike Douglas Show* to go public with his grievances against NBC. (*Photofest*)

The Big One: Fred Sanford suffers one of his many "heart attacks" during a surprise visit from "The Horne" (Lena Horne). (*NBCU Photobank*)

Redd teamed with Pearl Bailey for the 1976 movie *Norman, Is That You?* They bickered constantly on the set. (*Author's collection*)

Fred Silverman and Redd cement the deal that brought TV's highest-paid star to ABC for *The Redd Foxx Comedy Hour*, which premiered in 1977 and quickly flamed out. (*Author's collection*)

Redd and third wife Yun Chi Chung (Joi) on their wedding day in Las Vegas, 1976. (*Globe Photos*)

NBC failed in its attempt to recapture the old magic with *Sanford*, starring Redd and Dennis Burkley (left). (*Photofest*)

In *The Redd Foxx Show*, which aired on ABC in 1986, Redd (here with guest star Vanessa Williams) played the owner of a New York City newsstand/restaurant. (*Author's collection*)

Redd and Della Reese teamed for *The Royal Family* on CBS. The sitcom was poised for success until Redd's death in October 1991. (*Author's collection*)

Most of the other television critics agreed, and *Sanford* didn't make much of a splash in the Nielsen ratings, though NBC was pleased enough with the show's numbers to give it a second-season renewal. "The show did reasonably well for NBC, and the two of them, Redd and Dennis Burkley, were very good," said Fred Silverman. "They had really good chemistry together, because you had Redd Foxx and this big redneck with a beard . . . and Dennis was a very skilled comedy actor."

The season finale of *Sanford* aired on May 31. Several weeks before, Redd's million-dollar home in Las Vegas was vandalized. The house was splashed with red paint, with the letters "KKK" and the words "Fuck You" scribbled on the outside walls, just hours after Redd's housekeeper called police to report a threatening phone call. Redd was shaken up. "They painted all over the yard and the walls and the house," he said. "They called my office here in Los Angeles and they called a few other places. They say they're going to kill me, that's what they say." Producers beefed up security on the set of *Sanford*, and "his entourage would go in and out and make him feel better," said Stuart Sheslow. Las Vegas police didn't have any suspects in the case, but Redd thought it might have something to do with the 1978 incident at the Silverbird Hotel, when he was accused of sexually harassing a fifteen-year-old waitress in the hotel coffee shop. "I don't know if that was that, or the Ku Klux Klan wanting to kill me for cussin' this girl out or what," he said, referring to the 1978 incident.

Redd took the threat seriously, but was back on stage in Las Vegas after *Sanford* wrapped its season. He opened at the Landmark in June (in a show called "The Best of Burlesque") and, in July, returned to the Copacabana in New York for the first time in over a year, where he opened to good reviews. "Foxx is funny. He's more earnest and honest than he has been of late, and if he lacks Rodney Dangerfield's musical rhythms of comedy, he has a good head for what works," wrote the *New York Post*. "He can be racial (he dislikes his thin lips because 'I can barely taste barbecue') or racy."

He also took his commitment to his friends seriously, and in early July, Redd announced plans to stage a two-day telethon for his protégé Richard Pryor. A month before, Pryor was burned on over half his body, nearly killing himself, while freebasing cocaine in his house in Los Angeles. (It was initially believed that Pryor accidentally caused an explosion while freebasing; he later admitted to pouring cognac over himself and lighting himself on fire during a drug-induced psychosis.) Pryor required several expensive skin-graft operations. Redd hoped to raise $1 million to offset Pryor's medical costs, and said he had the support of Frank Sinatra, Sammy Davis Jr., and other celebrities. "We don't want Pryor to go into debt," Redd said, all-too-knowingly. "We think that with the pleasure he has brought to millions they will want to contribute to his welfare."

Redd went through the trouble of lining up a closed-circuit broadcast of the Richard Pryor Burn Foundation telethon, which originated in Los Angeles and was seen in several California cities and in Hartford, Connecticut. He also donated $13,000 worth of sound equipment. But there was trouble from the start.

The hastily organized telethon didn't turn out as planned—not a great shock, considering Redd was in charge of organizing the fundraiser. Originally scheduled to last two days, it aired for only ten hours and raised just $140,000, with Stevie Wonder donating a $10,000 harmonica and Muhammad Ali calling in several pledges (Pryor insisted the funds go to needy burn victims and to research). Doomed by a weak broadcast signal from KHOF in suburban Glendale, California, the telethon couldn't be seen in many sections of Los Angeles. Redd, who was billed as the telethon's organizer, never even bothered to show up for the broadcast, blaming a "bad back" for his absence, while Sammy Davis Jr., who was supposed to co-host, was also a no-show because he was performing in Indianapolis. He contributed two filmed appearances and was replaced by his wife, Altovise. Redd then scheduled a press conference the next day to discuss the telethon—and didn't show up for that, either. In typical Redd Foxx fashion, he was sued in Los Angeles Superior Court for $100,000 in damages for allegedly failing to pay Showtime Scenery, the company that provided the backdrops he ordered for the telethon.

Redd was also up to his old tricks once *Sanford* was renewed for its second season. He failed to show up for four rehearsals, which forced Tandem Productions chief Alan Horn to cancel the taping of an episode, hitting cast and crew members hard in their wallets (since they only got paid for the days they worked). His erratic behavior wasn't limited only to the *Sanford* set; he showed up forty-five minutes late for an appearance on *The Merv Griffin Show*, sending Griffin's production team scrambling to find a replacement in case he didn't show up (he eventually materialized).

NBC, meanwhile, decided to tweak *Sanford's* format for its upcoming second season. The network moved the show from Saturday to the old *Sanford and Son* timeslot on Friday night, and decided to downplay Fred's relationship with Evelyn, who now became a recurring character (they were supposed to get married the first season but never did). *Sanford* now turned its focus back to Fred's life at the junkyard at 9114 South Central. Old *Sanford and Son* stalwarts including LaWanda Page—who appeared in the two-part season opener as Aunt Esther—Don "Bubba" Bexley, and Whitman Mayo were brought in to guest-star in a stab at capturing some of the old magic.

An actor's strike that fall delayed *Sanford's* second-season premiere until January, and when the show finally aired, the format changes failed to generate much viewer interest. NBC officially cancelled *Sanford* on January 29, 1981, four episodes into its second season. The remaining episodes were aired that summer. "We never really had the quality of writers because NBC, at that point, was in third place," said Stuart Sheslow. "Redd and [Dennis] Burkley were hysterical . . . and they had a funny combination, but the show just wasn't up to their comedic talents."

Redd wasted no time hightailing it back to Las Vegas, opening at the Hacienda Hotel almost to the day that NBC announced the *Sanford* cancellation. There was talk that he and Demond Wilson would reunite on the big screen for a movie called *Slick*, in which they would play two generations of con men, but the project, supposedly to be produced by Roy Radin, never got off the ground. (Radin was murdered two years later.)

Meanwhile, there were the usual Redd Foxx money problems. In August 1981, a California attorney named David W. Williams Jr., who'd been hired by Redd on a retainer, pleaded no contest to ripping off over $20,000 from Redd and actor Mickey Rooney by forging their names on checks. Williams was accused of forging Rooney's signature on a $10,000 check, and of forging Redd and Prince Spencer's signatures on two blank Redd Foxx General Account checks, which Williams made out to himself for $5,000 each. He was also accused of intercepting a $1,100 check mailed to Redd and forging the star's signature. "Hell, I tried to help him. I knew about the trouble he was in with Mickey

Rooney and I thought this would be a way he could sort of redeem himself," Redd said. "You know, I think along the lines of helping my fellow man. I gave him a break, but he did me in. I think all that law he studied might have tangled up his brain."

The spring of 1981 also brought some more trouble from Taft, the all-black town in Oklahoma that Redd "adopted" in 1974. In April, the town's mayor, Lelia Foley Davis, publicly blasted her association with Redd as "a bad dream," saying that the two Plymouth police cars Redd donated to the town in 1975 never worked properly, and were now "rat-infested eyesores" that sat behind city hall, hadn't been used in three years and cost the city over $1,000 in repairs. "It's just created some bad memories for Taft," she said. "It has hurt us. He's not the police chief and never was." According to Davis, the town's relationship with Redd went downhill after it refused to change Taft's name to Reddfoxxville. "A black celebrity has made it to the top and tried to use a small black community with black people to get farther, and it just hurts me to think about it," she said.

Redd fired back, calling Davis a "lousy" mayor and saying he could do a better job of running the town. "I'd like to go down there and run the city," he said. "I'd be a better mayor—anyone would. She is undoubtedly one of the worst persons to represent that town. Everything she said is stupidity." Redd claimed that he owed the city nothing—and had, in fact, not only donated the two police cars, but also a fifteen-seat van to transport the city's elderly people around town. "She's the mayor, and a good mayor would keep the cars running," he said. The Plymouth police cars were later sold for $115 to a local garage owner.

The divorce from Joi, meanwhile, was still dragging on in the courts, nearly two years later. While dealing with the David Williams Jr. forgery case, Redd asked the Las Vegas District Court to terminate his $2,500 monthly payments to Joi, saying he couldn't afford them and contending that Joi should be working and supporting herself. Joi maintained she needed the monthly payments to "maintain my standard of living," and Redd's request was tossed out when he failed to submit a financial statement. Finally, in September 1981, the divorce was finalized. Redd agreed to pay Joi off with a lump sum of $300,000. He kept one of his two houses in Las Vegas and his houses in Los Angeles and Saint Louis.

Redd's legal troubles continued into the New Year. In the spring of

1982, one of his former secretaries, Carol Whitsett, filed a $500,000 lawsuit, accusing Redd of sexually harassing her and, according to Whitsett, occasionally calling her into his office while he was naked. The story appeared in the *National Enquirer*, and Redd filed a countersuit, suing the magazine for $30 million for slander and libel and also naming Whitsett in the suit. Redd's countersuit was dismissed in Los Angeles Superior Court and he was given thirty days to amend the complaint and re-file. Redd's lawyer insisted he would file again on Redd's behalf and clear his client's name.

With no television prospects in sight, and no movie roles forthcoming, Redd hit the club circuit with abandon. In late July 1982, he opened for what was supposed to be a ten-day run at Dangerfield's, the surprisingly successful New York comedy club owned and operated by Redd's friend and fellow comic, Rodney Dangerfield. Always a flashy, "foxy" dresser, Redd wasn't about to let his money woes, lawsuits, and his ongoing battles with the IRS cramp his style. He performed on stage as he always did, the ever-present cigarette clenched between his teeth, his fingers adorned with huge diamond rings, his neck dripping with a cluster of gold chains. Sometimes he wore his special pair of pants embroidered with a gold, license-plate-sized Mercedes-Benz logo. Critics praised the Dangerfield's shows. "He both sustains and destroys stereotypes, but with the off-handedness of a grandparent tossing back a lifetime to a young pair of ears," wrote the *New York Post*, and Redd was held over at Dangerfield's another two weeks based on audience demand.

Offstage, though, he projected the image of a sad, lonely man searching for some elusive happiness that seemed just out of his grasp. A *New York Times* profile described him as "bitter about his career," bitter about being exploited by "unscrupulous" business associates—*and* bitter about being victimized by racism in Hollywood. "I've been cheated more than most people because I'm gullible and I'm a target," he said. "My heart is open, and I listen to people and I believe their sob stories." He described the industry's racism as "strong as the stench of a skunk's armpit" and said it had affected every facet of his life. "He is courteous, even courtly, but he seems depressed," the article noted. "Asked what he wants for the future, Mr. Foxx shrugs as if it didn't matter. 'Not too much,' he says. 'All you can gain is material things, and when you get to be sixty, material things don't mean so much; you don't have that long left to enjoy them. I'd just like some peace of mind.'"

When he was in Los Angeles, one of Redd's favorite haunts was the Laugh Factory, a comedy club that opened on the Sunset Strip in 1979. The club was run by Jamie Masada, an Iranian-born stand-up comic who came to the United States in 1977 at the age of fourteen and opened the Laugh Factory two years later after borrowing $10,000 from screenwriter Neal Israel. Richard Pryor inaugurated the club in 1979, and Redd would often hang out there with Pryor and writer Paul Mooney—and sometimes get up on stage to perform a set.

"He came in one night and he was a little bit stoned, and he started talking to this lady [while he was onstage]," Masada recalled. "Her breasts were big and unusual breasts, to put it nicely, you know, a lot of plastic surgery, and Redd started joking around about it and he told me to bring him a drink. So I brought him a drink and he said, 'Hey, Hymie,' he called me Hymie, 'how do you jerk off in your country? Do you jerk off like this or like this?' and he actually unzipped himself on the stage and he actually started jerking off. It was amazing. The people were laughing and enjoying it . . . and he did it for a while. And the girl was kind of playful and she actually started joking around and said, 'I bet you can't shoot all the way here' and she was showing him her breasts. And he said, 'I could shoot across the room.' The conversation was pretty raunchy. All kinds of crazy stuff like that."

Redd turned sixty on December 9, 1982, and three months later he filed for bankruptcy in Nevada, citing $1.6 million he owed the IRS from taxes before 1983 and more than $800,000 he owed to other creditors. At the same time, the state of California, after examining his tax returns for the previous ten years, determined that Redd owed the state $400,000. His financial planner, Dempsey Mork, said Redd did, in fact, pay his California income taxes, but only on his earnings in the state—and not on his earnings from Nevada and elsewhere. "Redd didn't like to file tax returns," said Paul Whitford, who became Redd's attorney in late 1982, and remained part of his inner circle until Redd's death. "I filed many returns for him, delinquent, after the IRS insisted on it. He filed delinquent returns so there were huge penalties in interest. He had a sort of resentfulness of authority. He never paid anything."

Soon thereafter it was determined that Redd also owed $600,000 in alimony payments, and before long the IRS had placed a lien on his house in Las Vegas. Redd Foxx Enterprises, and its many offshoot companies, had long since ceased to exist, and Redd's "staff" now consisted mainly of his manager/Guy Friday Prince Spencer, who handled everything from his boss's dry cleaning to paying the bills to arranging deals.

There was one positive note in Redd's bankruptcy filing—the dismissal of Carol Whitsett's sexual harassment case against her former boss. "I went to state court with him that day and I informed the judge that Redd was in Chapter 11 and there was an automatic stay," Whitford said. "The judge said, 'This is dismissed' and that was the end of it."

The spring of 1983 brought more bad news, the type which could only happen in the strange world of Redd Foxx. First, a driver lost control of his car and plowed through an eight-foot-high brick wall at Redd's house. The car ended up in Redd's bedroom. Then, in March, Redd's house in Las Vegas was robbed by three men who tied up a guest, John Reid, ransacked the place, and stole valuables worth an estimated $200,000. "They stole guns, antique swords, and Foxx's stereo system," Reid said. "They were looking for his jewelry."

But despite his financial and legal woes, Redd continued to draw big audiences in the clubs. He returned to Dangerfield's several more times—in January and October 1984—and then inked a deal to headline at the Sahara Hotel in Las Vegas for a six-week run. He was still big enough to merit a short profile in *Newsweek*, which used his success at Dangerfield's as a jumping-off point to take a look back at Redd's long career and rehash some of his more memorable stand-up lines. (On cheating: "Show me a husband who won't and I'll show you a neighbor who will"; on flatulence: "The Lord put a smell in it so the deaf could enjoy it.")

The demise of *Sanford* in 1981 signaled a shift in Redd's career, but his absence from television, and from the movies, was more a product of Redd's stubbornness than a lack of interest on the part of Hollywood. He was offered several projects in the mid-1980s that, for a variety of reasons, never worked out.

"We used to get calls, probably about a dozen over the years, from *Saturday Night Live*. They wanted Redd to host," said Paul Whitford. "But they didn't pay much for their host—I think it was like $5,000—and even though it was such an honor to be on that show, Redd wouldn't do it. He wasn't going to spend a week of his life for $5,000."

In 1985, Redd and Whitford were approached by movie producer

Harold Hecht, who was interested in having Redd star in an all-black remake of the 1967 movie *Guess Who's Coming to Dinner?*, which starred Spencer Tracy, Katharine Hepburn, and Sidney Poitier. Redd and Whitford met with Hecht, and Redd seemed interested, but he made a prescient prediction. "When Harold Hecht left, Redd said, 'That man is not gonna make that movie. He's dying.' And Hecht died about a month later," Whitford said. "That was an interesting bit of observation for Redd."

Around that same time, Redd and Whitford also met with director Ron Howard and producers Richard and Lily Zanuck, who were casting their new movie, *Cocoon*. "We went out there and met them, and then got a call from the casting agent, saying that the script had been re-written and that the African American character was minor," Whitford said. "And they didn't think Redd would want to do it and they couldn't pay him enough." They were right. Redd passed. *Cocoon*, meanwhile, went on to gross over eighty-five million dollars and spawned a 1988 sequel.

And there were television executives who were still convinced, even at this stage of his career—even with all the past contract nonsense, the high-maintenance drama, three cancelled shows, and one failed pilot—that Redd Foxx could still be a viable draw on television. They figured that Redd Foxx, even at half-speed, was still better—and still funnier—than nearly any other performer around.

In 1980, Redd returned to NBC to resurrect Fred Sanford for a third-place network; now, five years later, he was about to return to ABC—the scene of *The Redd Foxx Comedy Hour*. The network now found itself mired in third place and about to be taken over by Capital Cities Communications, which bought the struggling ABC for $3.5 billion in March 1985.

Redd's new series would be produced by Lorimar Productions under the watchful eye of Stuart Sheslow, who'd worked with Redd at NBC on *Sanford* before leaving for Lorimar. Sheslow was eager to be in business with Redd for a second time, and reached out to him in the summer and early fall of 1985 to see about making a deal for a new television show.

"I wanted to do something with Redd again and I started corresponding with him and he made like, 'Oh, I don't know who-the-hell you are' and I finally said, 'I'm coming to Vegas,'" Sheslow said. A meeting was arranged to discuss some possible ideas for the new series. Redd was legendary for his business meetings—when he bothered to show up for them—and one never knew exactly *what* to expect when finally meeting Redd in person. It was often a surreal experience, like Bob Einstein's meeting with Redd years before, when he'd watched on security cameras as Redd's dogs chased Slappy White into the swimming pool. And Sheslow's first meeting with Redd wasn't lacking in entertainment value.

"I went to his house and I'm sitting in the waiting room and it's all mirrors," he said. "The walls are mirrors, the table was a mirror and all of a sudden a mirror opens and a head pops out, I think it was Prince Spencer, and he says, 'Redd will be right with you' and the mirror closes. I'm thinking, this must be *Laugh-In*, I'm on a show. So the wall opens up, Redd escorts me in and I sit there with him and we're talking and he's smoking one cigarette after another. I tell him that we want to bring him back and want to do a half-hour comedy and all he was concerned about was, 'How much am I going to get paid?'"

Redd wanted $50,000 per episode. The executives at Lorimar were only willing to go as high as $35,000 per episode. "I won't be their nigger for $35,000 a week," Redd told a friend. After much back-and-forth negotiating, Sheslow got Lorimar to agree to Redd's $50,000 asking price, and then took the Redd Foxx series idea to his mentor, Brandon Tartikoff, president of programming at NBC.

"He loved Redd, he really did," Sheslow said. "He loved people who make you laugh." Tartikoff told Sheslow he envisioned Redd's new show airing behind *The Cosby Show*, one of the top-rated series on television in only its second season. But, in the meantime, Lorimar president Lee Rich had wangled a thirteen-episode commitment from ABC for Redd's still-unnamed show. "He was the boss and he took the ABC deal," Sheslow said of Rich.

ABC made the deal official in mid-December 1985, announcing that Redd would headline *The Redd Foxx Show*, a new midseason sitcom in which he would play Al Hughes, the curmudgeonly (what else?) "off-kilter but lovable" proprietor of a New York City coffee shop/newsstand who takes in a wayward, streetwise (white) waif named Toni, who would be played by nineteen-year-old actress Pamela Adlon. "The show mixes the relationships [Al] has with his regulars and the sharp humor of Foxx," ABC proclaimed in a press release trumpeting its new show, scheduled to air Saturdays at 8:00 p.m., leading into Robert Guillaume's sitcom, *Benson*. Actor Kevin Hooks joined Redd on ABC's midseason schedule, headlining the Friday-night sitcom, *He's the Mayor*, about a college graduate who's elected the mayor of his hometown.

To create *The Redd Foxx Show*, ABC brought in Rick Kellard and Bob Comfort, a writing-producing team who had a deal with Lorimar. Kellard would co-produce Redd's new show with Sheslow. "They still wanted to do a family thing and they wanted Redd Foxx because Bill Cosby was rocking on NBC," Kellard said. "And they thought, 'Hey, let's get Redd Foxx, if we can get him in a situation where he can be funny and not be Fred Sanford.' And he didn't want to be Sanford again, either. So we met with Redd and we started designing the show."

Redd was wary, at first, of his new production team, but eventually let his guard down a bit once he met Kellard and Comfort and they hashed over some ideas. "Redd's a guy who has to trust you. I mean, a lot of times you think he's okay and he's not," Kellard said. "He's also—through his own kind of self-destructive aspects—caused himself a lot of problems. [But] he liked what we did and I also think at the time he needed the money. He was supporting a lot of people. And he was not a stranger to being in tax trouble."

If ABC wanted a piece of the same vibe that Bill Cosby was "rocking" on NBC, they knew that Redd's on-screen demeanor would have to be softened. Cosby's character, Dr. Cliff Huxtable, was a gentle, fatherly soul with a wry sense of humor; Kellard and Comfort would have to find the right balance of curmudgeon and caring for Redd's new character, Al Hughes. "We put together the show of a guy who kind of runs this little newsstand and coffee shop in New York and mentors kids," Kellard said. "So I think that was a stretch for Redd, because he was an adult comic. It was tough, because you had to try to capture Redd Foxx, and what made Redd Foxx likeable to the audience was his edge and his cantankerous nature.

"But [we] also [had] to bring in sort of a gentler comedy with the kid. So we decided to let him be cantankerous with the kid and we tried to be as edgy as we possibly could, given the fact it was on at eight o'clock. So working that out was kind of a puzzle, but we finally got the right sort of mix, the right percentage of 'Redd' and 'gentle.' He'd surprise you— Redd was actually brilliant, a very brilliant comic, and he was a gifted actor."

The role of the wayward teen who was taken in by Al was originally written for a male actor. Pamela Adlon, who'd played several tomboy roles, including a guest-starring role on NBC's *Night Court*, auditioned for the role in drag. "I went into the first audition as Paul Segal, and I had an Ace bandage on my chest and I was in full drag all the way up to the network," Adlon recalled. "In my second meeting, I went in and met Redd and he said, 'I always knew. I know women. I knew you was a girl!' Then when I went to the network, it was me and like four or five guys [up for the role] and I kind of sequestered myself away so they wouldn't figure it out. They were like, 'This is Paul Segal' and I was like, 'Hey!'" Once Adlon won the part her secret was revealed, and the role was re-written as Toni. Rounding out the cast were Rosana DeSoto as Al's co-worker, Diana; Barry Van Dyke as Sgt. Dwight Stryker, a cop; and Redd's old *Sanford and Son* cast mate Nathaniel Taylor as Jim-Jam, who owned a competing newsstand.

To help with the show, Stuart Sheslow also brought in an old friend, Anthony Major, who would become one of the primary figures in Redd's life for the next five years. Sheslow and Major knew each other from their days as graduate students at New York University; they'd promised each other that whoever "made it" first in Hollywood would bring the other guy out to join him. Sheslow held firm to the promise, and in the fall of 1985, he called Major with an offer to come work on *The Redd Foxx Show*, as either a director or an assistant producer. Major, who'd co-written and directed the 1975 blaxploitation spoof, *Super Spook*, knew Redd only in passing. Years before, when Major owned a record shop in New York City, he was introduced to Redd Foxx by old-time comedian Pop Foster, who claimed to have helped Redd and Flip Wilson hone their comedy chops.

By the time Major arrived in Los Angeles, Redd was busy shooting the pilot for *The Redd Foxx Show*. "My first encounter with Redd was, he was standing on the set one day and he said he wanted some coffee," Major said. "There were no production assistants around, so as the assistant producer on the show, I said, 'I'll go get it for you. How do you like it?' And he said, 'Make it the color of Lena Horne.' He loved her. So here I go off to the craft service table to get Redd some coffee and he told me to bring the sugar on the side. And I'm there mixing in the powder to lighten the coffee up and I'm saying, 'Is Lena this dark? This light?' And he says, 'Oh, I think she's a little lighter than that,' so I went back and put a little more creamer in and stirred it up and took it to him. And he said, 'Perfect.'"

There was the usual backstage drama leading up to the premiere of *The Redd Foxx Show*, and just getting Redd onto the set to shoot the pilot turned into an ordeal. He'd learned, through the grapevine, that ABC was in the habit of giving Louis Vuitton luggage as gifts to the stars of its pilots. Where was his Louis Vuitton luggage? It was a reasonable question that no one could answer and, on the day the pilot was scheduled to shoot, he refused to come out of his dressing room until the luggage arrived. "I said, 'We better get him the Louis Vuitton luggage, because he's not coming out,'" Sheslow said. "And I knew when he said he wasn't going to do something, he wasn't going to do it." Sheslow's wife had connections to a local store that, despite being closed because it was Sunday, opened its doors so the Louis Vuitton luggage could be purchased. "I put a bag every three feet, leading out of his dressing room, onto the stage so he could pick it up like a little boy picking up sugar, to get him to the set," Sheslow said. "'No motherfucker is gonna get Louis Vuitton luggage unless I get it!' Other people got it, he was going to get it. That was Redd."

Rick Kellard remembers the incident a little differently. Redd, he said, demanded the Louis Vuitton luggage because he wasn't being paid to tape promotional spots for *The Redd Foxx Show*. "And we had to get it for him, because he was in his trailer—and that means he ain't coming out," Kellard said. "With Redd, it was just something every day. He'd either be hustling you for something or he wasn't going to show up, but at the end of the week, all I can tell you is, he hit that stage and he was funny as hell."

The Redd Foxx Show debuted on January 18, 1986, a week later than originally scheduled (after Redd and Pamela Adlon missed a week of work battling the flu). The ratings were decent, but critical reaction was mixed. "You've got to like cantankerous to enjoy *The Redd Foxx Show*. That's what Foxx plays," wrote the *Los Angeles Times*. "It worked well enough in *Sanford and Son*, but in his new ABC comedy series . . . it doesn't jibe with the premise."

Stan Lathan, who'd directed several *Sanford and Son* episodes, was brought in to direct *The Redd Foxx Show*, and noticed some marked changes in Redd's physical appearance. "I noticed that he seemed to have aged a lot," Lathan said. "I remember feeling he had kind of lost a certain bounce in his step. I mean that metaphorically—he seemed tired, he seemed like . . . he really wore himself down. Maybe it had a lot to do with [drug] abuse, but he'd been through a lot of stuff with his ex-wife and all kinds of financial challenges. His star was not as bright in the sky as it had been."

Several episodes into the run of *The Redd Foxx Show*, ABC and the show's producers decided to drop Pamela Adlon's character, Toni, who didn't seem to fit into the show's emotional framework. "The show goes on the air and the first week, huge numbers," Sheslow said. "And I'm saying, 'Well, people love Redd.' No doubt about it. And then the show goes on the second week and it takes a nosedive. And I'm sitting in my office and I realize, right star, wrong show. They don't like the little girl. The audience is uncomfortable with Redd and her because in all of his other shows, he's always interacted with adults."

Redd was also uncomfortable with the relationship between his character, Al Hughes, and the white runaway, Toni. And he let the producers know in no uncertain terms. "I remember we did a scene in the bedroom, where she came out . . . she had some emotional problem and she came up to talk to Redd. And you could see Redd didn't want to do the scene," said Rick Kellard. "I said, 'Redd, you gotta get into it, you gotta listen, she's talking to you, she's opening up her heart and you're her mentor.' He said, 'Listen, Ricky, look at the picture here. I'm an old black guy and I got a white chick, a white kid, sitting on my bed.' And he was totally right. And I would imagine that to some sections of this country, possibly all [of the country], that's a disturbing shot. So he was very sensitive to that and he was actually smarter than we were about it."

Redd also wasn't comfortable with the fact that Al and Toni's bedrooms were both on the second floor. "And he didn't want the public to think that this old man is upstairs with this young girl," said Anthony Major. "So now they had to redo the set and change the script so that her bedroom was down in the back of the store. The other problem with the show was that America wanted to see Redd as Fred Sanford, the cranky old man who called his son 'Big Dummy' and all that kind of stuff. He wouldn't do it with the girl. He said, 'I'm not going to speak to her that way—you don't speak to women that way and I'm not going to do it.' So of course the ratings suffered."

Adlon was let go, and ABC gave Sheslow and Kellard one week to re-cast the show and basically shoot an entirely new pilot. Toni was written out of the show with one line, with Al explaining that she was away at school. With Toni gone, two new characters, Al's ex-wife, Felicia, and his son, Byron, were added to the cast. "We were trying to find the wife, and a friend of mine, Barbara Montgomery, who ended up on *Amen*, came in and Stu [Sheslow] kind of hired her for the role of Felicia, but Redd said, 'No, I don't want her,'" Major said. "He was looking for somebody that looked like Phylicia Rashad, because of *The Cosby Show*. So then we had to call up every beautiful girl that we knew in Hollywood and get them in there, because Redd was due to start rehearsal that Sunday. He was trying to get another friend of his the part, but she couldn't act, so he worked with her and convinced Stu to let her have a last shot and she came in that day and was terrible."

Beverly Todd and Ursaline Bryant eventually competed for the role of Felicia. Redd preferred Bryant, and told producers he wanted "the one with the sweater" because she reminded him of his first wife, Evelyn Killibrew. The producers, though, misunderstood; they thought "the one with the sweater" was Beverly Todd, so when it came time for the table read, with both actresses sitting next to each other, Beverly was placed next to Redd as Al's wife. Redd balked, but by then it was too late; Todd had already signed her contract to play Felicia. To assuage Bryant, who only had one line in that episode, Sheslow told her that she would have a stronger presence on the show in later episodes and, sure enough, she was signed to play Felicia's best friend.

With Beverly Todd now hired to play Felicia, the producers brought in comedian Sinbad to play Al's son, Byron. Sinbad had been a contestant on *Star Search*, a syndicated television talent show hosted by Johnny Carson's *Tonight Show* sidekick, Ed McMahon (Sinbad beat Dennis Miller in head-to-head competition). He was originally hired to warm up *The Redd Foxx Show* audience before each taping began. Now, after some intensive work with Anthony Major, he was moved in front of the cameras in the reshuffle. "He was a standup comedian and couldn't really interact with people that well, so Stu told me to take him in the next room and work with him . . . and he ended up getting the part," Major said. Vanessa Williams, nearly two years removed from her Miss America controversy (she was forced to relinquish her crown after lesbian photos resurfaced), appeared in one episode as a waitress. Nathaniel Taylor, who played Al's friend, Jim-Jam, also left the show and was replaced by Theodore Wilson (playing the same character).

One of Redd's primary concerns on his television shows, dating back to *Sanford and Son*, was to make sure there were no negative stereotypes of African Americans. It was no different on *The Redd Foxx Show*, and he let the writers and producers know, in no uncertain terms, when he was unhappy with something he deemed offensive. One script, for instance, had a reference to a water-skiing raccoon. Redd objected to the word "raccoon." "He kind of sat there and schooled us about it," Kellard said. "He said, 'You don't understand what this means. Doesn't mean shit to you, but here's what this means in another universe, another world.' And at the end of the day . . . he was right."

Redd took the show's format change in stride, and tried to make the best of what appeared to be a losing proposition. One of the first episodes in which Sinbad appeared was built around a scene in the kitchen, with Al turning on a gas stove, which then explodes.

"Redd said, 'I want a blanket over here,' and he shows me right where the seats on the counter are," Sheslow said. "He said, 'Put a blanket over here. When that stove explodes, I'm going over the counter.' I said, 'You're *what?*' He said, 'Just put a camera over here.' I call the director, I said, 'Redd's going over the counter, make sure you have him on two cameras. We'll pick up Sinbad later.' The scene starts, Redd turns on the oven—explosion. Redd goes flying, and I mean *flying*, over the counter and lands on the ground as if he was shot out of a cannon. We had to stop tape. The laughter lasted five minutes until the audience calmed down. He wasn't going to let Sinbad get the laugh. That's Redd Foxx."

But all the hard work in retooling the show didn't make a difference. "They were trying to recreate *Sanford and Son* and it just wasn't working," Major said, "especially once we changed the format of the show." There were script problems—even former *Sanford and Son* writer Ilunga Adell was brought in to help out—and ABC didn't seem to know what type of show it wanted to put on the air.

"Sinbad was really good—you just knew this kid was going to be a star—and Redd was great, he was totally on-board with [the changes]," Sheslow said. "He never missed a beat. And the third show goes on the air and we get no promotion. None. If you ever wanted to talk about racism against a star or . . . a network that just didn't like the guy they had on the air, this was it. It was blatant. No matter who I spoke to to get [a promo] done, I couldn't get it done."

In a last-ditch effort to jack up the show's ratings, Sheslow and Kellard brought former *All in the Family* star Carroll O'Connor in to guest-star with Redd (and direct) an episode called "Old Buddies." But pairing two of the biggest sitcom stars of 1970s didn't move the needle. "They bounced us around, they changed our night, nobody can find the show and they successfully kill it," Sheslow said. In May, ABC announced it was canceling *The Redd Foxx Show*, along with *He's the Mayor*, *Hardcastle & McCormick*, *Ripley's Believe It or Not*, and *The Fall Guy*.

After *The Redd Foxx Show* was cancelled, Anthony Major went over to say hello to Redd, who, despite the tax troubles and the multiple lawsuits, still kept office space in the building on North La Brea. Redd offered him a job ("I guess he remembered that I got the coffee right!" he joked) and Major agreed to become the vice president of Redd Foxx Productions. "He fired everybody," Major said. "He cleaned house and the only people left were me, him, and Prince Spencer."

Redd was loyal to a fault, though, and there were some people he kept on the payroll, including Iron Jaw Wilson, who worked as a custodian and maintenance man in the building on North La Brea after retiring from show business. When Iron Jaw suffered a stroke in 1988, Redd started a trust fund for his old friend and eventually moved him to a nursing home in Las Vegas. "He put him on an airplane, paid all that money because he said Iron Jaw couldn't drive there, and the Medevac came and Redd flew him to Vegas and put him in a nursing home," Major said. "Redd didn't miss a week without going to see Iron Jaw. And he wouldn't work without Slappy opening the show for him. He just would not do a show without Slappy, unless they got mad at each other, which they did a couple of times."

Whenever Redd did a show in Las Vegas, he would always make sure that his aide-de-camp Prince Spencer, the onetime member of The Four Step Brothers, had his moment in the spotlight. Prince would introduce Redd (and Slappy) and, in the middle of the show, would perform a few dance numbers.

While Redd made a clean sweep of his production company, there were still the hangers-on who loitered around the building, looking for a handout, drugs, or anything else they could sponge. "When Redd didn't have work you didn't see anybody, but every time he would get work, people would show up," Major said. Redd would give odd jobs to Gene "Poo-Poo Man" Anderson, a struggling musician who ostensibly ran a recording studio downstairs but really only slept there. Redd would sometimes send Poo-Poo Man to a health food store for what, some suspected, was some kind of pill or powder that would cut the strength of Redd's cocaine.

On one occasion, Poo-Poo Man borrowed the company car to pick up some food for Redd—and disappeared for two weeks. "And it was okay," Major said. "Now he took Redd's car and Redd gave him the money. He comes back two weeks later with the food. We didn't know if Poo-Poo Man was in jail or what, 'cause he would sometimes call Redd collect from jail. And Redd would accept the calls. He felt sorry for him. Redd would always bail him out and let him come stay [in the building on La Brea]. Even when Redd would get mad with him and curse him out, he'd come back the next day and Redd would say, 'Yeah, okay. Take care of Poo-Poo Man.'"

Redd's mother, Mary Carson, now in her mid-eighties, lived just a short cab ride away from the building on North La Brea and continued to be a presence in her son's life—whether he welcomed it or not. "It was a cantankerous relationship, although I don't know if that's the correct word, because Redd could hate you and love you at the same time," Major said. Mary, who was a regular visitor to Redd's office, sometimes never got further than the lobby, where she would sit with Iron Jaw Wilson while Redd pretended to be too busy to see her. Or he would instruct his secretary, Marte Augustus, to tell Mary he wasn't in the office.

"He was definitely taking care of her in terms of making sure her rent was paid and making sure everything was paid for, but then she always wanted to come and get more money," Major said. But it wasn't just Mary who had her hand out. "People would just come out of the woodwork in terms of all these so-called 'friends' because they knew Redd had a soft heart and he would just give," Major said. "Now I wish he felt the same about his employees like myself and Prince Spencer, because there was no steady income. When he worked, we did okay—when he didn't work, the salary wasn't the same."

In the wake of *The Redd Foxx Show* cancellation, Redd did manage to keep busy with other projects—and with fending off yet more lawsuits. In June 1986, he was sued in Rochester, New York for the ridiculous amount of $1 billion, by Granite Ltd. and William Thompson Productions, who claimed Redd reneged on a deal to promote barbecue sauce and seasoning salt bearing his name. The breach-of-contract suit claimed that Redd never showed up for commercials and other promotional appearances, although he'd signed a contract in 1983 to do so. "Those guys were crooks," said Redd's attorney, Paul Whitford. "The problem I had was that Redd agreed to do this barbecue thing, then he calls me and says, 'I don't know why I agreed to it, get me out of it.' So I had to break the news to them and they were not happy. They were just trading on his name. They had one [barbecue] stand out in Tujunga; I drove out there to see it and it had Redd's name and picture. But we got this stopped."

Redd starred in a television commercial for Craftmatic Beds, and Stuart Sheslow hooked him up with the Miller Brewing Company, which hired Redd to host its first Miller Lite Comedy Search Contest. He didn't seem to be missing the daily grind of a television series. "He could sleep in his bed and get up and take a shower and get in his car and in ten minutes make a million dollars," Major said. "So going on television was hard work, to memorize a script, to be on the set, and carry a show. He could always go to Vegas anytime he wanted to . . . just show up and work in Vegas at either the Hacienda or the Sahara, because they were owned by the same guy."

But Redd was still a highly valued television commodity, even at this stage in the game and despite his post-*Sanford and Son* track record. In 1987, he was approached by Motown to replace comedian David Brenner as the host of *Night Life*, a syndicated, late-night half-hour talk show produced by Suzanne De Passe (who later bought Motown Productions). Redd was nervous about meeting the Motown bosses, and asked Stuart Sheslow to accompany him to the meeting. "He says, 'Just walk into the meeting with me, man, they'll think you're my lawyer,'" Sheslow said. "Redd says to me, 'You walk in first,' so I walk in and Redd follows me in and the guy from Motown says, 'You didn't have to bring your lawyer.'" Motown offered Redd $25,000 a week to take the show over from Brenner. Redd countered with $50,000 a week. "He doubled it immediately," Sheslow said. "But it was just another example of Redd being Redd."

The executives at Motown didn't balk at Redd's demands, and gave his management team—namely Anthony Major—a week to come up with a workable deal. "They wanted Redd to finish the season [of *Night Life*], and were going to pay him either $600,000 or $900,000," Major said. "But then they were going to spend a million dollars on the set and also give Redd a musical director . . . and he could pick the set, he could pick his director, he could pick whatever and he could put his group in the show, guys like Slappy White and Pat Morita and The Unknown Comic. And Redd said, 'Tony, go back and get me more,' so I went back and got more for him and I had gotten to where I had squeezed every ounce."

But Redd refused to budge unless he was given more money, and the negotiations with Motown broke down. The deal was never signed. "To this day I think that he knew it was a lot of work and responsibility and I don't know if he really wanted to take all that on," said Major. "Even for that money."

More to Redd's liking was a deal to co-star with Dick Van Dyke in a CBS television movie called *Ghost of a Chance*. In the movie, developed by Stuart Sheslow and written by Hank Bradford, Redd played Ivory Clay, a honky tonk jazz pianist accidentally shot and killed by a narcotics detective, Bill Nolan (Van Dyke). In a plot turn reminiscent of the movie *Heaven Can Wait*, Ivory, who wasn't supposed to die just yet, returns to earth—where only Nolan can see and hear him. "It would take a train wreck to make these two guys [Redd and Van Dyke] unfunny, and we found the train wreck," said Sheslow. "But Redd was really funny and Dick Van Dyke was terrific and the two of them on screen together was magic. But the director wouldn't have known a joke if it hit him on the head."

Redd and Dick Van Dyke got along famously during the shoot, and would come up with little bits of shtick here and there as the cameras were rolling. But the movie's director, Don Taylor—"a John Wayne type," Major said—didn't want his two stars to improvise. "He pissed both of them off and they stopped doing it altogether," Major said. "So finally Redd stopped learning his lines. And they had to send to Hollywood and bring in the guy with the [cue cards]. They wanted to get a teleprompter, and Redd refused. He said he wouldn't use it because it makes your eyes go up and down." Redd insisted the producers hire the cue-card man who'd worked on *Sanford and Son*, which they did in order to placate their star and finish the movie on time.

Off the set, Redd was having a good time. *Ghost of a Chance* was shot in Toronto, and Stuart Sheslow's hotel room was just down the hall from Redd's suite. Early one morning, around 3:15 a.m., Sheslow got a call from Prince Spencer. "He says, 'Oh, man, Foxx is hurt, you gotta come down here, man,'" Sheslow recalled. "I said, 'Foxx is hurt? It's three o'clock in the morning!' So as is my tradition, I'm thinking to myself, 'This is going to be really funny.' So I walk into Redd's room, and there's the head of security. There is a naked woman sitting in the corner, an Asian woman, dripping wet, with a towel around her. The only thing left is [for] a Barnum & Bailey clown to come out of the closet.

"I look into the bathroom, and there is Redd, sitting on the toilet, with a towel wrapped around him, smoking a cigarette. I start to laugh and I say to Redd, 'What's up?' He said, 'I hurt my back.' I said, 'What happened?' He said, 'I flew her in from Vegas. She's a beautiful babe, and I'm fucking her from the back, you know what I mean? And the shower is going and all of the sudden I feel this thing in my nose start moving. I can feel it moving but I don't want to stop, you know, I'm fucking her man, and I can feel this rock moving in my nose and all of a sudden I sneeze and this fucking rock of cocaine comes shootin' out of my nose and I can see it hit the tub and it starts getting near the drain and I try to stop it with my foot and I slip and fall on my ass.' He says, 'I can't work tomorrow.' I said, 'Don't worry, Redd, we'll shoot around you.' He says thanks and I go back to bed."

But despite all the women—and there were many—Redd never really got over the divorce from Joi. Even now, six years after their marriage was officially dissolved, they were still in touch with each other. In March 1985, Joi was one of the guests invited by Redd to a party in honor of his mother's eighty-second birthday. "Joi was the love of his life," Major said. "He was just in love with her and would go visit her, even though they were divorced. I remember one weekend it was her birthday, and he had me driving all over Los Angeles trying to find her a gardenia. She loved gardenias. I mean, I rode all over the place trying to find a white gardenia to take to her."

Even after their divorce, and all the courtroom drama, Redd was still helping Joi financially. He bankrolled his ex-wife's new restaurant in Los Angeles, which was located at the Corner of Pico and La Cienega, and named it Joi's Oriental Express. "I think whenever she needed anything Redd was there to provide for her," said Paul Whitford. "He cared very much for her. We went out to her restaurant one night and Redd was bending jokes, it was a wonderful night. It was in an area that has a very integrated population . . . and was in a corner shopping place

like we have thousands of out here. What amazed me was Redd's reputation. As we walked down the sidewalk, he was mobbed by the black
kids. It was good to see. This was before Eddie Murphy came to prominence, and Redd used to brag about being the number-one TV star."

The women who flocked to Redd didn't seem to care that he was
nearly sixty-five years old. And, as time went on, the groupies seemed to
get younger and younger. "They could have been his granddaughters.
They were always on his case and showing up," Major said. "I didn't
see any older women." One young woman even followed Redd all the
way from Los Angeles to New York, where he was preparing to open a
show. Major and Prince Spencer sent her away.

Despite his advancing years, Redd still lived his life like a man
half his age, refusing to make any concessions to age. He smoked the
occasional joint, and his daily cocaine habit was now more of mundane
routine than a thrilling high (the powder he snorted was diluted to
lessen its impact, according to many in his inner circle). Still, there were
the occasional gaffes when he got careless, when Tony Major or Prince
Spencer had to motion for him to brush some errant white powder off
his mustache at the start of a television or newspaper interview.

Ghost of a Chance aired on CBS on May 12, 1987, but no one seemed
to notice, except the critics. "Most of the humor is weak, and some is
painfully dated and insensitive," the *New York Post* opined. Redd was
non-plussed. He'd been paid for the job, which was almost as important
to him as the end product.

Besides, he was about to open a new show—on Broadway, no less.

chapter fourteen

"They've Taken Everything"

The closest Redd Foxx had ever come to performing on Broadway was in 1976, when he co-starred in *Norman, Is That You?*, which was based on a short-lived Broadway flop. Now, The Great White Way was beckoning, and this time it was the real deal—a legitimate run in a legitimate Broadway theater. Redd Foxx, thespian. It was a million miles and a lifetime away from telling jokes for twenty-five bucks a night at the Brass Rail.

The show was called *Redd Foxx and Friends* and was co-produced by Tony Major and Prince Spencer. In the late spring of 1987, Major and Spencer were approached by the Brandt Organization, which owned several theaters on Broadway. The manager of the organization was a big Redd Foxx fan, and he wanted Redd to perform his act, or some variation thereof, to help celebrate his upcoming fiftieth year in show business. "The guy really wanted Redd and he needed to make some money at the time and he had the theater available," said Major.

That was the easy part. But nothing in the world of Redd Foxx was ever easy. Something inevitably went wrong or took an unexpected detour, but it was never dull—especially when it was on the Broadway stage under the bright lights of New York City.

Redd's Broadway show was originally intended for a theater on Forty-second Street, but that particular venue was being renovated, and wouldn't be ready in time for the opening of *Redd Foxx and Friends*, which was scheduled for November. The show was moved to the Academy Theater on Forty-third Street, which was a bit off the beaten path, at least in its proximity to other Broadway theaters. The Academy had a checkered history and had been through several incarnations as the

Apollo, the New Apollo, and as a "grind house" showing movies twenty-four hours a day.

Anthony Major negotiated a six-week deal for Redd to headline *Redd Foxx and Friends*. The bill would also include Slappy White, LaWanda Page, and Prince Spencer (who'd do a bit of hoofing). "I'll talk about my young life in show business, about my three marriages, three divorces, two hundred shack-ups," Redd said. "I say in the show that when I went to Hollywood I left my first wife and my car in New York—because neither of them was working." He promised "a triple-X-rated show" with the usual Foxx bravado: "Now I'm on Broadway and I think I'm qualified, and I'll give the audiences what my fifty years have given me. If they wanna compare me with somebody else, they can't get more laughs than I do, I'll bet you that."

The show was beset by problems from the get-go. For starters, Redd and LaWanda Page were bickering with each other over how to open the show. For the first several performances, *Redd Foxx and Friends* began with Page coming out into the balcony, as Redd was onstage, and interrupting him as they launched into some back-and-forth, *Sanford and Son*-type banter. (Page: "Father Time's been kind to me." Redd: "Maybe so, but Mother Nature's been fuckin' you up!"). That was fine, but if anyone came late to the show they missed it—*and* Page, since that was the extent of her involvement.

Page then started pushing Redd to let her perform her stand-up routine, which, at times, surpassed Redd's material in terms of its blue overtones. "Redd said, 'What kind of jokes are you going to tell?' and she said, 'Well, I do my own act,' but he wouldn't put her on without hearing what she was going to say," Major said. "So we brought her up one night to Redd's suite and had her perform and tell jokes. So Redd said, 'No, I'm not going to embarrass myself,' because she was dirtier than he was. They would fuss back and forth, like, 'You tell her so-and-so' and then, 'You tell him so-and-so.'" The original opening stayed.

But it didn't make much of a difference. *Redd Foxx and Friends* opened on November 19, 1987, to wildly diverse reviews by those critics who even bothered to show up. "The entertainment world of Las Vegas is so far removed in spirit from Broadway that performers who have become fixtures in Nevada often arrive in New York pathetically unprepared to translate their showroom acts into theatrically coherent variety shows," Stephen Holden wrote in the *New York Times*. "One of the most painful illustrations in recent memory was provided on Thursday evening by Redd Foxx . . . "

The review went downhill from there, with Holden writing that the show was "undermined by poorly engineered sound that often rendered Mr. Foxx's gruff, husky delivery unintelligible" and noting that Redd, who chain-smoked throughout the evening, "shuffled back and forth across the stage . . . growling out a shtick that has shown essentially no change in decades." It was also noted that, "long before" the show ended, many people had already walked out of the theater.

The *New York Post* was kinder, noting that "though a few of his stag party routines may be over-the-hill, Foxx is still king of the mountain . . . he manages to make it all seem fresh and satisfying . . . what the show lacks in theatricality, it more than makes up for in laughs."

Behind-the-scenes, Redd was being pressured by theater management to cut down on his stand-up routine and introduce more Fred Sanford-type material into the stage show. "But Redd wouldn't do it. He would only do that little bit with LaWanda Page," Major said. "Redd said, 'No, that's over and done with and I'm not doing that anymore.' And the audiences began to fall, and when the audiences started to fall, the money got funky, even though we had guaranteed money and stuff like that. So the money started to come in late."

Once the money dried up, Redd was gone. One thing he would never stand for was not being paid, regardless of the consequences. If they wanted to sue, let them sue. And get in line. Within days, Redd was on a plane back to Los Angeles, leaving the show and its producers in the lurch. "Redd just got up and said, 'We're going home,'" Major said. "Which we did. We got some fairly decent houses for a minute, but I think it was the combination of the publicity, the expectations of *Sanford and Son* by the audience and then Redd would do something like that and get bored with it, or tired with it, unless it was in Vegas."

Redd turned sixty-five on December 9, 1987, and he was now starting to take stock of his legacy with a combination of typical Foxx-style braggadocio and pride—mixed with increasingly public bitterness and anger. While he was proud of how far he'd come from his humble beginnings in Saint Louis, and especially of his multi-millionaire status (at least on paper), he sounded a note of resentment. He targeted the younger generation of "dirty" comics who, while talented, were profiting from a genre he brought to the forefront, and an industry which he felt had chewed him up and spit him out because of the color of his skin.

"If Eddie Murphy or Richard Pryor had gone into Basin Street East then they'd have been handcuffed and taken off stage for saying some of the things they say now," he told one reporter. "I love what they're doing, but I had to kick the door down to let them in. I pioneered this kind of stuff, and I never changed . . . I'm not putting them down," he said. "I like to listen to them. I seen them all. Most of them make me laugh. But I think I handle the four-letter words a little more sophisticatedly than they do." He still railed about never getting paid the royalties he felt were owed to him by Dooto Records and all the other fly-by-night record companies who'd profited off his party albums. And, a decade later, the specter of Fred Sanford still haunted him.

"I'd still be Sanford if they paid me the kind of money they paid other artists with shows not as good as *Sanford*," he said, stopping just short of playing the race card. "It wasn't black, it was green. They're hogs, they wanted it all," he said of the networks. "I was number one at NBC. I was supposed to get the number one money. Right or wrong? So now *Sanford and Son* is doing good in reruns, and here I am live, and I haven't worked in five, six months. I'd work in nightclubs if the money was fair, but they don't want to pay the right salary."

To Redd, the "right salary" meant being paid more than everyone else on a given project; the fact that a celebrity working with Redd might be a bigger star didn't make any difference—he was REDD FOXX, dammit, and he demanded to be paid top dollar, even now, when his career was in a marked decline and the offers were few and far between. Anthony Major, who was running Redd Foxx Productions, often had to think out of the box to guarantee that his boss would get paid more than everyone else. And it wasn't always easy.

After abandoning his Broadway show and heading back to Los Angeles, Redd was booked to appear on NBC's *The Motown Merry Christmas Special* along with Natalie Cole, Smokey Robinson, Lola Falana, *Miami Vice* star Philip Michael Thomas, Ronnie Spector, The Pointer Sisters, Stephanie Mills, and others. "Redd would never settle for what other folks were making," Major said. "And when we did *The Motown Merry Christmas Special*, I had to come up with another way to pay Redd more money, without letting *them* know, and without breaking the law."

Several years earlier, Redd had written a song called "When You

Love Someone (It's Christmas Everyday)," based on his philosophy that, "If I can afford it now, and I love you now, then that means Christmas is everyday." He even kept a Christmas tree in his house year-round (and had plans to cut a version of his song with rapper Kurtis Blow; Gladys Knight recorded a version of Redd's song in 1988). In order to make sure Redd was paid more than anyone else on the Motown special, Stephanie Mills was talked into singing "When You Love Someone (It's Christmas Everyday)"—thereby insuring Redd was paid songwriting royalties in addition to his fee for appearing on the show. He also insisted on being paid for any promotional appearances he made on behalf of the show (which wasn't standard practice, but wasn't an unusual stipulation in a Redd Foxx contract).

The New Year got off to an inauspicious start. Redd's ongoing problems with the IRS were beginning to take an ominous turn when someone broke into his house in Las Vegas in early 1988, absconding with nearly $3 million in jewelry and cash. Redd was out of town at the time.

"Someone called and said, 'If you want your stuff, go to the fence and get it before someone else does,'" he said. "My neighbor, Dan Parker, went outside and a garbage bag was hanging from the fence." Most of the items were recovered and were in the garbage bag, including a watch Elvis Presley had given to Redd years before. The watch, which Presley designed himself, included four lion heads with diamonds around their necks; a personalized note to Redd from Presley was engraved on the inside. The burglars had also taken nearly $110,000 in cash Redd had lying around the house. No arrests were ever made, and no one, apparently, thought to ask why robbers would go through all the trouble of breaking into Redd Foxx's house and stealing millions in property, only to leave it all hanging on a fence in a garbage bag.

Redd suspected two "well-dressed" black men who'd rung his doorbell some time before and stood off in the shadows, as if to hide their faces. "They told me, 'God sent us here to save Lola Falana [from multiple sclerosis] and we want her address. We just got in from Houston.' That automatically made me suspicious, because if God sent them from Houston to save Lola, why didn't God give them her address?"

The "robbery" wasn't the first time Redd's house in Las Vegas was targeted for criminal activity. There was the incident ten years earlier, when someone scribbled "KKK" and "Fuck You" on the outside walls of Redd's house. In 1976, one of Redd's beloved dogs, an eight-year-old St. Bernard named Saint, was killed when he scarfed down a piece of poisoned hamburger meat thrown over the wall into Redd's backyard. "[The meat] had enough poison in it to kill an elephant," said Redd's secretary, Kathy Chase. That crime, too, went unsolved. Redd would complain intermittently of harassing phone calls and unexplained threats—the result, perhaps, of an unpaid debt (and there were plenty of those). It was one of the reasons he always carried a gun. The threats were there—whether real or imagined.

But there was one debt that *would* be repaid—and this time Redd was the beneficiary. Eddie Murphy, one of the young, profane comedians for whom Redd paved the way, counted Redd Foxx as one of his major influences. And now that he was in a position to call the shots, Murphy reached out to Redd in early 1988 with an offer to co-star in his newest movie, *Harlem Nights*.

Murphy, a breakout star on *Saturday Night Live*, had segued seamlessly onto the big screen in 1982 with *48 Hours*, and followed that up with *Trading Places*, *Beverly Hills Cop*, *Beverly Hills Cop II*, *The Golden Child*, and *Coming to America*—all major box-office hits. *Harlem Nights* would be Murphy's $40 million vanity project: not only was he co-producing and starring in the movie, but he wrote the screenplay and would direct himself as Quick, a smooth-talking, sharp-dressed, 1930s-era owner of a Harlem speakeasy who butts heads with the mob. The young comedian (he was only twenty-seven) envisioned *Harlem Nights* as a comedic dream-team project showcasing three generations of legendary African American funnymen: himself, Richard Pryor, and Redd Foxx. Pryor, already diagnosed with the multiple sclerosis that would eventually confine him to a wheelchair, agreed to co-star in the movie as Sugar Ray, Quick's mentor; snaring Redd to play their croupier pal Bennie Wilson would insure the triumvirate. The cast also included Redd's old friend Della Reese, who signed on to play Vera, the madam who ran the brothel behind Quick's club.

"When I wrote my film I had in mind who I wanted to play each character," Murphy said. "Redd's character is Bennie and when I was writing I envisioned Redd saying everything that I was writing on paper. I grew up admiring and laughing at Redd so everything was tailor-made for him. Redd is a brilliant comedian even though most people think of him as Sanford."

But if Murphy thought Redd would jump at the chance to partner on-screen with him and Richard Pryor to make his first movie since *Norman, Is That You?* in 1976, he was sorely mistaken. The problem wasn't Redd's interest in the project; work was work, he liked Murphy and he was particularly fond of Pryor. And it was also a chance to work again with Della Reese. The issue, as it usually was with Redd, boiled down to money—and the veneer of respect that went along with that money. And Paramount's initial offer of $250,000 just wasn't enough.

"We said Redd would be interested because he liked Eddie," said Anthony Major, who was now Redd's *de facto* manager. "But, you know, we weren't going to work for that kind of money." Redd, accompanied by Major and Prince Spencer, flew in from Las Vegas for a meeting on the Paramount lot with studio officials. Eddie Murphy was there, along with a bevy of lawyers who showed up late, which Redd interpreted as a lack of respect. "We had this meeting and I remember walking in with the nasty attorneys, you know, making all the comments, pulling out the yellow [legal] pads," Major said. "And they made us wait, because they said they were across town doing some other big deal, and Redd said, 'Look, let's get this thing going, otherwise . . . '"

The first proposal put on the table was the original $250,000 offer. "Prince and I looked at each other and said, 'Redd, let's go.' How insulting is this?" Major said. "We come all the way here; your casting person offered us that $250,000, we know good and well you didn't bring us here to offer us the same money. That's why we're having the meeting." The trio got up, left the room and were on their way out of the building when they were chased down by a few of the Paramount attorneys. Redd told them to "Talk to Tony."

Major and the Paramount attorneys went back-and-forth over the contract for the next several weeks, with Major eventually getting them to double their original offer to $500,000. But Redd then pressed for another $50,000, representing that magical monetary marker he used for nearly every business deal. The studio balked. "They were saying that Redd was not a movie star, that he was a TV star and that there was a difference," Major said. "I said, 'He's Redd Foxx. So I don't even want to hear any of that. So you pay him what he's worth. Otherwise, he can go to Vegas and make a million dollars a year. He's losing money to come here anyway.' So, anyway, they finally went back and I think the last word I got was that Eddie kicked in the other $50,000." Redd got his $550,000.

Major was even able to wangle his client another $10,000 when production on *Harlem Nights* began a day earlier than planned. "He was working in Vegas and he had a payroll and he had to let the hotel know that he was leaving [a day early] because they had to fill in with somebody," Major said. "So we ended up getting another ten grand for him."

With Redd's contract ironed out, another minor kerfuffle erupted over his trailer—or the lack thereof. The studio wanted Redd to share a trailer with co-star Danny Aiello, but had gone ahead and negotiated with Aiello and given him his own trailer before talking to Redd. (Richard Pryor, eight years removed from his horrific self-immolation, needed his own trailer for specific makeup purposes.) "Redd wasn't about to share a trailer with anybody, because he wanted his privacy," Major said. "So they were going to cut a trailer in half and give one side to Redd and one side to Danny Aiello, because they claimed that Aiello's contract said that no one could have a bigger trailer than him other than Richard and Eddie. And I said, 'No way, Jose, y'all go find Redd a trailer, or Redd ain't coming.' So finally they brought one in."

Shooting on *Harlem Nights* began in late 1988 in Los Angeles and was, by all accounts, a positive experience for everyone involved. Redd showed up on time, knew his lines, and behaved himself on Eddie Murphy's set. If there were problems, Redd kept them to himself, or shared them with Della Reese. "I think Della and Redd got a little frustrated because Eddie wanted to do it his way and he never really asked them, 'How did it go?'" Major said. "I mean, you're talking about an era that Redd and Della lived through . . . so as good a movie as it was, it could have been much, much better if Eddie had just asked them. They were willing to give the information to him." Pryor himself admitted in his autobiography that he "never connected with Eddie," even while praising the star's acting chops.

Redd's decades-long friendship with Della Reese translated into an easy, comfortable relationship strengthened by years of mutually shared experiences. They knew the slings and arrows of racism—both inside and outside the world of entertainment—and had worked their way up from the Chitlin' Circuit to attain major stardom. They ribbed each other mercilessly—like an old married couple—and their good-natured banter on the set of *Harlem Nights* kept Eddie Murphy so entertained that he dashed into his trailer one day and, within a half hour or so, wrote a treatment for a television show in which Redd and Della would co-star as husband-and-wife.

"We were just playfully going at it during a break," said Reese. "Richard Pryor was sitting on the side. When I got a good line in on Redd, he said, 'I wouldn't let no woman talk to me like that.' And then, Redd would get one in on me. He [Pryor] kept instigating and we kept signifying with each other. Eddie Murphy was standing on the side and he was cracking up. The whole cast came in and everybody was laughing. We stopped production. Eddie said, 'This is a television series.' And he began to write it."

Harlem Nights opened in theaters in mid-November 1989 to solid box-office receipts but tepid reviews. The hoped-for magical trio of Eddie Murphy, Richard Pryor, and Redd Foxx fizzled; most movie critics complained about the film's weak writing, its overabundance of violence and, most of all, Murphy's preening. Redd, for the most part, emerged unscathed; Murphy—as the movie's producer, director, screenwriter, and star—absorbed the lion's share of the vitriol. "In this buddy-buddy-buddy movie—with three generations of stand-up comics (Murphy, Pryor, and Redd Foxx) together—two buddies always melt into the background," wrote the *Los Angeles Times*. "Pryor grays over into a grinning paterfamilias. . . . Foxx, at first funny as a cantankerous craps croupier too blind to read the dice, turns from instigator of jokes to the butt of them. If he's going to confine himself to bad movies like *Harlem Nights*, it's probably better that [Murphy] writes and directs them himself. At least he's learning new skills."

The *New York Times* was a bit kinder in its assessment of the movie: "Though *Harlem Nights* may be an ego trip, it is a generous one. The only problem is that it's seldom as funny as it should be. The gangster comedy, set in Harlem in the 1930s, is a self-designed star-vehicle that is also a tribute to Mr. Murphy's great co-stars: Richard Pryor, Redd Foxx, and Della Reese. It's Mr. Murphy's apparently genuine enjoyment of his associates that keeps one amiable throughout *Harlem Nights*, even while waiting for the belly laughs that erupt no more than once or twice."

Most of the $550,000 Redd earned for his work on *Harlem Nights* went to the IRS, which was dunning a large chunk of his paychecks for the back taxes he still owed. "As some lawyers will say, it would have been better if he never filed [his tax returns]," said Major. "But he filed and then he didn't pay, so they knew how much he made."

Redd's friend George Schlatter, who'd directed him in *Norman, Is That You?* was aware of Redd's squabbles with the IRS—because Redd contacted him, from time to time, to complain about his battles with the government. "He called me up one day and said, 'I got a problem. The IRS is on my ass.' I said, 'What's the matter?' He said, 'Fuck 'em. I'm not paying any more taxes to a white president. Fuck 'em—you elect a black president, I'll pay the taxes.' I said, 'Redd, they're going to come get you.' And he said, 'No, fuck them, they're not going to get me. I got a dog. I got a man name of Mr. White and he weighs four hundred pounds and he has a cannon in his belt.' I said, 'Redd, pay the fucking taxes' and he said, 'Fuck them, George, you're just like they are.'"

Redd went to great lengths to hide a portion of his earnings from the IRS, including giving a chunk of cash to a woman in Las Vegas who kept it for him. "He had another woman that he trusted with his money," Major said. "So I had to make arrangements to keep the IRS off him and he would give this woman some money, and every time he needed something, I would just go meet her and get it and bring it back to him. I could get a bunch of money orders for nine thousand dollars and that would keep [the IRS] out of his money because he couldn't have a bank account, he couldn't get any money like that because they would come and take it."

Despite his chicanery, the IRS was convinced Redd wasn't paying as much as he should, or could, in order to liquidate the nearly $800,000 it claimed he still owed the government. Redd's bankruptcy proceedings from 1983 were still dragging on, six years later, and he'd lost one of his Los Angeles homes in the process. He later claimed that all of the property he owned in Los Angeles, including the Redd Foxx Productions building on North La Brea, was sold for $3 million after he declared bankruptcy; that money, he argued, should have gone a long way toward paying off a big chunk, if not all, of his IRS debts. He was still earning over $1 million a year, and continued to be a top draw in Las Vegas, where he opened for a long run at the Hacienda Hotel, at $20,000 a week, after finishing his work on *Harlem Nights*.

But while Redd was cash-poor, his generosity toward anyone looking for a break didn't waver—even though his own star was falling. During his run at the Hacienda—where he was joined on the bill by Slappy White, Prince Spencer, and Bernie Allen—a young comedian named Bernie Mac, a huge Redd Foxx fan from Chicago who was trying to make a name for himself, approached his idol one night. "I was rambling on, and he just shut me up real quick: 'You want to go on?'" Mac said. "Slappy White didn't dig it . . . he didn't give me too much love at all."

But Mac went onstage, did his routine, and "had this feeling in my heart and the back of my head that I held my own." Redd came out, told the audience, "That's a funny motherfucker" and sealed, for Mac, his "legitimacy" as a comedian. "That gave me the heart and gave me the confidence I needed to not second-place myself to anything and anybody."

At 7:30 a.m. on the morning of November 28, 1989, IRS agents stormed Redd's corner-lot ranch house on Eastern Avenue in Las Vegas, swooping in while Redd and a woman friend were asleep in the bedroom. Agents raided the three-bedroom house and began carting off nearly everything they could find while Redd stood there in his underwear, his bewilderment slowly turning to anger. Paintings were ripped off the walls, Redd's collection of exotic cars was loaded onto a truck and one IRS agent literally ripped the diamond-encrusted watch Elvis Presley had given Redd off the comedian's wrist. "They took everything," Redd said. "All the stuff they thought was of value. . . . They took Lena Horne's picture off the wall. That picture was of her kissing me at the door [on *Sanford and Son*]. And they took the picture of me with Demond Wilson and Frank Sinatra's autographed picture. They even took the plants—and the watch off my wrist."

Neighbors gathered to watch the surreal scene, which was punctuated by the cacophony of Redd's barking dogs (who *weren't* carted off when Redd convinced the agents he could care for the animals, who he thought of as his "children"). Television crews, alerted to the raid, arrived in time to film Redd's cars being towed away. By the time the IRS agents were done several hours later, Redd was left with little more than his bedroom set and some of his mother's belongings, which he kept boxed up in the garage.

Las Vegas auctioneer Guy Deiro accompanied the IRS agents on their raid and helped to remove Redd's belongings, which would be auctioned off by Deiro's company, Robert Deiro and Associates, if Redd couldn't come up with a plan to save his possessions. "It was early in the morning and they got him out of bed and put him on the couch," Deiro said. "He wasn't happy about it and he was cussing everybody out, like Redd Foxx would do. And he was standing in just his underwear. So then we went through the house and left only what was necessary for him to live off of—in other words, you leave the fridge, one TV, you take the other TV and you take everything else: jewelry, rings, watches, things like that. He had a lot of pornographic gold jewelry, which was interesting. The furniture that he had wasn't anything special, but his jewelry and his watches and rings and things were valuable."

According to an affidavit released in federal court the following week, Redd owed the IRS nearly $1 million in back taxes for the years 1983, 1984, and 1986. He'd ignored four requests for payments. Among the three hundred items taken from his house were $12,769 in cash, a dozen guns—including a semiautomatic pistol—a grand piano, six vehicles (among them a 1983 Zimmer Opera Coupe, 1927 Model T, 1975 Panther, a Vespa motor scooter, and a knockoff of the famous red *Sanford and Son* pickup truck) and seventy-six pieces of jewelry, including the Elvis Presley watch and the 14-carat erotic baubles. The IRS also filed a lien on Redd's property for $755,000. The agency gave Redd thirty to forty-five days to square his accounts in order to prevent it from auctioning off his belongings—including his $200,000 house.

Some of the IRS agents on the raid that day carried out their duties only grudgingly. The agency was well aware of its public perception and hated this kind of publicity, but felt it had exhausted every other avenue in getting Redd to repay his taxes. "He'd been in trouble before and, believe me, I don't stick up for the IRS, but I knew the guys who were in charge back then, and they tried to make a deal with Redd every which way possible," Deiro said. "He never lived up to it. They didn't want to do [the raid]. They knew it was a high-profile case and they didn't want to get in the newspaper. They wanted just anything, a thousand bucks . . . they just knew they were going to be all over with the publicity and they knew it was going to be a nightmare. So they tried to give Redd every opportunity to make some kind of token payment—a grand a week. He wouldn't do it. Just wouldn't do it."

Redd told a different story to the local television news crews who arrived on the scene to record his public humiliation. The gravel-voiced comedian, dressed in a white T-shirt, blue pants and black boots, stood on his driveway, squinting in the Las Vegas sun, looking as if he was about to burst into tears. But he was still defiant toward the IRS. "I think someone should come and do something to help me, 'cause I've helped a lot of folks, you know?" he said plaintively. "Who knows, if they'd a given me a chance, I could've gotten in touch with Eddie Murphy, or Richard Pryor, or Frank Sinatra, or somebody who knows that I've been helpful to a lot of people." He conveniently ignored the many warnings he'd received from the IRS through their years of tangling with each other. "They've taken everything," he said. "This is so unfair."

Several weeks went by, and Redd continued to perform his midnight show at the Hacienda (in a denim jacket and jeans—"Forgive me, they took my tuxedo," he joked). He was reminded of his precarious plight every morning when he awoke in his nearly empty house. His pleas for help from his show-business friends fell on deaf ears, with very few exceptions, among them fellow comedian George Carlin and longtime friends Pat Morita and George Schlatter. "Two of the strongest supporters were Pat Morita and George Carlin—Carlin very much so," said Redd's attorney, Mark Risman. Redd claimed that musicians Carlos Santana and British rockers the Who also contributed some money to help cover his tax debts, but this was denied by their publicists.

"He calls me up and says, 'They came and took my bed! They came to the house! George, you gotta help me—I need money!' Schlatter said. "I said, 'Well, Redd, what about the brothers?' and he said, 'Fuck them—they aren't going to loan me any money. There are no black people that are going to loan me money.' So I loaned him money a couple of times."

But Redd needed more than some cash from Schlatter, Carlin, and Morita, and when none of his other show-business friends came forward, his melancholy turned to anger. He'd helped so many people over the years—a weakness that contributed heavily to his financial downfall—so where was everyone when *he* needed *them*? "I haven't heard from anyone. That's remarkable," he said. "I just look for a telegram to say: 'Hey, man, look, I'm sorry, keep a chin up.' But I haven't received anything. I've been in the business for fifty years. I've helped a lot of people, started them off."

Sounding an almost plaintive note, Redd said he'd reached out to his *Harlem Nights* co-star Eddie Murphy—but, so far, he hadn't heard back from the wealthy actor. "Eddie is in a position to totally get me out of this," he said. "It wouldn't hurt him any. I could sign up with him for five years of work, doing something until I pay him back. Or he could get my stuff out and take what he likes. He wouldn't lose a quarter. He's the only one I know who has that kind of bread."

Seeking advice, and a donation to the cause, Redd called his friend Stuart Sheslow, who'd produced *Sanford*, *The Redd Foxx Show*, and *Ghost of a Chance*. "He called me up and said, 'Can you get some guys to help me?' And I said, 'What about Cosby?' Redd said, 'He turned his back on me.' Pryor was too sick. . . . Redd broke ground for these guys and they should have helped him. Especially Cosby. He needed somebody big. He didn't need an executive making one hundred grand a year, if you know what I mean. He needed some political heavyweight like Cosby."

Redd was happy to report, somewhat pointedly, that while his celebrity pals were nowhere to be found in his time of crisis, total strangers were chipping in with whatever they could afford—including a neighbor who gave him $200 and a group of local students at nearby Chapperal High School, who banded together to raise eighty dollars (which he didn't accept). He lashed out, playing the race card and accusing the IRS of targeting him because of his skin color. He insisted he was "whitelisted" and "whiteballed"—not "blacklisted" because, he said, "nobody black hurt me." "There have got to be some whites in town that owe taxes," he said. "Why don't they go to their houses and tear it up and throw stuff on the floor? Because they got big attorneys."

Back in Chicago, Louis Pittman, a young IRS revenue officer, was at home watching the news footage of the IRS raid on Redd's house. Pittman was dedicated to his job and believed in the work the IRS was doing—but something didn't seem right to him as he watched Redd's cars being hauled off. Pittman thought the raid was illegal—and he picked up the phone and called Redd to tell him so. "Believe it or not, I was able to talk to him," Pittman said. "And I told him that I couldn't advise him, but I could answer any questions that he might have and that I felt that some of the things that happened [in the raid] weren't right, from what I could see on TV . . . [that] the seizures were out-of-line and that the IRS was just out for blood."

Redd asked Pittman if he could come out to Las Vegas to meet with him and his attorney, Mark Risman. As luck would have it, Pittman was due to be in Las Vegas on vacation the following week. They scheduled a meeting and, by the time it was over, Pittman had quit his job with the

IRS to become Redd's personal accountant. And it wasn't long before he found out just *why* Redd's finances were in such tangled disarray. "I was making like $4,500 a week [with Redd], but I wasn't getting $4,500 a week," he said. "We just *said* that I was making $4,500 a week. I was actually making $2,500 a week, but I was giving Redd $2,000 under the table." Redd, though, could be generous to a fault, even to a new employee like Pittman. "He would buy us clothes, leather jackets, and a lot of the time it wasn't something I would wear," he said. "But he would buy it and I would just go ahead and accept it."

It was standard practice for any of Redd's new employees to see their boss perform live, and Pittman went to one of his midnight shows at the Hacienda. "It was kind of disappointing because you would think he was like his [*Sanford and Son*] character, but I saw the dirty side, the drugs," he said. "He was snorting cocaine on the stage of the Hacienda. He was on the stage and he had filled a Vicks inhaler with cocaine . . . and he sniffed it right there on stage."

Redd's possessions were scheduled to be auctioned off by the IRS at Cashman Field Center, in downtown Las Vegas, in late January 1990—two months after the raid. Redd continued his defiant stance toward the IRS, and was now fighting to keep the agency from sharing in the proceeds from the sale, in Los Angeles, of the Redd Foxx Productions building on North La Brea (which sold for $1.6 million). Redd's Los Angeles attorney, Paul Whitford, claimed the IRS failed to document back taxes it had received from Redd.

Whitford was also trying to short-circuit the Cashman Field Center auction, claiming the IRS auction would conflict with any rights that creditors had in Redd's bankruptcy case, which dated back to 1983. There was, finally, some good news, when U.S. Bankruptcy Judge Clive Jones issued a thirty-day stay of the auction, despite objections from auctioneers Robert Deiro Associates and, of course, the IRS. The agency now amended Redd's tax bill to around $3 million—up drastically from the previous $1 million figure, with interest and penalties factored in.

The planned IRS auction dragged on through the spring, with court delays and injunctions. Finally, in mid-May, the IRS held the first of two auctions, this one for the eight cars seized from Redd's house the previous November. The auction raised nearly $50,000, with one unidentified buyer shelling out $16,500 for the 1983 Zimmer Opera Coupe.

The second auction, held in late July, raised around $34,000. The big-ticket item here was the personalized, diamond-encrusted watch given to Redd by Elvis Presley, which netted $17,500. The two auctions had brought in around $85,000, which made only a small dent in Redd's massive, $3 million tax bill. The IRS eventually returned most of the unsold items to Redd.

Whitford, meanwhile, managed to fend off the IRS from taking Redd's house, and short-circuited the planned larger auction of Redd's possessions. "He knew that I was gay, and when they tried to take his house I was over there and my associate was with me and we had a trial and we won so they couldn't take his house," Whitford said. "So he tells my associate, 'Hell, I'm so happy I'd buy Paul a whore but he wouldn't want one.' That was pure Redd Foxx."

In the meantime, Redd's Las Vegas attorney, Mark Risman, and his accountant, Louis Pittman, worked out a payment plan with the IRS. "Eddie Murphy's people came in and the IRS wanted them to just pay it all, without a payment plan," Pittman said. "Eddie Murphy's people were thinking about just doing it, but they were also getting ready to make Redd sign his life over . . . so I convinced Redd not to do it and go ahead and let me finish [working on the payment plan]."

"We did two things," Risman said. "We worked out a reduction [in Redd's payments] and a payment schedule. The liability was reduced approximately by ninety-cents per dollar owed and then a payment schedule was made for the remaining ten-cents on the dollar. Redd was allowed to remain in his home and enjoy a certain lifestyle based on . . . we'll call it a 'salary,' for lack of a better term. But on the same hand, I believe there was a great deal of humanity involved in the consideration of the amount [Redd owed] by the IRS—but Redd wasn't free to hoard or spend foolishly or have extra money for gambling or whatever."

chapter fifteen

"God Has Plans of His Own"

Things were starting to look up. The IRS was finally off Redd's back—as long as he behaved himself and stuck to the payment plan—and he was no longer threatened with losing his Las Vegas house, which was feeling a little more like home now that the IRS had returned many of the items seized in the raid. "I'm happy," Redd said. "They kept the watch Elvis Presley gave me. That hurts. It wasn't about the monetary value. I've had that since 1977. If it was about the money I could have sold it a long time ago." He owned 90 percent of his short-lived ABC variety show, and talked about editing some of *The Redd Foxx Comedy Hour* tapes for a "Best Of" collection, featuring stars like Bill Cosby, Milton Berle, and Pat Morita, which he could sell in stores.

There was also a new woman in his life. Her name was Kaho Cho, and they'd met at Bally's Hotel and Casino in Las Vegas. Like his ex-wife Joi, Kaho was a Korean native who emigrated to the United States with her family. And, like Joi, she was in her early thirties when she and Redd began their relationship. Kaho obviously didn't mind their difference in age—Redd was sixty-seven—nor the fact that her new boyfriend was in dire financial straits.

It meant a lot to Redd that Kaho was there for him through all his trials and tribulations with the IRS. His last two wives had taken him to the cleaners when their marriages dissolved, and he was suspicious of ulterior motives—*especially* when it involved money. "She stuck with me through the IRS mess and everything," he said. "She didn't run like some women would do. She stuck with me and helped me in a whole lot of ways. She saw me when I didn't have a quarter. She saw me with a nickel. And hopefully, she will see me with a dollar. I'll give her seventy-five cents of it."

Redd made a habit of borrowing Anthony Major's 1988 Toyota Cressida—"He loved my car," Major said—and taking Kaho on shopping sprees. It wasn't unusual for him to blow a couple of thousand dollars at a time, but Redd's generosity was legendary, and that extended not only to his love interests but to his trusted friends and employees. "He would go down there and get boxes of clothes and come back and give them to Kaho, but he would always bring some back for you," Major said. "He would walk in and say, 'Tony, take this hat,' and he would give me a Kangol hat or a shirt or a sweater. He would say, 'Oh, Tony, I think this will fit you. If it fits you, you can have it.'"

With his IRS problems under control, Redd could relax a bit. He continued to perform his midnight shows at the Hacienda, while back in Hollywood, Eddie Murphy was hammering out a deal with Paramount to produce the television series he'd written for Redd and Della Reese on the set of *Harlem Nights*. Murphy wanted to call the series *Chest Pains*—a nod to Fred Sanford's chest-clutching antics on *Sanford and Son*—but ABC already had the established sitcom *Growing Pains*. Murphy changed the show's name to *The Royal Family* and sold it to CBS, with the stipulation that he be credited as the show's creator and executive producer. "Once we signed the contract we never saw Eddie again," Major said.

For Redd Foxx, the new series was a win-win situation. It had been nearly twenty years since the premiere of *Sanford and Son*, and his television track record since then—*The Redd Foxx Comedy Hour*, *Sanford*, and *The Redd Foxx Show*—were all short-lived failures. He was almost sixty-eight years old, with a shaky financial future and worsening health. His breathing was noticeably more labored now, his voice extra-gravelly, his energy visibly sapped. The years of hard living were taking their toll. But Redd still refused to give in to Father Time: he chain-smoked, snorted coke, smoked some dope, and indulged in the occasional glass of Grand Marnier. Eddie Murphy was giving Redd perhaps his final shot at capturing some of the old *Sanford and Son* magic, to prove he still had it, to prove he was still a marketable commodity off the Las Vegas stage. He couldn't say no.

"I just negotiated with Eddie's people and what we had to do was work it out so that Redd could work, because this was the time of the taxes and the IRS and all that stuff and we were in and out of court in Vegas," said Anthony Major. "Redd needed the money. So the IRS said, 'Okay, he can work,' as long as a certain amount of that money went to them. And each week that Redd got paid, a certain amount would go to the IRS and it was fine. So he was actually working to pay off the debt and get in good and all that kind of stuff."

Besides, Redd would be working with his old friend, Della Reese. "He loved Della and he loved Eddie . . . so now he's torn between loving to do the show and loving to work with Della and thinking that Eddie is going to show up any day, which he never did," Major said. "But Redd came to work. He did his job."

In the show, Redd and Della would play Alphonso "Al" Royal and his wife, Victoria. Al, a mailman, is on the verge of retirement, and he and Victoria are looking forward to spending their golden years together, bickering in peace and quiet. Their plans, however, are thrown into disarray when their daughter, Elizabeth (Mariann Aalda), who's divorcing her husband, moves in with her three kids: teenagers Kim (Sylver Gregory) and Curtis (Larenz Tate) and preschooler Hilary (Naya Rivera). The comedic conflict would play out not only between the curmudgeonly Al and the more empathetic Victoria, but between Al, his daughter Elizabeth, and her children.

Redd sounded a note of caution regarding his upcoming return to prime time television. He'd been there, done that, with only one hit show on his resume—but he sounded grateful to be getting another chance, if only to take another very public swipe at the IRS. "Well, it feels good that I'm going back [on television]," he said. "But I don't know what's going to be happening. It's been so long. Twenty years is a long time to wait. They'll [the IRS] come in and take the money anyway, and have me living poor like a bum. Whatever comes out [of *The Royal Family*] comes out. I'm so disillusioned about the last one that I don't have any thoughts, really."

In late May 1991, CBS announced its fall schedule, including its pickup of *The Royal Family*, which was slotted to air Wednesdays at 8:00 p.m. up against the ABC sitcom *Dinosaurs* and NBC's hour-long *Unsolved Mysteries*, hosted by Robert Stack. CBS president Jeff Sagansky called his new show "the best-testing comedy in years," and there was a good feeling on the set going into the new season. "The show was funny, it was up-to-date, it was about what was happening during a time when children were going back to their mother's and father's because they didn't have enough money from their jobs and they had families they couldn't take care of," said Della Reese. "It was right in the midst of what was happening at that time."

In July, as rehearsals began for *The Royal Family*, Redd became a groom for the fourth time when he married Kaho in Las Vegas at the Little Church of the West. She wore a traditional white wedding dress, Redd an all-white tuxedo. The reception was held in the Granada Room at the Hacienda Hotel and was attended by over one hundred-and-fifty friends and family members (mostly Kaho's extended clan). Slappy White, Prince Spencer, George Carlin, and Della Reese were there; after the reception, Redd and his new bride went to visit Redd's mother, Mary, now eighty-eight and lying unconscious in the hospital after suffering a stroke. They also stopped off at the cemetery where Kaho's parents were buried, and talked about honeymooning in Hawaii during a break in Redd's *Royal Family* shooting schedule. Redd was sounding a more upbeat tone after a psychic told him that 1991 would be his best year yet. "It's started out slowly but things have picked up," he said after the wedding reception. "Everything seems like it's going to be alright."

The atmosphere on *The Royal Family* set was positive from the get-go. Notwithstanding Redd and Della's long history together, the rest of the cast were relative newcomers to television (Naya Rivera was only four-and-a-half years old) and were working together for the first time. Redd made everyone feel at ease, joking around and sharing stories about his life in show business. "You didn't work with him and not get to know him as a person because the person you saw, that was it," said co-star Mariann Aalda. "He would always encourage us in whatever way that he possibly could."

Aalda was playing Al and Victoria's daughter, Elizabeth, and the character was written as prissy—which Redd latched on to, and projected onto Aalda herself. When the cast got together for their first photo shoot, and each co-star was asked to wear something appropriate for their character, Aalda wore a loose-fitting dress. "And Redd looked over at me and he said, 'Is that what you're wearing?' He said, 'Well, can't we get her something better than this?' And I said, 'Redd, this is my dress,' and he said, 'Well, can't we take up a collection to buy this child some clothes?' He looked at the dress and he said something to me that I have not forgotten to this day. He looked at me and he said, 'Listen, you got a nice figure. Get some pins or something and tie this up in the back' so the dress would be form fitting.

"And then he looked at my chest and he said, 'Can't we get her some socks or something? It doesn't make sense for the daughter to have more than the mama has.' He was talking about Sylver [Gregory], who was quite voluptuous. And they did. They went and got me some socks and plumped me up and gave me a little bit of cleavage, and he looked at me and said, 'Now that's better. Don't ever forget this is show business, baby, you gotta show 'em something.' And I've never forgotten that. "

Aalda eventually wore what she called her "California Boobs," a special bra for when the cameras rolled. "Sometimes I would come out on the set and Redd would say, 'Where's your chest?' I would say, 'Redd, this is rehearsal,' and he'd say, 'Don't tease me, baby, I gotta look at you all the time.'"

The Royal Family premiered on September 18, 1991 to mixed reviews, but solid numbers in its debut. "*The Royal Family* has energy, but not much else," critic Howard Rosenberg wrote in the *Los Angeles Times*. "And if the theme isn't familiar enough, there's Foxx himself, who is more or less a middle-class reincarnation of the crass, cantankerous junkman who conned his way through *Sanford and Son* on NBC in the mid-1970s. Foxx still has the gift, and he and Reese are fine together. But he looks, walks, and talks like Fred Sanford, except that the material isn't nearly as funny."

The critic for *Variety* agreed. "Nice as it is to see Redd Foxx grousing and bellowing again, why does it have to be in such a thin, pandering vehicle?" he wrote. "This isn't exactly 'Grandfather Knows Best,' since Foxx's character can be downright nasty with the little dears, but it still tugs at the heart and turns the stomach in all the wrong places. Foxx has his moments, especially with some of the bluer material. . . . Older viewers who aren't interested in *Unsolved Mysteries* may be tickled by seeing the *Sanford and Son* star up to his old antics, but that should be a meager audience—particularly after the novelty wears off."

CBS officials, though, were pleased with the show's performance. The network was struggling in prime time, especially on Wednesday night, and while *The Royal Family's* opening-night numbers weren't spectacular, they were respectable enough to give CBS a much-needed mid-week lift. It looked like Redd's television comeback could become a reality if the show continued on its positive path.

But there was trouble brewing behind the scenes. Redd was getting along famously with his co-stars, but was having issues with the writing staff and, according to some who were present on the set, with executive producer Greg Antonacci. "We were doing okay with the numbers and it was getting better each week, but they were just driving him by working him," said Anthony Major, who was a constant presence on the set. "He could have done what [Bill] Cosby did, work three days a week, come in and shoot the show. Because he would get his lines and I would help him with the script and rehearse it with him and . . . it would be funny. Because Redd could say 'hello' and make it funny. But he had to put up with the scripts and put up with rehearsals and five days a week, nine to five . . . working him that way, it was crazy."

According to Antonacci, adjustments were made to Redd's schedule to accommodate what even he acknowledged was a taxing schedule. "A five-day-a-week, half-hour comedy is pretty grueling, and at the time he was sixty-eight," he said. "If there's a villain in the piece, it's the IRS. At that age, Redd had to work five days a week, do three or four shows and then come back. We did try to adjust [his schedule]. Normally, you come in on Monday and read at the table and then go to work on the scenes you think will work. You read two scripts, an advance script and that week's script. What we did was, we wouldn't work on Monday but would come back on Tuesday to give [Redd] that little break. There were adjustments made but they didn't hurt the show. Redd was there but he did tire. It was difficult on him."

It was no secret that CBS and Paramount were leaning hard on Redd, based on his past on-set television squabbles, and the network expected Antonacci, Major, and Prince Spencer—who was seventy-four at the time—to keep *The Royal Family* star focused on the task at hand. There would be no walkouts and no "illnesses" this time around. "I had control of that. I mean, that's why I was there," Major said. "So when people tried to get between me and Redd, that's when the big problems would occur. Prince was smart about show business and I'd have to pass things by him, but, you know, Prince . . . at his age would just turn it over to me and say, 'Well, you figure it out.'"

Redd's biggest complaints on *The Royal Family* set, besides his rigorous work schedule, were the show's scripts. Twenty years earlier, on

Sanford and Son, he was quick to object to lines that didn't ring true, or which, in his opinion, demeaned the image of African Americans. He was usually right, and his attitude hadn't changed, even now when he was being given a final shot at reclaiming some of his former glory. It was important to Redd that Al Royal and everyone else on the show speak to each other as realistically as possible—and that meant making some changes to dialogue he considered insulting.

Redd preferred to see each week's script ahead of time, so he could make any changes he felt were necessary before the table read. But he felt that some of his suggestions were being ignored and, in some cases, that the writers were trying to pull one over on him.

In one script, the show's writers had Al calling his grandson, Curtis, "boy" and "kid," terms Redd thought demeaning—"boy" for its obvious racial connotations and "kid" because, "to black folks, 'kid' is a goat," Major said. Redd told the writers Al would call his grandson by his proper name. But, the next morning at the table read, the words "boy" and "kid" were back in the script. Redd exploded in anger. "So he pushed back from the table and cursed everybody out and was going home," Major said. The writers implored Major to chase after Redd and get him to come back—they would remove the offending words. But the damage had been done.

It got worse from that point on. Major got a call one Sunday afternoon from Kaho, pleading with him to rush over to the Universal Hotel in Universal City, where she and Redd were staying while he taped the show. Redd, she told Major, had tossed that week's *Royal Family* script across the room after reading it through, and was furious. "Redd had told them the second act wasn't any good, and they were supposed to change it," Major said. "So, instead of changing it, they sent him the script and it was identical. They hadn't changed anything. They tried to trick him into thinking they had worked all night to finish the second act and sent him the same second act. He said, 'They think I'm stupid. If somebody don't go over there, I'm going to Vegas and I'm going to take the phone off the hook and lock the door.' So I immediately called the producers and said, y'all better get over here to his hotel, otherwise you're gonna lose Redd. So they come over there, trying to apologize. Redd said, 'We had this discussion.' Every week there was something in the script [he objected to]."

Della Reese, too, noticed Redd's unhappiness over some lines of dialogue he felt were insulting—and she agreed with her co-star. "They had a line about my youngest granddaughter, and they wanted [Al] to call her 'peanut shell.' Redd said, 'I'm not going to call this baby "peanut shell." That's garbage.' The writer said, 'Well, I call my niece peanut shell. Redd said, 'I don't care what you call your niece, I am not calling this beautiful child "peanut shell." Well, now, we didn't work for about three hours because the producer had to be placated, which is stupid. It was always something like that. [The producer] was always telling Redd how to be black, and he was white—so he didn't know how to be black."

Antonacci was aware of Redd's antagonism toward him during their first meeting. But, he said, both men eventually came to understand each other, which led to a better working relationship. "The first time I met him was when we were preparing to work together, and he was leery of me," he said. "And I felt that. The white guys who ran things had done him dirty. He said that to me once. So I go in to give him the first run-through and he puts a pistol on the table. The next day, I brought a pistol with me and put it on the table and he laughed. I said, 'Redd, look, you gotta understand where I'm coming from. My job is to write for Redd Foxx and I need to make you happy, because if you succeed, we succeed.' And he said to me, 'I thought you were one of those wise guy white guys, Antonacci.'

"And we began to have a better relationship. I told him, 'You've forgotten more comedy than I know.' I developed a great fondness for him, and he a fondness for me. He loved that I called people 'knucklehead.'"

Despite the backstage tensions, *The Royal Family* continued to draw solid numbers and, after a month on the air, it had given a considerable ratings boost to CBS's Wednesday-night schedule. There was talk of giving the show a full-season pickup, even this early in the new television season. "It was a hit," said Della Reese. "I was so glad that it was a hit, that Redd got a chance to go out the way he deserved to go out—at the top of the scale."

And then came October 11, 1991.

Redd complained of feeling warm earlier in the day, which wasn't surprising, since Los Angeles was in the grip of a fierce heat wave. Otherwise, he seemed to be his usual irascible self on *The Royal Family* set. He was scheduled to be interviewed that afternoon by *Lifestyles of the*

Rich and Famous—further validation that his comeback was a success—and a half hour of time was set aside for the interview to be conducted in a back room off the main set.

A *Lifestyles of the Rich and Famous* camera crew shadowed Redd—wearing a blue paisley shirt and blue cap—around the set that day, getting some shots of him rehearsing a kissing scene on the couch with Della Reese, and clowning around with co-star Larenz Tate and with some onlookers in the studio bleachers. As usual, Prince Spencer and Anthony Major were on the set with Redd. Louis Pittman, Redd's accountant, was also there to watch that day's taping. Major was sent out to get "The Chief" something to eat. "I had gone to get him some chicken cacciatore, and when I came back with it, the place was freezing and he was lying there, nothing wrong with him," Major said. "Prince was in his overcoat and I said, 'Prince, why is it so cold?' He said, 'Redd said he's hot.' So, anyway, he ate what I brought him and he said, 'Yeah, Tony, I'm still gonna eat my hamburger.' He said he was tired, so I left him in the dressing room and went outside."

While the rest of *The Royal Family* cast gathered for rehearsal, Redd went in for his interview with *Lifestyles of the Rich and Famous*. In footage from the interview he seems short of breath, his familiar voice more gravelly than usual. He doesn't look very happy to be there, but, then again, Redd never cared much for interviews. He's asked about his new cast mates. "Fabulous. Everybody fell in love the first day," he says. "You know, so it's been like that ever since. Like family, a real family."

"And you're a newlywed?" he's asked.

Before Redd could answer, a voice can be heard off-camera, abruptly interrupting. "I'm sorry, guys. We really need . . . it's been half an hour."

"It's not been a half hour, it's been five minutes," the *Lifestyles* interviewer shoots back.

Redd, visibly pissed off at being interrupted, shoots daggers at the unseen voice interrupting him. He looks at the camera, and then looks back at the interviewer. "I'm sorry about the interruption, but I'll be back," he growls. Later footage shows him taking off his glasses, wiping them down with a handkerchief, and muttering, "Boy, that ticks me off, you know, really. Dumb-ass brother."

"They came to interview him and we had a producer who will remain nameless because I can't remember his name—that's how important he was to me," said Della Reese. "He was forever on Redd about something or other. This particular day, we had this scene where I was in the scene and the girl who played my daughter was in the scene, and we were talking about Redd. He was supposed to come in, Redd was, and walk behind us where we did not see him and [he would] hear what we were saying. And he was in the middle of this interview . . . and this man went in and insisted that Redd had to rehearse this. And *you* could have walked back there. It was not required at all. And when Redd discovered how unnecessary it was for him to be there, he got absolutely livid."

"There wasn't even a line [for Redd to say]—it was just mumbling, and Redd could do that in his sleep," Major said. "And when he found out what it was, he just went off. And so Della and I had to calm him down and we said, 'Redd, go back and finish the interview.'"

What happened next on the set of *The Royal Family* has a *Rashomon*-type subtext, with several people who witnessed the events each telling their version of the story just a little differently.

It was around 4:15 in the afternoon when Redd was called to the set to rehearse a scene with Della Reese. Everyone who was there agrees on one thing: Redd suddenly clutched his chest, like Fred Sanford having one of his famous "heart attacks" on *Sanford and Son*. But this time it was no joke.

Della Reese: "The producer said, 'We gotta get the camera, we gotta see this' and Redd said, 'Ah, give me a break' and reached for the chair and did what we thought was a pratfall, 'cause he did that all the time. And we all stood there laughing while he was laying on the floor. He'd had a heart attack."

Anthony Major: "Later in the afternoon we were rehearsing that particular show. He and I were sitting [on the set] and he said, 'Tony, I'm tired. People are stealing from me, I'm getting tired of it.' I think at that point he probably got so upset he went in and had a snoot [of cocaine] or whatever. It was supposed to be a scene about the father taking the daughter to the prom or the dance or something, parent night, and her daddy wasn't there, so [Redd's character] Al was filling in. So she was teaching him the new dances and he was teaching her the old dances. So they rehearsed that scene and when they finished, they were moving to the next scene which took place in the living room. So he and I walked over to the chair that he normally used, and we're standing and talking. Della was up on the steps and he fell. And we thought he was playing. We said, 'Redd, get up and stop.' By the time I turned, and Della said, 'Yeah, Redd, get up and stop playing and acting like a fool,' he had already turned blue. His face had contorted and his dentures were coming out. And I screamed for Kaho, and then that's when they rushed over."

Louis Pittman: "He was pretty upset. He was trying to get hold of some drugs and he was angry with everyone and he came out on to the set after he got some drugs. He got the cocaine and he was fine after that. He came out real jolly and happy and went to do the scene, and there was a little baby doll on the seat; it was a play doll that urinates. It wet the seat when he was getting ready to sit, and he started cracking a joke about it and picked it up and went to sit down and he passed out. He fell over. They hustled around him and they got the ambulance and they took him to the hospital."

Mariann Aalda: "Redd and I had just finished rehearsing a scene and I remember it was really hot that day. It was one of those Indian summer, really hot days in October and there was something wrong with the air conditioner, because I remember the doors being open to ventilate [the set]. We had just finished our scene in the kitchen and Redd was going into the living room set to do a scene with Della. He was coming through the door and somebody had put a bunch of boxes that were sitting on Grandpa's chair. Because it was just rehearsal, the boxes were not supposed to be there. So when Redd comes in and he goes to sit in Grandpa's chair, we thought he was doing a pratfall. We were just laughing hysterically, because it would be like Redd to say, 'Motherfucker, who put this crap in my chair?' And it went on a little too long so we just laughed and laughed and Della said, 'Okay, Redd, that's enough' and he didn't move. And she said, 'Redd!' And it took us a good twenty seconds before anybody realized what was wrong."

Greg Antonacci: "I was in the [writers'] office and we got a call that Redd had collapsed on the set. I ran down to the set as quickly as I could get there—the Paramount lot was pretty big—and [episode director] Shelley [Jensen] thought he was doing his 'I'm coming, Elizabeth!' and everyone thought it was a joke. Shelley said he tried to get up and went down again. The paramedics from Paramount revived him and got him in the ambulance. I heard he flatlined in the ambulance and they brought him back again."

Anthony Major: "His mouth was all twisted, so I screamed for Kaho right away because she said that the night before, he had been hot and cold, hot and cold, in the hotel room. But nobody paid any attention to it. And there was no nurse to check him out that morning. I mean, that's how fast it happened. Somebody called for an ambulance and it took them forever to come. And there was no oxygen, so the Paramount people had to go all the way back across wherever they came from to get the oxygen. By that time the 911 people were on the set. And then they worked on him there and then they took him to the hospital."

Mariann Aalda: "I remember running to the refrigerator to get some ice to put on his head and ran back. By that time there was a crowd around him and Della was saying to get back, let him breathe, and somebody took the ice from me to put on his head and that's when the paramedics came in and they took him to the hospital and we all carpooled to go to the hospital, the cast and some of the crew. And I remember when we were driving out, I looked up and there were all these black crows that flew up away from the studio. You know sometimes images make an impact on you? I remember that image."

Redd was rushed to Queen of Angels-Hollywood Presbyterian Medical Center. He was alive, but unconscious, and the situation looked bleak. "We stayed at the hospital for several hours and then they called us into this room, like a conference room at the hospital," Aalda said. "And Della said that the doctor said that Redd suffered a massive heart attack and that if he came out of it, he would not be the Redd that we knew, that he would be in a vegetative state. And I remember Della saying, 'That is not what Redd would want, but God has plans of His own, let's just pray for his best outcome' . . . and we all joined hands and prayed and then we left."

Redd lingered, clinging to life for several more hours. Anthony Major, Prince Spencer, Della Reese, and Greg Antonacci remained at the hospital, hoping for the best. At 7:45 p.m. that night, Redd died, with Kaho at his side. He was sixty-eight years old. He was survived by his wife of three months, Kaho, and his mother, Mary Carson, who was eighty-eight.

"The doctor came out and said, Mrs. Foxx, your husband is gone," said Reese. "And they pulled aside and they said, 'Well we gotta do something about this script, it's written for Redd and Della'—we're sitting in the hospital lobby there, a man just died . . . that still makes me mad."

"I was the last one there with his wife," said Antonacci. "At some point Della held a prayer circle and was sure that God had saved him. Kaho didn't speak much English and I sat with her and waited for the doctor, and out comes this Pakistani or Russian doctor. His accent was impenetrable . . . trying to explain the embolism. It was a nightmare."

The cause of death was listed as cardio respiratory arrest, cardiogenic shock, and acute myocardial infarction.

Redd's death made headlines around the country. "Redd Foxx was blessed with the ability to make people laugh and audiences everywhere loved him for it," said Brandon Tartikoff. "Within a short period of time, Redd and his *Royal Family* had won their way into millions of homes and hearts."

The *New York Times* devoted half a page to Redd's obituary, calling him the "Cantankerous Master of Bawdy Humor": "While Mr. Foxx was best known as the bow-legged, raspy-voiced star of *Sanford and Son* . . . he had had a long career on the black theater and cabaret circuit, where he was known as the dean of X-rated comedians . . . With the first of his party records, in 1956, Mr. Foxx began to be heard by larger audiences, eventually selling twenty million records. He was a bridge between a decades-old burlesque-show tradition of scatological party humor and a younger generation of comics and social satirists from Lenny Bruce to Andrew Dice Clay."

"Foxx . . . was a comedian's comedian, infinitely closer to the spirit of Rabelais and Henry Miller than the ostensibly liberated gross-out comics who parade through the clubs today," Lawrence Christon wrote in the *Los Angeles Times*. "A lot of his stand-up stuff is unquestionably dated, an expression of hang-ups different from our own. But what redeems it is his sense of sex as a tease, an embarrassment, something ineluctable and incomparable fun."

Redd's body was flown back to Las Vegas, where an open-casket funeral was held four days later on October 15. Anthony Major and Louis Pittman were among the pallbearers, and nearly one-thousand people filled the Palm Valley View Chapel to say goodbye, including Mike Tyson, Gladys Knight, Cholly Atkins, Lola Falana, blues singer Joe Williams, and Redd's former *Sanford and Son* co-star, Don "Bubba" Bexley. Betty Jeanne and Debraca showed up with Debraca's son, Paul Hiles. Slappy White was there, of course, as was LaWanda Page, Prince Spencer, and other members of Redd's inner circle, including attorney Paul Whitford. Colonel Tom Parker, the late Elvis Presley's manager— and Redd's Las Vegas gambling buddy—showed up with a cap Redd had given him ten years earlier.

Bill Cosby, Richard Pryor, and Eddie Murphy were nowhere to be found—though Murphy did send a telegram of condolence and later said he paid for the funeral. "Eddie didn't come to the funeral and I didn't like that at all," said Paul Whitford. "I didn't think that was fair, because so many black entertainers did turn out for the funeral." Maya Angelou sent a telegram, and Flip Wilson, who credited Redd with giving him his start in show business, also failed to materialize—but a Flip Wilson impostor *was* there. Even in death, Redd's world was infiltrated by the surreal and bizarre.

"LaWanda Page was there and signing autographs. I liked her a lot but she was kind of the center of attention at the funeral," Whitford said. "The funeral was open to the public and you've heard the term 'The Great Unwashed Masses'? A great deal of them came to the funeral. I looked up, and there was a woman walking down the aisle—this was a hot day in October—she had on shorts, a halter top, flip-flops, and she was carrying a baby with a bottle in his mouth. She was walking down to see the casket. There were a lot of people there who wanted to see a celebrity—dead or alive. I'm not so sure Redd wouldn't have gotten a kick out of it."

"They let me go in by myself and see him, because I wanted to be alone with him," said Page. "I stood next to the casket and talked to him just like he was living, because it just didn't seem like he was dead. And I said, 'Redd, I told you this and I told you that and what are you doing lying up here in this casket. You got no business laying up here in this casket.' And it's like I could hear him say, 'Oh, shut up, bitch!'"

Redd's funeral service was filled with lots of laughter, gospel music, and tears. Della Reese, who sang and led the service, delivered a stirring eulogy and also read "Ode to Kaho," a poem Redd had written to his new wife. It reduced everyone to tears. "He was a very sensitive man," said Reese. "If he had a dime and you wanted a dime, you had a dime. Everybody kept saying how happy he looked. He was doing what he wanted to do. He was in his proper place. He was on top."

Comedian Bernie Allen, who'd worked in Las Vegas with Redd many times over the years, joked about his friend's willingness to help others, usually as they streamed through Redd's dressing room after a show: "He handed out one hundred dollar bills to all of them. He must have thought he was giving them to the IRS."

"The funeral itself turned out to be kind of like a roast, but it was really quite interesting," said Whitford. "Della conducted it and she was wonderful, and Mike Tyson spoke very eloquently, which kind of surprised me. He didn't say a lot but what he said was from the heart."

Stuart Sheslow was there, too, and the sight of Redd lying in his casket reduced him to a fit of giggles. "The Pointer Sisters and I are in line as we're waiting to go up to the coffin," he said. "Well, I get up to the coffin and I crack up. I start laughing. And I'm looking down at Redd and he looks like Colonel Peanut. His hair is coiffed up, his beard is fluffed up. I said, 'They finally got him. They couldn't get him in life, but they got him. Look at him!' He was wearing a white suit, I mean, it was so un-Redd Foxx.'"

Redd was buried in Palm Valley View Memorial Park in Las Vegas. His headstone was adorned with the chiseled head of a red fox, with an upper-case "R" and a curved, lower-case "f" on either side of its head as the fox's eyes (the "f" on the right-hand side makes it appear that the fox is winking). Underneath the words "REDD FOXX: DEC. 9, 1922–OCT. 11, 1991" reads the inscription: "You are my ♥ always."

As his casket was lowered into the ground, a series of red balloons were released, floating upwards and out of sight into the clear blue sky.

At the time of Redd's death, four of the seven *Royal Family* episodes he taped had already aired, and CBS now had to decide how, or even if, to proceed with a series bereft of its star attraction. There was talk that Sherman Hemsley, the former star of *The Jeffersons*, would step in to replace Redd (in another role), or that *Good Times* star John Amos would be hired to play an uncle.

CBS and Paramount officials decided to continue with the show, and to work Redd/Al's death into the storyline. CBS ran on-air promotional spots touting the decision: "Like any family, *The Royal Family* will go on." Redd's final three episodes aired sporadically from October 30 through November 20. In the meantime, former *227* star Jackee Harry was brought in to play Ruth, the estranged half-sister of Victoria Royal (Reese's character).

Jackee made her *Royal Family* debut in "New Beginnings," the first episode without Redd, which aired on November 27, 1991. In the episode, news of Al's sudden death at the post office was delivered to Victoria by several of his co-workers—played by Don Bexley and Prince Spencer. The episode featured Al's funeral (Slappy White and Reynaldo Rey played two of Al's buddies) as Victoria grappled with her grief and Ruth was immersed into the show's plotline.

Following the "New Beginnings" episode, *The Royal Family* went on a five-month hiatus while the writers retooled the show. When it returned on April 8, 1992, Jackee was no longer Victoria's half-sister, but Al and Victoria's oldest daughter, which was more believable, considering the twenty-five-year age difference between her and Della Reese. But the show never regained its footing. CBS aired four more new episodes of *The Royal Family* before pulling the plug in May. Two remaining episodes never aired.

The tangled financial web that defined Redd Foxx later in life proved just as problematic to those he left behind. Redd's estate was, to no one's surprise, in total disarray, to the point where insurance policies and benefits named Betty Jeanne, the wife he'd divorced nearly twenty years before, as Redd's beneficiary. "What happened was, unfortunately, Redd had never gone to the Screen Actors Guild and changed the beneficiary," said Anthony Major. "When he joined [SAG], he and Betty Jeanne were married. He had her as the beneficiary. So there was $50,000 that went to her when he died. It went to Betty Jeanne, not Kaho. Because he and Kaho had been married less than a year."

The IRS was still expecting its share of a reported $3.6 million that Redd owed in back taxes, and had questions of its own regarding who owed what. Meanwhile, Betty Jeanne and Debraca battled Kaho over the estate, or what was left of it. "There were so many players and so much disarray . . . it was a no-win situation for any members of the [legal] team," said Mark Risman. "After Redd passed away, even though a lot of the items could have been under Prince Spencer's control, I think he just got tired of it and decided to move on. There was nobody there to expertly market what could have been [marketed] in 1991."

Redd had not provided for Kaho in his will, leaving his wife of three months saddled with his debts, and with the house on 5460 Eastern Avenue in Las Vegas. After the funeral, Kaho asked Prince Spencer, Slappy White, and Anthony Major to stop by. There was something troubling her. "She said, 'Well, Redd came to me last night and he said, 'Nigger with a black neck,'" said Major. "And we looked at each other and said, 'What?!' And she didn't know what it meant and she was asking us if any of us knew what it meant, or what he was trying to say to her. She said, 'He's not gone, he's in this house.'" Years later, several people who lived in the house after Kaho moved out claimed the place was haunted by Redd's ghost.

On November 18, 1991, Kaho filed a petition with the Clark County District Court, stating that she was entitled to keep the house, "all of the wearing apparel and provisions on hand" and all of the furniture. Among other possessions, she also petitioned to keep Redd's private library, "necessary yard equipment," four pickup trucks and Redd's claim to a mine in Jean, Nevada.

"Everybody tried to help her," Louis Pittman said of Kaho. "Eddie Murphy's people gave her some money. The IRS allowed her to stay in the house. But she felt that the mortgage company and the IRS should have let her stay there for free. She didn't want to make a mortgage payment. It wasn't going to work like that. I stuck around for a little bit and then I just left, because they were starting to fight over whatever junk was there and it just disgusted me."

postscript

The battle over the Redd Foxx estate continues to this day. In 2006, Debraca was removed as the administrator of the estate after failing to provide an accounting of revenue received in royalties, residuals, and licensing deals dating back to Redd's death. Kaho, meanwhile, went to court again, this time accusing Debraca of keeping money that should have gone toward paying off Redd's $3.6 million IRS debt.

After some legal back-and-forth, a Nevada probate court—in a last-ditch attempt to resolve Redd's outstanding debts—put the Clark County Public Administrator in charge of managing the Redd Foxx estate. The administrator managed to collect over $100,000 in fees for the estate, including a $5,000 fee from CBS Studios—for using a video clip of Redd in an episode of the Chris Rock-produced UPN/CW series, *Everybody Hates Chris*—and $3,000 from Hallmark for using Redd's likeness on a greeting card. The administrator then took the bizarre step of trying to "sell" Redd's life story to the highest bidder, but that effort went nowhere. The Redd Foxx estate remains a tangled mess.

"The other ladies in his life that he trusted with his money probably ended up with it," said Anthony Major. "A couple of times when Redd would run short, he would have me go get it for him. There was one woman, I don't remember her name, I just remember she had a finger missing. But there was another Korean lady that lived almost down in Long Beach somewhere. She would keep [some of Redd's cash] and I would go get it from her from time to time and he would then have money and cash and stuff so the IRS and everybody couldn't get to it."

But the legacy of Redd Foxx extends far beyond his monetary debts and his battles with the IRS. A whole new generation of fans has been exposed to Redd's television work through reruns of *Sanford and Son* on cable's TV Land network, which continue to draw solid ratings—a remarkable feat for a series that premiered nearly forty years ago. In 1992, a year after his death, Redd was honored in his native city with a star on the Saint Louis Walk of Fame.

In 1999, the *E! True Hollywood Story* television series devoted an entire episode to Redd; that was followed two years later by the A&E series *Biography*, which spent an hour retelling Redd's life and gave old friends including Della Reese, LaWanda Page, Prince Spencer, and boyhood pal Steve Trimble the chance to share their memories of Redd on camera.

As the 1990s segued into the new millennium, Redd's legacy also entered the digital age. He is a strong presence on the Internet, with dozens of links related to Redd, including YouTube—which has many video clips and recordings of Redd, including entire *Sanford and Son* episodes—and www.reddfoxx.com, a Web site devoted to "The Chief."

The fall of 2011 will mark the twentieth anniversary of Redd's death. Sadly, many of Redd's friends and contemporaries are gone now, although some outlived him by many years.

Redd's first manager, Bardu Ali, passed away in October 1981 in Inglewood, California, at the age of seventy-five from kidney failure. Ali guided Redd's career from the late 1960s through the turbulent *Sanford and Son* years. He kept in touch with Redd after retiring from show business, and was a frequent guest at events honoring his former client.

Although I searched high and low, I was unable to find Redd's first wife, Evelyn Killebrew, or his third and fourth wives, Joi and Kaho. So, for them, I'll just assume "whereabouts unknown." Betty Jeanne still lives in Las Vegas, where she and Redd spent most of their years together. Her daughter, Debraca, lives nearby.

Redd's boyhood pal, Steve Trimble, one of the original Four Bon Bons, died in May 2002 at the age of seventy-eight. Trimble spent most of his adult life working as a doorman for a Chicago condominium complex and gained a local reputation as a jazz musician of some note. Whenever Redd was performing in Chicago at a theater without a house band, he would call Trimble and have him put a band together as his opening act. The friends remained close throughout their lives, and Redd put Trimble in an early episode of *Sanford and Son* (in a non-speaking role), and named series character "Reverend Trimble" after his old friend. Redd encouraged Trimble to move out to California or Las Vegas to further his musical ambitions, but Trimble chose to stay in Chicago. He cherished the electric stand-up bass Redd had given him as a gift.

Slappy White, Redd's onetime comedy partner as half of Foxx and White, died in November 1995 at the age of seventy-four after suffering a heart attack at his home in Brigantine, New Jersey. After Redd became famous on *Sanford and Son*, he rarely opened a show without Slappy on the bill. The two men remained the closest of friends up until the day Redd died.

LaWanda Page, Redd's childhood friend whose show-business career benefited the most from Redd's friendship and generosity, passed away in September 2002 at the age of eighty-one after battling diabetes and suffering a stroke. Page parlayed her *Sanford and Son* role as Aunt Esther ("Watch it, Sucka!") into a successful television career, starring in the short-lived *Sanford Arms* and returning as Fred Sanford's foil on *Sanford*. She later appeared on many television shows including *Amen*, *Martin*, *Family Matters*, *227* and *Diff'rent Strokes* and had small roles in several movies (including *Shakes the Clown* and Steve Martin's *My Blue Heaven*).

Prince Spencer, who spent over thirty years as Redd's friend, confidante, *de facto* manager, and Guy Friday, has, as of this writing, survived into his mid-nineties. After Redd's death, Prince retired from show business. He and his wife Jerri live quietly in Las Vegas.

Redd's mother, Mary Sanford Carson, outlived her only surviving son by two years. She passed away in 1993 at the age of ninety, lingering in and out of a coma for several years before her death. She's buried next to Redd in Palm Valley View Memorial Park in Las Vegas.

Dee Crawford and Anthony Major, who both worked closely with Redd during their tenures as Presidents of Redd Foxx Productions— Dee in the mid-to-late 1970s and Anthony in the mid-1980s until Redd's death—have thrived in their respective fields.

Dee, who was married to the late Los Angeles Dodgers star Willie Crawford, is a star in her own right as a successful real estate agent in Beverly Hills, California.

Anthony, who continued to work behind-the-scenes in television, movies, and the theater after Redd's death, is now Program Director for the Zora Neale Hurston Institute for Documentary Studies and Associate Professor/Film Department at the University of Central

Florida. He and his mentor, Stuart Sheslow—who produced, directed, and wrote for *Sanford* and *The Redd Foxx Show*—hope to eventually turn Redd's life story into a Hollywood movie. Their love and admiration for Redd remains strong even now, twenty years after his death.

"He lived and did everything his heart wanted to even *think* it wanted to do, and he had a lot of fun along the way," said Crawford, summing up her memories of her former boss. "He helped a lot of people. He was Redd being Redd in live, living color. He didn't pull any punches and he didn't hold anything back. What you saw was what you got. He was cool. He was it. He was funny. Most of all, he was creative. He was such a natural-born comic. He had a lot of ups and downs, a lot of hangers-on. He had some demons. What would he do without three or four guys around? What would he do without his cocaine and reefer? What would he do without a place to stand up and tell a joke? Those guys were his audience—all the rest was a stage.

"He was *always* Redd Foxx."

notes

chapter one

1 "That name just fell on my heart": *Jet* (25 December 1980).

2 "My folks worked regularly": *New York Daily News* (7 October 1973).

2 "There's some white in the family, too": Joe X Price, *Redd Foxx, B.S.*, (Contemporary Books, 1979).

2 "He was one of the best first basemen ever": *Penthouse* (March 1971).

2 "I remember an ice cream cone, two for a nickel": *The Barbara Walters Special*, ABC Television (31 May 1977).

4 "It was across the street from a brewery": Price, *Redd Foxx, B.S.*

4 "I remember one time [Fred] came into the cafeteria": *Biography*, A&E (2000).

5 "School meant nothing to me . . . ": Price, *Redd Foxx, B.S.*

5 "Sometimes if the teacher would get on him about something he would try to jive":*Biography*, A&E (2000).

5 "After school I'd dig around the market for old cabbage leaves": Price, *Redd Foxx,B.S.*

6 "I was so raggedy I was too ashamed to go and pick up my diploma when I got out": *Penthouse* (March 1971).

7 "We called him 'Smiley,' because he always smiled": *Biography*, A&E (2000).

7 "He could talk about you, your mother, and other members of your family in derogatory language": Travis J. Dempsey, *The Life and Times of Redd Foxx* (Urban Research Press, 1999).

9 "We played on the street corners and passed the hat": Bronzeville interview with Steve Trimble, Charles Walton (jazzinstituteofchicago.org. 2002).

9 "I was working professionally, because I was making money": Interview with Jane Ardmore, archives of The Academy of Motion Picture Arts & Sciences. 1972.

10 "I don't think I have ever gotten to know her": Interview with Jane Ardmore.1972.

10 "Cried all the way there": Price, *Redd Foxx, B.S.*

11 "A group of detectives chased us": *Penthouse* (March 1971).

11 "They framed us": *Biography*, A&E (2000).

11 "Because I could run pretty fast": Interview with Jane Ardmore. 1972.

11 "As we got closer to Manhattan I saw it turn black": *Penthouse* (March 1971).

chapter two

14 "For a while we did pretty well with the group": Penthouse (March 1971).

16 "Now here's the Jump Swinging Six": *Major Bowes Original Amateur Hour* (27 July 1939).

17 "Whenever I had the bread, I would spend all my time at the Savoy Ballroom on 140th and Lennox": *Penthouse* (March 1971).

17 "We saw some of the greatest bands in the world": *Penthouse* (March 1971).

17 "We kept going until the war broke up the group": *Penthouse* (March 1971).

18 "I went to a draft board in Harlem": *Penthouse* (March 1971).

18 "It became just a fight for survival": *Penthouse* (March 1971).

18 "And I like to starved to death waiting for my salary": *Penthouse* (March 1971).

19 "My mother knew about this": *Penthouse* (March 1971).

19 "I wasn't guilty. I know that's what all cons say, but this is true": Price, *Redd Foxx, B.S.*

19 "Just a bunch of kids, alongside some of the baddest group of folks I ever met": Price, *Redd Foxx, B.S.*

20 "It was hard to stay away from pot, knowing how much you could make with it": Price, *Redd Foxx, B.S.*

20 "I was watching the Buddy Johnson band that night": Price, *Redd Foxx, B.S.*

21 "No realistic goal for a nigger": Bruce Perry *Malcolm X: The Last Speeches* (Pathfinder Press 1989).

21 "A jam-packed four-thirty a.m. crowd at Jimmy's Chicken Shack": Malcolm X. and Alex Haley, *The Autobiography of Malcolm X* (Ballantine Books 1987).

21 "He was a beautiful": *The Barbara Walters Special*, ABC Television (31 May 1977).

22 "Chicago Red was the funniest dishwasher on this earth": *The Autobiography of Malcolm X.*

22 "Malcolm was about the same color as me": *Penthouse* (March 1971).

22 "They used to rob places together and sleep on rooftops together": Author interview with Anthony Major.

22 "We had about five hundred pounds of newspapers up there": *Ebony* (April 1967).

22 "There was a bunch of guys in the neighborhood": *Penthouse* (March 1971).

22 "Malcolm didn't have the showbiz talent": *Penthouse* (March 1971).

23 "We'd sell one or two of them a day off the roof": *Penthouse* (March 1971).

23 "They hung around us 'cause they were shoveling pot": Tammy Kernodle, *Soul on Soul: The Life and Music of Mary Lou Williams* (Northeastern 2004).

23 "What was going on in America wasn't on Malcolm's mind or mine": Price, *Redd Foxx, B.S.*

23 "I remember one time Malcolm and I joined the Communist Party": *Penthouse* (March 1971).

NOTES

24 "You'd dance with the chicks, smell the perfume and eat the sandwiches": *Penthouse* (March 1971).

24 "I was always the one that would up with the black chick": *Penthouse* (March 1971).

chapter three

25 "I didn't like Jon or Elroy so they called me 'Smiley'": Interview with Jane Ardmore. 1972.

25 "I added the extra letters onto both names": *Photo Screen* (October 1972).

26 "Baltimore was tough": *Ebony* (June 1988).

26 "They wanted to hear something that they're used to down there on the docks": *Biography* (A&E 2000).

26 "I had never done a nightclub comedy routine before": *Baltimore Afro-American* (3 November 1959).

26 "As a kid in Baltimore": Ralph Matthews, *Baltimore Afro-American*.

27 "Folks, we have a celebrity in the house": *Baltimore Afro-American*, (February 1972).

27 "Redd liked to party and Redd could be arrogant": David Ritz, *Faith in Time: The Life of Jimmy Scott* (Da Capo Press 2003).

27 "In the morning he'd bang on my door": Author interview with Jimmy Scott.

27 "He was telling jokes and everybody was crazy about him": Author interview.

28 "Redd did so much for so many people that he worked with": Author interview.

28 "'This boy's gotta sing in the Big Apple'": Author interview.

30 "He was going to rape her": *Penthouse* (March 1971).

31 "My father-in-law was so good [at supporting us that] pretty soon I didn't have to hustle": *Penthouse* (March 1971).

32 "I began to get tired of this whole idea": Price, *Redd Foxx, B.S.*

32 "It was hard to get work, and I hated sitting around idle": Price, *Redd Foxx, B.S.*

32 "For a few hours": Guy Sterling, *The Newark Star-Ledger* (15 April 2007).

32 "Redd Foxx, Ace of Comic Emcees": *Baltimore Afro-American* (30 October 1948).

32 "Gamby's is drawing good weekend crowds": *Baltimore Afro-American* (7 August 1948).

33 "Fellow entertainers often wondered": *Baltimore Afro-American* (13 September 1949).

34 "Colored boys whose comedy pantomime": *Billboard* (10 July 1943).

34 "Ah was so tahred, ah wuz so lazy": Jack Schiffman, *Harlem Heyday* (Prometheus Books 1984).

35 "When I took the hat off": *Penthouse* (March 1971).

35 "Redd and I marched out onstage": Price, *Redd Foxx, B.S.*

36 "We died like dogs": *Penthouse* (March 1971).

37 "It wasn't that they were raggedy, dirty and lowdown": Author interview.

37 "As good as Dean Martin and Jerry Lewis": *Los Angeles Times* (18 March 1973).

38 "Nobody wanted to hire us on a white job": *Los Angeles Times* (18 March 1973).

38 "The white public's concept of black comedy": *Penthouse* (March 1971).

NOTES

chapter four

42 "As luck would have it": Price, *Redd Foxx, B.S.*

42 "She looked like something": Price, *Redd Foxx, B.S.*

42 "All I could see was they looked like money": Price, *Redd Foxx, B.S.*

43 "California was a drag": *Penthouse* (March 1971).

43 "Man, there just wasn't enough money:" Price, *Redd Foxx, B.S.*

44 "He was the greatest third baseman that ever lived": *New York Daily News* (7 October 1973).

44 "But they didn't really give him a chance": *Penthouse* (March 1971).

46 "That's the humor I heard in the ghettos": *New York Times* (30 July 1982).

47 "These were three rather large women singers": *Metroactive.com* (27 December 2006 to 2 January 2007).

47 "Frequently sullen, grumpy and morose": George Lipsitz, *Midnight at the Barrelhouse: The Johnny Otis Story* (University of Minnesota Press 2010).

48 "I can't stand that bitch": Lipsitz, *Midnight at the Barrelhouse.*

48 "I was doing so bad": Interview with Robert Bennett (June 1972).

49 "I wasn't allowed to work in white places": *Sepia* (January 1976).

49 "Foxx removed the rural black dialect": Christine Acham, *Revolution Televised: Prime Time and the Struggle for Black Power* (University of Minnesota Press 2005).

49 "He was the first of the *urban* black comics": Acham, *Revolution Televised.*

51 "I listened to this guy, and he wasn't really obscene": George Lipsitz and Johnny Otis, *Upside Your Head: Rhythm and Blues on Central Avenue* (Wesleyan University Press 1993).

51 "While I was in a club at 38th and Western": *Penthouse* (March 1971).

51 "They went crazy!": Lipsitz and Otis, *Upside Your Head.*

51 "So the next day I see him": Lipsitz and Otis, *Upside Your Head.*

chapter five

53 "Marcene, 'Dimples,' the little one, she had the talent": Interview with author.

53 "We worked more classy clubs, more high-class things": Interview with author.

53 "I looked up there and I loved her": Interview with Jane Ardmore. 1972.

54 "I didn't like the jokes he was telling": *Biography*, A&E.

54 "I was young and handsome": Interview with Jane Ardmore.

54 "He would come in the dressing room": *Biography*, A&E.

54 "I would see Redd backstage and he would never pay any attention to me": *Biography*, A&E.

54 "I was cussing": Interview with Jane Ardmore.

54 "He was just chasing her down": Interview with author.

54 "But I was happy because he was a nice guy": Interview with author.

58 "There was a black color line in Vegas": Interview with author.

NOTES

59 "I could perform in Vegas, but I could not eat there": Interview with author.

60 "The first thing I did [at NBC]": Interview with author.

60 "The material I did was the stuttering bit": *Baltimore Afro-American* (3 November 1959).

60 "Stay off the South, white women, the Congo, and the President": Mel Watkins, *On the Real Side: A History of African American Comedy* (Lawrence Hill Books 1999).

61 "I had no idea the first album would sell like it did": *Penthouse* (March 1971).

61 "Everybody bought the records": Interview with author.

61 "The Redd Foxx albums": Watkins, *On the Real Side.*

63 "Foxx, an ace comic, performs several times nightly": *Chicago Daily Defender* (31 March 31 1959).

64 "The 20 Grand held about three thousand people ": Interview with author.

64 "Some of the big companies have tried to get me to split": *Baltimore Afro-American* (3 November 1959).

65 "That was a powerhouse place at the time": Penthouse (March 1971).

65 "Better laugh now": *Jet* (19 April 1962).

66 "One club on the Strip": *Los Angeles Times* (18 March 1973).

67 "The Crescendo engagement promises to be a historic one": *Chicago Daily Defender* (28 September 1960).

67 "This is an important break for me": *Chicago Daily Defender* (28 September 1960).

chapter six

69 "There are good Negro comics": *New York Times* (30 April 1961).

70 "If it had not been for Dick Gregory": *Chicago Daily Defender* (23 January 1963).

70 "Working clean doesn't pay anything": *Ebony* (April 1967).

70 "If your lips were filled with quarters": *Chicago Daily Defender* (11 February 1961).

71 "I just don't think I've been treated right": *New York Amersterdam News* (20 May 1961).

72 "He's just trying to break his contract": *Chicago Daily Defender* (3 June 1961).

72 "Distasteful and crude": *Los Angeles Times* (6 August 1961).

72 "Foxx willingly signed his contract with us": *Chicago Daily Defender* (9 July 1962).

73 "We recovered two years of over-payment to Foxx": *Chicago Daily Defender* (25 September 1963).

74 "Redd Foxx, in his first Vegas appearance": *Las Vegas Review-Journal* (25 October 1963).

75 "I had seen Foxx": Author interview.

75 "I said I wanted to invite him on the *Today Show*": Author interview.

75 "I put him on the air and it worked": Author interview.

76 "I knew all of Redd's material": Author interview.

76 "I thought he would be much more comfortable": Author interview.

76 "He said he didn't believe in black power": Author interview.

76 "I admonished him": Author interview.

77 "I said to Foxx": Author interview.

77 "TV is nice, but I love the applause": *Chicago Daily Defender* (3 August 1974).

77 "What my husband gets": *Photo Screen* (August 1973).

78 "There was always the question": Redd Foxx and Norma Miller, *The Redd Foxx Encyclopedia of Black Humor* (W. Ritchie Press, 1977).

78 "I've always had the feeling": Interview with Robert Bennett.

78 "Sophisticates will have a field day": *Variety* (21 April 21 1964).

79 "I stayed out there two weeks": *Chicago Daily Defender* (9 February 1965).

79 "He was just a street urchin": *Biography*, A&E.

79 "When my brother died": Interview with Jane Ardmore.

80 "Frank Sinatra changed my whole recording scene": *Penthouse* (March 1971).

80 "He became quite a heavy gambler": Interview with author.

80 "Redd Foxx, some people swear": *Baltimore Afro-American* (31 October 1970).

81 "Foxx, who is notorious": *Los Angeles Times* (22 December 1966).

81 "The ghetto talk moves into two other areas": *Chicago Daily Defender* (28 March 1967).

82 "It's the best thing that happened": *Las Vegas Sun* (2 May 1967).

chapter seven

85 "I spent many nights": Todd Gold and Richard Pryor, *Pryor Convictions: And Other Life Sentences* (Pantheon 1995).

85 "Ever get ejected out of a joint": Price, *Redd Foxx, B.S.*

86 "Los Angeles is a rotten town": Price, *Redd Foxx, B.S.*

86 "We wore red patent-leather mini skirts": Author interview.

86 "I used to go to his club": Author interview.

87 "He ran the club like a gangster": Gold and Pryor, *Pryor Convictions.*

87 "It was the Troc or the Grove": Price, *Redd Foxx, B.S.*

87 "As long a hike as it is from here to Forest Lawn": Price, *Redd Foxx, B.S.*

87 "It was The Queen who brought me to California": Price, *Redd Foxx, B.S.*

88 "Redd's Place became a kind of rallying point": Price, *Redd Foxx, B.S.*

88 "Just as casual as you like": Price, *Redd Foxx, B.S.*

88 "Redd would stand outside": Price, *Redd Foxx, B.S.*

88 "Battling each other for the attention": Gold and Pryor, *Pryor Convictions.*

88 "Because you're a junkie": Gold and Pryor, *Pryor Conviction.s*

89 "Redd used to call him": Price, *Redd Foxx, B.S.*

89 "Steve Allen is a prince of a man": Price, *Redd Foxx, B.S.*

89 "Redd used to smoke marijuana": Author interview.

90 "He was the epitome": Gold and Pryor, *Pryor Convictions.*

90 "I hung around there often": Price, *Redd Foxx, B.S.*

90 "Talk about intimate": Price, *Redd Foxx, B.S.*

91 "He would hire a lot of his friends": *Biography*, A&E.

91 "Money is not green with Redd Foxx": Price, *Redd Foxx, B.S.*

91 "Money and him just ain't on the best of terms": Price, *Redd Foxx, B.S.*

91 "Now the two black guys jump": Price, *Redd Foxx, B.S.*

92 "For about an hour, Redd rattled off joke after joke": *New York Amsterdam News* (30 September 1967).

92 "A lot of you don't know:" *Chicago Daily Defender* (14 October 1967).

93 "So I said to Redd": Price, *Redd Foxx, B.S.*

94 "If somebody walks out of this hotel": Price, *Redd Foxx, B.S.*

94 "He was a businessman, it was just the wrong business": Author interview.

95 "I saw Redd and Bardu": Price, *Redd Foxx, B.S.*

95 "A tragedy because I may have to close it up": Price, *Redd Foxx, B.S.*

96 "Aesop's Fox, when he had lost his tail": *Los Angeles Times* (2 January 1968).

96 "The stars came to Redd's rescue": Author interview.

97 "We tried everything": Price, *Redd Foxx, B.S.*

97 "I remember one night": Price, *Redd Foxx, B.S.*

98 "When Bill Cosby became active": *Penthouse* (March 1971).

98 "What the writers had to do": *Los Angeles Times* (13 October 1968).

98 "We're not trying to prove anything": *Los Angeles Times* (13 October 1968).

101 "We had a screening": Author interview.

101 "Most of the comedy": Los Angeles Times (18 October 1968).

101 "We ran it for NBC": Author interview.

101 "I can only remember one time": *Penthouse* (March 1971).

102 "One executive told me": *New York Times* (14 June 1998).

102 "I was doing the *Della* show": Author interview.

102 "That was insulting": *Biography*, A&E.

102 "From a theatrical point of view": *New York Times* (28 December 1969).

103 "What prisoners want to hear": *Los Angeles Times* (12 January 1973).

104 "Redd was a tremendous jazz fan": Author interview.

104 "My little son, Philip": Author interview.

104 "Of course we would bring Redd out": Author interview.

104 "Get a round ball of cocaine": Author interview.

105 "There were bills under there": Price, *Redd Foxx, B.S.*

105 "I bought that place": Interview with Jane Ardmore.

106 "They weren't, but of course": Author interview.

106 "The way we heard it": Price, *Redd Foxx, B.S.*

chapter eight

108 "I ain't working for no peanuts!": Price, *Redd Foxx, B.S.*

109 "It was Ossie's first movie script": Author interview.

109 "He was cast": Author interview.

109 "My introduction to Redd Foxx": Author interview.

110 "A conventional white movie": *New York Times* (11 June 1970).

110 "The pace is fast": *Los Angeles Times* (23 July 1970).

110 "We had more people": Author interview.

112 "Flip and the other young comedians": Author interview.

113 "There was a friendship": Author interview.

115 "Mainly, we had in mind Jewish or Italian actors": *Los Angeles Times* (29 October 1972).

116 "We were either going to get Italian, Jewish or Black": Author interview.

116 "Believe me, he lived hard": Author interview.

117 "That made him feel better": Price, *Redd Foxx, B.S.*

117 "He came in": Author interview.

117 "After learning about the series format": Demond Wilson, *Second Banana: The Bitter Sweet Memoirs of the Sanford & Son Years* (Demond Wilson Enterprises 2009).

118 "[Redd] liked the script": *Los Angeles Times* (29 October 1972).

118 "I cooked dinner for everyone": Interview with Jane Ardmore.

118 "We were rehearsing ": Author interview.

118 "We had a problem with Fred Silverman": Author interview.

118 "It was one of the stupidest things I did at CBS": Author interview.

119 "Redd played a reporter": Author interview.

119 "We had committed to a pilot": Author interview.

119 "Well, when he said that": Author interview.

120 "Herb said, 'I can't go to CBS'": Author interview.

120 "I said, 'OK, you guys are going to sit and watch . . .'": Author interview.

120 "The *All in the Family* cast fell on the floor": Author interview.

120 "And as were walking out the door": Author interview.

121 "Veteran black comedian Redd Foxx": *New York Post* (28 September 1971).

121 "Redd Foxx stars": *Los Angeles Times* (10 November 1971).

122 "Just as soon as I put those big heavy shoes on": *New York Times* (20 June 1976).

122 "Fred Sanford is Mary Sanford": *Sammy and Company* (1975).

123 "I anticipate we've got that audience": *Los Angeles Times* (16 December 1971).

123 "They'll be saying things": *Baltimore Afro-American* (28 December 1971).

123 "We paid him": Author interview.

123 "I don't think that's a putdown": *Los Angeles Times* (16 December 1971).

124 "He said, 'I'd like you to write": Billboard.com (4 November 2010).

125 "If you remember": Author interview.

126 "A lot of whites": *Los Angeles Times* (18 March 1973).

126 "In America it's got to be black or white . . .": *Sepia* (January 1976).

126 "Veteran black comedian Redd Foxx": *New York Post* (15 January 1972).

126 "It's the funniest show": *Los Angeles Times* (15 January 1972).

127 "A warm, funny show": *New York Daily News* (15 January 1972).

127 "If overnight ratings mean anything": *Los Angeles Times* (18 January 1972).

127 "Niggas don't leave the house": *Second Banana*.

127 "To say that the younger man": *Soul* (28 February 1972).

128 "Redd became a star": Author interview.

NOTES

129 "In Vegas, there's nothin' to do": *New York Times* (6 February 1972).

129 "Fred Sanford is just an infant": *Los Angeles Times* (18 March 1973).

129 "Some people say": *Second: Banana.*

130 "Although he's paid his dues": *Chicago Daily Defender* (8 May 1972).

130 "The place was jammed": Author interview.

130 "We played fair dates": *Second Banana.*

131 "Kiss me. Kiss me": Rich, John. *Warm Up the Snake: A Hollywood Memoir* (University of Michigan Press 2006).

131 "Don't blame me, ma'am": *Los Angeles Times* (6 October 1972).

132 "It's an agreeable show": *Life* (21 April 1972).

132 "He's a warm, lovable, saucy": *New York Daily News* (6 February 1972).

133 "Redd could string together": Author interview.

134 "We had a nine o'clock table read": Author interview.

134 "The old man, played by Redd Foxx": *Time* (25 September 1972).

chapter nine

135 "He's not an idiot": *Los Angeles Times* (10 October 1972).

136 "'Sanford and Son' Is White to the Core'": *New York Times* (17 June 1973).

137 "I'm a guy who got rid of his slave name": Author interview.

137 "Aaron Ruben reads the Sunday *New York Times*": Author interview.

137 "The writers are beginning to learn": *Time* (25 September 1972).

138 "In order to eliminate the word": *New York Daily News* (6 February 1972).

138 "I am not gonna eat watermelon on TV": Interview with Robert Bennett (June 1972).

138 "We sit around a table and I tell them": *Los Angeles Times* (18 March 1973).

138 "The first time I said 'nigger'": *Los Angeles Times* (18 March 1973).

138 "They would say that they didn't think": *Los Angeles Times* (13 March, 1974).

138 "He was making a lot of noise": Author interview.

139 "It was a big deal that Redd": Author interview.

139 "I did not want to do that": Author interview.

139 "He was very down-to-earth": Author interview.

140 "It was rampant": Author interview.

140 "Redd Foxx used a lot of cocaine": Author interview.

141 "In between the readings": Author interview.

141 "There would be a lot of people": Alan Rafkin, *Cue the Bunny on the Rainbow: Tales from TV's Most Prolific Sitcom Director* (Syracuse University Press 1998).

141 "We could never get any insurance on him": Author interview.

141 "He was a man who openly did drugs": Rafkin, *Cue the Bunny on the Rainbow.*

142 "Oftentimes we wouldn't know what to expect": Author interview.

142 "When we cut the show together": Author interview.

143 "Redd would say things like": Author interview.

143 "There was a woman": Author interview.

144 "Almost had a heart attack for real": *Los Angeles Times* (12 January 1973).

144 "So in comes Redd": Author interview.

144 "She said, 'I'll tell you what'": Author interview.

145 "And he came back": Author interview.

145 "Redd touched so many lives:" Author interview.

145 "He did look after his old friends": Author interview.

146 "Most of my friends:" *New York Daily News* (7 October 1973).

146 "A lot of people retired": *Sammy and Company*.

146 "Bubba, Don Bexley": *Sammy and Company*.

146 "One day, NBC took a bus": Author interview.

148 "I hadn't seen Redd": *Jet* (6 May 1976).

149 "She was a sensational gal": Author interview.

149 "I remember when she came onto the show": Author interview.

149 "They had a ball together on stage": Author interview.

150 "I ran into a *Sanford and Son* Seabees battalion": *Los Angeles Times* (12 January 1973).

150 "Hope told me to take it easy on the tour": *Los Angeles Times* (12 January 1973).

150 "Soldiers are just like prisoners": *Los Angeles Times* (12 January 1973).

150 "Now that Redd Foxx on *Sanford and Son*, he's amazing": *Los Angeles Times* (6 May 1973).

151 "I remember one day": Author interview.

151 "Like drinking about fifteen cups of coffee": Patsi Bale Cox and Tony Orlando, *Halfway to Paradise* (St. Martin's Griffin 2002).

151 "That was the heyday of cocaine": Author interview.

151 "He was addicted to Keno": Author interview.

152 "They needed somebody to work": Author interview.

chapter ten

155 "That show was monstrous": Author interview.

155 "There was a show": Author interview.

156 "We probably don't have": Author interview.

156 "I come from a job": *Ebony* (June 1974).

157 "I think part of the problem": Rafkin, *Cue the Bunny on the Rainbow*.

157 "I can make over $35,000 a week": *New York Daily News* (16 July 1973).

158 "We couldn't pay him": Author interview.

158 "My arguments were simple": *New York Daily News* (16 July 1973).

158 "Hit in the mouth with a clenched fist": *Soul* (24 November 1975).

160 "Bud had such an annoying way of speaking": Author interview.

160 "We never argued": *Ebony* (June 1974).

160 "I think you need to see this for yourself": *Second Banana*.

161 "At least ten young women": *Second Banana*.

161 "For years while I did nothing": *New York Daily News* (16 July 1973).

161 "One must remember": *Jet* (22 February 1973).

161 "He came to me and said": Author interview.

162 "He's much better": *Soul* (1 April 1974).

163 "I was in a theatre troupe": Author interview.

163 "For some reason": Author interview.

163 "That was a weird time": Author interview.

164 "It was strange": Author interview.

164 "We got so mad": Author interview.

164 "Most of my enjoyment": *Los Angeles Times* (2 April 1974).

165 "The rash is gone": *New York Daily News* (22 February 1974).

165 "They're making a lot of bread": *Chicago Daily Defender* (25 February 1974).

165 "Like a boy and not a man": *Associated Press* (7 March 1974) and *Biography*, A&E.

166 "Until today, nobody could say": *Ebony* (June 1974).

166 "If I have to work": *Ebony* (June 1974).

166 "When people make a comment": *Sammy and Company* (1975).

166 "Twenty five grand a week ain't bad": *Los Angeles Times* (13 March 1974).

167 "They had one show": *Los Angeles Times* (13 March 1974).

167 "As for the working conditions": *Los Angeles Times* (13 March 1974).

167 "This prolonged the season": *Los Angeles Times* (13 March 1974).

167 "The series seems to be alive": *Ebony* (June 1974)

168 "It certainly must open up": *Ebony* (June 1974).

168 "All I want to do": *New York Post* (2 May 1974).

168 "But if I owned one-fourth of myself": *Ebony* (30 May 1974).

169 "I've had to change the script many times": *Jet* (9 May 1974).

169 "But I hope to honor my other commitments": *Soul* (15 April 1974).

170 "This is why he has a problem": *Ebony* (June 1974).

170 "Not only can Redd tough it out": *Ebony* (30 May 1974).

170 "She has a Mercedes that isn't a year old": *New York Post* (2 May 1974).

171 "There seems to be another woman involved": *Jet* (9 May 1974).

171 "A lot of it was the friends": *Biography*, A&E.

171 "I'm going home to Las Vegas": *Jet* (30 May 1974).

171 "I won't say it's settled yet": *Soul* (8 July 1974).

173 "They knew that we got along": Author interview.

173 "He came in and we did the show together": Author interview.

173 "We just don't get along": *Los Angeles Times* (26 August 1974).

173 "The easiest thing I can say": *Ebony* (30 May 1974).

174 "My wife handled all of my business affairs": *Jet* (14 November 1974).

chapter eleven

175 "It was a decent building in a great location": Author interview.

176 "He wanted the best for her": Author interview.

176 "She is a reverend. Like a preacher": Interview with Jane Ardmore.

176 "He would say, 'Man, how am I supposed to feel'": *Biography*, A&E.

NOTES

176 "I never knew her, knew nothing about her": *Biography*, A&E.

177 "I don't like to say this": *Sammy and Company*.

177 "He did not like her at all": Author interview.

177 "When Mama Carson": Author interview.

178 "It was called 'car flocking'": Author interview.

178 "Redd had such an inflated ego sometimes": Author interview.

179 "She stayed with Redd": Author interview.

179 "When my wife managed his beauty parlor": Author interview.

180 "Redd wouldn't come down": Author interview.

180 "I seen him just give people": *Biography*, A&E.

180 "If you walked up to Redd": Author interview.

181 "I could see he was good:" *Chicago Defender* (3 August 1974).

181 "He was just like an old pop:" Author interview.

181 "He kept my name in the news": Author interview.

182 "I think they handed Redd a check": Author interview.

182 "So I started to run his company": Author interview.

183 "Just about everybody": Author interview.

183 "Each day was a new circus:" Author interview.

183 "It was just something": Author interview.

183 "It just wasn't the right time": Author interview.

184 "He's helped so many people": *Los Angeles Times* (16 November 1975).

185 "Redd brought me back": *Las Vegas Review-Journal* (10 November 2006).

185 "I went to see Redd": Author interview.

185 "He became an instant hit with Redd": Author interview.

187 "Redd's show was in the Top Three": Author interview.

187 "He said, 'Why don't you and my lawyer'": Author interview.

188 "The head of WEA": Author interview.

188 "I got tired of being the same old dude": *Sepia* (January 1976).

189 "We're homebodies": *Baltimore Afro-American* (27 December 1975).

189 "He has been plagued": *Sepia* (January 1976).

189 "I don't see no color": *Sepia* (January 1976).

190 "A few years ago": *Sepia* (January 1976).

191 "There was no *Sanford and Son* without Redd Foxx": Author interview.

192 "I really didn't want to do another year": Author interview.

192 "He is a consummate entertainer": *New York Daily News* (9 April 1976).

192 "I changed networks": *New York Post* (9 April 1976).

192 "I flew to New York": *Los Angeles Times* (12 April 1976).

193 "They never asked me": *New York Times* (20 June 1976).

193 "These things happen to you": *New York Times* (20 June 1976).

193 "I spoke to Redd last night": *Los Angeles Times* (12 April 1976).

193 "Some people 'go Hollywood' awfully fast": *New York Post* (21 June 1977).

194 "I felt we should spend less money": *Jet* (December 1975).

195 "I met him in the hallway": *Jet* (3 February 1977).

NOTES

195 "Redd was a womanizer": Author interview.

195 "I remember going up there to Redd's house": Author interview.

chapter twelve

198 "Already most of the world": *Ebony* (November 1976).

199 "They really resented": Author interview.

200 "I didn't know this": Author interview.

200 "Pearl said, 'That's a terrible word!'": Author interview.

200 "So Pearl said": Author interview.

200 "Next time, I'm going to work with Burton!": *Los Angeles Times* (12 September 1976).

201 "Any time we had to stop": Author interview.

201 "This is a great thing for Redd's career": *Los Angeles Times* (12 September 1976).

201 "He should have had an award": *Jet* (27 May 1976).

201 "I said, 'Redd, why?'": Author interview.

202 "It is possible to imagine *Norman, Is That You?*": *New York Times* (30 September 1976).

202 "We can now gaze in wonder and mixed emotions": *Los Angeles Times* (30 September 1976).

203 "I don't, but I think she does": *Jet* (20 January 1977).

203 "I just opened my wallet": *Jet* (20 January 1977).

203 "This is my third wife": *Jet* (3 February 1977).

204 "Talk about dirty tricks": *New York Post* (11 November 1977).

204 "No way they send two bottles of booze": *The Barbara Walters Special* (31 May 1977).

206 "I was the funny one in the group": *The Barbara Walters Special* (31 May 1977).

207 "We were in New York, we were clean": *The Barbara Walters Special* (31 May 1977).

208 "When you take the hells and damns away": *New York Daily News* (31 August 1977).

208 "Supposedly the deal that Fred made with us": Author interview.

"So we go to the meeting": Author interview.

209 "Outside the windows of this house": Author interview.

210 "Blye and Einstein were first-class producers": Author interview.

210 "Let me tell you what he did": Author interview.

210 "So I said, 'Can you go out and just talk to the audience?'": Author interview.

210 "Redd insisted they use so many of his people": Author interview.

211 "Before, I couldn't be there": *Jet* (3 November 1977).

212 "Could be going down the tubes": *Baltimore Afro-American* (21 June 1977).

212 "Foxx wants to put in as many of his ideas as possible": *Baltimore Afro-American* (21 June 1977).

212 "If we started a day at nine o'clock": Author interview.

213 "Richard said, 'Man, I don't know what I'm gonna do'": Author interview.

213 "So we do all that": Author interview.

213 "We were taping": Author interview.

214 "Think of his life": Author interview.

215 "This Allan Blye-Bob Einstein concoction": *Los Angeles Times* (15 September 1977).

215 "The blue is gone": *New York Post* (15 September 15 1977).

215 "Relaxed and amiable, the veteran comedian": *New York Times* (15 September 1977).

215 "He's not the same funny man": *New York Daily News* (15 September 1977).

216 "Satire is satire": *Los Angeles Times* (22 October 1977).

216 "What's Bob Hope been doing all these years": *New York Post* (11 November 1977).

216 "I'm just here closing up": *Soul* (5 December 1977).

216 "No one's standing up for me": *Soul* (5 December 1977).

216 "I'm down, but it's not a terminal case": *New York Post* (11 November 1977).

217 "Redd gets up with a knife": Author interview.

217 "Berle is all over Redd": Author interview.

218 "We did a 'Best Of' show": Author interview.

218 "Tell 'em Foxx wants the black vote": *Jet* (29 December 1977).

219 "They mounted a good show": Author interview.

219 "To most viewers": *New York Times* (31 December 1978).

220 "Redd has been protesting": *Soul* (13 November 1978).

220 "We agreed in principle": *Soul* (13 November 1978).

221 "I'm not going to be another Martin Luther King Jr.": *New York Times* (21 March 1978.

221 "The father was going to head down": Author interview.

222 "He said using the word 'cherry'": Author interview.

223 "I'm making $30,000 for three shows": *Jet* (16 November 1978).

223 "All kinds of things went wrong": *Soul* (28 August 1978).

223 "There were a lot of people who predicted": *Jet* (25 January 1979).

224 "He would file his returns": Author interview.

225 "He certainly was aware of the problems": Author interview.

225 "He said to me": Author interview.

225 "He decides that if he performs": Author interview.

226 "That's stupid": Todd Bridges, *Killing Willis: From Diff'rent Strokes to the Mean Streets to the Life I Always Wanted* (Touchstone 2010).

226 "Shortly after we were married": *Jet* (22 November 1979).

227 "There was a little bit of activity": *Jet* (22 November 1979).

227 "I got used to living in a certain style": *New York Post* (3 December 1979).

227 "Oh, I can't say anything against the woman": *Jet* (22 November 1979).

chapter thirteen

229 "At NBC, we desperately needed shows": Author interview.

230 "I'd do anything for money": *New York Daily News* (17 January 1980).

231 "Mort [Lachman] told me": Author interview.

231 "Basically the writers": Author interview.

NOTES

231 "When I was offered the show": Author interview.
232 "I wasn't a big fan of cocaine": Author interview.
232 "Always asking me": Author interview.
232 "Redd hated to rehearse": Author interview.
232 "Fred Sanford is back": *Los Angeles Times* (15 March 1980).
233 "The show did reasonably well": Author interview.
233 "They painted all over the yard": *Jet* (15 May 1980).
233 "His entourage would go in": Author interview.
233 "I don't know if that was": *Jet* (15 May 1980).
233 "Foxx is funny": New York Post (3 July 1980).
234 "We don't want Pryor to go into debt": *New York Daily News* (15 July 1980).
235 "We never really had the quality of writers": Author interview.
235 "Hell, I tried to help him": *Los Angeles Times* (12 August 1981).
236 "It's just created some bad memories": *Washington African-American* (7 April 1981).
236 "I'd like to go down there": *Washington African-American* (7 April 1981).
237 "He both sustains and destroys stereotypes": *New York Post* (26 July 1982).
237 "I've been cheated more than most people": *New York Times* (30 July 1982).
238 "Redd didn't like to file tax returns": Author interview.
239 "I went to state court": Author interview.
239 "They stole guns, antique swords": *Jet* (4 April 1983).
239 "Show me a husband": *Newsweek*, (4 November 1984).
239 "We used to get calls": Author interview.
240 "When Harold Hecht left": Author interview.
240 "We went out there and met them": Author interview.
240 "I wanted to do something with Redd again": Author interview.
241 "I went to his house": Author interview.
241 "He loved Redd, he really did": Author interview.
242 "They still wanted to do a family thing": Author interview.
242 "Redd's a guy who has to trust you": Author interview.
242 "We put together the show": Author interview.
242 "But [we] also [had] to bring in sort of a gentler comedy": Author interview.
243 "I went into the first audition as Paul Segal": Author interview.
243 "My first encounter with Redd": Author intervivew.
244 "I said, 'We better get him the Louis Vuitton luggage'": Author interview.
244 "And we had to get it for him": Author interview.
244 "You've got to like cantankerous": *Los Angeles Times* (17 January 1986).
244 "I remember feeling": Author interview.
245 "The show goes on the air": Author interview.
245 "I remember we did a scene": Author interview.
245 "And he didn't want the public to think": Author interview.
246 "We were trying to find the wife": Author interview.
246 "He was a standup comedian": Author interview.
247 "He kind of sat there": Author interview.

247 "Redd said, 'I want a blanket over here'": Author interview.

247 "They were trying to recreate *Sanford and Son*": Author interview.

247 "Sinbad was really good": Author interview.

248 "They bounced us around": Author interview.

248 "I guess he remembered": Author interview.

248 "He put him on an airplane": Author interview.

248 "When Redd didn't have work": Author interview.

249 "And it was okay": Author interview.

249 "It was a cantankerous relationship": Author interview.

249 "He was definitely taking care of her": Author interview.

250 "Those guys were crooks": Author interview.

250 "He could sleep in his bed": Author interview.

250 "He says, 'Just walk into the meeting'": Author interview.

250 "They wanted Redd to finish": Author interview.

251 "To this day I think": Author interview.

251 "It would take a train wreck": Author interview.

251 "He pissed both of them off'": Author interview.

252 "He says, 'Oh, man, Foxx is hurt": Author interview.

252 "Joi was the love of his life": Author interview.

252 "I think whenever she needed anything": Author interview.

253 "They could have been his granddaughters": Author interview.

253 "Most of the humor is weak": *New York Post* (12 May 1987).

chapter fourteen

255 "The guy really wanted Redd": Author interview.

256 "I'll talk about my young life": *New York Post* (19 November 1987).

256 "Redd said, 'What kind of jokes are you going to tell?'": Author interview.

256 "The entertainment world of Las Vegas": *New York Times* (20 November 1987).

257 "Though a few of his stag party routines": *New York Post* (21 November 1987).

257 "But Redd wouldn't do it": Author interview

257 "Redd just got up and said": Author interview.

258 "If Eddie Murphy or Richard Pryor": *New York Post* (19 November 1987).

258 "I'm not putting them down": *New York Daily News* (19 November 1987).

258 "I'd still be Sanford": *New York Post* (19 November 1987).

258 "Redd would never settle": Author interview.

259 "Someone called and said": *Jet* (28 November 1988).

259 "They told me, 'God sent us here '": *Jet* (28 November 1988)

260 "[The meat] had enough poison in it": Author interview.

260 "When I wrote my film": *Jet* (20 November 1989).

261 "We said Redd would be interested": Author interview.

261 "They were saying": Author interview.

262 "He was working in Vegas": Author interview.

262 "Redd wasn't about to share a trailer": Author interview.

262 "I think Della and Redd": Author interview.

262 "Never connected with Eddie": Gold and Pryor, *Pryor Convictions: And Other Life Sentences.*

263 "We were just playfully": *Jet* (23 September 1991).

263 "In this buddy-buddy-buddy movie": *Los Angeles Times* (17 November 1989).

263 "Though *Harlem Nights* may be an ego trip": *New York Times* (17 November 1989).

263 "As some lawyers will say": Author interview.

264 "He called me up one day": Author interview.

264 "He had another woman": Author interview.

265 "I was rambling on": *Las Vegas Review-Journal* (3 November 2000).

265 "They took everything": *Jet* (18 December 1989).

265 "It was early in the morning": Author interview.

266 "He'd been in trouble before": Author interview.

267 "I think someone should come and do something": *Biography*, A&E.

267 "They've taken everything": *New York Times* (2 December 1989).

267 "Two of the strongest supporters": Author interview.

267 "He calls me up": Author interview.

267 "I haven't heard from anyone": *Jet* (18 December 1989).

267 "Eddie is in a position": *Jet* (18 December 1989).

268 "He called me up": Author interview.

268 "There have got to be some whites in town": *New York Daily News* (5 December 1989).

268 "Believe it or not": Author interview.

269 "I was making like $4,500 a week [with Redd]": Author interview.

269 "It was kind of disappointing": Author interview.

270 "He knew that I was gay": Author interview.

270 "Eddie Murphy's people": Author interview.

chapter fifteen

271 "I'm happy": *Jet* (23 April 1990).

271 "She stuck with me through the IRS mess": *Jet* (29 July 1991).

272 "He loved my car": Author interview.

272 "He would go down there": Author interview.

272 "Once we signed the contract": Author interview.

272 "I just negotiated with Eddie's people": Author interview.

273 "He loved Della": Author interview.

273 "Well, it feels good": *Ebony* (October 1991).

273 "The show was funny": Author interview.

274 "It's started out slowly": *Jet* (29 July 1991).

274 "You didn't work with him": Author interview.

274 "And Redd looked over at me": Author interview.

275 "Sometimes I would come out on the set": Author interview.

275 "*The Royal Family* has energy, but not much else": *Los Angeles Times* (18 September 1991).

275 "Nice as it is to see Redd Foxx grousing and bellowing": *Variety* (17 September 1991).

276 "We were doing okay with the numbers": Author interview.

276 "A five-day-a-week, half-hour comedy": Author interview.

276 "I had control of that": Author interview.

277 "So he pushed back from the table": Author interview.

277 "Redd had told them": Author interview.

278 "They had a line about my youngest granddaughter": Author interview.

278 "The first time I met him": Author interview.

278 "It was a hit": Author interview.

279 "I had gone to get him some chicken cacciatore": Author interview.

279 "Fabulous. Everybody fell in love": *Biography*, A&E.

279 "They came to interview him": Author interview.

280 "There wasn't even a line [for Redd to say]": Author interview.

280 "The producer said": Author interview.

280 "Later in the afternoon": Author interview.

281 "He was pretty upset": Author interview.

281 "Redd and I had just finished rehearsing": Author interview.

281 "I was in the [writers'] office": Author interview.

282 "His mouth was all twisted": Author interview.

282 "I remember running to the refrigerator": Author interview.

282 "We stayed at the hospital for several hours": Author interview.

283 "The doctor came out": *Biography*, A&E.

283 "I was the last one there": Author interview.

283 "Redd Foxx was blessed": *Los Angeles Times* (12 October 1991).

283 "While Mr. Foxx was best known": *New York Times* (13 October 1991).

283 "Foxx … was a comedian's comedian": *Los Angeles Times* (14 October 1991).

284 "Eddie didn't come to the funeral": Author interview.

284 "LaWanda Page was there": Author interview.

284 "They let me go in by myself": *Biography*, A&E.

285 "He was a very sensitive man": *Biography*, A&E.

285 "The funeral itself": Author interview.

285 "The Pointer Sisters and I are in line": Author interview.

286 "What happened was, unfortunately": Author interview.

286 "There were so many players and so much disarray": Author interview.

287 "She said, 'Well, Redd came to me last night'": Author interview.

287 "Everybody tried to help her": Author interview.

289 "The other ladies in his life": Author interview.

292 "He lived and did everything": Author interview.

index

INDEX

INDEX

INDEX

INDEX

INDEX

INDEX

INDEX

INDEX

INDEX

INDEX

INDEX

INDEX

INDEX

INDEX